THE SUPERCOMMANDOS
First Special Service Force • 1942-1944

THE SUPERCOMMANDOS
First Special Service Force • 1942-1944
An Illustrated History

Robert Todd Ross

Schiffer Military History
Atglen, PA

For Tracy
This book is dedicated to the men of the First Special Service Force

• • •

Color Maps and Graphics Prepared by:
Rick Brownlee, R&B Graphic Design
12838 W. 88th Circle, Apt. 49
Lenexa, Kansas 66215
Phone: (913) 859-9979, Fax: (913) 859-9981
E-mail: rbgrafic@unicom.net

Studio photography and book design by Robert Biondi.

Copyright © 2000 by Robert Todd Ross.
Library of Congress Catalog Number: 00-101170.

Printed in China.
ISBN: 0-7643-1171-9

We are always looking for people to write books on new and related subjects. If you have an idea for a book, please contact us at the address below.

Published by Schiffer Publishing Ltd.
4880 Lower Valley Road
Atglen, PA 19310
Phone: (610) 593-1777
FAX: (610) 593-2002
E-mail: Schifferbk@aol.com.
Visit our web site at: www.schifferbooks.com
Please write for a free catalog.
This book may be purchased from the publisher.
Please include $3.95 postage.
Try your bookstore first.

In Europe, Schiffer books are distributed by:
Bushwood Books
6 Marksbury Ave.
Kew Gardens
Surrey TW9 4JF
England
Phone: 44 (0)208 392-8585
FAX: 44 (0)208 392-9876
E-mail: Bushwd@aol.com.
Free postage in the UK. Europe: air mail at cost.
Try your bookstore first.

Contents

Special Feature #9   *279*
Campaigns, Battle Honors, and, Decorations and Awards of the First Special Service Force

APPENDICES

Introduction

"Enterprises must be prepared, with specially trained troops of the hunter class, who can develop a reign of terror . . . leaving a trail of German corpses behind them." These were British Prime Minister, Sir Winston Churchill's instructions to General Ismay, his Chief of Staff, on June 6, 1940. They came at a time during World War II when Great Britain was, by Churchill's own admission, "a struggling country beset by deadly foes." Undaunted, Churchill advocated *offensive* action, in the form of bold, viscous raids as the best means to keep his enemies at bay while more decisive countermeasures could be organized.[1]

To carry out such raids Churchill envisioned a light infantry force using tactics borrowed from the hard-hitting guerrilla types of modern warfare's recent past – primarily those of the Afrikaner *Kommandos* of the Boer War and the German *Sturmtruppen* of World War I. Now, in the current war, German triumphs could again be attributed to shock troops; example, the breathtakingly swift capture of the Belgian fortress Eben Emael on 10 May 1940.[2] Though the British had formerly resisted the concept of guerrilla warfare, they were first among the Allies to grasp fully this idea and make it their own. During the early years of World War II the British Commandos kept their enemies off balance by executing a series of highly successful, "butcher and bolt" raids against the fortified coastal areas of German-occupied Europe.[3]

In order to confront the diverse tactical challenges that were inherent to World War II, the proliferation of distinctive raiding formations spread throughout the Allied armies. Notable among these were the U.S. Army Rangers, Special Operations Executive Detachments, Office of Strategic Services Operational Groups, the Special Air Service, the Jedburghs, and the U.S. Marine Corps Raiders. Their common thread being that all were intended to accomplish unusual missions beyond the scope of larger, less wieldy, regular formations.[4] Elaborating on earlier examples, these Allied raiding forces received specialized weapons, training and equipment. With shock and aggressiveness, they were used to exploit weaknesses in the enemy's defenses, to by-pass his strong points, and drive hard and fast into his rear areas cutting vital communications and isolating his front lines. The resulting confusion and fear among the enemy's troops would set the stage for more sweeping military operations to follow.[5]

Throughout the course of the war, the role of the Allies' raiding forces was continually modified from that of raiders, to one of shock troops, to one more consistent with light infantry. By the addition of support weapons, motor transport, and administrative adjuncts these troops were, during the middle and latter stages of the war, often committed to conventional, sustained operations, deployed in the same way as standard troops.[6]

Of all "hunter class" formations born during World War II, perhaps the most remarkable was the joint Canadian-American First Special Service Force. The Force was activated at a remote United States Army post in Helena, Montana on July 20, 1942, in conjunction with Operations PLOUGH and JUPITER. The former involved the development of an experimental snow vehicle; the latter, the use of this vehicle to mount an audacious sabotage scheme aimed at crippling hydroelectric and oil producing facilities across enemy occupied Europe during that coming winter. Made up of "rugged individualists," hand-picked volunteers drawn from the various branches of both armies, the First Special Service Force was strenuously and exactingly trained, and charismatically led by aggressive, capable officers and noncommissioned officers from both nations. Remembers one Force officer: "The individual soldier, almost to a man, had resourcefulness, mental and physical toughness, and an initiative that surmounted all obstacles."[7]

Designated as a separate branch of service of the United States Army, and operating directly under the auspices of the War Department, the First Special Service Force's personnel, both Canadian and American, were completely mixed within its ranks. The Force was the only combat unit within the Allied fold whose variegate training rendered its combat men all qualified parachutists, skiers and demolitionists, as well as experts in hand-to-hand fighting, mountain and winter warfare. Ex-

ceeding this overall training, individual Forcemen received further instruction in a wide variety of technical skills.[8] While in the midst of training, the project for which the Force was originally conceived was abruptly canceled. Rather than disband the unit, it was re-organized for an assault infantry role, one that would be played out in the campaigns for the Aleutian Islands, Italy, and southern France. To effect this, the Force added an amphibious landing capability; and, to its relatively small number, it added an inordinate abundance of automatic weapons rendering it, arguably, the most capable and deadly infantry organization in the Allied forces during World War II – North America's supercommandos.[9]

CHAPTER 1

Snow Plough to Jupiter

Shortly after the United States entered the war, joint military planning between England and America began. Immediate and important achievements included the establishment of the Combined Chiefs of Staff in Washington, DC, and the commencement of meticulous planning for a limited cross-Channel invasion, Operation ROUNDUP, advocated primarily by the United States and tentatively scheduled for early Spring 1943. On 7 April 1942, Army Chief of Staff George C. Marshall, accompanied by Harry Lloyd Hopkins, a special advisor and close confidant to President Roosevelt, proceeded to London to confer with the joint Anglo-American Staff over development of the cross-Channel plan. Introduced during the course of these sessions was the subject of diversionary attacks that might be mounted to coincide with the Allied reentry onto the continent. General Marshall was solicited by Admiral Lord Louis Mountbatten, Chief of Britain's Combined Operations, and presented with a plan that this organization had been studying for the Commandos.[1]

The author of the plan was Geoffrey Pyke, an eccentric English scientist whom Mountbatten had taken under his wing at Combined Operations. Pyke considered snow, along with air, sea, and land, to be a fourth element over which war could be effectively waged, provided one had the means. Taking into account that up to seventy percent of Europe lay under snow for periods varying from 60 to 250 days out of each year, Pyke concluded that he who could best cope with the snow, would dominate that considerable portion of European territory.[2]

Pyke's plan illustrated how a small force of specially trained, uniformed (rather than clandestine) troops, equipped with lightly armored snow vehicles, might be dropped by parachute over the scattered snow areas of Europe during winter to carry out widespread, systematic and aggressive sabotage of vital enemy installations. As no vehicles such as envisioned in Pyke's plan currently existed, they would have to be built. However, British engineers, already struggling to meet current wartime demands, would need an estimated four years to produce the required vehicles, and so the plan was offered to the United States.[3]

PLOUGH, as the secret plan was code-named, was set forth in Pyke's thesis titled, *Mastery of the Snows*. Beyond describing a revolutionary new over-the-snow vehicle, it went on to list a number of possible economic and military targets. Primarily, these were located in Norway, but other targets, in Rumania and northern Italy, were also noted.

High-head electrical stations powered Norway's electro-chemical and electro-metallurgical industries. Nearly half of Norway's hydro-electric production was concentrated at fourteen stations. Occupied by the Germans since 10 June 1940, Norway was their irreplaceable source for a tremendous variety of important ores and minerals such a molybdenum, essential for strengthening steel armor, and deuterium or *heavy water*, critical to the Nazis in their effort to produce an atomic bomb. The world's only factory then turning out deuterium, the Norsk Hydro in Vemork (Rjuken), was PLOUGH's number one target. The second major objective represented the single richest target in Europe, the Ploesti oil fields in Rumania. Ploesti was a complex of oil storage depots, refineries and cracking plants supplying the Nazis with nearly half of the oil that fueled their war machine. Oil wells, pipelines, and as many as six refineries and their power stations at Ploesti were to be weighed as possible targets. Also targeted for destruction was Italy's hydro-electric power, almost seventy percent of which was produced in a few large plants on the southern Alpine slopes. This power mainly supplied industry in Turin, Milan and the whole of the Po River watershed. It also fed the electrified railroads. As diversion was PLOUGH's chief intent, it was hoped that these raids would force vast numbers of enemy troops to be redirected from coastal defense duties to anti-sabotage efforts.[4]

On 9 April 1942, General Marshall accepted the PLOUGH project for consideration by the United States Army and upon his return to the U.S. devoted his attention first to the development of a snow vehicle. Marshall assigned the task jointly to the Office of Scientific Research and Development (OSRD) and the War Production Board, both directed by General Staff G-4 Brigadier General Raymond G. Moses. The Canadian National Research Council was also recruited to help in the work. PLOUGH's timetable mandated that production commence on a standardized design, one fully tested and approved, by no later than 1 October 1942.[5]

Combined Operations representative, Brigadier Nigel Duncan, and Commando Major E.A.M Wedderburn, Combined Operations Assistant Director of Research, with Geoffrey Pyke along ostensibly as technical advisor, arrived in Washington, DC, on 24 April 1942, to continue discussions and planning on the snow vehicle. Almost immediately Pyke registered misgivings about the way the Americans were proceeding with PLOUGH. Pyke's doubts were, in point of fact, rooted in his unwillingness to accept the U.S. Army's considerations in vehicle production, that, while being militarily expedient, were divergent from his own views. Self-admittedly, Pyke's persona was, at best, difficult for others to tolerate. Yet he was disinclined to moderate his outward contempt for the way in which *his* idea was being supposedly *fobbed* by the Americans. The results of a June visit by Lord Louis to Washington, DC, seemed to ease Pyke's conscience as to the American's resolve, but by now the American's tolerance for Pyke had been strained to the breaking point.[6]

Despite this peripheral friction, scientists were moving closer to generating an acceptable snow machine. Principal requirements for the vehicle were that its armor be up to proof against small-arms fire, that it be capable of movement over both snow and non-snow terrain, that it be highly maneuverable, and that it be capable of sustained cross-country speeds faster than that of enemy ski troops. After considering what models were available, a low-silhouetted, track-laying *Weasel*, designed by Palmer C. Putnam of OSRD, met with approval. Motor car builder Studebaker Corporation of South

T-15 Cargo Carrier mounted under the fuselage of a C-54 Skymaster prior to the first parachute test drop. (Courtesy Frederick-Hicks)

Bend, Indiana was approached by OSRD and asked if they could manufacture the necessary number of vehicles by the October deadline. Studebaker had on hand a quantity of their six-cylinder *Champion* motors that its engineers calculated were adequate to power the Weasel, and, after some deliberation, agreed to produce the new vehicle, designated by the Army as the Cargo Carrier, Light, T-15. Four pilot models (the first of which was delivered to OSRD in late June 1942) were ordered right away with which to conduct extensive trials. Subsequently modified, the improved model was classified as the T-24 (this model being the model the Force would use most extensively). A third version, produced during the mid-to-late-war period, was the M-29.[7]

While the Weasel was not of the radically new design that Pyke had anticipated, it evolved as the best snow machine to see service during the war. It was a versatile vehicle, its "low center of gravity, smooth underside, and its low pressure on the ground – only one-fourth that of a fully-equipped infantry soldier [enabled] the machine to break its own path through underbrush and second growth timber." Inclines of up to forty-five degrees were, at low speeds, easily traversed by the Weasel. It weighed 4,077 pounds, and measured ten and one-half feet long by six and one-half feet wide. With its canvas top raised it stood at just under six feet. With seating for four, the Weasel's top-end speed was thirty-six miles per hour with a range of 175 miles.[8]

As vehicle development progressed, attention shifted to Operation JUPITER, the new code-name for PLOUGH's spin-off military campaign. Burden for that portion of the plan was dumped in the lap of Major General Dwight D. Eisenhower,

Weasel descends to earth by four cargo parachutes after being dropped from the Skymaster. (Courtesy Frederick-Hicks)

Crumpled remains of a T-15 Weasel after initial parachute test drop. (Courtesy Frederick-Hicks)

then Deputy Chief of the War Department's War Plans Division. Eisenhower, in turn, assigned Lt. Colonel Robert T. Frederick, a former Coast Artilleryman serving on his staff, to conduct a feasibility study of the proposal. In early May 1942, after twelve days of thorough examination, Frederick presented his findings in a memorandum to Eisenhower.[9]

Frederick's report led off by pointing out that PLOUGH's proposed targets in Italy and Rumania could be more easily reduced by employing Allied air power. After taking this into account, the balance of his assessment dealt with the operation only as it pertained to Norway. Nonetheless, Frederick deemed that even a strictly Norwegian venture was unlikely of success given the short amount of time in which to prepare. The PLOUGH scheme had other shortcomings according to Frederick, including the unavailability of air transport for the, as yet to him unspecified, snow vehicles, as well as leaving unsolved the problem of how the raiding force would be organized, trained and equipped to carry out the mission. Most problematical to Frederick was that the proposal offered no sound method for withdrawing the would-be saboteurs once their foray was completed; presumably leaving the men to escape as best they could on their own.[10]

Political insistence by Churchill and Mountbatten rather than sound military judgment overrode Frederick's findings, and PLOUGH was ordered to proceed unaltered. In early June 1942, General Marshall directed General Eisenhower to select a commander to commence with activating the military force necessary for the operation. At Eisenhower's behest Army Ground Forces submitted a number of candidates who interviewed for the post. Of these, Lt. Colonel H.R. Johnson was chosen. Yet, within twenty-four hours, Johnson found himself unable to stomach Pyke's difficult personality and so stepped down.[11]

But if the U.S. Army could find no one suitable, perhaps Lord Louis had. Earlier in June, during meetings on the project, Lt. Colonel Frederick had been introduced to Admiral Mountbatten. Intuitively, Mountbatten sensed in Frederick the mettle to lead PLOUGH to fruition, and made his sentiments known to Eisenhower. Eisenhower coalesced, and on 16 June 1942, relieved Frederick from his duties at the War Department ordering him, "Frederick, you take this Plough project. You've been over the whole thing. You're in charge now. Let me know what you need." Frederick was told to write a directive to this effect and to begin with utmost speed. Having craved adventure all his life, Robert Tyron Frederick, though momentarily stunned by the irony of the decision, was "also terribly happy."[12]

CHAPTER 2

Ploughshares into Swords

" The urgent necessity for speed in all phases of the project [made] it mandatory that all development and procurement of material and supplies, and the procurement and training of all personnel be accomplished under the highest priority." To that end, Frederick composed a remarkably wise directive that in ten paragraphs granted him unusual and important latitudes placing the full facilities of all agencies of the War Department at his disposal. The PLOUGH force would be under the direct assignment of the War Department and would have highest priority (an AA-1 rating) for procurement of personnel and items of equipment. Frederick could select training areas anywhere in North America and had the power to deal directly with the representatives of the participating governments and their agencies. He had the document signed and authorized both by U.S. Army Chief of Staff Marshall and by Major General Eisenhower, now acting in the capacity of Assistant Chief of Staff. As the PLOUGH force was designated as a parachute unit, and in order that the Force would be assured table of organization strength of fitted personnel at the end of training, Frederick requested and was authorized a 30% overstrength of combat personnel. At once, he was apprised of progress on the Weasels, and informed that 600 would be ready by October. The PLOUGH force was to move from its training area to the combat area as soon as practicable after 15 December 1942.[1]

Frederick secured office space in the Munitions Building in Washington and immediately set about gathering a staff around him to organize the new unit and to begin detailed planning. Captain Robert D. Burhans arrived on 17 June as S-2, Intelligence Officer. Two days later Captain Kenneth G. Wickham, one of Frederick's old acquaintances from his Coast Artillery days, arrived as Adjutant or S-1. Also arriving on 19 June was Major Orval J. Baldwin as S-4, Administrative Officer in charge of supplies and logistics. On the 23rd, Captain Harry M. (*Tug*) Wilson and Lieutenant Robert Ellis arrived from Fort Benning as parachute instructors. Rounding out the initial staff were Lieutenant Finn Roll as specialist on the Norwegian situation, and Captain Alcide M. Touchette as office adjutant. Major John B. Shinberger came aboard as temporary training officer on 26 June. Each at his own task, the assembled staff began eighteen hour work days.[2]

Borrowing the epithet, in part, from the British Commandos who were at that time organized within the *Special Service Brigade*, Frederick christened his command the First Special Service Force. The designation was appropriate as the unit was indeed the first of its kind and was of the same predilection as its namesake; and while the name was notably less striking than *Ranger*, *Commando* or *Parachute Infantry*, it suited Frederick's aim to as much as possible keep the Force's intent secret from both press and public. It was during the process to choose a name that an officer on Frederick's staff suggested naming the Force's subordinate units after Indian tribes and to refer to individual Forcemen as *Braves*. This idea was set aside in favor of standard Army nomenclature, but, however unofficially, the *Braves* moniker stuck.[3]

Frederick's directive reasserted the proposal of Mountbatten and Churchill, that United Kingdom, Canadian, and Norwegian, as well as American personnel might constitute the force to carry out the PLOUGH campaign. An ensuing meeting in Ottawa between Frederick and Mountbatten, and

The first volunteers arrive at Fort William Henry Harrison to see the camp literally being built around them, c. July 1942. (Author's Collection)

Earth-moving equipment and civilian workers labor before one of Fort Harrison's partially completed tar-paper and rough-lumber buildings, c. July 1942. (Author's Collection)

Canadian officials regarding Canadian participation in the enterprise brought their affirmative response. On 14 July 1942, Canadian Defense Minister Ralston gave his final approval that 47 officers and 650 enlisted personnel would be made available to Frederick.[4]

The participation of United Kingdom and Norwegian soldiers in the Force was never to evolve. However, Frederick was able gain the expert help of a number of Norwegian ski instructors, as well as both Norwegian and English intelligence specialists and scientists. Conspicuously absent among the later was Geoffrey Pyke, having been removed from the project for its own good. As well, Mountbatten had ordered Brigadier Duncan returned to other duties in England, and, in mid-July,

had promoted Wedderburn to Lt. Colonel to better carry on in his current role.[5]

The finite number of cargo carriers that were to be available for the PLOUGH campaign, approximately 600, was of major importance in organizing the First Special Service Force as it worked to set a limit on its potential authorized strength. It was left to Captain Wickham to draw up the unprecedented unit's Table of Organization – T/O (Special) or 'War Establishment' the Canadians call it – that prescribed in detail the allocation of men, and assigned to them their various jobs, required skills, and grades of rank. The Force was divided into two echelons – one being combat, and one being service.[6]

First group of Canadian volunteers arrives at Fort William Henry Harrison, 5 August 1942. (Author's Collection)

Another group from the first Canadian contingent of 35 officers and 451 other ranks to arrive in Helena. Five days later, a second group of some 200 Canadian volunteers would arrive and begin training. (Author's Collection)

On paper, Wickham organized the Combat Echelon into three identical Regiments, one to tackle each of PLOUGH's proposed strategic areas – Norway, Rumania, and northern Italy. The most basic component of the Combat Echelon was a nine-man *Section* (Canadian terminology roughly interchangeable with the U.S. Army's designation, 'Rifle Squad') each equipped with four Weasels. Two sections were organized into a Platoon commanded by a Lieutenant. Three platoons formed a Combat Company led by a Captain. Three companies, under a Lt. Colonel, made a Combat Battalion; and two battalions formed each of the three Special Service Regiments, each under a full Colonel. Attached to each regiment was a fifteen-man Regimental Supply Detachment and a two-man Regimental Medical Detachment. Filling out the Combat Echelon was a four-man Combat Force Communications Detachment and an eight-man Air Detachment. The Headquarters Detachment of twelve men tied the various parts together. In all, the Combat Echelon was comprised of 108 officers and 1,167 enlisted men. 432 Weasels were equally distributed among the combat regiments with the balance assigned to the headquarters and various service and support elements.[7]

Due to time constraints, the combat troops could do nothing but train and would have to be totally supported by another group. A separate battalion was formed for this task. The Service Battalion contained three companies: Headquarters, Service, and Maintenance. Headquarters Company (twelve officers, 120 enlisted) served administrative functions providing clerks, personnel and records people, and a publications staff. It operated the post office, contained the Military Police Platoon, intelligence sections, and radio and telephone people. The Service Company (five officers, 268 enlisted) was comprised of cooks and permanent K.P.s, barbers, carpenters, a cobbler, a butcher and a plumber, a Field Music Detachment (soon nicknamed, *Rodehaver's Rhythm Rascals* in honor of the Service Battalion's CO), ammunition and supply personnel and parachute riggers. Maintenance Company (four officers, 122 enlisted) was to maintain all the Force's equipment, run the motor pool, and oversee fuel supply, ordnance, and signal repair. The aggregate strength of both Combat Echelon and Service Battalion was 133 officers and 1,688 enlisted men. On 4 July, the T/O (Special) was approved and published by the Office of the Adjutant General.[8]

Personnel for the Service Battalion were assigned through normal channels by requisition submitted on 6 July 1942. Within the Service Battalion grades of rank, appropriate to each position, were assigned to personnel as per Army status quo. Men of the Combat Echelon were to acquire a more unique variety of specialized skills and thus the lowest enlisted rank, as per the table of organization, was to be equal to that of a buck sergeant. In practice, however, the presence of the overstrength personnel within the ranks always kept at least one-third of the Combat Echelon in the rank of private.[9]

Organic to the Force's Combat Echelon, the Air Detachment was authorized six Army Air Corps officers, all pilots, and two enlisted air mechanics; all of whom were to undergo the same rigorous training as the rest of the Force. The Air Detachment operated from neighboring Helena Municipal Airport and drew on the Army Air Corps Depot at Great Falls,

Colonel Frederick (left) with Lt. Colonel John G. McQueen, Commander of the Canadian contingent and the Force's original Executive Officer. McQueen broke his leg during parachute training and left the Force. (Author's Collection)

The Fort Harrison Post Canteen with pyramidal tents in the background. (Author's Collection)

Tug of war with a static line to demonstrate its strength. (National Archives)

Force Parachute Officer, Lieutenant James W. Wallace of Service Company, gives instruction to a group of would-be jumpers from the doorway of an aircraft mockup. (National Archives)

Montana for all Army Air Force supplies. It was planned that its aircraft, including two Douglas C-47 Skytrains, two twin-motor Cessna C-78 Bobcats, two Stinson L-9B Voyagers, and an L-74 single-engine cabin high wing Fairchild, were to be used for air-ground liaison, aerial supply, and reconnaissance in support of the ground troops, both in training and eventually in the combat area.

In addition to the Force's Air Detachment, a request to the Commanding General, Army Air Forces brought the arrival to Fort Harrison, on 29 July 1942, the first of six C-47 troop transports from nearby Great Falls Air Depot, complete with external delivery unit racks and six WI-100 aerial delivery containers, for use in parachute training and in shuttling men and materiel to and from the main base and the various training areas. These troop transports were to remain on detached service to the Force through August 31, 1942. Support for these crews, in contrast to the Force Air Detachment, was the responsibility of the Army Air Force. Subsequent movement of the Force from Fort Harrison, Montana, to Camp Bradford, Virginia, resulted in its loss of ground crew personnel which had been provided by an Army Air Force detachment from Great Falls, Montana. To make the Force Air Detachment self-sufficient, it was allowed fourteen additional personnel, including one officer, and the full complement of tools and equipment necessary to provide full maintenance facilities. However, the Air Detachment was dissolved after the Force finished parachute training for its newly arrived replacements at Fort Ethan Allen in Burlington, Vermont. Lieutenant (later Major) Brandon N. Rimmer stayed on as Colonel Frederick's personal pilot to fly the one Stinson that was retained. The members of the deactivated Air Detachment were reassigned back to various Army Air Corps units.[10]

On 30 June, Major D.D. Williamson, Canadian Army, flew to Washington to meet with now-Major Wickham, Force S-1. Together they hammered out the guidelines by which American and Canadian would be integrated into a single unit. The agreement established that the United States would provide all personnel for the Force-component Service Battalion, save for a separate Canadian paymaster and records group there attached. The Canadians would furnish men for the Combat Echelon only. The 2nd Canadian Parachute Battalion – as, from August 1942, through April 1943, the Canadian component was designated for Canadian administrative purposes – although serving in a United States Army unit, would remain subject to Canadian law for disciplinary matters and pay. The United States would provide all clothing, equipment, travel expenses, food and shelter, and medical support for the troops, but would be reimbursed by Canada for food and hospitalization costs as well as for funds provided by the United States to the Canadian paymaster. Formally adopted by both the United States and Canada in January 1943, this understanding was recorded as the *Wickham-Williamson Agreement* and was the basis on which the unit operated henceforth.[11]

Within the Combat Echelon, Canadian and American command positions would be divided as evenly as possible at the outset with subsequent promotions based on merit regardless of nationality. At the outset the Canadians were able to provide more senior Majors and Captains, while American officer strength proved to be in junior officers. With guidelines in hand, Williamson left for Canada to muster the 600+ officers and men.[12]

Getting a feel for hanging in the harness was one aspect of the abbreviated parachute course at Fort Harrison. (National Archives)

Proper technique of exiting the aircraft is practiced one last time by a group of Forcemen who are about to make their first jump. Note that the men wear standard M-1 helmets, as stocks of M-1C helmets designed specifically for airborne troops have apparently not yet arrived. (National Archives)

OPPOSITE:
INSET TOP: Standing in a line, each Forcemen checks the parachute harness of the man in front of him. (National Archives)

INSET BOTTOM: Force "sticks" pass the time while waiting for their turn to jump. (Author's Collection)

Meanwhile, Major Shinberger's search for a suitable training area ended at Fort William Henry Harrison, a derelict National Guard Post near Helena, Montana. Remote, the camp was surrounded by ample flat lands well-suited for both an airfield and a parachute dropping zone, and, nearby to the mountains of the Continental Divide, offered a perfect venue for rock climbing and ski instruction. On 5 July, a station compliment of 350 military personnel was detailed to Fort Harrison and given two weeks in which to prepare the camp in advance of the soon-to-be arriving troops.[13]

American Army units training in the southwest and along the Pacific coast were canvassed by examiners from the Adjutant General's Office who screened and selected appropriate men from prospective volunteers. They wanted no raw recruits. Volunteers had to be tough, self-reliant young men who had completed all their basics and who were willing to undergo parachute training. They were, preferably, single, separated or divorced, between the ages of twenty-one and thirty-five who had completed at least three years or more of grammar school.

The examiners sought those whose pre-military experiences were within the occupational range of lumberjacks, forest rangers, hunters, northwoodsmen, game wardens, prospectors, and explorers. Intelligent, if not necessarily academics, the kind of men the Force was in need of were warriors.[14]

For junior officers, Wickham and Lieutenant Ellis first traveled to the Infantry School at Fort Benning, Georgia on 9 July, where they interviewed and selected fifty-five men from Benning's Officer Candidate program. On 12 July, they proceeded to Virginia where another fifteen prospects were chosen from Fort Belvoir's Officer Candidate School program. These newly confirmed Second Lieutenants, in return for volunteering, received their commissions regardless of their standings in OCS, and were soon on their way to Montana. Frederick (now at the rank of Colonel, another recipient of recent promotion), for his part, reviewed the records of prospective Combat Echelon senior officers. Many of the field grade officers were chosen for their prior experience and special training such as ski training. These officers received transfers and orders to

A batch of Forcemen board a transport aircraft for one of their two qualifying parachute drops. (Author's Collection)

report to the First Special Service Force, of which most new nothing but would soon be informed. Frederick's original executive officer was Lt. Colonel John McQueen, the Force's senior Canadian officer.[15]

On 19 July 1942, a rapid inflow of personnel began. Frederick, Shinberger and Wickham, themselves recently arrived in Helena, were there to meet them. On 20 July 1942, Frederick officially activated the First Special Service Force. Men poured into Fort Harrison by train and bus – all as individuals on secret orders – all to be fitted into the units that had been devised. The camp was literally being built around them. By 25 July, the Service Battalion was formed and up to strength. New U.S. Second Lieutenants were coming in and formed into groups for orientation and intensive training. On 5 August, the first Canadian contingent of thirty-five officers and 451 other ranks arrived. The second and what was believed at the time to be final Canadian group arrived on 10 August. Overall, the Canadians who arrived at Helena were an outstanding group; some later arrivals being veterans of combat in Europe having participated in the raid on Dieppe. According to K.G. Wickham, "what had been an administrative madhouse since 16 June was settling down. Much had been accomplished."[16]

One of the Force Air Detachment's C-47 Dakotas, dubbed "High Yaller," taxies down the runway with a load of jumpers, c. August 1942. (Author's Collection)

RIGHT: View from inside the cockpit of a Force Air Detachment C-47 Dakota troop transport. (Thomas W. Hope)

Awaiting their turn to jump, Forcemen cheer on their comrades. (National Archives)

ABOVE: "Stand up, hook up." View from inside the fuselage of a C-47 Dakota at a stick of Forcemen about to make their first parachute drop. (Thomas W. Hope)

With progress now underway at Fort Harrison, Frederick allotted much of the responsibility for training the Force to his Headquarters staff officers, freeing himself to attend to other aspects of the PLOUGH project, either in Washington, DC, or wherever else his presence was required. For the time being, Force S-4 (Supply) and S-2 (Intelligence) sections stayed in Washington in close interaction with the government agencies supplying specialized equipment and material, and information to those FSSF offices.[17]

Training in the First Special Service Force was divided into three phases. The first phase, conducted by specially selected instructors covered a nine week period that was to last from 3 August to 3 October 1942, and was devoted to the fol-

A broken leg, the result of a hard parachute landing, ends the career of this volunteer to the Force. (Author's collection)

lowing subjects: parachute jumping, defense against chemicals, demolitions orientation, vehicle operation and maintenance, bayonet, hand-to-hand combat, scouting and patrolling, first aid and hygiene, and range qualification in small arms. All weapons were American and included the automatic pistol, the carbine, the Thompson submachine gun, the Browning machine gun, and the Garand rifle. Running and work on the obstacle course to build stamina and fitness was an underlying current; and administration, inspections, and close order drill rounded out the training regime. "Motor vehicle instruction was conducted by civilian experts and included care and maintenance, driving, trouble shooting by the driver, and training second echelon mechanics. . . . Officers were required to undergo the same training as the enlisted men. Lectures and films, as well as practical work, were used extensively during this

training phase which ended with tests for each individual. The tests were a combination of written and practical examinations. Men who did not pass the tests initially were given extra instruction during the evening and re-tested. This continued until all men qualified."[18]

According to then Captain Ed Thomas, 2 i/c of 2nd Battalion, Second Regiment: "There was an unaccustomed intensity and focus to the training. While no official announcement had been made it was obvious that we had a definite mission assignment, that Norway was our battlefield, and a plywood power plant mock-up left forecast our targets. And the training tempo left no question that the time of testing was coming and coming soon, the kind of situation that tends to concentrate the mind and training."[19]

At Fort Harrison was developing what one American officer described as "a different culture." Both Yanks and Canadians, initially surprised to discover themselves in the company of one another, found their differences so minor as to be unnoticeable. At twenty-six years, the average age of the Force's volunteers was older than that of any other U.S. Army airborne outfit. This overall maturity proved to be an asset to the Force, both in its quick amalgamation and, later, in its steadiness on the battlefield. Discipline, while strict, was not *martinet*, there being "little emphasis on spit and polish." For minor infractions, punishment was most often meted out in the form of fines or restrictions to post rather than by stints in the stockade – there was no time for this.[20]

LEFT: Forceman showing good form as he descends; his feet are held together, considerably lessening his chance for injury upon landing. (Thomas W. Hope)

BELOW: After a successful landing this Forceman hurries to collapse his 'chute, c. August 1942. (Thomas W. Hope)

The differences between the commands for close order drill used by the American and Canadian Force officers proved quite a nuisance during the early days at Helena. Commands issued by officers from the nation opposite of given enlisted personnel, in many instances, proved to be quite baffling. From his experience, Lieutenant William S. Story recalls that, "Canadians were accustomed to hearing: 'Company will move to the right in column of threes by platoon. Right turn! By the left, quick march!' Americans would mutter: 'What in hell does he mean, 'by the left''? So if the platoon commander was a Canadian the Americans learned to operate by Canadian commands, and vice versa. Same was true of the companies. But this happy, if somewhat confusing state of affairs could not continue. . . ." As a result, a composite close-order drill was created by the First Special Service Force using elements of both the Canadian and American Armies' drills. "The line formation and turns were U.S.; the long arm swing, some of the commands, and the about-face were Canadian." As well, the Force lexicon became one of commingled jargon and slang.

Colonel Frederick and Lt. Colonel McQueen during early wing pinning ceremony. Force junior officers were among the first to make their jumps. Once qualified, some became jump masters and helped to train the enlisted personnel. (Author's Collection)

Robert Tyron Frederick (center) had graduated from West Point in 1928 and was now in his mid-thirties. Though his early soldiering gave little hint of his future exploits, taking command of the First Special Service Force would be the turning point in his military career. (Author's Collection)

Force officers receiving demolitions training from Engineer Board instructors, c. October 1942. (Author's Collection)

Marching quick time was at a cadence of 140 steps per minute, more rapid than the U.S. Army's normal 120, while maintaining a thirty-inch stride. According to Robert D. Burhans: "If the uniforms, weapons, and equipment were visibly U.S. issue, the Force character had evolved into something international in flavor."[21]

Parachute training at Fort William Henry Harrison shared little in common with the U.S. Army's Parachute School at Fort Benning, Georgia. Because of time restraints, the Army's standard four week schedule was thrown out the window. While, as was the case throughout all phases of Force training, the men underwent vigorous physical training (copious condition-

"Powder River, let 'er blow!" Abandoned mine equipment is blasted high above the Montana prairie by a Force demolitions class. (Author's Collection)

RS explosive came in the form of blocks connected by an internal vein of primacord. (Author's Collection)

ing runs in the nearby Scratch Gravel Hills and up "Muscle Mountain," as well as calisthenics and workouts on the obstacle course), there were neither jump towers nor the requirement for the men to learn how to pack their own 'chutes. In a few short days the men were taught the rudiments of parachuting, got the feel of hanging in their harnesses, learned from mock-ups and parked planes how to exit the aircraft properly, and got a taste for what landing would be like. The whole process, from orientation to the final jump, took about one week. While the rest of the U.S. Army required five jumps to qualify, the First Special Service Force required but two. The idea was that if a man jumped successfully on his first attempt, and then had the nerve to, usually on the next day, board an aircraft and make another leap, that was sufficient to earn him his parachute qualification badge.

With the exception of men from Service Company's Parachute Platoon (who, on 31 July 1942, were the first men to jump at Fort Harrison), only personnel of the Combat Echelon took parachute training. It was deemed that Service Battalion's support functions were, to the organization as a whole, too indispensable to be compromised by the inevitable casualties that parachute jumping caused. Even Force Headquarters Detachment S-1, Kenneth G. Wickham, a member of the Combat Echelon, was, by Colonel Frederick, not allowed to jump for the same reason. Regardless of prior qualification (as was the case with a number of Canadian Forcemen who had either taken jump training at Fort Benning, Georgia, or Ringway, England), all combat men men had to complete two successful parachute drops at Fort William Henry Harrison.[22]

Force demolitions class prepares to destroy the Elk Point Bridge with RS explosive, c. October 1942. (Author's Collection)

Forcemen examine a large piece of debris hurled from the blast of a mine demolition. (Author's Collection)

The power of RS is demonstrated on a railroad bridge near Libby, Montana, felling the massive structure into the Kootenai River, 5 October 1942. (Lew Merrim)

Ruins of railroad bridge at Libby, Montana, 5 October 1942. The blast was so powerful that over three miles away plate glass store windows along Libby's Main Street were shattered. (Author's Collection)

Initially, casualties from parachute jumping ran high, some weeks as high as twenty five percent – everything from sprained ankles to broken legs. The landing technique, peddled by the Parachute School, and initially adopted by the Force, was found to be the culprit. The men had been taught to land with their feet eighteen inches apart, and to tumble forward or backward upon making contact with the ground. Motion picture film of parachute landings was quickly ordered. Produced by Sergeant Tom Hope of Force Headquarters Company's photo unit, the resulting footage showed that one parachutist's foot usually hit the ground a split second before the other. The impact of landing on an unsupported leg, however briefly, was in many cases enough to cause serious injury. At this point the influence of those Canadian Force members who had had the benefit of Royal Air Force parachute training at Ringway, England, came into play. The landing stance was changed to the British style, that being one with both feet together. This simple alteration turned the trick and casualties immediately dropped to about one percent. The Force photo unit produced a short film demonstrating this 'new' landing technique and sent it to the Parachute School, where it became the new standard.[23]

On 31 July, the Force conducted its first parachute jumps with Colonel Frederick being among the first out the door. By 3 August, almost all U.S. officers had become qualified parachutists, and the enlisted men had begun their training in earnest. On 29 August a parade formation was held where 1,200 Forcemen, both Canadians and Americans, received their parachute wings. Incidentally, early on in parachute training, the Force lost its original Executive Officer, Canadian Lt. Colonel John McQueen, to a broken leg. On 1 September 1942, he was replaced by a no-nonsense American, Lt. Colonel Paul D. Adams, who was one of Frederick's West Point classmates. McQueen transferred to Washington, where even though being dropped from the Force, he lent his assistance to the Force Intelligence and Supply staffs, contributing to planning for Operation PLOUGH.[24]

On 3 September 1943, Colonel Frederick flew to England for deployment planning. "There he found the climate for PLOUGH greatly changed." In the months that led up to this moment it had come to pass that both Rumania and Italy had been, for numerous reasons, dropped from consideration as objectives for the PLOUGH campaign. Hence, all energy and planning had been focused on Norway. However, the Norwegian government in exile had soured to PLOUGH. Having reconsidered its position on the matter, it now contended that widespread raids would invite harsh reprisals by the Germans upon the Norwegian people, and that mass destruction of power producing facilities would cause undue hardship among the already hard-pressed populace. Moreover, Great Britain's reluctance to mount a cross-Channel invasion in the Spring of 1943 (a position in no small way influenced by the sobering results of the Dieppe raid of August 1942), and the insistence on the part of the Russians that a second front be opened as soon as possible, forced the postponement of the cross-Channel invasion for one year. The focus of the Joint Chiefs was now on a long ranged plan that would immediately place Anglo-American forces in North Africa as a prelude to landings on the Italian mainland.[25]

With the justification for the PLOUGH force's existence removed, to say nothing of other factors – including resistance

Dermont M. O'Neill (left) taught the Force a highly effective form of self defense based on jujitsu. The O'Neill method included kicks to the groin, and devastating eye and throat punches that could down an opponent in a matter of moments. (Author's Collection)

Techniques of unarmed combat are practiced under the expert tutelage of Dermont M. "Pat" O'Neill (center) who was seconded to the Force from the O.S.S. Here, a Forceman learns how to overcome an opponent armed with a pistol. (Author's Collection)

RIGHT: Bayonet drill at Fort Harrison. Note that Canadian Forcemen still wear tam-o'-shanters, and that there appears to be as yet no piping on the American's overseas caps. All four men wear A-2 leather flight jackets, olive drab wool ski trousers, and ski-mountain boots. (National Archives)

An unarmed Force trainee squares off against an opponent armed with a bayonet. (Author's Collection)

on the part of the Royal Air Force with regard to air transport for the Weasels – Frederick and Mountbatten agreed to lay the PLOUGH campaign to rest. After returning to Washington, Frederick reported to General Marshall, in whose hands he left the fate of the First Special Service Force. When, on 8 October 1942, Ottawa was notified of the operation's cancellation, it considered withdrawing the Canadians from the Force. However, an appeal to the Canadian Government by General Marshall, who envisioned a new role for Frederick's command, perhaps as assault infantry, kept the Force alive.[26]

Armed with a new purpose, Frederick and his staff, "set about changing the tables of organization and equipment to fit the Force more readily into a versatile assault group." Training was altered accordingly, and the new tables reflected not only an increase in authorized strength, but the addition of the necessary organic support weapons at the section and platoon level. While the sections would be led, as before, by a Staff Sergeant, the personnel strength of each section was raised to include as many as sixteen men. The Service Battalion would likewise receive an infusion of personnel, and by December, 97 Canadian volunteers (from the 1st Canadian Parachute Battalion) and 236 American volunteers would arrive to fill the ranks of the newly reorganized companies. A number of the Canadians in this forthcoming batch would be signed aboard by Captain R.W. Becket from contingents undergoing parachute training at Fort Benning.[27]

Training's second phase, began in October and "was designed to train the subordinate units. During this phase the regularly assigned unit commanders conducted the instruction except in specialized subjects, such as skiing, demolitions, and motor maintenance." Originally this training period had been scheduled to last from 5 October to 21 November 1942, but in light of PLOUGH's demise and due in part to certain snow conditions, it would last through January 1943. A four-week-long ski training was carried out under very rigorous conditions. Troops were trucked into a remote railway pass in the Rocky Mountains near Blossburg, Montana. They familiarized themselves with various articles of winter equipment including their eider-down-filled mountain sleeping bags. Living out of boxcars that lay on the railway siding, the Forcemen were led in their training by a group of Norwegian Army ski instructors commanded by Captain Einer S. Kiil. The Forcemen dubbed their instructors "ski-Wegians". Proficiency, especially by Canadians, many already accustomed to snowy conditions, was gained rapidly.[28]

Forceman drills on the bayonet course. (Author's collection)

Amidst cries of *Powder River, let 'er blow!*, demolitions training had commenced with TNT (*trinitrotoluene*). A few weeks later, Pentolite, and a new, concentrated explosive called *Ryan's Special* (RS) were introduced. RS was three to four times as powerful as a comparable weight charge of TNT, and, in the form of sticks, was carried in thirty-pound packages. The Force had procured the first seventy tons of RS (the total current production) from the Ordnance Department. In late September, Lieutenant Dan Ryan, inventor of RS, along with three other officers, was sent to Fort Harrison to instruct the Forcemen on its uses and capabilities. Connected by primacord (resembling fuze but which was actually filled with TNT allowing multiple charges to be detonated simultaneously) it was very effective against both steel and concrete.[29]

Trainees setting up the M-1919A4 Browning machine gun, Fort William Henry Harrison, Montana. (Author's Collection)

ABOVE LEFT: Checking his accuracy with the M-1911A1 automatic on the pistol range at Fort Harrison. (Author's Collection)

ABOVE RIGHT: Machine gunners move their M-1919A4 machine gun into firing position. (Author's collection)

BELOW: Light machine gun crew prepares to fire at a towed target during antiaircraft training. (Lew Merrim)

Other elements were added including combat principles, field exercises, camping, field firing and combat firing, map reading, foreign weapons (primarily German), grenades, combat signals, extended order drill, and the continuation of marksmanship practice as well as marching and physical training. The training marches were, for the most part, carried out over the rough Montana countryside making use of compass bearings to maintain course. Elaborate combat courses, comprised of moving targets, smoke, booby traps, and explosive charges, gave a realistic environment in which to practice fire and maneuver, introduced as *Battle Drill* by the Canadians. In order to successfully complete combat problems on these courses, small unit leaders were encouraged to develop personal initiative and resourcefulness.[30]

The third and final training phase at Fort Harrison, from January 1943, through March 1943, involved almost continuous field work that combined the utilization of special equipment such as vehicles, radios, and skis. New weapons were introduced including the 60mm mortar, the Bazooka, and the portable flame thrower. Other new elements included mountain climbing, antiaircraft and anti-mechanized defense, intelligence and communications, rules of land warfare, and large-scale field exercises. Second Lieutenant Lincoln Washburn, of National Geographic mountaineering fame, and more recently of the Army Specialist Corps, was secured by the Force to assist the Quartermaster Corps in selecting the items of winter clothing and equipment that the Force required. Having had wide experience in this field, Washburn lectured to the Force on how to survive under conditions of extreme cold. Forcemen learned to use ice axes, pitons, various ropes and slings, and became skilled at scaling vertical rock faces and rappelling down cliffs on single lines. The latter had to be practiced while supporting the weight of a simulated casualty on one's chest. Later, as a number of select men completed their general training, they were formed into separate groups and sent to U.S. Army schools, including – as in the case of Intelligence and Reconnaissance Sergeants and Officers – the Intelligence School at Fort Ritchie, Maryland, where they received specialized individual instruction.[31]

"Tactical problems were drawn to stress raiding an objective and getting away, as opposed to standing and fighting it out with the enemy. Demolition training intensified. Instructors provided by the Engineer Board gave advanced training to fifty selected officers who were taught the complete technique, including photo or map reconnaissance of the target, planning the attack, and actual placing and firing of the charges. Bridges,

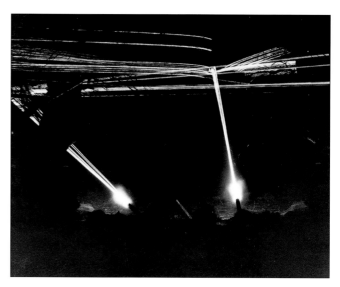

Tracer rounds paint the sky during a live fire exercise at night with light machine guns. (Lew Merrim)

Forcemen were trained to use enemy weapons at a time when this practice was unheard of in most other units. Here a man squeezes off a burst from a German MP-40 9mm submachine gun. (Author's Collection)

The German MG-34 machine gun is tested by a Force Canadian. The weapon's 1,200 round per minute cyclic rate was approximately twice that of the American Army's standard light machine gun. (Author's Collection)

Canadian member of the Force about to test-fire a German 28-20 Gerlich-principle antitank rifle. (Author's Collection)

mills and heavy machinery which had fallen into disuse were used as targets." Every Forceman was trained to cut girders, to demolish dumps, and to destroy industrial equipment by having actually placed and fired such charges. "All types of training, including demolitions, was conducted during darkness," a measure that was to pay great dividends when the Force was finally committed to combat operations.[32]

Late arrivals and training replacements were grouped together to form what was called the Training Regiment and followed an especially intensive compressed training schedule to bring them up to speed on Force drill, tables of organization, and U.S. military courtesy and terminology. On 11 January, after completing its course, the Training Regiment was broken up and the men were dispersed throughout the companies. The arduous training pace set at Helena, in the words of the Force

S-2, "separated the sheep from the goats." Any member of the Force who could not adapt to the climatic conditions that were encountered, or who was unable to continue the rigorous training, was reassigned immediately. Few men would allow themselves this personal disgrace and out of that determination and camaraderie grew a strong *esprit de corps*.[33]

In the interest of morale of the entire group, released individuals were reassigned, and those individuals left the Force, on the day that the decision was made to take such action. "Officers who [became] available for reassignment during the training period of the First Special Service Force [were] reported to the Commanding General of the component Ground Force, Air Forces or Services of Supply," and were then reassigned back to the station from which the officer had come. Warrant officers and enlisted men who became available for reassignment

"Hang, Fire!" Forcemen learn how to operate the M-2 60mm mortar. (Author's Collection)

An M-1 antitank rocket launcher is shown to a class of trainees. (Author's Collection)

The 2.36" antitank rocket that is launched by the M-1 Bazooka. (Author's Collection)

Test firing the M-1 Bazooka. The men wear light weight gas masks in order to protect their faces from any back blast from the rocket as it leaves the tube. (Author's Collection)

were reported to the Adjutant General who promptly issued orders for the men, so affected, to be transferred out to a unit of the appropriate arm or service. According to Stanley Dziuban: "Throughout the training process in Montana, a substantial rate of transfers from the Force was maintained as individuals showed lack of will, stamina, or other qualifications." It is estimated that the Force, during the weeding out process, went through twice as many men as it eventually kept.[34]

On 11 April 1943, orders were issued by the War Department for the First Special Service Force's movement to Camp Bradford, near Norfolk, Virginia, where it arrived on 15 April 1943, to commence amphibious training. Upon its arrival, the Force was assigned to the Second Army, except for amphibious training which was conducted under the direction of the Commander, Amphibious Force, Atlantic Fleet. The purpose of this training was to "prepare the Force for ship-to-shore and shore-to-shore landings with its present winter equipment and vehicles" and to develop within the Force the capability to "gain access to enemy areas by means of amphibious landing . . . and

thereafter [to] operate in small groups, employing infiltration tactics to perform acts of sabotage, disrupt communications and transmit to friendly sources such elements of military information as possible."[35]

The first phase of training at Camp Bradford was directed towards familiarizing the Forcemen with basic Naval terminology as well as to acclimate them to existence aboard ships. The second phase, which included night operations, rehearsed the methods that would make possible the ". . . landing of the First Special Service Force at unexpected places by rubber

RIGHT: Closeup view of M-1 portable flame thrower showing the main fuel tanks and the smaller nitrogen propellant tank. (Author's Collection)

BELOW: Forcemen ignite a patch of Montana prairie to test out the M-1 portable flame thrower. (Author's Collection)

boats," and emphasized the tactical advantages of its deployment onto "rocky shores in widely separated small groups." In late April, ten days after arrival at Bradford, the Amphibious staff proclaimed the Force had finished its essential work a week ahead of schedule. From that time until middle May, from anchorages off of Solomons Island, Maryland, and Fort Story, Virginia, the Force took part in simulated combat landings along the Chesapeake coast. With praise for the "high state of efficiency with which [it] had assimilated its water training," the First Special Service Force "was declared thoroughly quali-

fied for all types of amphibious operations" by the Amphibious Force staff.[36]

From the Chesapeake Bay area, the Force moved to Fort Ethan Allen, near Burlington, Vermont, there to wait for what most of the Forcemen expected would be their transfer to the United Kingdom and then to somewhere in the European Theatre of Operations and an inevitable meeting with the Germans. During their short stay at Ethan Allen, from 23 May 1943, to 28 June 1943, the Forcemen were kept busy plying their newly acquired skills in raiding and scouting exercises along the shores

On the road to Marysville, Montana, September 1942. The Forcemen marched 47.6 miles this day, getting a feel for ski poles along the way. (Canadian War Museum)

Forcemen fall out for a ten minute break along the roadside during one of the extended conditioning marches, September 1942. (Canadian War Museum)

of Lake Champlain, and in testing the new section-level weapon that had been issued to them while at Camp Bradford – the M-41 Johnson light machine gun. The Force, as well, took on further replacements, in this case all U.S. volunteers. Like the men who had been placed in the Training Regiment at Fort Harrison, these men were given a crash course in Force doctrine and customs, including parachute jumping which was performed out of a C-47 Dakota troopship using Ethen Allen's parade ground as the dropping zone.[37]

Over the months following PLOUGH's cancellation, Frederick tirelessly undertook to employ his command. He closely watched the developments of Operation TORCH and the situation in North Africa. Action on the Russian Front, especially in the Caucuses, held his attention. New Guinea was briefly offered as the locality for a possible operation but quickly dropped. The Force, it was suggested, might even take part in an operation to wrest Kiska, one of the western-most islands in the Aleutian chain, back from the Japanese.

In January 1943, in a meeting between Colonel Frederick and Lt. General Simon B. Buckner, Jr., commander of the U.S. Army Alaska Defense Command, the latter expressed notable enthusiasm over the possible inclusion of the Force in an Aleutian operation during the coming spring. Meanwhile, General Eisenhower, who was immersed in planning Operation HUSKY – the invasion of Sicily – had sent several communiqués to the War Department requesting use of the First Special Service Force.

But no matter how anxious Frederick might have been to prove the worth of his command, he remained patient as his men continued to hone their skills to a precise edge. When the moment arrived that it had completed the entirety of its training, the First Special Service Force had achieved a readiness for combat unmatched throughout the Allied armies. With training behind them, Frederick and his men awaited their ultimate test. Trial by fire.[38]

Forcemen tackle one of many apparatus on Fort Harrison's obstacle course, c. August 1942. (Author's Collection)

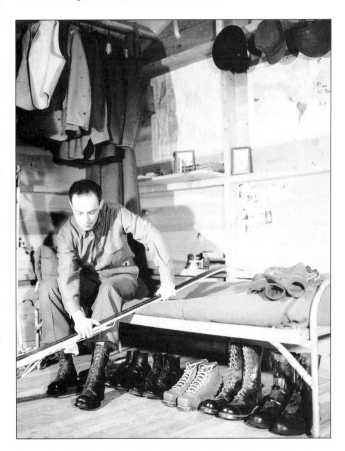

View of enlisted man's quarters, Fort William Henry Harrison, Montana. (Thomas W. Hope)

Double retreat ceremony is performed at Fort William Henry Harrison as both United States and Canadian national flags are lowered. (National Archives)

Fort Harrison classroom: Second Lieutenant Lincoln Washburn discusses the items of clothing and equipment that are to be carried in the framed rucksack. (National Archives)

Rows of T-15 Weasels parked at Fort William Henry Harrison, winter 1942-1943. (Author's Collection)

Studebaker representative gives motor maintenance instruction to group of Force combat mechanics, c. October 1942. (Author's Collection)

OPPOSITE: Forcemen carrying rucksacks and rifles practice rappelling in the rocky terrain of the Continental Divide. (National Archives)

INSET TOP: Using ropes to lower themselves down a ledge. (Thomas W. Hope)

INSET BOTTOM: Captain Einer S. Kiil, Norwegian Army, leads Force ski instruction at Blossburg, Montana, c. January 1943. (First Special Service Force Association)

BACKGROUND: Ski-borne Forcemen glide over a slope. According to the Force S-2, Lt. Colonel Robert D. Burhans, by the end of February 1943, 99% of the Force had been declared competent skiers by Norwegian Army standards. (National Archives)

LEFT: With rifles slung, Forcemen learn how to cross country ski during training at Blossburg, Montana, c. January 1943. (Lew Merrim)

Forcemen use an SCR-694 ground radio set powered by a hand-cranked generator operated by the man on the left, c. January 1943. (National Archives)

Force rifleman with M-1942 bayonet hunkered down in deep snow during winter exercises, c. January 1943. (National Archives)

Cleaning weapons and drying out after day-long training, Blossburg, Montana, c. January 1943. (Author's Collection)

Ski trainees warm themselves around a pot-bellied stove inside of one of the boxcar-barracks at Blossburg, Montana, c. January 1943. (Author's Collection)

ABOVE: Forceman stands guard during a Second Regiment command post exercise in the hills near Fort Harrison, 17 March 1943. (Author's Collection)

ABOVE RIGHT: Headquarters personnel inside of Second Regiment CP during a command post exercise, 17 March 1943. (Author's Collection)

RIGHT: T-15 cargo carrier in winter camouflage paint scheme parked beside the Second Regiment CP during a command post exercise on 17 March 1943. The Forceman is concealing the Weasel against aerial observation. (Author's Collection)

Saying goodbye to Helena, 6 April 1943. Force color guard carries before it the national flags of the United States and Canada. Missing from this picture is the Force's Organizational Colors which would be completed and delivered to the Force when it arrived at Camp Bradford, Virginia. (Author's Collection)

Procession of Force companies passes down Last Chance Gulch. Rather than shouldering their arms in the standard U.S. Army fashion, on the few occasions that Forcemen marched under arms in service dress uniform, they simply slung their weapons. (Author's Collection)

HELENA, MO
APRIL 6, 19

Closeup of Force company marching past throngs of Helenites. (Canadian War Museum)

Force parade passes reviewing stand occupied by Governor Ford of Montana; General Weeks of the Canadian Forces General Staff; Colonel Eaton, Great Falls Air Base Commander; Colonel Biles, Post Commander of Fort William Henry Harrison; Colonel Frederick; and Mr. A.T. Hibbard of the Union Bank and Trust Company, a strong supporter of the Force during its stay in Helena. (Canadian War Museum)

OPPOSITE: First Special Service Force's farewell parade down Last Chance Gulch, Helena, Montana. (Canadian War Museum)

OPPOSITE: Lowering a rubber boat from a transport ship onto the deck of an LCT during amphibious training, vic. Camp Bradford, Virginia. (Author's Collection)

INSET TOP: Forcemen board a transport ship via a scramble net during amphibious exercises, Norfolk, Virginia. Overhead in the background an LCVP hangs suspended by its davits. (Author's Collection)

INSET BOTTOM: Forcemen wait their turn to board the transport ship. (Author's Collection)

RIGHT: Forcemen lounge about the deck of an LCT transport. Once in position offshore of the landing beach, the rubber boats will be carried down the ramp of the LCT and launched into the water. (Author's Collection)

RIGHT: Force platoon descends net scramble into an LCVP during amphibious training on the Chesapeake Bay. (Author's Collection)

BELOW: An LCA carrying a Force section plows through the bay water toward Solomons Island. (Author's Collection)

LEFT: Rubber boats are stacked aboard the LCT, Chesapeake Bay, vic. Camp Bradford, Virginia. (Author's collection) RIGHT: Boarding a landing craft via a scramble net was a tricky business, but one in which the Force became quite proficient. Here Forcemen and rubber boats quickly crowd the deck of an LCT off the coast of Camp Bradford, Virginia. (Author's Collection)

Seven-man teams practice landing techniques using rubber assault boats off Camp Bradford, Virginia. These rubber boats were officially designated as LCR(S), or Landing Craft Rubber-Small. (Author's Collection)

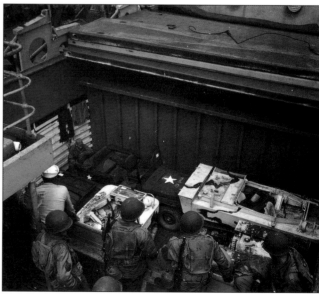

Forcemen peer into the hold of their transport at jeeps and T-15 cargo carriers. (Author's Collection)

T-15 Weasel is hoisted from the hold of the transport. (Author's Collection)

T-15 cargo carrier is lowered to the deck of an LCVP. (Author's Collection)

LEFT: Force section scrambles from the LCA onto the beach during maneuvers at Solomons Island, Maryland. (Author's Collection)
BELOW: Naval crewmen of an assault landing craft signal to other vessels. Meanwhile, Forcemen, with bayonets bared, make ready to land at Solomons Island, Maryland. Note that the Forcemen wear Arctic field jackets, and that the man at the rear right of the landing craft utilizes a formed plywood packboard. (Author's Collection)

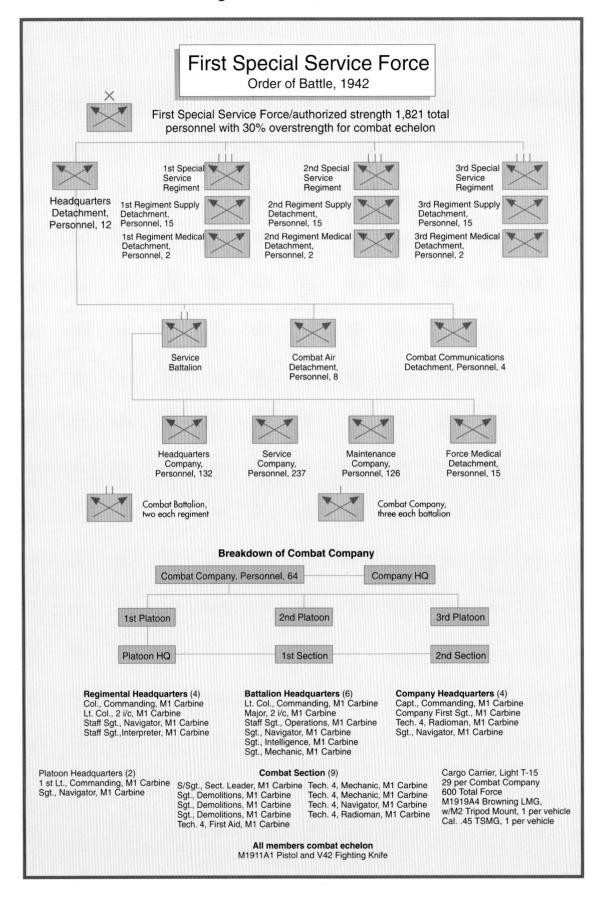

First Special Service Force
Order of Battle, 1942

First Special Service Force/authorized strength 1,821 total personnel with 30% overstrength for combat echelon

Headquarters Detachment, Personnel, 12

1st Special Service Regiment

1st Regiment Supply Detachment, Personnel, 15

1st Regiment Medical Detachment, Personnel, 2

2nd Special Service Regiment

2nd Regiment Supply Detachment, Personnel, 15

2nd Regiment Medical Detachment, Personnel, 2

3rd Special Service Regiment

3rd Regiment Supply Detachment, Personnel, 15

3rd Regiment Medical Detachment, Personnel, 2

Service Battalion

Combat Air Detachment, Personnel, 8

Combat Communications Detachment, Personnel, 4

Headquarters Company, Personnel, 132

Service Company, Personnel, 237

Maintenance Company, Personnel, 126

Force Medical Detachment, Personnel, 15

Combat Battalion, two each regiment

Combat Company, three each battalion

Breakdown of Combat Company

Combat Company, Personnel, 64

Company HQ

1st Platoon

2nd Platoon

3rd Platoon

Platoon HQ

1st Section

2nd Section

Regimental Headquarters (4)
Col., Commanding, M1 Carbine
Lt. Col., 2 i/c, M1 Carbine
Staff Sgt., Navigator, M1 Carbine
Staff Sgt.,Interpreter, M1 Carbine

Battalion Headquarters (6)
Lt. Col., Commanding, M1 Carbine
Major, 2 i/c, M1 Carbine
Staff Sgt., Operations, M1 Carbine
Sgt., Navigator, M1 Carbine
Sgt., Intelligence, M1 Carbine
Sgt., Mechanic, M1 Carbine

Company Headquarters (4)
Capt., Commanding, M1 Carbine
Company First Sgt., M1 Carbine
Tech. 4, Radioman, M1 Carbine
Sgt., Navigator, M1 Carbine

Platoon Headquarters (2)
1 st Lt., Commanding, M1 Carbine
Sgt., Navigator, M1 Carbine

Combat Section (9)
S/Sgt., Sect. Leader, M1 Carbine
Sgt., Demolitions, M1 Carbine
Sgt., Demolitions, M1 Carbine
Sgt., Demolitions, M1 Carbine
Tech. 4, First Aid, M1 Carbine

Tech. 4, Mechanic, M1 Carbine
Tech. 4, Mechanic, M1 Carbine
Tech. 4, Navigator, M1 Carbine
Tech. 4, Radioman, M1 Carbine

Cargo Carrier, Light T-15
29 per Combat Company
600 Total Force
M1919A4 Browning LMG,
w/M2 Tripod Mount, 1 per vehicle
Cal. .45 TSMG, 1 per vehicle

All members combat echelon
M1911A1 Pistol and V42 Fighting Knife

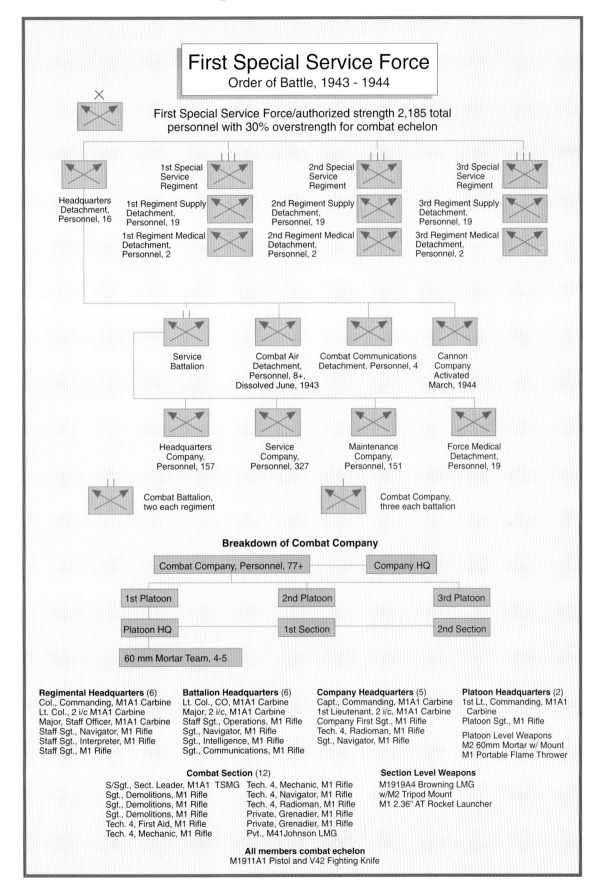

First Special Service Force
Order of Battle, 1943 - 1944

First Special Service Force/authorized strength 2,185 total personnel with 30% overstrength for combat echelon

1st Special Service Regiment

2nd Special Service Regiment

3rd Special Service Regiment

Headquarters Detachment, Personnel, 16

1st Regiment Supply Detachment, Personnel, 19

2nd Regiment Supply Detachment, Personnel, 19

3rd Regiment Supply Detachment, Personnel, 19

1st Regiment Medical Detachment, Personnel, 2

2nd Regiment Medical Detachment, Personnel, 2

3rd Regiment Medical Detachment, Personnel, 2

Service Battalion

Combat Air Detachment, Personnel, 8+, Dissolved June, 1943

Combat Communications Detachment, Personnel, 4

Cannon Company Activated March, 1944

Headquarters Company, Personnel, 157

Service Company, Personnel, 327

Maintenance Company, Personnel, 151

Force Medical Detachment, Personnel, 19

Combat Battalion, two each regiment

Combat Company, three each battalion

Breakdown of Combat Company

Combat Company, Personnel, 77+

Company HQ

1st Platoon

2nd Platoon

3rd Platoon

Platoon HQ

1st Section

2nd Section

60 mm Mortar Team, 4-5

Regimental Headquarters (6)
Col., Commanding, M1A1 Carbine
Lt. Col., 2 i/c M1A1 Carbine
Major, Staff Officer, M1A1 Carbine
Staff Sgt., Navigator, M1 Rifle
Staff Sgt., Interpreter, M1 Rifle
Staff Sgt., M1 Rifle

Battalion Headquarters (6)
Lt. Col., CO, M1A1 Carbine
Major, 2 i/c, M1A1 Carbine
Staff Sgt., Operations, M1 Rifle
Sgt., Navigator, M1 Rifle
Sgt., Intelligence, M1 Rifle
Sgt., Communications, M1 Rifle

Company Headquarters (5)
Capt., Commanding, M1A1 Carbine
1st Lieutenant, 2 i/c, M1A1 Carbine
Company First Sgt., M1 Rifle
Tech. 4, Radioman, M1 Rifle
Sgt., Navigator, M1 Rifle

Platoon Headquarters (2)
1st Lt., Commanding, M1A1 Carbine
Platoon Sgt., M1 Rifle

Platoon Level Weapons
M2 60mm Mortar w/ Mount
M1 Portable Flame Thrower

Combat Section (12)
S/Sgt., Sect. Leader, M1A1 TSMG
Sgt., Demolitions, M1 Rifle
Sgt., Demolitions, M1 Rifle
Sgt., Demolitions, M1 Rifle
Tech. 4, First Aid, M1 Rifle
Tech. 4, Mechanic, M1 Rifle

Tech. 4, Mechanic, M1 Rifle
Tech. 4, Navigator, M1 Rifle
Tech. 4, Radioman, M1 Rifle
Private, Grenadier, M1 Rifle
Private, Grenadier, M1 Rifle
Pvt., M41Johnson LMG

Section Level Weapons
M1919A4 Browning LMG
w/M2 Tripod Mount
M1 2.36" AT Rocket Launcher

All members combat echelon
M1911A1 Pistol and V42 Fighting Knife

Historical Document #1: The Wickham-Williamson Agreement

C
  O
    P
      Y

Washington, D.C.
15 Jul 42.

To: D.S.D.

From: Williamson.

Certainly hope the enclosed "agreement" will meet with approval. It gives us a definite working basis. A copy has also gone forward to General Marshall for his approval.

It looks, at the moment, as though I would be leaving Washington Sunday for Helena, Montana. I will confirm this later.

The project is moving ahead by leaps and bounds here, and from my observations is in very capable hands.

Col. Frederick is most anxious that the Canadian personnel arrive in Helena by August 1, as all training schedules have been drawn up on that date, and believe me they are plenty tough.

Col. Frederick mentioned to me that mail moved very lowly via our Diplomatic Bag -- he cited the case of a letter written by you or Col. Anderson to him on July 3, which was not in his hands until July 11.

The necessary information re our troops' date of departure, port of entry, expected time of entry, numbers, etc., will be necessary in good time to make the necessary arrangements re Customs and Immigration.

This is being written in haste in long hand, as no one is available to type it.

Your comments are awaited.

HEADQUARTERS, 1ST SPECIAL SERVICE FORCE

Washington, D.C.

July 15, 1942.

MEMORANDUM FOR THE DIRECTOR OF STAFF DUTIES,
    GENERAL STAFF, OTTAWA, CANADA:

The following proposals have been agreed upon by Major Kenneth G. Wickham, U.S. Army, and Major D.D. Williamson, Canadian Army, and approved by Colonel Robert T. Frederick, U.S. Army, as a system of handling Canadian personnel of the 1st Special Service (official U.S. War Department designation), in relation to discipline, records, pay, allowances, rations, quarters, clothing and equipment, travel, hospitalization and dental care, and men for various reasons found unfit for service with this force and returned for duty in Canada.

1. The Canadian members of the force having enlisted in the Canadian Army and taken the <u>oath of allegiance</u> will not be required to take the American oath of allegiance.

2. <u>Discipline</u> for all members of the force will be in accordance with U.S. regulations as laid down in the 1928 "Manual for Courts-Martial, U.S. Army".

3. Records of Canadian personnel will be maintained and posted in accordance with the existing Canadian system.
    This entails the addition to the force of a Canadian paymaster, pay sergeant, and records sergeant, who, along with their other routine duties in connection with the force, would be responsible for this work.
    The paymaster would also provide a valuable link with the Canadian Pay Corps for accounting purposes and be available to the Canadian personnel to aid in straightening out dependents allowance difficulties, etc.

4. <u>Pay</u> for all members of the force will be in accordance with Bulletin No. 28 (June 25th, 1942), U.S. War Department,

-1-

---

3 (three) copies of which are enclosed.
    Inasmuch as it is the intention of the Canadian Government to reimburse the U.S. Government in this respect, and that the force will be homogenous, a simple system has been defined and has received the tentative approval of Colonel E.W. McLarren, Office, Chief of Finance, U.S. Army, Advisory and Regulations Division.

5. <u>Dependents allowances</u> for the Canadian members of the force will be subject to the same regulations and system of payment as is in use in Canada under P & A regulations. This has also been taken into consideration in the system mentioned in the preceding paragraph.

6. <u>Rations</u> - Standard U.S. Army rations will be used for the force and the Canadian Government will be billed for the value of these rations by the Finance Department, U.S. Army.
    The pay vouchers and ration accounts will be submitted together from the above-mentioned office.

7. <u>Quarters</u> will be furnished to Canadian personnel on the same basis as to American personnel. (See Sec. 6, page 3 of enclosed Bulletin No. 28.)

8. <u>Clothing and Equipment</u> will be furnished to all members of the force at the expense of the U.S. Government.
    Canadian personnel, on receiving their instructions to report at the location chosen for their concentration, should be instructed to bring the following articles ONLY:

Summer drill with long trousers and black tie. This is to be worn, as it means puttees can be turned in before departure from the man's station.
    1 pair boots.
    3 pair socks.
    2 complete sets summer underwear.
    2 summer shirts (short sleeves).
    Personal toilet articles.
    1 pair shorts.
the summer drill, black ties, and boots will be returned to the nearest Canadian Ordnance Corps Depot at the expense of the Canadian Government.

9. <u>Travel</u> - The total cost of the original movement of the Canadian personnel to HELENA, MONTANA, to be borne by the Canadian Government. Subsequent traveling costs for all personnel to be borne by the U.S. Government.

10. <u>Hospitalization and Dental Care</u> will be provided at the expense of the U.S. Government, but Canadian personnel

-2-

---

hospitalized and found unfit for further service with the force will be returned to Canada when capable of traveling. Their further care will then be the responsibility of the Canadian Government.

11. <u>Pensions</u> - The U.S. Government assumes no liability for pensions liable owing to injury or death of Canadian personnel while members of this force.

12. Canadian personnel found unfit owing to physical or temperamental reason, etc., will be S.O.S. this force and returned for duty in Canada at the discretion of the Commanding Officer. Travel warrant will be issued and paid for by the U.S. Government to the nearest Canadian Depot.

13. In the event of any death while in the United States among the Canadian personnel, either by accident or through natural causes, the agreement recently reached by the United Nations will be adhered to.

Respectfully submitted,

KENNETH G. WICKHAM, Major, CAC   D.D. WILLIAMSON, Major,
                                  1st Bn, Dufferin & Haldimand Rifles,
                                     Canadian Army.

Approval:

Robert T. Frederick,
  Colonel, Commanding,
1st Special Service Force.

-3-

Historical Document #2: Drill Regulations

DRILL REGULATIONS

FIRST SPECIAL SERVICE FORCE
FORT WILLIAM HENRY HARRISON
HELENA, MONTANA

DRILL REGULATIONS

GENERAL

The drill prescribed herein is for the use of the First Special Service Force. The drill constitutes select movements of the U. S. Dismounted and Canadian Drill. It is of a general nature and should be used as a common sense solution of minor points which are not specifically covered in this memorandum. Necessary adaptations should be simple and should not complicate the drill. Stress should be placed on precision and unison in execution of commands, and in marching in step with proper alignment. Commanders are reminded that the drill should reflect the smartness, efficiency and the highly select quality of the personnel composing this force.

Section I

DEFINITION

1.   ALIGNMENT.- A straight line upon which several elements are formed or are to be formed; or the dressing of several elements upon a straight line.
2.   BASE.- The element or point on which a movement is regulated.
3.   COLUMN.- A formation in which the elements are placed one behind another.
4.   DEPTH.- The space from head to rear of any formation or of a position, including the leading and rear elements.
5.   DISTANCE.- Space between elements in the direction of depth. Distance is measured from the rear rank of the unit in front to the front rank of the unit in rear.
6.   DOUBLE TIME.- Cadence at the rate of 180 steps per minute.
7.   FILE.- A single column of men one behind the other.
8.   FLANK.- The right or left of a command in line or in column, or the element on right or left of the line.
9.   FORMATION.- Arrangement of elements of a command.
10.   FRONT.- The space occupied by an element measured from one flank to the opposite flank.
11.   GUIDE.- The person upon whom the command regulates its march.
12.   INTERVAL.- Space between individuals or elements of the same line.
13.   LINE.- A formation in which the different elements are abreast of each other.
14.   MASS FORMATION.- The formation of a company or any larger unit in which the sections in column are abreast of one another.
15.   PACE.- A step of 30 inches, the length of the full step in quick time.
16.   QUICK TIME.- Cadence at the rate of 140 steps per minute.
17.   RANK.- A line of men placed side by side.
18.   STEP.- The distance measured from heel to heel between the feet of a man walking. The steps in quick and double time are 30 and 36 inches respectively.

Section II

POSITIONS

1. POSITION OF THE SOLDIER, OR OF ATTENTION. a. Heels on the same line and as near to each other as the conformation of the man permits.
     b. Feet turned out equally and forming an angle of 45 degrees.
     c. Knees straight without stiffness.
     d. Hips level and drawn back slightly; body erect and resting equally on hips; chest lifted and arched; shoulders square and falling equally.
     e. Arms hanging straight down without stiffness. Hands closed but not clenched. Backs of the finders touching the thigh lightly, thumbs to the

---

front and close to the forefinger; thumbs immediately behind the seam of the trousers.
     f. Head erect and squarely to the front; chin drawn in so that the axis of the head and neck is vertical; eyes straight to the front.
     g. Weight of the body resting equally on the heels and the balls of the feet.
     h. In assuming the position of the soldier, or of attention the heels are brought together smartly and audibly.

2. RESTS. Being at a halt the commands are: BREAK OFF; 1. Stand At, 2. EASE; and REST.
     a. At the command BREAK OFF, the men leave the ranks but are required to remain in the immediate vicinity. On them resume their former places at attention at the command FALL IN. On the march, men will fall in At Ease unless they were at attention when the command Break Off was given.
     b. At the command of execution, EASE, of 1. Stand At, 2. EASE, move the left foot smartly 12 inches to the left keeping the leg straight. Keep the legs straight so that the weight of the body rests equally on both feet. At the same time, clasp the hands behind the back, palms to the rear, thumbs and fingers of the right hand clasping the left thumb without constraint, fingers extended and joined, preserve silence and immobility.
     c. At the command REST, one foot is kept in place. Silence and immobility are not required.

3. FACINGS. All facings are executed from the halt and in the cadence of quick time.
     a. To the Flank. (1) The commands are: 1. Right (Left), 2. FACE. At the command FACE, slightly raise the left heel and the right toe; face to the right, turning on the right heel, assisted by a slight pressure on the ball of the left foot. Hold the left leg straight without stiffness. (TWO) Place left foot beside the right. (2) Execute 1. Left, 2. FACE on the left heel in a corresponding manner.
     b. To the Rear. The commands are: 1. About, 2. FACE. At the command FACE, slightly raise the left heel and the right toe; face to the rear by the right-about, turning on the right heel, assisted by a slight pressure one the ball of the left foot. Hold the left leg straight without stiffness. (TWO) Place the left foot beside the right.

4. SALUTE WITH THE HAND. The commands are: 1. Hand, 2. SALUTE.
     a. At the command SALUTE, raise the right hand smartly until the tip of the forefinger touches the lower part of the headdress or forehead above and slightly to the right of the right eye, thumb and fingers extended and joined, palm to the left, upper arm horizontal, forearm incline at 45 degrees, hand and wrist straight; at the same time turn the head and eyes toward the person saluted. (TWO) Drop the arm to its normal position by the side in one motion, at the same time turning the head and eyes to the front.
     b. Execute the first position of the hand salute when six paces from the person saluted, or at the nearest point of approach, if more than six paces. Hold the first position until the person saluted has passed or the salute is returned. Then execute the second movement of the hand salute.

Section III

STEPS AND MARCHING

1. GENERAL. a. All steps and marching executed from the halt, begin with the left foot.
     b. The instructor indicates the proper cadence when necessary by calling "ONE", "TWO", "THREE", "FOUR", as the left and right foot strikes the ground.

---

2. QUICK TIME. Being at the halt, to march forward in quick time, the commands are:
     a. 1. Forward, 2. MARCH. At the command Forward, shift the weight of the body to the right leg without perceptible movement. At the command MARCH, step off smartly with the left foot and continue the march with 30 inch steps taken straight forward. Swing the arms naturally from the shoulders, elbows straight, so the hands reach the height of the waist belt in front and a natural swinging height to the rear. Hands should be kept closed but not clenched, thumbs always to the front.

3. DOUBLE TIME. a. Being in march in quick time, to march in double time the commands are: 1. Double Time, 2. MARCH. At the command MARCH, given as the right foot strikes the ground, take one more step in quick time and then step off in double time, raise the forearms, fingers closed, knuckles out, to a horizontal position along the waist line, take up an easy run with the step and cadence of double time, allowing a natural swinging motion to the arms.
     b. To resume the quick time from double time the commands are: 1. Quick Time, 2. MARCH. At the command MARCH, given as the right foot strikes the ground, advance and plant the left foot in double time, resume the quick time, dropping the hands by the sides.

4. TO HALT. To halt when marching in quick time, the commands are: 1. Section (Platoon, Company, Battalion), 2. HALT. At the command HALT, given as the right foot strikes the round, execute a halt in two counts by advancing and planting the left foot and then bring the right foot beside the left.

5. TO FACE TO THE REAR IN MARCHING. Being in march, the commands are: 1. To the Rear, 2. MARCH. At the command MARCH, given as the right foot strikes the ground, advance and plant the left foot; turn to the right about on the balls of both feet and immediately step off with the left foot. The arms must be kept close to the sides during the turn.

6. TO CHANGE STEP. The Commands are: 1. Change Step, 2. MARCH.
     a. Being in march in quick time, at the command MARCH, given as the right foot strikes the ground, advance and plant the left foot, plant the toe of the right foot near the heel of the left and step off with the left foot.

7. TO MARCH OTHER THAN AT ATTENTION. a. Marching at Attention, the command is: MARCH AT EASE. On this command men are required to keep in step and properly closed up, but are not required to march at attention and maintain silence.
     b. Marching at Ease, to march at Attention the command is: MARCH AT ATTENTION. On this command Attention is resumed and quick time cadence is executed.

Section IV

DRILL FOR FOOT TROOPS

Part I   The Section
Part II   The Platoon
Part III   The Company

Historical Document #2: Drill Regulations

Part I

THE SECTION

1. GENERAL.
    a. The section is a group of soldiers organized as a combat team. It consists of one Section Leader and other personnel as authorized. When the section leader is absent he is replaced by the next senior.
    b. The normal formation of the section is a single rank or single file.
    c. The section in line marches to the left or to the front only for minor changes of position.

2. TO FORM THE SECTION.
    a. The command is: FALL IN. At the command FALL IN, the section forms in line as shown below.

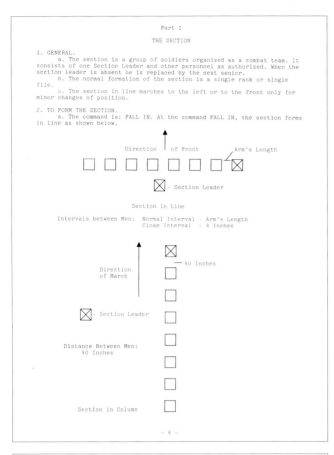

Direction of Front   Arm's Length

⊠ - Section Leader

Section in Line

Intervals between Men: Normal Interval - Arm's Length
                         Close Interval - 4 Inches

Direction of March

— 40 Inches

⊠ - Section Leader

Distance Between Men:
40 Inches

Section in Column

On the command: FALL IN, each man except the one on the right flank extends his right arm laterally at shoulder height, hand closed in the form of a fist. Each man, except the one on the right, turns his head and eyes to the right and places himself in line so that his right fist touches lightly the left shoulder of the man on his right. As soon as proper interval has been obtained each man drops his arms quietly to the side and turns his head to the front.
    b. The section falls in on the section leader or the right file if the section leader is not in ranks.
    c. To form close intervals, the commands are: 1. At Close Interval, 2. FALL IN. At the command FALL IN, the men fall in as in (a) above, except that close intervals are obtained by placing the right hand on the hip. In this position the heel of the palm of the hand rests on the hip, the finger and thumb are extended and joined, and the elbow is in the plane of the body.

3. TO COUNT OFF. The command is: COUNT OFF. At the command COUNT OFF, each man of the squad, except the one on the right flank, turns his head and eyes to the right. The right flank call out, "One". Each man in succession calls out, "Two", "Three", etc., turning his head and eyes to the front as he gives the number.

4. TO ALIGN THE SECTION. a. In line the commands are: 1. Dress Right (Left), 2. DRESS. At the command DRESS, each man except the one on the right extends his right arm (or if at close interval places his right hand upon his hip), and turns his head and eyes to the right and aligns himself to the right. The section leader places himself on the right flank one pace from and in prolongation of the line and facing down the line. From this position he verifies the alignment of the men, ordering individual men to move forward or backward as necessary. Having checked the alignment, he faces to the right in marching and moves three paces forward, halts, faces to the left and commands: 1. Ready, 2. FRONT. At the command FRONT, arms are dropped quietly and smartly to the side and heads turned to the front.
    b. In column the command is: COVER. At the command COVER, men cover from front to rear with 40 inches distance between men.

5. BEING IN COLUMN, TO CHANGE DIRECTION. The commands are: 1. Column Right (Left) (Half Right) (Half Left), 2. MARCH.
    a. Being at a halt, the leading man faces to the right by turning to the right (Left) or, (Half Right) or, (Half Left) on the ball of the right foot and at the same time steps off in the new direction with the left foot.
    b. Being in march, at the command of execution, given as the right foot strikes the ground the leading man advances and plants the left foot, then faces to the right in marching and steps off in the new direction with the right foot.
    c. In movement the other men in the column execute the same movement successively and on the same ground as the leading man.

6. PREVIOUS INSTRUCTIONS APPLICABLE. The section executes positions and steps and marching in the same manner as previously explained.

Part II

THE PLATOON

1. COMPOSITION AND FORMATION OF THE PLATOON.
    The platoon headquarters and two sections. For purposes of drill and ceremonies, a two rank formation should be arranged and the size of the sections equalized.

- 4 -

- 5 -

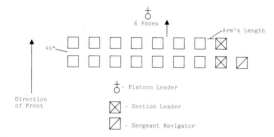

6 Paces   Arm's Length

40"

♀ - Platoon Leader

⊠ - Section Leader

⊠ - Sergeant Navigator

Direction of Front

Platoon in Line

2. TO FORM THE PLATOON. a. The command is: FALL IN. The platoon leader stands two paces in front of and facing the point where the section leader of the front section is to fall in. At the command FALL IN, the section leader of the front section takes position as indicated. The remaining men of the front rank section fall in on the section leader and extend arms laterally at shoulder height, back of hands up, hand closed in the form of a fist. Each man except the one on the right, turns head and eyes to the right and places himself in line so his knuckles touch the left shoulder of the man on the right. As soon as proper interval and alignment has been obtained, each man drops his arm smartly to the side and turns his head to the front. The other section forms in rear of the front section and in the same manner, with 40 inches distance between ranks. Members of the rear section extend arms to obtain their approximate interval but cover the corresponding members in the front section. The men of the rear section drop arms and turn heads to the front with the corresponding man of the front section.
    b. TO FORM AT CLOSE INTERVAL. The commands are: 1 At Close Interval, 2. FALL IN. At the command FALL IN, the movement is executed as prescribed in (2a) above except that sections form by placing the right hand on the hip.

3. TO DISMISS THE PLATOON. a. Being at attention, the command is: DISMISSED. At the command DISMISSED, given by an officer the platoon executes right face, right hand salute and leaves the formation.
    b. If the command DISMISSED, is given by a noncommissioned officer the platoon executes right race and leaves the formation without saluting.

4. TO MARCH THE PLATOON. a. The normal formation for marching is in a column of two with sections abreast, section leaders at the head of their sections.
    b. The platoon being in line to march to the right the commands are: 1. Right, 2. PACE, 3. Forward, 4. MARCH.

5. BEING IN LINE TO OPEN AND CLOSE RANKS. a. To open ranks the commands are: 1. Open Ranks, 2. MARCH, 3. Ready, 4. FRONT. At the command MARCH, the front rank takes one step forward and executes Dress Right. The rear rank

stands fast executes Dress Right, coming to the dress right with the front rank. The platoon leader places himself on the flank of the platoon toward which the dress is to be made, one pace from and in prolongation of the front rank and facing down the line. From this position he aligns the front rank. The second rank is aligned in the same manner. In moving from front to rear rank, the platoon leader faces to the left in marching. After verifying the alignment of the rear rank, he faces to the right in marching, moves three paces beyond the front rank, halts, faces to the left and commands: 1. Ready, 2. FRONT.
    b. TO CLOSE RANKS. The commands are: 1. Close Ranks, 2. MARCH. At the command MARCH, the front rank stands fast; the second rank takes one step forward and halts. Each man covers his file leaders. The platoon leader takes position six paces from and opposite the center of the platoon to give the command.

6. BEING IN COLUMN, TO CHANGE DIRECTION. a. The commands are: 1. Column Right (Left), 2. MARCH. The right flank section guide is the pivot for the movement. At the command MARCH, he faces to the right in marching takes one full step and takes up the half step until the man on his left comes abreast, then takes up the full step. The man on the left executes right oblique, advances until opposite his place in line, executes a second right oblique when abreast of the pivot man and takes up the full step. Succeeding men execute the movement on the same ground and in the same manner as the leading file.

Part III

THE COMPANY

1. GENERAL. a. The company consists of a company headquarters and three platoons. Sections and platoons are numbered consecutively within the company from right to left or from front to rear.
2. TO FORM THE COMPANY. a. The first sergeant takes position two paces in front of and facing the point where the right file man (section leader, first section) is to be posted and commands: SECTION LEADERS. At this command the section leader, first section, first platoon takes position two paces in front of and facing the first sergeant. The section leader, second section, first platoon takes position 40 inches in rear of and covering the section leader, first section. The section leaders of the second and third platoons take position on line and on the left of the section leaders of the first platoon; the section leader's odd numbered sections in the front rank, and the section leader's even numbered sections in the rear rank. The first sergeant then commands: 1. Section Leaders at ____ Paces, 2. MARCH. At the command MARCH, the section leaders of the second and third platoons face to the left in marching, section leaders of second platoon step off the number of paces designated, section leaders of the third platoon step off twice the number of paces designated. Section leaders of the second and third platoons face to the front simultaneously. Then the first sergeant about faces, marches seven paces forward, executes a left face in marching, and takes position nice paces in front of and opposite the center of the company and commands: FALL IN. At the command FALL IN, each platoon takes position on the section leaders as prescribed in platoon drill.
    b. The first sergeant then commands: REPORT. The section leaders in succession from front to rear beginning with the first platoon, salute and report "All Present" or "Private (____) absent."
    c. The company commander moves to his position twelve paces in front of and opposite the center of the company (three paces in front of the first sergeant) while the reports from the section leaders are being received.
    d. All sections having reported, the first sergeant then faces the company commander, salutes and reports, "Sir, all present or accounted

- 6 -

- 7 -

Historical Document #2: Drill Regulations

for," or "Sir, _____ men absent."
e. The company commander commands: POSTS. The first sergeant about faces, faces to the right in marching and marches forward. When opposite his position in the formation, indicated in the diagram, he faces to the left in marching and marches to position, halts and about faces. The platoon leaders move around the right flank of the platoon to a point six paces in front of the right of the platoon, execute a left face in marching, move to a position opposite the center of the platoon, and execute a right face.
f. The company may be formed at close interval.

Direction of Front

12 Paces

6 Paces

3 Paces

● - Company Commander
○ - Platoon Leader
⊠ - First Sergeant
⊠ - Section Leader
⊡ - Sergeant Navigator

Company in Line

3. BEING IN LINE, TO MARCH TO THE RIGHT. a. The company is faced to the right. The platoon leaders move to a position in front of the file leader of the left section. (See Diagram) All extra men move to a position in column in rear of the last platoon. Extra officers form in rear of enlisted men.
b. In ceremony or parade extra officers will exchange positions with Sergeant Navigators. All company officers except company commanders will be in the front rank in mass formation.
c. The company marches to the left from line only for minor changes of position.

4. TO DISMISS THE COMPANY. a. The company being in line at a halt, the company commander directs the first sergeant, "Dismiss the Company." The officers fall out. The first sergeant moves to a point nine paces in front of the center of the company, salutes the company commander, faces toward the company and commands: DISMISSED. The company executes right face, right hand salute and leaves the formation. The senior officer present returns the salute.

5. TO ALIGN THE COMPANY. a. The company being in the line at a halt, to align the company, the command is: DRESS RIGHT (Center or Left). At the command DRESS RIGHT, given by the company commander, the platoon leader of the base platoon dresses his platoon immediately. When the base platoon has executed FRONT, the platoon next adjacent to the base platoon executes the dress toward the base platoon. This movement is executed successively by other platoons.

- 8 -

Direction of Front

3 Paces

● - Company Commander
○ - Platoon Leader
⊠ - First Sergeant
⊠ - Section Leader
⊡ - Sergeant Navigator
○ - Extra Officers
□ - Extra Enlisted Men

Company in Line

6. PREVIOUS INSTRUCTION APPLICABLE. The company marches, executes change of direction, opens and closes ranks, executes facing, and steps in marching as in section and platoon drill.

7. TO PREPARE FOR INSPECTION. The company being in line, the company commander commands: PREPARE FOR INSPECTION. On this command the platoon leader of the first platoon commands: 1. Open Ranks, 2. MARCH, 3. Ready, 4. FRONT. The second and third platoons execute the open ranks successively after the platoon on the right has completed the dress. This dress must be expedited by platoon leaders.

8. BEING IN COLUMN OF TWO, TO FORM COMPANY MASS. a. The company being at a halt, the commands are: 1. Company Mass Left (Right), 2. MARCH. At the command MARCH, the leading platoon stands fast. The rear platoons move to position along side the leading platoons at normal interval by executing Column Half Left then Column Half Right. Each platoon is halted when its leading rank is on line with the leading rank of the platoon(s) already on line.
b. The company being in march, the commands are the same as given in (a) above. The movement is executed as described above except that immediately after the command MARCH, the leading platoon is halted by the commands: 1. Platoon, 2. HALT, given by its own leader.
c. Platoon leaders will give the appropriate commands for individual movements of the platoon.

9. BEING IN MASS FORMATION TO CHANGE DIRECTION. a. The commands are: 1. Column Right (Left), 2. MARCH. 3. Forward, 4. MARCH. The right flank man of the line of guides and platoon leaders is the pivot of this movement. At the command MARCH, he faces to the right in marching, takes one full step, and then takes up the half step. Other first rank men execute a right oblique, advance until opposite their place in line, execute a second right oblique on arriving abreast of the pivot man, and take up the half step. Each succeeding rank executes the movement on the same ground and in the same manner as the first rank. All take up the full step at the command MARCH, which is given after the entire company has changed direction.

- 9 -

b. In turning to the left on a moving pivot, each rank dresses to the left until the command MARCH, after that the dress is to the right unless otherwise announced.
c. The company commander faces to the rear and marches backward until the change in direction has been completed.

Direction of Front

Company Mass

6 Paces

40 Inches

● - Company Commander   ⊠ - Section Leader   ○ - Extra Officers
○ - Platoon Leader   ⊡ - Sergeant Navigator
⊠ - First Sergeant   □ - Extra Enlisted Men

10. BEING IN COMPANY MASS, TO FORM COLUMN OF TWOS.
Being at a halt, the commands are: 1. Column of Twos, 2. Right Platoon Forward. 3. MARCH. At the command MARCH, the right platoon marches forward. The other platoons stand fast and follow in column in their normal formation successively by executing Column Half Right and Column Half Left upon the commands of their respective leaders.

By Order of Colonel FREDERICK:

J. B. SHINBERGER,
Lt. Col., Infantry,
Training Officer.

OFFICIAL:

J. B. SHINBERGER,
Lt. Col., Infantry,
Training Officer.

- 10 -

CHAPTER 3

Operation Cottage

On 9 June 1943, Frederick received orders, the like of which he had for so long waited – his Force was to be committed for Operation COTTAGE: the assault on Kiska Island in the Aleutians. Stretching from the western tip of the Alaskan Peninsula across the northern Pacific for more than a thousand miles, the Aleutians offered an island bridge over which Japan had struck at North America. With a maneuver designed to divert at least part of the U.S. Fleet away from the imperiled American Naval Base at Midway Island and to perhaps "screen a northward thrust by Japanese forces into Siberia's maritime provinces and the Kamchatka Peninsula," Kiska and Attu, the two western most islands of the Aleutian chain, were occupied by the Japanese on 6 and 7 June 1942, respectively.[1]

Though the Japanese threatened no further expansion in the northern Pacific region, the Joint Chiefs of Staff, in mid-June 1942, directed that General Buckner's Alaska Defense Command, along with the Northern Pacific Force (Naval) and the Eleventh Air Force, begin a concerted effort to retake Attu and Kiska. Valued above what military success might be achieved was the possible psychological blow that could be dealt by decisively sweeping the Japanese from their only foothold on North American soil. The first step in this campaign began in mid-May 1943, when "Kiska was bypassed in favor of an invasion of [less heavily defended] Attu."[2] The inhospitable northern Pacific weather proved to be of major consequence during the ensuing three-week-long battle. Ill prepared to cope with the enemy or the elements, sixteen-hundred desert-trained and equipped American soldiers struggled to retake the island while enduring bitter hardship. But for twenty-nine Japanese who were taken prisoner, all of the island's 2,650 defenders fought to their deaths. American casualties were appallingly high – the ratio being second only to that of the battle of Iwo Jima.[3]

Now it remained only for Kiska to be taken. Possessing superior harbor facilities and what was believed to be an operational airfield, Kiska was more valuable to the Japanese and as such was more heavily defended by shore batteries and a larger garrison. Not wishing to repeat the hollow victory that Attu had become, Allied leaders strove to ensure that the assault on Kiska would be made under more favorable conditions. Troops of the landing force would be more suitably trained and equipped. "The landing force would consist of either combat veterans from Attu or troops trained at Adak in the type of fighting that had developed on Attu."[4] Beginning with summer 1942, General William C. Butler's U.S. Eleventh Air Force, operating from airfields in the central Aleutians, mounted continuous air attacks against Kiska pausing only for bad weather. During the same period, the island was also heavily bombarded by U.S. warships and was the stage for an elaborately contrived U.S. propaganda campaign. American planners were certain that the Japanese on Kiska knew full well of the Allied intent to reclaim the island. They also believed that the Japanese were steadily increasing Kiska's garrison to meet that coming threat. In mid-March 1943, the Northern Pacific Force under the command of Rear Admiral Thomas C. Kinkaid established a Naval blockade around Kiska, that in due course might limit the Japanese outpost, cut off from its lines of communication, to "wither on the vine."[5]

The Force moved from Fort Ethan Allen by rail to San Francisco where it arrived on 3 July 1943. From there the regiments and Service Battalion were ferried out to Fort McDowell,

Angel Island, Port of Embarkation in San Francisco Bay. Most of the men were still in the dark as to their final destination, but when they began to receive issues of clothing and footwear suited for cold and wet weather – rainsuits, heavy wool socks, and shoepacks – the picture became somewhat clearer. Additionally, Forcemen were issued the shoulder insignia of Amphibian Training Force 9 which they were to sew on both shoulders of their uniforms. Between 3-11 July the Forcemen received new equipment and shots, and underwent a final shake down before the Force departed as member of a small convoy en route to the Aleutians – First and Third Regiments aboard the newly commissioned Liberty ship S.S. *Nathaniel Wyeth*, and Second Regiment and Service Battalion aboard U.S.A.T. *John B. Floyd*. All told the Force sailed from "San Francisco with 169 officers, 8 warrant officers, and 2,283 enlisted men. . . ." The Force's Canadian component, having for record-keeping purposes been redesignated as the 1st Canadian Special Service Battalion in May 1943, numbered 42 officers and 552 other ranks.[6]

Troops, supplies, and logistics for Operation COTTAGE were being massed on Adak Island. The Force was assigned, as were the other Army units to take part in the operation, to Amphibian Training Force 9, under the command of Major General Charles H. Corlett. Once the ground troops gathered for training under ATF 9 became operational, Corlett's command would be redesignated as Landing Force 16.8. Comprised of the 17th Infantry, 53rd Infantry, 87th Mountain Infantry (Reinforced), 184th Infantry, 13th Infantry Brigade (Canadian), a detachment from the Alaska Scouts (2 officers and 18 enlisted men which were to be sprinkled throughout the leading elements of the landing force) and the First Special Service Force (as well as a motley assortment of other smaller units), ATF 9 totaled some 34,426 men, of whom approximately 5,300 were Canadian. But "with the exception of the First Special Service Force and the 17th Infantry who had taken part in the Attu fight, these units had had no significant amphibious training."[7]

After enduring a wearisome voyage, punctuated by sea sickness, high winds, rain squalls, crowded conditions and little comfort, the *Wyeth* and the *Floyd* finally pulled into the harbor at Adak on 23 July 1943. Colonel Frederick, who had flown to Adak aboard his personal aircraft, was there to meet his men. Beckoning Canadian Adjutant Sergeant Gordon Sims of Force Headquarters down from the *Floyd*, Frederick had him scrounge up some transportation, and in a borrowed jeep the two set off to make a survey of the island. As one jeep would run low on

Communications tent, Amchitka, c. July 1943. (Lew Merrim)

All the comforts of home, including knee-high shoepacks to keep one's feet dry and a board walk to keep from sinking into Amchitka's slimy muskeg. (Lew Merrim)

gas, they would find another. After three jeeps, Frederick determined that the island was far too crowded by other troops, and was lacking in suitable terrain on which to bivouac his men.[8] Leaving an administrative section with Captain Richard Whitney of HQ Company, and a Force S-2 complement to establish a separate headquarters on Adak and to maintain communications with Headquarters ATF 9/Landing Force 16.8, Frederick next day moved the Force to Amchitka, some 70 miles to the west of Adak and only some 40 miles east of Kiska.[9]

Digging a revetment within which will be erected a pyramidal tent, Amchitka, Aleutian Islands, c. July 1943. (Author's Collection)

Headquarters Company Communications Platoon personnel running telephone wires to a central switchboard, Amchitka, c. July 1943. (Author's Collection)

Living on Amchitka was not easy but the Forcemen made do. After exiting their ships at Amchitka's harbor, the men formed up and began marching inland along what passed for a road – a muddy track that had been scraped out of the tundra by bulldozers. After about five miles they came to the area which was to be their new home for the next month. Treeless, damp and almost constantly blanketed with fog, it was a rather gloomy place. In order to erect the pyramidal tents in which the men would live, and to offer protection in the event of a Japanese attack, it was necessary to remove the layer of muddy, mossy tundra down to the sandy ground. In some places it was as much as 18-20 feet deep. Those that were lucky enough to select a spot where there was not much muskeg might only have to dig down about two feet. Some were forced to dig their

tents in so deeply that they were literally below ground level. Williwaws, fierce pacific ocean winds common to the Aleutians and which often began without warning required that the men secure all of their equipment in order to keep it from being blown away. To ease some of their toil the men constructed raised walkways about their encampments, but marching in the muskeg was an entirely different matter. With each step one sank six inches into the mire and "released a swarm of mosquitoes."[10] A point of interest to the Forcemen, but one which did not better their situation, was the discovery that the Weasels, which had been issued to every other outfit stationed on Amchitka, were excellent "mudders." Ironically the Force, for which the cargo carriers had been originally designed, were not furnished any. The arrival of Service Company's Field

Good example of the clothing worn by the Force during its stint in the Aleutians. Coveralls, mountain trousers, Arctic field jackets, jump boots and shoepacks are all in evidence. (Lew Merrim)

Drinking water is drawn from one of Amchitka's many fresh-water lakes. (Author's collection)

Kitchen was met cheerfully by all, but despite the fact that a Japanese attack seemed to most unlikely, the taunting radio messages of Tokyo Rose prompted many men to ponder their uncertain futures.[11]

During the Force's voyage from Angel Island, "all units [had been] given a complete map of the Aleutians and a portfolio of information concerning Kiska and other targets. They were drilled in this information until each man could draw a map of the island from memory."[12] Likewise, a book of pointers on living in the Arctic and conduct on the battlefield, the *Soldiers' Manual (How To Get Along In the Field)*, was issued to all men of ATF 9. After the men settled in to their new surroundings on Amchitka, training marches and rubber boat work commenced bent on hardening limbs and regaining stamina as the men "practiced the techniques that they would soon be called upon to use in similar terrain on Kiska Island."[13] Sand tables were closely studied, as were available maps and intelligence reports. The Forcemen also "spent time and ammunition"[14] sharpening shooting eyes with their various small arms. A night exercise beginning aboard the APD U.S.S. *Kane* was conducted by First Regiment under full battle conditions on the north side of Amchitka. The *Kane* was one of a number escort destroyers of World War I origin that had been converted especially for the purpose of launching troops for rubber boats landings, and that now were reclassified as Assault Personnel Destroyers, or APDs. Third Regiment men, paddling through the kelp that ringed Amchitka's shores – there was a great deal of seaweed in these waters – practiced landings from LSTs (Landing Ship Tank) – the front ramp would drop and the men would carry their seven-man rubber boats down the ramp and into the wa-

Service Company personnel prepare to serve a hot meal on Amchitka. (Author's Collection)

Forcemen moving through the chow line on Amchitka. Note that over their green herringbone mechanic's coveralls, both of the men standing in the center of the frame wear Arctic field jackets with standard Force insignia. (Author's Collection)

Hot meals were welcome comfort amid the Aleutian's gloomy environment. (Author's Collection)

Reaching out his cup to be filled with hot coffee, the Forceman at center has stitched on an Amphibian Training Force 9 shoulder patch in place of his FSSF spearhead. (Author's Collection)

ter. These final pre D-day dress rehearsals were actively critiqued by all Force participants.[15]

By August 1943, Naval planners suspected there to be 11,925 Japanese on Kiska (the actual highest number being much less – approximately 2,600 army troops and 3,400 navy personnel). However, throughout late July and into August, it was apparent to experienced Army Air Force pilots who were familiar with flying missions over the island that Kiska "wasn't alive anymore." Indeed, aerial reconnaissance yielded no signs of recent enemy activity and the sudden cease of hostile ground fire hinted that the island might have been evacuated. Emboldened by this prospect, it was during this period that a flight of four P-40 Warhawks of the 18th Fighter Squadron, led by Captain George I. Ruddell, decided to find out for themselves the situation on Kiska and so landed on its airstrip. On foot, the foursome investigated the nearby area, during which time they visited the grave site of an American pilot who had been shot down roughly two weeks prior, and even posed for a snapshot next to a Japanese gun emplacement. The flight then climbed back into their fighters and returned to their base on Amchitka to report the incident to both their squadron commander, Major William Booth, and the group commander, Colonel Bill Elder. Still, in contrast to these reports, other pilots, particularly those of one Army Air Force Douglas SBD Dauntless squadron newly arrived to the theatre, attested to receiving ground fire from Kiska. It is likely that what these

Force Headquarters Detachment's S-3 section, Amchitka, c. August 1943. (Lew Merrim)

dive-bomber crews experienced was the result of flying through their own bomb debris. But in the end, possibly due to this confusion, Ruddell's startling report and others were disregarded.[16]

Though speculation mounted that Kiska may have been evacuated, this seemed highly unlikely as U.S. destroyers and cruisers had drawn a tight ring around the island. More plausible to Corlett's planners was the likelihood that the Japanese defenders had given up their coastal installations to take up more defensible positions along the island's central ridgeline. Further complicating matters, Frederick found himself becom-

Aerial view, looking south at Kiska Harbor and the island's Southern Sector terrain. (Courtesy William S. Story)

ing increasingly frustrated by what he perceived to be interservice rivalry and pettiness on the parts of members of other headquarters. Confounded by the sloth with which critical intelligence reports trickled down to his staff, and concerned for the well being of his men, Frederick pressed his superiors that a small scouting party should be landed on Kiska prior to D-day to verify the situation on the island. But his proposal was flatly rejected on the grounds that such a maneuver might jeopardize the operation's element of surprise and as such Operation COTTAGE would get underway as scheduled on 15 August 1943. The results of Kiska influenced Frederick to such an extent, that in all future Force operations he would insist that thorough reconnaissance be conducted prior to an attack, and would often undertake the job personally.[17]

"It was believed that the enemy positions had been laid out to meet attack from the south and east. An interesting plan was evolved to capitalize on this concentration of defensive power. Major fire support was to be delivered from the south and east against known Japanese gun positions. Simultaneously one transport group was to make a feint from the southeast. The actual landings, however, were to be made on the southwest and northwest sides of the island, facing our major fire support."[18]

Once established ashore, the two major elements of Landing Force 16.8, Northern Sector and Southern Sector, would move toward one another in a giant pincer movement with the jaws set to close on the main Japanese camp at Kiska Harbor.

Aerial view of Kiska looking south with lines denoting Third Regiment's objectives and planned routes of advance. (Courtesy William S. Story)

The First Special Service Force would assist the attack of Landing Force 16.8 by putting its First and Third Regiments ashore well ahead of H-hour on D-day and D+1 to mark the landing areas and to seize and hold the high ground guarding the beaches in advance of the main landings.

Second Regiment was ordered to stand by at the Air Base on Amchitka as Force reserve, ready to assist either First or Third Regiment or to "exploit any emergency tactical situation" by parachute or amphibious deployment. At their disposal were ten C-47 Skytrains, aircraft and pilots alike furnished to the First Special Service Force by the Eleventh Air Force. Enplaned in them on D+1, ready to take off at a moment's notice, would wait the men of 1st Battalion (less one company) with attached medical and supply personnel. The rest of the regiment would wait trussed in their 'chutes on the runway. The entire Second Regiment was to be ready to make a quick transition to an amphibious landing should it be ordered. Standing by at the Air Base too were the men of Service Company's Parachute Platoon, prepared to undertake aerial resupply missions in support of the regiments. Also remaining at Amchitka was the rest of Service Battalion which was to guard the bivouac area and to perform its normal supply and administrative duties. However, in the event of a crisis, Service Battalion was to be ready to move immediately by troop transport to the combat zone and to, if circumstances dictated, engage in combat.[19]

Having made all final preparations, the Force's two assault regiments moved by truck from bivouac to Amchitka harbor arriving in late afternoon 13 August there to board waiting transports, the First Regiment assigned to the U.S.S. *Kane* and

Rubber boat training from LCMs and LCVPs off Amchitka. (Lew Merrim)

Their boats beached, the landing parties quickly move toward simulated objectives on the high ground, Amchitka, c. July/August 1943.

Practicing tactics that will be used on Kiska, Forcemen dash through a waist-deep sea of shore grass on Amchitka. (Lew Merrim)

one LST, and the Third Regiment to be loaded onto a single LST. Their faces streaked with camouflage paint, and fitted out with all the impedimenta of war, the Forcemen de-trucked and marched down the long pier to board the ships which would carry them to points just off the shore of Kiska. At the appointed time these ships slipped from their berths and steered out of the harbor to join the larger assault convoy that had steamed from Adak to meet them. Heading westward, the invasion force, comprised of nearly one hundred vessels of all types, sailed into the darkness.[20]

The attack on Kiska commenced on 15 August 1943, amidst a heavy Naval bombardment and a demonstration by troop transports directed along the shore of Vega Bay – a feint that threatened a landing on Kiska's eastern approach. Five hours before H-hour, First Regiment SSF, embarking from the APD U.S.S. *Kane* and an LST, rubber-boated ashore at Quisling Cove (Beach 9-Blue) on the island's western side where it was to clear, secure and, using colored panels and lamps, mark Southern Sector landing Beaches 9-Blue, 9-Yellow, and, 10-

First or Third Regiment Forcemen carrying full combat loads entruck for the trip from their Amchitka camp to waiting Naval transports, 14 August 1943. (Author's Collection)

Section from First Regiment, entrucked and rolling to Amchitka Harbor. (Lew Merrim)

Scarlet (Lily Beach) and their dominating hills (the ridgeline connecting Link, Lawson, Larry, and Lame Hills) ahead of the main landings that would occur at 0630 hours. Organized into three provisional two-company battalions, First Regiment SSF was directed to operate independently until the main force established itself ashore.[21]

Lt. Colonel Alfred C. Marshall's First Regiment Headquarters, with a detachment of Alaska Scouts, 1st and 4th Compa-

nies, and advance parties from the soon to be landed Battalion Landing Groups touched ground and scrambled across the rocky beach moving inland to seize Larry Hill. 2nd and 3rd Companies, accompanied by artillery forward observers and air-ground liaison teams penetrated Quisling Cove and landed at the mouth of Limpid Creek, then advanced along its bed to Lame and Lard Hills. 5th and 6th Companies with like attachments traversed Lily Beach's kelp lined shore to quickly ascended Link

At Amchitka Harbor, Forcemen move down the dirt road toward the pier. (Lew Merrim)

Forcemen of the assault landing regiments on their way to Amchitka Harbor. Note the chincup of one of the men's M-1C helmet, the dual-type life preservers, and the improvised ammunition carrying vest worn by the man second from left. (Author's Collection)

Hill. Once on their initial objectives First Regiment's men dug in emplacing their weapons for defensive fire. Immediately Force reconnaissance patrols were sent forward to Lief Cove some two miles southwest of the landing beaches, while others moved south across the island toward the Japanese Army Barracks at Gertrude Cove.[22]

Frederick and Force headquarters landed close on the heels of First Regiment, less two rubber boats carrying the balance of his Headquarters staff and signal equipment. Burdened down by radios, generators and other heavy gear, and struggling against the strong current, these had drifted seaward but all were safely recovered at dawn by a Navy minelayer. Meanwhile, Forcemen led by Lt. Dan Ryan, set to work with RS blasting a path through the large rocks that hampered the entry of landing craft to Lily Beach. Still more landing craft were making their way toward beaches at Quisling Cove.[23]

At 0621 hours, just ahead of schedule, the first soldiers of the 87th Mountain Infantry and 17th Infantry Regiments waded ashore. By late afternoon of 15 August some 6,500 troops had been landed and the Southern Sector was signaled secure. Rather unexpectedly there as yet had been no firing and no contact with the enemy. Returning Force patrols reported signs that suggested what enemy had been on the island had been hurriedly evacuated, apparently "in the very recent past."[24]

Mindful, however, that Japanese defenders might still remain hidden somewhere on the northern half of the island, the high state of vigilance was maintained and the landings scheduled for next morning were to proceed as planned. By the order of General Corlett further patrolling was held south of the line formed by Middle Pass (the strip of lowland between Beach Cove and Trout Lagoon) and the operation's principal objective, the main Japanese camp at Kiska Harbor. This measure would, perhaps, keep what Japanese who might be holed-up there from being flushed out into the formidable terrain of the surrounding hills. The Southern Sector force now waited like the anvil with the hammer blow that was to be the Northern force set to strike. Colonel Frederick and Force Headquarters departed Kiska for the *Kane*, leaving First Regiment under the control of Southern Sector commander Colonel E.M. Sutherland.[25]

On D+1 the Northern Sector convoy carrying troops under the command of Brigadier General J. L. Ready was poised

LCIs crowd the harbor at Amchitka. At the pier, Forcemen step into a landing craft to be ferried out to their designated transport. (Lew Merrim)

First Regiment group in high spirits, about to make the trip to one of the larger vessels. (Lew Merrim)

off Kiska to make the second series of landings just north of Witchcraft Point. Again the landings would be spearheaded by Forcemen. Shortly after midnight men of Colonel Walker's Third Regiment with a detachment of Alaska Scouts disembarked from their waiting LST into rubber boats. Paddling through a darkness made all the more impenetrable by the ever present Aleutian fog they steered for the rock bight, nearly a mile distant, that separated West Kiska Lake from the Bering Sea. Once they reached this narrow sea wall, they were to carry their boats and equipment across and re-embark onto West Kiska Lake and make for their assigned landing beach near the mouth of Robin Creek which lay at the foot of Ranger Hill.[26]

Lieutenant Mark Radcliffe's platoon from 1st Company, Third Regiment, accompanied by a pair of Alaska Scouts, was designated to lead the way and as such were first to reach the

The Assault Personnel Destroyer U.S.S. *Kane*. A converted destroyer of World War I vintage, the *Kane* bore part of First Regiment to Kiska. (Official U.S. Navy Photograph)

rock bight. They quickly discovered that what Naval planners had claimed was to be an easily traversed strip of rock shingle was in fact a formidable mass of huge boulders some 10-12 feet in height. It took some effort, but the men, many of them shouldering individual combat loads in excess of ninety pounds,

LEFT: First Regiment officers, wearing the shoulder sleeve insignia of ATF9 – "Corlett's Long Knives" – have breakfast shipboard in the officer's mess prior to landing on Kiska Island, August 1943. (National Archives) RIGHT: Forcemen make themselves up with camouflage face paint prior to landing on Kiska Island, August 1943. ATF9 shoulder sleeve insignia were issued for wear to all men of the landing force. The issue insignia was simply manufactured, the cartoon stamped directly onto denim fabric. Embroidered ATF9 insignia could be purchased from post exchanges on Amchitka or Adak. (National Archives)

BACKGROUND: Part of a Second Regiment stick. (Lew Merrim)

INSET TOP: Second Regiment men geared up in white T-5 parachutes, Amchitka, 15 August 1943. (Lew Merrim)

INSET BOTTOM LEFT: Boarding drill for Second Regiment men on Amchitka, 15 August 1943. (Lew Merrim)

INSET BOTTOM RIGHT: Men of 1st Battalion, Second Regiment wait enplaned, ready to take off at a moment's notice. (Lew Merrim)

succeeded. Picking up their paddles once more Radcliffe's men set out onto the lake. With their landing beach nearly two miles distant the Forcemen steered onward aided only by compass bearings as darkness and otherwise poor visibility permitted no visual landmarks on which to guide. As 1st Company neared the middle of West Kiska Lake, and with the rest of Third Regiment approaching the rock bight from the Bering Sea, the mantle of clouds which planners had been dependent on for concealment suddenly split wide open to reveal a full moon which shone brightly down upon the Forcemen silhouetting them exposed and helpless in the water. Fully aware of their situation the Forcemen nevertheless remained composed but pulled harder on their paddles. Arriving at its selected landing area, 1st Company beached its boats and set off up the steep ridge line toward their objective, Ranger Hill's crest, some 1,433 feet high. Upward progress was difficult, made all the more so as the men had to work against an incredibly strong Aleutian wind that began to blow. So strong was it in fact that it nearly toppled some of the burdensomely equipped Forcemen. Yet Radcliffe remembers that his men made little noise. Practicing strict noise discipline they had even chosen to forgo the comfort of their rustling rain suits. Feeling their way forward, Radcliffe's men had within an hour gained the crest of the hill.[27]

While most of Third Regiment followed 1st Company's course across the fresh water lake and inland to occupy Riot and Ranger Hills, a platoon sized detachment broke off and struck southwest toward Witchcraft Point following the shoreline with Broad Beach 14 Green and Red as their destination. Arriving there they placed markers to guide ashore the soldiers of the main landing force comprised of elements of the 184th Infantry, the 87th Infantry, the 301st Reconnaissance

An American flag flies over Kiska's bluffs where men of the FSSF's First Regiment came ashore during the assault. (National Archives)

"Toots." One of ten C-47 transport aircraft reserved for use by the Force at Amchitka Airfield for Operation Cottage. (Lew Merrim)

Second Regiment Forcemen break the tension with a joke while waiting under the fuselage of a transport aircraft. (Author's Collection)

Troop and the 13th Brigade (Canadian). By 0400 hours Third Regiment had dispatched patrols to Rose Hill to the east and was digging in along the ridge line which connected Ranger and Riot Hills, the latter overlooking Kiska Harbor. Third Regiment men found much the same situation as was in the south – a bomb and shell cratered landscape replete with signs of a timely evacuation, but no enemy; only little stuffed dummies left behind in the dugouts to meet the invaders.[28]

How mystified the Forcemen were by not finding any Japanese on the island was told by one of them:

Colonel Robert T. Frederick, his face streaked with camouflage makeup, rests in the grass near Kiska's Quisling Cove, 15 August 1943. Note that, as per the Landing Force directive, the rank insignia fastened to his helmet net has been blackened. (National Archives)

Forceman, standing in an abandoned enemy fighting hole, shoulders a Japanese Type 96 machine gun, Kiska, 16 August 1943. (Official U.S. Navy Photograph)

"'Once ashore there was no sign of the enemy. We lost no time in proceeding with the next step of the operation, climbing the heights of a very steep mountainous ridge where we were to dig in along the crest. After the beach was secured with the landing of the main force, we then moved from the ridge and searched for the Japanese, who had puzzlingly failed to show up. By that time the initial

OPPOSITE TOP: First Regiment Headquarters Group on the beach near Quisling Cove, 15 August 1943. A beach-marking panel stands erected just behind the group, in the upper, right-hand portion of the frame. (National Archives)

BELOW: A trio of First Regiment Forcemen clean weapons after returning from a patrol on Kiska, c. 16 August 1943. The men wear jump boots, mountain trousers with Air Corps type suspenders, wool knit toques, and, in the case of the man on the left, an Arctic field jacket. The insignia of ATF9 was to be worn on both shoulder sleeves in place of other unit insignia. In practice it was sometimes stitched below the Force spearhead, sometimes directly atop the spearhead, or even omitted altogether. (National Archives)

delight of having succeeded in making a surprise landing had turned into bewilderment. Where were they?"

"'In deserted dugouts we saw clothes hung on walls and even bits of food in plates on the tables; food that hadn't yet begun to mildew and looked as though it hadn't been set out for so many hours. It was all very mysterious, and the mystery was not cleared any by the ghostly fog which at times almost completely blanketed the area'"[29]

At 1000 hours on the 16th, as Force patrols from both Northern and Southern groups converged on the main enemy camp all doubts that there were any Japanese left on Kiska were confirmed. Fortunately the enemy had had little time to leave behind mines and booby traps in any quantity; and the steadiness and fire discipline displayed by the Forcemen had undoubtedly saved lives. Having suffered just two casualties the Force's luck had run high. These unfortunate two had both

LEFT: In a trench atop LULU Hill in the First Regiment zone, a corporal of the First Special Service Force examines an enemy machine gun and other equipment left behind by the Japanese, 16 August 1943. The Forceman's cartridge belt and other web gear is slung across his Yukon packboard and leans against the wall of the trench. (National Archives) RIGHT: Forcemen brew coffee in their canteen cups, Kiska, 16 August 1943. (National Archives)

been the results of accidents: the first occurred when a First Regiment Forceman named Conchola, being of Mexican-American descent, was mistaken for a Japanese by a member of the 87th Mountain Infantry who shot him in the hand; the second caused when a grenade went off in another Forceman's back pocket. Six of his comrades carried him on a stretcher to the beach. As told by one Forceman, other units of the landing force had not faired as well: "In a small world of extremely limited visibility, suspicion raised dark monsters, and several shooting incidents occurred."[30] Although First and Third Regiment Forcemen had by now surmised that the island was deserted, tragically that first night on the island witnessed an eruption of so called "friendly-fire" between companies of the 87th Mountain Infantry whose men, frightened and confused, peppered each other with mortars, machine guns and rifles until the exchange could be stopped. In fact, during the first four days of the operation casualties among the landing force totaled some 21 dead and 121 sick or wounded.[31]

Throughout 15-16 August Second Regiment, as Force Reserve, had remained by their C-47s at the airfield on Amchitka ready to land by parachute to assist First or Third Regiment if the need arose. Frederick's order to them to stand down, "baby needs a new pair of shoes," was met with feelings of both disappointment and relief. Kiska secured, Corlett sent First Regiment less 1st Battalion on 16 August to search neighboring Little Kiska Island. The next day Segula Island, some twelve miles to the northeast of Kiska, was swept by 1st Battalion of First Regiment. Results were negative in both cases. On the evening of the 18th, Frederick received a radiogram instructing him to return the First Special Service Force to San Francisco with all speed.[32]

The current status of the Force had been the topic of heated discussion at the First Quebec Conference which coincidentally had gotten underway simultaneously with the landings on Kiska. It had been suggested that the Force would serve a more valuable role in the Mediterranean Theatre of Operations possibly under the command of General Eisenhower. Departing Kiska, First and Third Regiments boarded the Attack Transport *J. Franklin Bell* and on the 19th steamed for Adak. By 22 August Second Regiment and the Service Battalion had closed camp on Amchitka and had embarked aboard the *Floyd* en route to Adak as well where they transferred to the *Heywood*, another Attack Transport. On the 23rd and 24th respectively, *Bell* and *Heywood* weighed anchor and slipped out of Adak's harbor. Though taking part in only its first operation, the First Special Service Force had proven its readiness for actual combat by performing its missions with great skill, flexibility and efficiency while under adverse conditions of darkness, weather, and terrain. The Force's next mission, and its true baptism of fire, would come in little more than three months' time in Italy.[33]

As a footnote to the Kiska escapade, the question lingered of how had the Japanese escaped? Attu had been lost and with Kiska, their last remaining foothold in the Aleutians, growing ever more untenable, on 19 May 1943, the Japanese High Com-

mand decided to abandon its efforts in the region and to evacuate the Kiska garrison. Beginning on 27 May 1943, numerous evacuation attempts were undertaken by submarine. These attempts resulted in the evacuation of some 820 men from the island, but the growing pressure of Allied Naval patrols soon made this method too risky so on 23 June 1943, further attempts by submarine were called off. The moment of deliverance for the defenders of Kiska finally came at 1735 hours on 29 July 1943, when 5,183 Japanese personnel were evacuated *en masse* aboard the light cruiser *Abukuma* that, cloaked by a thick blanket of fog, had slipped through the U.S. blockade into Kiska Harbor and then out again undetected. Miraculously, the evacuation operation had been carried out in less than one hour's time.[34]

D+1. Two Forcemen examine an enemy knee mortar left behind by the Japanese as they fled Kiska. Note that the man seated on the left of the frame wears an M1918 trench knife (a.k.a. "knuckle knife") on his left waist. (National Archives)

BACKGROUND: Casualties caused by so-called friendly fire are evacuated across Lilly Beach, Kiska, to waiting landing craft, 16 August 1943. Close scrutiny of one man on the right of the frame reveals him to be a member of the First Special Service Force, wearing jump boots, mountain trousers, and a V-42 fighting knife strapped to his right calf. (National Archives)

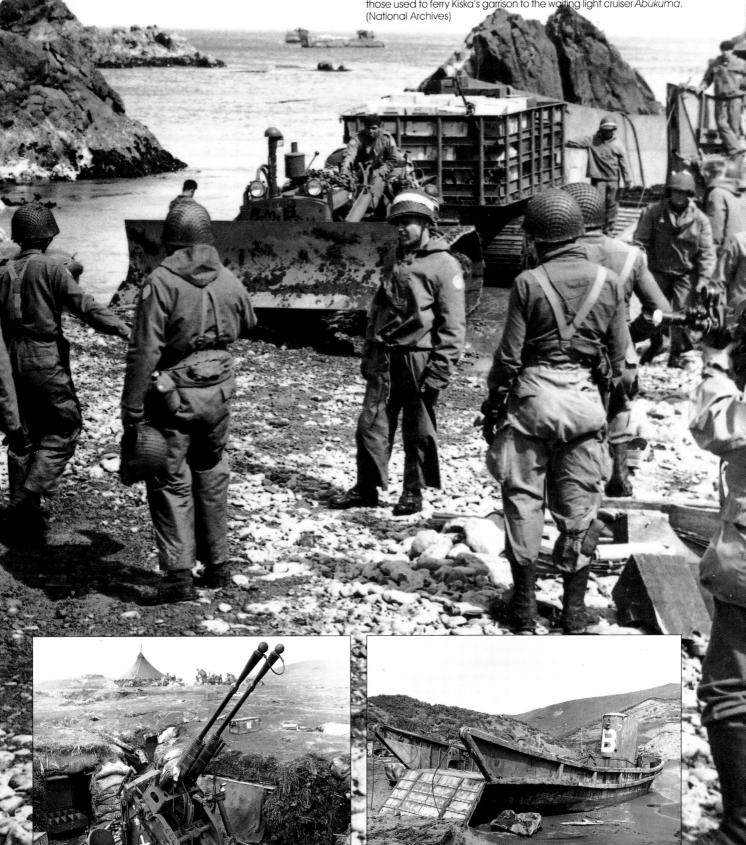

OPPOSITE BELOW
INSET LEFT: Japanese field artillery emplacement on Kiska. (National Archives)

INSET RIGHT: Abandoned Japanese shore battery on Kiska Island. (National Archives)

BELOW
INSET LEFT: Japanese antiaircraft weapon still points skyward, its crew long escaped. Troops of the occupation force have erected a pyramidal tent in the background. (National Archives)

INSET RIGHT: Japanese landing craft beached in Kiska Harbor; one of those used to ferry Kiska's garrison to the waiting light cruiser *Abukuma*. (National Archives)

Map #1

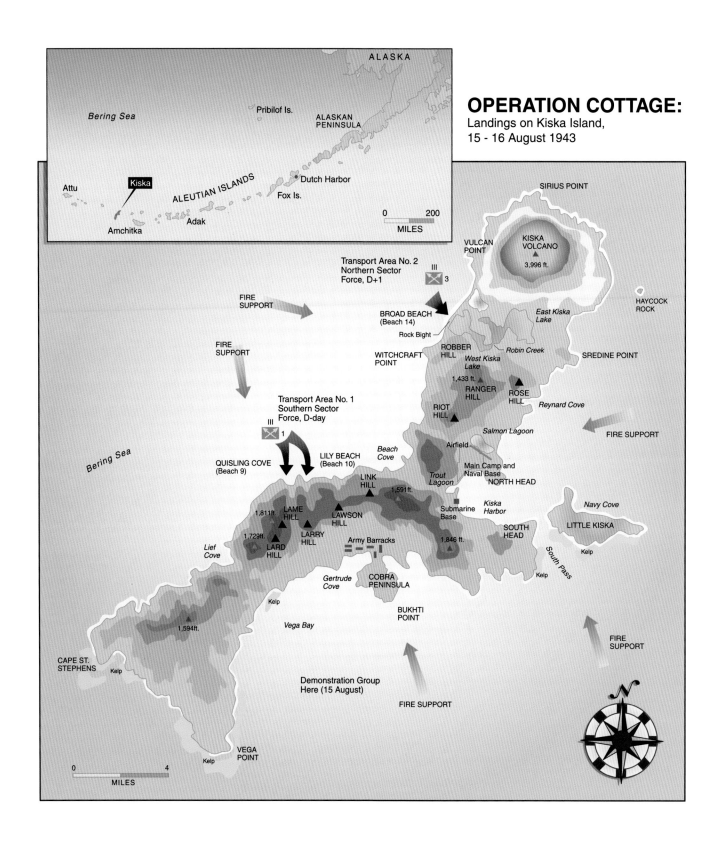

OPERATION COTTAGE:
Landings on Kiska Island,
15 - 16 August 1943

ALASKA

Bering Sea

Pribilof Is.

ALASKAN
PENINSULA

Attu

Kiska

ALEUTIAN ISLANDS

Dutch Harbor

Fox Is.

Amchitka

Adak

0   200
MILES

SIRIUS POINT

KISKA
VOLCANO
3,996 ft.

VULCAN
POINT

HAYCOCK
ROCK

Transport Area No. 2
Northern Sector
Force, D+1

III
3

East Kiska
Lake

FIRE
SUPPORT

BROAD BEACH
(Beach 14)

Rock Bight

SREDINE POINT

FIRE
SUPPORT

WITCHCRAFT
POINT

ROBBER
HILL

Robin Creek

West Kiska
Lake

1,433 ft.

RANGER
HILL

ROSE
HILL

Reynard Cove

Transport Area No. 1
Southern Sector
Force, D-day

III
1

RIOT
HILL

Salmon Lagoon

FIRE SUPPORT

Beach
Cove

Airfield

Bering Sea

QUISLING COVE
(Beach 9)

LILY BEACH
(Beach 10)

LINK
HILL

1,591 ft.

Trout
Lagoon

Main Camp and
Naval Base

NORTH HEAD

1,811 ft.

LAME
HILL

LAWSON
HILL

Submarine
Base

Kiska
Harbor

Navy Cove

LITTLE KISKA

1,729 ft.

LARRY
HILL

SOUTH
HEAD

Kelp

LARD
HILL

Army Barracks

1,846 ft.

Kelp

Lief
Cove

Gertrude
Cove

COBRA
PENINSULA

South Pass

1,594ft.

Kelp

Vega Bay

BUKHTI
POINT

FIRE
SUPPORT

CAPE ST.
STEPHENS

Kelp

Demonstration Group
Here (15 August)

FIRE SUPPORT

VEGA
POINT

Kelp

0   4
MILES

N

Special Feature #2

Service Uniforms & Distinctive Insignia of the First Special Service Force

Blazon & Organizational Colors

Authorization for the Organizational Colors of the First Special Service Force was by "Tables of Equipment T/E 60-50S, dated 10 February 1943, as confirmed informally by the Assistant Chief of Staff, G-1 (Colonel Nowland) Office of the Quartermaster General at the Pentagon Building on February 1943."[1] Manufactured by the Philadelphia Quartermaster Depot, the specifications for the flag are as follows: Cut from scarlet wool, rather than out of the standard silk or rayon, it measures 4'4" by 5'6". The blazon, or coat of arms, is comprised simply of an argent background upon which is superimposed in sable the prominent figure of the Force's distinctive fighting knife, set at a perpendicular angle. Trimming three sides is a knotted yellow fringe of standard length. The scroll for the motto of the organization, clutched in the eagle's beak, was left blank.

Organizational Colors of the First Special Service Force. (Courtesy John F. Kennedy Special Warfare Museum)

Special Feature #2

Frederick wanted no feign-glorious battle cry behind which to rally his men; the words: "For God's sake, man, show the Helena spirit," were a genuine tonic. "Inscribed on the scroll carrying the unit designation [are] the words 'First Special Service Force.'" An 8'6" cord with a tassel on each end was attached to the pike. It was not until April 1943, when stationed at Amphibious Training Base, Camp Bradford, Virginia, that the Force received its organizational colors.[2]

The Force carried before it three flags: its Organizational Colors, and the National Banners of both Canada and the United States. (Lew Merrim)

BELOW: Regimental Guidon Pennant, 1st Company, First Regiment, FSSF. (Courtesy Hayes Otoupalik)

Special Feature #2

Shoulder Sleeve Insignia

The shoulder sleeve insignia, worn by all members of the Force, "consisted of an Indian spearhead in red on which appeared the words USA-CANADA in white." The design was prepared by the U.S. Army's Heraldry Section and was authorized after it received the approval of the National Defense Headquarters in Ottawa and the War Department. "The use of this insignia bearing the words USA-CANADA was agreed to by Canadian officials as a suitable replacement for the shoulder sleeve insignia bearing the word CANADA normally worn by Canadian Forces."[3]

Sewing on the Force's distinctive red spearhead shoulder sleeve insignia at Fort Harrison. (National Archives)

Special Feature #2

OPPOSITE: Cloth Insignia. Six examples of First Special Service Force Spearhead shoulder sleeve insignia, including (1) privately made beaded design on doe-skin backing, (2) privately made velvet with white embroidery, (3) narrow U.S. Government manufacture, (4) standard U.S. Government manufacture, (5) crudely fashioned wool felt with white embroidery on olive drab wool flannel backing, and (6) variation theatre made in Italy. Also shown are two variations of the shoulder sleeve insignia of the 99th Infantry Battalion (Separate): one (7) being of private manufacture, and the other (8) being standard U.S. Government issue; (9) shoulder sleeve insignia of the U.S. 3rd Ranger Infantry Battalion (1st and 4th not pictured); (10 and 11) two variations of shoulder sleeve insignia of the 474th Infantry Regiment (Separate); (12) round shoulder sleeve insignia of Amphibian Training Force 9 – "Corlett's Long Knives" – with design stamped on denim cloth; (13) Canadian Parachute Qualification Badge; (14) Canadian national shoulder sleeve insignia; examples of U.S. Army chevrons: (15) Staff Sergeant being of green thread embroidered on dark blue wool felt backing, and (16) Technician 4th Grade being of silver thread embroidered on dark blue cloth backing; and (17) broad Canadian Army Corporal chevrons. Canadian national cloth insignia and chevrons were commonly worn by Canadian enlisted personnel of the Force until about October 1942 when these men were required to assume their equivalent U.S. Army ranks. (Courtesy Hayes Otoupalik/W.S. Story/Author's Collection)

Cap Braid, Shoulder Cord and Jump Wing Oval

To replace the assorted branch-of-service piping that had formerly adorned the enlisted men's overseas caps, the Force was authorized a red, white, and blue cap braid that it acquired from the Office of the Quartermaster General. Officers' overseas caps were trimmed in the standard Army gold and black piping. As a further embellishment to their service uniforms, all men of the Force were required to wear a red, white, and blue braided shoulder-cord, or *aiguillette*, fashioned from dyed cotton parachute suspension line. In the case of the Canadian members of the Force, these shoulder-cords supplanted their regimental cords. The Force's tri-color jumpwing oval was also of red, white, and blue; its border was of finely embroidered gold-colored thread, as were the pair of holes arranged in its center through which passed the hasp-pin of the sterling silver parachutist's qualification badge or 'jumpwings.' Both the shoulder-cords and the jumpwing ovals were manufactured by A.H. Dondero, Inc. of Washington, DC.[4]

Enlisted man's overseas cap belonging to PFC August C. Erdbrink. (Courtesy August C. Erdbrink)

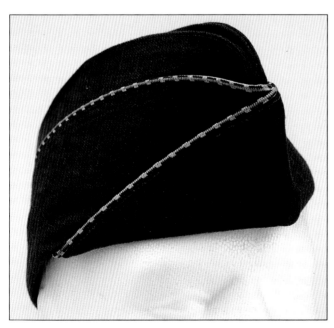

Olive drab wool overseas cap of Sergeant T.H. Harrison, 5th Company, Third Regiment. (Courtesy Hayes Otoupalik)

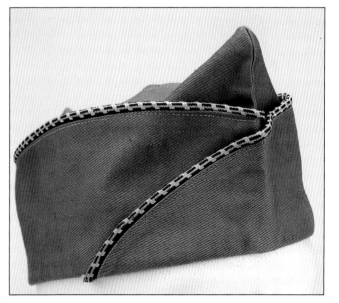

First Special Service Force enlisted man's overseas cap with red, white and blue piping. Caps, such as this example, were issued for tropical wear, and constructed of cotton in khaki shade 1. (Courtesy Hayes Otoupalik)

Special Feature #2

Shoulder cord – or *aiguillette* – manufactured of dyed parachute suspension line. The cords cost $1.50 apiece; and it was required that each Forceman purchase one of his own before being given a pass. (Courtesy Hayes Otoupalik)

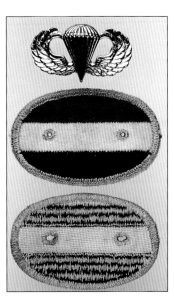

U.S. Parachute Qualification Badge with First Special Service Force wing backers, showing detail of both front and back. (Courtesy Hayes Otoupalik)

ABOVE RIGHT: Closeup of privately manufactured embroidered FSSF wing backer and U.S. parachute qualification badge. (Courtesy BG Edward Burka Collection)

RIGHT: Captain Carl A. Brakel, Third Regiment Surgeon, receives his parachute qualification badge – also known as "buzzard claws" by the Forcemen – c. August 1942. (National Archives)

Collar Brass

The separate insignia of the First Special Service Force was designed to raise the morale of its men and to secure 'homogeneity' within an organization composed of dual nationality. "Inasmuch as the entire motif of [the Force] was set up along Indian lines," Frederick's command was authorized the "former insignia of the [U.S. Army's] U.S.S. Indian Scouts, such being two crossed arrows, in lieu of a branch of service pin." As in the case of the shoulder cord, the various metal insignia was manufactured by A. H. Dondero, Inc. of Washington, DC. Worn on the left coat collar of the enlisted men's service uniform was the Force's crossed arrow insignia, embossed on a one-inch gold metal disc. Officers wore pierced branch of service gold arrows on either coat lapel. One differentiation was drawn between U.S. and Canadian personnel. On the right coat collar of the service uniform, American enlisted men wore the "U.S." cipher embossed on a one-inch gold metal disc; Canadian enlisted personnel a "CANADA" cipher. In the case of officers, Canadians wore pierced "CANADA" national ciphers, while Americans wore pierced "U.S." national ciphers on both coat collar points, above the branch of service devices. The nature of the Force's insignia prompted some outsiders to dub them the 'bow and arrow boys,' but to one another they were, simply, Forcemen.[5]

U.S.S. Indian Scouts ceremonial dress helmet with crossed arrow insignia. (Courtesy BG Edward Burka Collection)

Original U.S.S. Indian Scouts insignia. "U.S.S." and crossed arrow collar insignia are flanked on either side by two variations of the hat badge. (Courtesy BG Edward Burka Collection)

Special Feature #2

A pair of Canadian Forcemen mix with two members of the Canadian National Forces, c. late 1942. The latter wear standard Canadian Army battle dress uniforms – what the men called the "Queen's Burlap" – while the Forcemen wear standard U.S. service uniforms with First Special Service Force insignia. (National Archives of Canada)

ABOVE: First Special Service Force branch of service insignia. Enlisted men's clutch-back embossed disk, and officer's pierced version. (Courtesy A. Erdbrink/Hayes Otoupalik)

RIGHT: First Special Service Force collar insignia including Canadian enlisted men's "CANADA" screw-back collar disk – standard embossed "U.S." collar disk for American enlisted personnel not pictured; Canadian officer's pierced "CANADA" national cipher; American officer's pierced "U.S." national cipher; officer's clutch-back branch of service collar devise (crossed arrows), unmarked and manufactured by A.H. Dondero, Inc. of Washington, DC; stamped crossed arrows with lug-back fasteners and cotter pins privately manufactured in London, England, by Skully for Canadian former Forcemen subsequent to the deactivation of the First Special Service Force. (Courtesy Hayes Otoupalik/W.S. Story)

ABOVE: Joined by two local girls, Canadian (left) and American members of the Force enjoy a double-date in Helena, Montana, c. October 1942. (National Archives)

RIGHT: Waiting for transportation into Helena, Montana, this American Private of the Force wears the standard enlisted man's wool service uniform, c. October 1942. Features of the uniform include the red, white, and blue shoulder cord; and parachute wings pinned through a red, white, and blue FSSF wing backer. In most cases, the only thing that distinguished a Canadian enlisted man of the Force from an American was the embossed national cipher on his right coat collar; that, and possibly a Canadian parachute qualification badge earned by a Canadian Forceman who had undergone parachute training at Ringway, England. The service cap was a strictly non-regulation item, but was very popular off post with enlisted personnel. (Reconstruction)

Souvenir silk "sweetheart" pillow case. (Courtesy Hayes Otoupalik)

Special Feature #2

LEFT: Sergeant Tom Prince (2-3) explains the M-1 portable flame thrower to an interested Helenite, 6 April 1943. Prince went on to become Canada's most highly decorated Canadian native of World War II. (Author's Collection)

RIGHT: Four-pocket wool service coat with brass buttons worn by Technician 5th Grade Charles E. Lay while a member of the First Special Service Force. (Courtesy Hayes Otoupalik)

BELOW: Service Company personnel demonstrate the workings of their field kitchen equipment, Helena, Montana, 6 April 1943. (Author's Collection)

Special Feature #2

ABOVE LEFT: Private First Class August C. Erdbrink (5-3) grouping showing two-day pass, identification tags with hand-made leather necklace and four-leaf clover, and snapshots. (Courtesy August C. Erdbrink)

LEFT: OD wool field jacket, more commonly known as the "Ike" jacket, of Private First Class August C. Erdbrink as a member of the 474th Infantry Regiment (Separate). Erdbrink joined the First Special Service Force in southern France as a replacement. Before that he had been a member of an antitank company of the 39th Infantry Regiment, part of the 9th Infantry Division, and had taken part in the invasion of North Africa. Captured by the Germans, Erdbrink later escaped and made his way back to friendly forces. Returned to the United States and then back to the European Theater of Operations, Erdbrink was in a replacement depot in Naples, Italy, when he answered the Force's call for volunteers. (Courtesy August C. Erdbrink)

ABOVE: Ike jacket of Technician 5th Grade Charles E. Lay as a member of the 474th Infantry Regiment (Separate). The Force shoulder cord was non-regulation in the 474th, but soldiers commonly added embellishments to their uniforms before they "stepped out" with passes or on leave. (Courtesy Hayes Otoupalik)

Special Feature #2

Full dress parade on McNarney Field, Helena, Montana, 17 October 1942. (Author's Collection)

Late arrivals who have recently qualified as parachute jumpers receive their wings. By this time all enlisted personnel of the Force wear standard U.S. Army service dress uniforms. Some Canadian officers, owing largely to a sluggish Quartermaster system, have yet to make the transition. (Author's Collection)

Captain Herbert B. Nichols, the Force's part-time Public Relations Officer and full-time counter intelligence chief, talks casually with members of the Canadian National Forces, 17 October 1942. (Author's Collection)

Officer's dark-green wool overseas cap with Captain's insignia. (Courtesy K. Ross)

Officer's "suntan" cotton overseas cap with Major's insignia. (Courtesy K. Ross)

Officer's "pink" wool overseas cap with Second Lieutenant's Insignia. (Courtesy J. Ranoia)

RIGHT: Company Commander, Combat Echelon at Fort Ethen Allen, Vermont, October 1943. This American Captain participated in the amphibious operation against Kiska Island in August as evidenced by his Asiatic-Pacific campaign ribbon with single battle star. Other ribbons include those for the American Defense medal and the American Campaign medal. The uniform is the U.S. Army's standard "Pinks and Greens" for officers. All other insignia is standard Force issue. (Reconstruction)

Pilot officer of the Force Air Detachment. (Author's Collection)

Two versions of the officer's overcoat. At left is Lt. Colonel Donald D. Williamson, Second Regiment Commander. At right stands Captain Eino O. Olson, Second Regiment Intelligence Officer.

This Canadian officer wears FSSF branch of service insignia, U.S. parachute qualification badge, and FSSF shoulder cord in conjunction with Canadian rank insignia, regimental necktie, and regimental crests. His uniform is also Canadian issue. Such mixing of uniform was overlooked until which time the purchase of standard U.S. Army uniforms could be completed. Henceforth such mixing of uniform and insignia was put to an end by order of Colonel Frederick. (Author's Collection)

Comparison view of early Canadian and American Force officer's dress. At left is Canadian Lt. Colonel D.D. Williamson, and at right is American Captain Eino O. Olson. (Author's Collection)

Special Feature #2

Captain Charles W. Heck, Force Medical Detachment Dental Officer. Note that his caduceus has been incorporated into his FSSF branch of service insignia. (Author's Collection)

Chaplains served in the Headquarters and Headquarters Company of the Force Service Battalion. This chaplain is believed to be First Lieutenant René P. Malboeuf. (Author's Collection)

Another Force Canadian, this gentleman wears Canadian service uniform, rank insignia, regimental crests and tartan regimental necktie, in addition to standard FSSF branch of service insignia and shoulder cord, and U.S. parachute qualification badge. (Author's Collection)

Second Lieutenant William P. Caskey, Force Provost Marshall, wearing Military Police armband. Caskey was nicknamed "The Sheriff" by his fellow Forcemen. (Author's Collection)

CHAPTER 4

"Like Wolfe at Quebec"

The Force arrived at San Francisco Harbor late on the afternoon of 31 August 1943. After the men disembarked from their transports they waited for several hours while arrangements were made for them to be loaded onto a ferry boat that by midnight would take them up the Sacramento River to a town named Pittsburg. After arriving there and again off loaded, they marched through the dark town with Camp Stoneman their destination. Along the way, however, the men were diverted to a sports stadium where, illuminated by bright banks of lights, they had to unceremoniously disrobe and submit to a venereal disease inspection. At Camp Stoneman, from 1-4 September, the men individually received tickets for travel. Those men whose homes were west of the Mississippi River were granted a delay en route and were instructed to report in one week to Fort Ethan Allen, Burlington, Vermont. Those who remained were charged with seeing all of the Force's supplies and other equipment aboard trains, and along with it to report immediately to Ethan Allen. Once there, these men would then be granted a five-day leave.[1]

While Colonel Frederick was satisfied by the overall performance that his command had turned in at Kiska, the operation had allowed him to evaluate his officers and men under actual combat conditions. As a result, he determined that a handful of men and officers simply had to be replaced and he took this opportunity to do a bit of house cleaning. The vast majority of officers had performed well as anticipated. For them promotions to the grades prescribed by the table of organization were in order. By and large, Company Commanders became Captains, Battalion Commanders became Lt. Colonels, and Regimental Commanders became Colonels. To fill the openings that had been left in the ranks, new replacements were taken on and these men were drilled in Force doctrine and otherwise brought up to speed.[2]

Quickly settling into Burlington's familiar surroundings, the Force wasted no time in returning to its training regime. Twenty and thirty mile route marches were served up. As well, fire and movement exercises were undertaken with an added element of realism provided by live-fired light machine guns and mortars; and with the lessons of Kiska taken into account. Once more the Force was scrutinized by Army inspectors who yet again acknowledged its preparedness for overseas movement. Lists of lost equipment were prepared and all such items were replaced. All of the men were issued various articles of kit appropriate to their forthcoming European assignment including the newly available M-1943 field jacket. The Forcemen were among the first soldiers in the United States Army to receive the long, dark green jacket.[3]

When the Force left Ethan Allen on 19 October 1943, this time it moved south to stage at Camp Patrick Henry near Hampton Roads, Virginia, arriving there on 21 October. Having left one week prior, Colonel Frederick, accompanied by two junior officers, had flown to Casablanca, North Africa to smooth the way for the Force's arrival there and to make preparations for its movement to Oran on the Mediterranean Sea. Upon receiving orders, the Force moved from Camp Patrick Henry to Hampton Roads Port of Embarkation and over the 27th and 28th of October loaded aboard the ocean liner *Empress of Scotland*. All aboard, the Force departed on the first leg of the journey that would take it to Italy. As the *Empress* possessed great speed, she proceeded to Casablanca unescorted except for two Destroyer Escorts. For the entire crossing, the ship's light armament, consisting of heavy machine guns and small caliber

Main gate of the artillery school compound, Santa Maria di Capua-Vetere, Italy. (Lew Merrim)

artillery, was manned by personnel from Force Maintenance Company.[4]

After a relatively uneventful passage, the liner pulled into Casablanca Harbor on the morning of 5 November. The Force disembarked and moved to Camp Don B. Passage, which presented little more than a collection of tents in the desert ringed by concertina wire but offering cover, water, and latrines. The perimeter wire was meant to discourage would-be native thieves from entering the camp. Several times during the night Force sentries mounting light machine guns were compelled to open fire resulting in the corpses of several desperate Arabs being discovered in the morning. Next day, as limited transportation would afford no movement of the Force *en masse*, the first of three separate daily contingents boarded trains that would take them across the Atlas Mountains to Oran, Algeria. The trains were old wood burning engines of World War I vintage pulling box cars labeled *Quarante Hommes/Huit Cheval* – 40 men or 8 horses. Along the line, the Forcemen traded briskly with the Arabs during the occasional stops. After a few days the Force moved into temporary bivouac in Oran's Assembly Area 1. On the night of the 16th, the Service Battalion and Combat Echelon, with their equipment secured aboard the Service Battalion's 110 newly issued 6x6 trucks, were loaded onto six Navy transports, including the U.S.S. *Barnett*, the U.S.S. *Jefferson*, and the U.S.S. *Dickman* and with barrage balloons flown overhead, set out for Naples, Italy. Arriving on the 19th of November, the Force took up temporary residence at nearby Bagnoli, Italy, housed in the vacant Collegio Constanzo Ciano.[5]

On 20 November the Force broke camp and moved out aboard trucks. The highway, which led northwest through Caserta, teamed with military traffic, as well as droves displaced Italian civilians. Several times during the twenty-one mile trip, German Focke-Wulf 190s, flying at low level, suddenly appeared and strafed the traffic on the highway. Two drivers from Force Service Battalion were wounded in the attacks before British fighters arrived overhead and drove the enemy off. The overwhelmed civilians faired far worse. The convoy finally came to a halt outside of Santa Maria di Capua-Vetere, the place that was to be the Force's permanent base camp throughout its tour in Italy. One-half mile west of the town, the Force took over the buildings and compound that originally had served as an Italian Artillery School Barracks.[6]

Before the Force, the barracks' previous occupants, *Fallschirmjäger* of the *Hermann Göring Panzer and Parachute Division*, had been forced to make a hurried departure, but not before doing a thorough job of demolishing the living quarters and utterly destroying the plumbing system and latrines. Water would be supplied by tank truck and the cracked shells of the buildings were covered over with tenting. There were no beds nor mattresses so the men would have to sleep in their mountain sleeping bags upon the hard tiled floors, but at least they would be dry. Over the next ten days, Capua-Vetere was transformed by a flurry of activity as the men quickly set about uncrating and storing equipment and weapons and making their quarters habitable. After nearly a month of constant travel, a succession of conditioning marches and range firing of weapons was in order to ready the men for battle. The Forcemen were also lectured to on the German's brand of mine warfare. In the midst of this preparation, war's horror was brutally demonstrated when a mishap on a firing range cost the lives of two Forcemen, decapitated when while preparing to test-fire their bazooka, both the rocket's propellant and its explosive charge went off in the tube.[7]

The Force was assigned to Lt. General Mark W. Clark's Fifth U.S. Army. Clark had been expecting the Force with "particular relish." Its reputation as highly skillful mountain warfare specialists and its "extraordinarily high morale" had impressed the Combined Chiefs of Staff to such an extent that they, at General Eisenhower's request, had secured its transfer to Clark's command with it in mind that they be used for raiding and special reconnaissance operations. In practice, however, opportunities for such a model employment of the Force – those best suited to its original intent – would prove to be few and far between. For at this moment, Clark was plainly desperate for troops. The foremost problem he faced, along with his counterparts of the British Eighth Army, was the fact that the Italian campaign was quickly being relegated to side show status. Overall supply and manpower resources that might otherwise have been utilized to wage a more successful campaign in Italy were now being shifted to the United Kingdom for Operation OVERLORD and elsewhere.[8]

Allied strategy for the Mediterranean Theatre dictated that what resources were expended would be utilized for achieving two principal goals: first, simply, to bring about the surrender of Italy (which was achieved with Operation AVALANCHE, the successful Anglo-American landings south of Naples at Salerno on 9 September 1943) and second, ill defined, to compel Germany to commit as many troops as possible to the defense of Italy, effectively preventing their use on either the Russian Front or the Atlantic Wall.[9] Allied policy makers wrestled with the dilemma of how best to translate strategy into tangible objectives for the armies in the field. Rome was the obvious choice. Rome, with its nearby airfields, for military as well as highly political reasons, became the principal objective in Italy, at least for the immediate future.

For Fifth Army, Highway 6 and the Liri Valley offered the most appealing route to Rome. Once through the Mignano Gap it was Clark's intention to exploit the mobility that the broad valley offered to mount a quick drive into Rome and in doing so claim, for Fifth Army as well as himself, the honor of liberating the first of the Axis capitals.[10] Pursuing the back-pedaling enemy, Fifth Army, in continual offensive, had by mid-

Forcemen tramp through the rubble of a semi-demolished barracks at the Capua compound, c. November 1943. (Lew Merrim)

October crossed the Volturno River. But, some forty miles northwest of Naples, Clark suddenly found the advance grinding to a halt as the Germans began to dig in their heels.

Before AVALANCHE the Combined Chiefs had concluded that the Germans would and could only make an effective defensive stand in Italy on or north of the Pisa-Rimini line, and in the face of successful Allied landings would carry out a fighting withdrawal from the south. The German reaction was quite to the contrary, and any illusions on the part of the Allies that the advance on Rome, some 120 miles distant, would be anything other than slow and painful, were soon swept away.[11]

German commander in chief in Italy, Generalfeldmarschall Albert Kesselring, held that a decisive stand by all means could be made south of Rome, and with the endorsement of Hitler hastily began the construction of the *Winterstellungen*, or winter positions. The Winter Line, as it came to be known to Allied soldiers, was in fact three separate defensive belts that girdled the Italian waist. The first of these, the Barbara Line, was a hodgepodge of outposts and strongpoints scattered east of the Garigliano River and on into the elevated terrain beyond Mignano and Venafro.[12]

Historian, Martin Blumenson, gives a vivid account of the first of the Winter Line battles. "The fighting took place in desolate mountains creased by narrow valleys and deep gorges; on brush-covered heights and bald slopes; along unpaved roads, mule tracks, and mountain ledges. Late autumn weather added fog, rain, and mud to the difficulties of terrain, and snow would soon bring more hazard and discomfort.

"Backing slowly, fighting skillfully – employing crossfires from mutually supporting defenses, extensive demolitions and mines, destroyed bridges and culverts, ambush and sudden artillery shell as their combat techniques – the Germans entered the Bernhard Line around November 1."[13]

The second of Kesselring's defensive walls, the Bernhard Line would prove to be many times more formidable an obstacle than had been the Barbara Line. A well planned and organized array of fortified mountain strongholds, its main line of resistance (MLR) was protected by 75,000 land mines of all types sewn along every conceivable avenue of approach. Fundamentally a forward extension of the Gustav Line – the third and most impressive of Kesselring's *Winterstellungen* – the Bernhard Line guarded the approach to the Liri Valley at its most defensible point, the Mignano Gap, a natural fortress formed by the Monte Camino-Monte Maggiori Hill Mass on the left, and Monte Sammucro on the right. In the narrow valley below these dominating peaks, through which ran Highway 6, were several smaller hills and the ancient farming village of San Pietro.[14]

Throughout the first two weeks of November, Fifth Army threw itself against the deeply entrenched Germans. "Winter fighting, under the conditions imposed by the mountainous terrain, had taxed the worn Fifth Army units to their limit. Non-battle casualties showed an increase, further reducing the combat strength of front-line units; fresh reserves were lacking to follow up initial successes. Supply and evacuation became more and more of a problem, and increasing efforts were needed in the struggle with snow and mud in the mountains, mud and rain in the valleys."[15] Repulsed in all attempts to dislodge the stubborn enemy, Clark called a halt to further attacks. During the second half of November 1943, as the front settled down to patrolling and artillery action, Fifth Army consolidated its gains in preparation for a renewed attack that was to be leveled against the Camino-Maggiori feature.[16]

On November 16th, the U.S. 36th Infantry Division, fresh from nearly two months of recuperation after its action during the Salerno invasion, arrived to bolster the Fifth Army front. The 36th, made up of the 141st, 142nd and 143rd Infantry Regiments, was a National Guard outfit commanded by Major General Fred L. Walker, a regular Army officer who had come up through the ranks. Next day, the headquarters of the U.S. II Corps, new to the Italian front, entered the line. It was commanded by Major General Geoffrey Keyes. II Corps took over control of the 36th and 3rd Infantry Divisions, of which the 3rd had been transferred to it from VI Corps. However, the 3rd

Division was so reduced from prolonged combat that it was sent to the rear for rehabilitation.[17]

At this juncture, the Fifth Army held down a front that stretched from a point near the mouth of the Garigliano River on the Mediterranean sea, northward in a general line falling across the foot of the Camino Hill Mass and Monte Sammucro, and then beyond to the towering peaks of Italy's Appennine range. Arrayed on the Army's extreme left was British 10 Corps composed of the 56 and 46 Divisions and the 23 Armored Brigade. The center of the line was the held by the U.S. II Corps comprised solely of the 36th Division. On Fifth Army's right was the zone of the U.S. VI Corps, which was made up the veteran 45th and 34th Divisions and the 1st, 3rd and 4th Ranger Infantry Battalions – Darby's Rangers. Elements of the U.S. 1st Armored Division were poised just behind the front as were other smaller units. Scheduled to arrive presently on the front were the U.S. 504th Parachute Infantry Regiment (part of the 82nd Airborne Division), the Italian 1st Motorized Group, and the French Expeditionary Corps. Across the Appennines, abreast of Fifth Army was the zone of the British Eighth Army made up of the 5 and 13 Corps.[18]

On 22 November, with its commitment to battle at hand, the First Special Service Force was assigned to the U.S. II Corps, and further attached to the 36th Division. At Fifth Army Headquarters in Caserta, plans were being drawn for a three-phase operation that would break the deadlock along the Bernhard Line. The first phase of the plan was, in view of the current weather situation, rather appropriately dubbed "Raincoat," and in it the First Special Service Force was to play a major part.[19]

Operation RAINCOAT called for a coordinated effort by elements of the British 10 Corps and the U.S. II Corps against the Camino-Maggiori Feature. The 56 Division (British) was to attack and capture Ridge 727, Hill 819 and Hill 963 on the night of D-1/D. The First Special Service Force, which was now attached to the 36th Division, was given the job of capturing the peaks of Monte la Difensa (Hill 960) and Monte la Remetanea (Hill 907) and then to hold them until relieved. The U.S. 142nd Regimental Combat Team of the 36th Division (reinforced), timing its attack with that of the Force's against Hill 907, would advance to the north across the Vallevona Plateau to capture the trio of peaks (Hills 510, 630, and 619) that comprised Monte Maggiori. The entirety of II Corps' artillery, as well as aviation, was to support the attack of the 36th Division and the Force. Additionally, the First Special Service Force's attack would be assisted by the fires from 1st Armored Division Artillery and one company of 4.2in mortars from the 2nd

Chemical Warfare Battalion, the barrage of the latter scheduled to commence against Monte la Difensa at 0200 hours on D-day.[20]

Monte la Difensa was the linchpin of the German defensive works in the Camino Massif. From its heights enemy observers could direct accurate and deadly artillery fire upon almost any point in the valley below. "La Difensa was an 'L' shaped mountain with the vertex of the 'L'" pointing in toward the Allied lines.[21] Nearing the top of the mountain the ridgeline that denoted the vertex rose almost vertically. As Colonel D.D. Williamson's Second Regiment SSF had for all intents and purposes been left out of the action at Kiska, it was given the dubious honor of leading the assault on Difensa. Waiting until darkness on D-1/D, Second Regiment was to rise from a concealed pre-assault position approximately halfway up the slopes of Hill 960 and advance up Ridge 368 to capture Monte la Difensa by daybreak on D-day. This maneuver would be accomplished under the cover of what was to be the heaviest artillery preparation of the Italian campaign thus far. Immediately the Second Regiment was to attack across the saddle that separated the Difensa and Remetanea peaks to capture Hill 907. Once atop 907, Second Regiment would be in a position to assist the attack of the 142nd Infantry.[22]

First Regiment SSF, as 36th Division reserve for the operation, was to dig in on the south side of Ridge 368, near the 36th Division's forward command post (CP), and just to the north of Difensa's peak. 1st Battalion of Third Regiment was designated as Force reserve and would also move up and dig in at the base of the mountain. Both of these assembly areas would be "within observation of the enemy and range of his mortar fire."[23] Two companies from 2nd Battalion, Third Regiment were assigned to duty as supply carriers. The men from the remaining company of 2nd Battalion, Third Regiment were designated as litter bearers. One platoon from this company was detailed to accompany Second Regiment throughout the operation, while the rest of the litter bearers were to bivouac in the vicinity of the Force Collecting Station that would be located in a farm house some 500 yards north of the village of Caspoli.[24]

The Force Service Battalion would leave a contingent at Santa Maria to provide security for the Force base camp and to perform its normal supply and administrative jobs. However, most of the battalion was detailed to the front to operate the forward supply base in support of the Combat Echelon. In fact, almost 300 Service Battalion personnel would participate in the forthcoming battle as members of carrying parties whose job it would be to man-pack supplies right up to the front lines for the regiments. The forthcoming action would earn for the men of the Service Battalion new respect from those in the Combat Echelon.[25]

Between 22 November and 1 December, Force patrols, for the most part drawn from Second Regiment's regimental and battalion headquarters were sent to the Mignano sector to take in first hand the fighting. Before Fifth Army had suspended its offensive, la Difensa had been unsuccessfully attacked by the 7th Infantry Regiment of the U.S. 3rd Division. Now, working with troops of the 36th Division, the Forcemen crept far forward to examine the routes over which the 7th Infantry had mounted its attacks against 960. The bloated bodies of American dead from those earlier attacks were still lying where they had fallen to the sides of the trails unable to be recovered. Clearly, this was not the way to go.[26]

The initial reconnaissance of Monte la Difensa by the First Special Service Force was undertaken by the command group of Second Regiment: Colonel D.D. Williamson, Regimental Commander; Major Walter S. Gray, Regimental Executive Officer; Lt. Colonel Tom C. MacWilliam, 1st Battalion Commander; and Lt. Colonel Robert S. Moore, 2nd Battalion Commander. Under Williamson's direction, the party secured jeeps and traveled to the front where they contacted the commander of that element of the 36th Infantry Division currently holding the line around the base of the mountain. Williamson's group was furnished with guides from the 36th who led them as far as the division's foremost outposts. With heavy fog obscuring their movements, Williamson's group began their exploration of Difensa's northern slopes. Higher up, forward progress was barred by sheer cliffs, but on the right-hand fringes of this obstacle they discovered a narrow trail leading to the summit that, while being quite precipitous, would be negotiable by the Forcemen if ropes could be employed.

Later, as his was to be the lead battalion in the forthcoming operation, Lt. Colonel Tom MacWilliam appointed his 1st Battalion 2 i/c, Major Edward H. Thomas, to take a small group and carry out a further, detailed, reconnaissance of la Difensa's northern approach, along the route that the regimental headquarters group had indicated from their prior inspection. Along with a guide from the 142nd Infantry Regiment, Thomas, with Assistant Intelligence Officer Finn Roll, Canadian Sergeant Tom Fenton, and Sergeant Howard C. Van Ausdale – part Native-American, and a man who, in Thomas's words, "could read terrain well" – set out on this mission. Fenton and Van Ausdale, both former prospectors in civilian life, were from

1st Company, Second Regiment and would lead the assault company during the actual attack. The party spent the first night of this patrol in a barn nearby the front. Next day they visited the 142nd Infantry's command post and conferred with its Commanding Officer, Colonel Lynch. The 142nd was holding two-thirds of the ridge, denoted as Ridge 368 on Army maps, stretching up la Difensa. To get to the uppermost parts of the 142nd's holdings on the mountain one had to cross stretches of open ground that in clear daylight were in plain view of the enemy on the adjacent peaks. Several times during the first leg of their climb, mules passed, descending the trail, carrying the bodies of U.S. dead wrapped in mattress covers. At the main line of resistance there was an open flank which ran south in the direction of Monte Camino, Hill 963, a peak in the British 10 Corps sector topped by a Benedictine Monastery of the same name. Thomas and his group explored as far forward on the mountain as they dared, surveying the route by which they might assail the hill. He and his party made a total of three reconnaissances of the mountain.[27]

The reconnaissance parties had done well, for like Wolfe at Quebec nearly two hundred years before, they had discovered what was to be the chink in the enemy's armor. Screened by a cleft in the north facing ridge was a precipice that rose almost perpendicularly for more than two-hundred feet. Previous attackers, having lacked the proper equipment and training to take on this, the mountain's most precipitous part, had avoided its treacherous heights. The Germans, too, considered these cliffs to be impassable to assault troops. An attack from this direction would outflank the main defenses on Hill 960 and would carry with it the crucial element of surprise. It was a daring plan, but after carrying out his own reconnaissance of the mountain, Frederick gave his approval.[28]

Loaded one section per 6x6 truck, Second Regiment pulled out from the Capua compound on the afternoon of 1 December and headed for the front. The rest of the Force followed at interval. There was no question in the minds of the Forcemen they could and would accomplish their mission. They were confident. "We're gonna kick those bastards off that hill," summed up the general consensus. But, naturally, at the same time the men had trepidation. As the shadows grew longer, rain began to fall. The line of trucks rolled urgently forward, their drivers pressing onward into the descending darkness with only blackout lights for assistance. Intermittently, the countryside was brightly lit by muzzle flashes from the massed Allied artillery pieces dug-in in the fields to either side of the muddy track. The noise, at times, was deafening. The regiments, each

Sand table of the Camino Hill Mass, including the Force objectives: Mounts la Difensa and la Remetanea. (Lew Merrim)

separated by about an hour, were trucked to a point near Presenzano. Second Regiment was the first there, arriving about dusk. Behind a hill, it detrucked and assembled, hidden from sight by observation from Monte la Difensa.[29]

Accompanied by a guide from the 142nd Infantry, the assault regiment began its approach march; across muddy fields and through streambeds, wearing ponchos, shouldering their blanket rolls, and carrying their weapons, rations, ammunition, and the *extra* ammunition that would surely be needed. The rain continued. After many hours of slogging through the mired countryside, and more than five miles, the column reached the base of the mountain and began the ascent. The regiment passed through the lines of 142nd along the lower reaches of la Difensa, and then proceeded up the mountain's eastern slope to about the 300 meter level reaching the pre-assault assembly area, a stand of trees and scrub that had been selected several days before. The regiment made it into the trees just as the sun was coming up on 2 December 1943 – there, in concealment, to wait out the day.[30]

2 December dawned clear and sunny and the men spent the day drying off, cleaning weapons and eating their K-rations. The clear weather also brought out Allied fighter-bombers that over the course of the day dropped a total of 500 tons of bombs on the Camino Hill and on targets as far to the rear as Cassino. The day passed and as the shadows lengthened, the men gathered themselves for the attack making final checks of equipment and weapons. With terrible ferocity, the guns of II Corps were unleashed against the forward slopes of the Camino Massif. "The II Corps opened its attack at 1630, . . . when 925 artillery pieces of all calibers began to pour high explosive, white phosphorus, and smoke on enemy positions, 820 of these weapons concentrating on the Camino-Difensa-Maggiore com-

plex. In a one-hour 'serenade' of massed fire, 346 pieces expended more than 22,000 rounds on Monte la Difensa. During the first forty-eight hours of the attack, the corps artillery, which had placed fourteen battalions in support of the 36th Division Artillery, would alone fire almost 75,000 shells in support, among them the shells of the new eight-inch howitzers, the first sustained combat use of the weapon."[31]

Troops later called la Difensa the "Million Dollar Mountain" alluding to the cost of the immense weight of ordnance that was expended on it. Though described by those it fell upon as being of "unprecedented violence," well dug in as they were, the four-hour barrage did little to harm the Germans atop Difensa save for robbing them of sleep. However, it did disrupt the flow of supplies and reinforcements to the front, thus isolating the German garrisons throughout the Camino Mass, as well as diverting their attention from the ascending Second Regiment.[32]

As soon as the light had faded sufficiently to conceal its movement, Second Regiment again got underway. With Lt. Colonel Tom MacWilliam's 1st Battalion leading, the regiment

made its way further up the eastern side of the mountain, to about the 650 meter level, and then began to work its way around to Difensa's northern face.[33]

The column was organized in order 1st, 2nd and 3rd Companies, Regimental Headquarters group, followed by 4th, 5th and 6th Companies. By approximately 2230 hours, after about four hours on the trail, Captain W.T. Rothlin's 1st Company arrived at a point below the north-facing cliffs. As planned, the artillery, which had kept the Germans' heads down atop Difensa, shifted its fire to more distant targets. Under the heavy artillery preparation, it was no secret to the Germans that they would soon be under attack. They simply expected that it would come from the same direction as had all of the previous attacks. German machine gunners, clearing and sighting-in their weapons, fired long bursts of tracer ammunition down upon the trails some distance to the left of Second Regiment. Other Germans, snipers hidden high up amongst the trees and rocks of Difensa's northeastern slopes, began to work along the trails. Tracer bursts from their Schmeisser machine pistols pointed out suspected targets for German mortar crews atop Difensa, and for their

Force officers are addressed by Major General Geoffrey Keyes, II Corps Commander, prior to the commencement of Operation RAINCOAT.

artillery counterparts hidden on the reverse slope of Mount Lungo. Limited German counter-battery fire also commenced.[34]

Now scouts, Sergeants Fenton and Van Ausdale, alone, explored ahead. Theirs was the task of investigating the final stretches of the plateau before the German positions. Silently up they went, raising themselves through chimneys and along fissures, gaining whatever purchase the hard limestone would offer. When the two had made it above the escarpment, they found that there was still about 350 yards of open, rocky slope to cross to get to what was a crescent-shaped lip overlooking Difensa's 'bowl' where the enemy was ensconced. Choosing each step with great care, the two scouts crept to this point, where, so close were they to the German sentries that the scouts could hear them chatting, lighting cigarettes, and changing the guard. The Germans had conspicuously left Difensa's backdoor open, and Fenton and Van Ausdale made their way back down to report. Immediately another pair of Forcemen, retracing the path of the scouts, scaled the cliff and this time placed ropes thus to aid the ascent of the companies and to hoist up the mortars, rocket launchers, and machine guns.[35]

While the regiment waited in the darkness, German fire, especially machine gun fire, continued to probe the trails to the south and east that had been the paths of previous American attacks. Agitated by this, Colonel Williamson turned to Regimental Headquarters group informing them that he felt the regiment had come under attack. Williamson then announced that he had to get down the hill to warn Colonel Frederick. Leaving his 2 i/c, Major Walter S. Gray, behind, Williamson started off down the hill taking along with him the regiment's Intelligence Sergeant. Presently, Gray sent Sergeant K.R.S. Meiklejohn up the hill to advise Lt. Colonel MacWilliam of Colonel Williamson's current action.[36]

One Forceman from 6-2 remembers that Williamson, ". . . whose nerved had been jangled . . . came barreling down the trail. . . . He would pause briefly, fire his pistol toward the origin of the tracers and yell, 'Get that sniper,' and continue on, exhorting the men to greater efforts." Some distance down the trail, Williamson met a rather puzzled Colonel Frederick, who, finding his Second Regiment Commander at this altogether unexpected place, announced his dissatisfaction, asking, "Colonel Williamson, what are you doing here?" Frederick took Williamson by the arm, and the two stepped around a bend in the trail to talk privately for a moment. The two reappeared, then Frederick, along with his command group, leaving Williamson trailside to collect himself, continued up the hill.[37]

Major George Evashwick, Second Regiment Surgeon, attends a wounded man on Monte la Difensa, c. 3-6 December 1943. (Courtesy Frederick-Hicks)

Meanwhile, 1st Company, under Captain W.T. Rothlin, had taken to the ropes. As the men strained against their own weight and that of their equipment, their officers and NCOs hissed at them to keep quiet. Captain Stan Waters' 2nd Company, and Captain D.A. Daugherty's 3rd Company (3-2 designated as the battalion reserve) each waited for their turn on the trail just below. Well before dawn on D-day, 1st Company made it atop the escarpment. There the word was passed to fix bayonets. Shortly, almost all of Water's men were up. With 3-2 beginning to take to the ropes, Rothlin and Waters gave the order for their companies to proceed to the lip overlooking the German positions. 1st Company closed the distance to the lip and got into position on the left. 2nd Company was completing their maneuver to extend the line to the right, when the sound of falling rocks and the challenge of a startled German sentry signaled the start of the battle.[38]

In the words of one Forcemen, "All Hell broke loose!" However, most of the enemy were still in their dugouts, and even those who were standing guard thought the attack was coming from another direction. The enemy's machine guns, anchored in place with stones piled around their tripods, were fixed to fire down the more likely approaches. Small fire fights erupted all around as confused and bewildered Germans, shaken from their limestone shelters were quickly overwhelmed. 2-2 soon joined the fight and the added pressure became too much for the Germans. The last holdouts made their stand in a system of caves and dugouts at Difensa's highest point. The Forcemen, wielding their organic supporting arms with great skill, blasted the enemy from these positions and there entered the enemy headquarters whereupon they were reported to have captured a German officer, who blurted out in disbelief: "You can't be here. It is impossible to come up those rocks."[39]

As early as 0440 hours, a message recorded as being sent by the "Special Service Force" had found its way to the Headquarters of the 36th Division: "Hill 960 captured – resistance light. Attack proceeding according to plan."[40] At 0500, Brigadier General William H. Wilbur, the 36th Division's assistant division commander, sent much the same message to 36th Division Headquarters. Inasmuch as MacWilliam's battalion had won a foothold at the top of Monte la Difensa the messages were accurate. However, pockets of enemy resistance still remained active over many parts of the hill. Against an expected counterattack, MacWilliam's men set about consolidating their gains and digging in. In the midst of the attack Lieutenant Lawrence J. Piette had taken over 1-2 after Captain W.T. Rothlin was bushwhacked and killed. Further reorganization of the companies, platoons, and sections was also in order. Meanwhile, the enemy headquarters, a nearly shell-proof bunker shored with huge timbers, was turned to use as an aid station. A nearby cave, sheltered by a large boulder, was earmarked to be used later as Second Regiment's command post. The enemy who had escaped death or capture retreated southward toward Monte Camino, or to the west across the saddle to Monte la Remetanea to take up defensive positions there. Scattered about the top of the hill were the bodies of at least 75 German dead. Dozens of enemy prisoners and wounded had been started down the mountain.[41]

Map #2

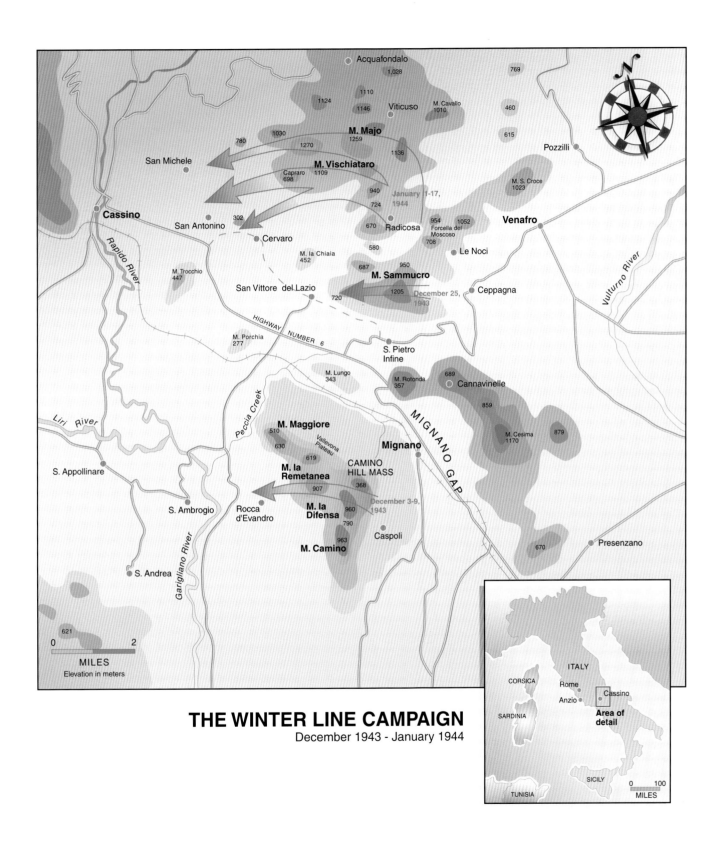

THE WINTER LINE CAMPAIGN
December 1943 - January 1944

Historical Document #3: Annex No.1 to Adiministrative Order No.2, Field Order 14

FIRST SPECIAL SERVICE FORCE
APO 4994, N.Y., N.Y.
27 November 1943

Annex No 1 To Administrative Order No 2

1. The following individual clothing and equipment will be carried to the front by personnel of Combat Echelon, and applies to both officers and enlisted men.

   a. To be worn.

      Band, helmet, camouflage
      Belt, cartridge, cal. .30, or pistol - as prescribed by T/E
      Boots, parachute
      Box, match, waterproof
      Cap, wool knit
      Spoon, M1926
      Drawers, wool
      Canteen, w/cup, cover and grate
      Gloves, wool o.d., leather palm
      Helmet, complete
      Handkerchiefs
      Insignia, shoulder sleeve, FSSF
      Insignia NCO or Techn.
      Knife, mountain
      Pockets, magazine, pistol - for personnel armed with pistol
      Pockets, magazine, carbine - 3 per officer Combat Echelon, 2
          per Officer Base Echelon
      Package, first aid, w/first aid packet and sulfadiazine
      Shirt, wool o.d.
      Socks, wool, heavy
      Sweater, wool, high neck
      Tags, identification, w/tape or necklace
      Suspenders, belt, M1936
      Trousers, mountain, w/suspenders
      Undershirt, wool

   b. To be Carried in a Blanket roll over the shoulder.

      1 Shelter Half, w/poles, pins and rope
      Bag, sleeping, mountain

   c. To be Carried in the Field Bag.

      Rations -   1 C
                1 D
                1 K
      Toilet Articles
      Poncho
      Extra socks

2. Rucksacks will be packed with a change of underwear and socks, remaining mess gear, remaining toilet articles and left stacked together at the unit storage point in the Base Camp available to the Supply Officer for delivery to advanced units in case the opportunity arises.

3. a. All troops will carry to the Assembly Area on their persons the items enumerated above in Paragraphs 1. in addition to their normal weapons and ammunition load.

- 1 -

Annex No 1 Adm O no 2 (Cont'd)

   b. The First and Third Regiments will retain the blanket roll with them until otherwise ordered.

   c. The Second Regiment will retain the blanket roll with them until the afternoon of D-1, at which time they will be stacked and turned over to carrying parties to be withdrawn by the carrying parties to the vicinity of the dump area where they will be kept in bulk, awaiting future use by the regiment. In preparing the rolls for withdrawal to the dump area, companies and detachments will make certain to keep their rolls together and carrying parties will make every effort to keep their rolls separated by organization.

   d. At any time that blanket rolls are ordered withdrawn to the supply area, regimental commanders will have them placed near the road or trails, sorted or stacked by company, where they may be kept segregated while being handled by supply personnel.

         By Order of Colonel FREDERICK:

                   PAUL D. ADAMS,
                   Colonel, 1st Sp Sv Force,
                   Executive.

OFFICIAL:
     K. G. WICKHAM,
       Lt. Col., 1st Sp Sv Force,
       Adjutant.

DISTRIBUTION:
   Same as Field Order No 14

- 2 -

CHAPTER 5

A Test of Endurance

L t. Colonel Moore arrived at Difensa's summit with his 2nd Battalion just prior to dawn (sunrise being 0700 hours). Without delay he began to maneuver his 4th, 5th, and 6th Companies onto a line facing the saddle connecting Hills 960 and 963 in preparation for the next phase of the attack. For the moment visibility was quite good, and of this the Germans, particularly those in the vicinity of Hill 790, were taking full advantage by turning mortar fire against their former stronghold. It was not long after sunrise that Lt. Colonel Moore learned from Sergeant Meiklejohn that Colonel Williamson would not be coming up, at least not for the time being. In light of this unexpected development, Moore sought out MacWilliam to discuss the situation. As MacWilliam was the senior officer then present on the hill, it was quickly decided that MacWilliam would take over command of Second Regiment and that the attack would be carried out as had been planned.

After their brief meeting, MacWilliam and Moore quickly resumed making final preparations for the next phase of the operation: MacWilliam for leading the 1st Battalion across the saddle to 907, and Moore for carrying out a supporting attack with his 2nd Battalion in the general direction of Monte Camino. Concurrently Moore began efforts to raise Force Headquarters by radio. Up to this point, communication between the various elements fighting on top of la Difensa had been carried out either by runner or in person, between the parties concerned. Contact between Force units engaged on Difensa, and Force Headquarters down the hill, had been nearly impossible. The SCR-536 radios that had been carried up with the platoon leaders and company headquarters were barely functioning if at all, and wire communication was constantly going out. Only after Lt. Colonel Moore was able to have use of an SCR-509

radio set, brought up the mountain by attached artillery forward observers, was he able to establish radio contact with Force Headquarters. However, the 509 radio was useless when it came to communicating with companies and platoons of Second Regiment spread out around the mountain top as none were equipped with these bulky sets.

By 0800 hours rain fell once more, and a heavy, clinging fog had moved in across the ridges at times limiting visibility to within twenty feet. Yet, by now, the Germans had the range zeroed in, and their mortaring was about to increase. Advance patrols from 1st Battalion, reaching toward 907, were run to ground by heavy German machine gun fire and mortaring coming in from the left of the 960-907 saddle. Snipers hidden amongst the rocks were coming alive as well. Accompanied by the rising pitch of the enemy's mortars, 1st Battalion began to form up for its approach to 907. It was during this process that Lt. Colonel MacWilliam was suddenly killed by mortar fire. Barely half an hour had passed since having last seen one another when word of MacWilliam's death reached Lt. Colonel Moore, to whose responsibility the leadership of Second Regiment now fell. Major Thomas, 1st Battalion's 2 i/c, was in the midst of taking over the battalion to carry through with the attack when a message from Lt. Colonel Moore arrived telling him to hold up and to dig in.[1]

Not long afterward, Lt. Colonel Moore was able, by radio, to get through to Colonel Adams, stationed at the base of the mountain. Adams asked Moore if reinforcements were needed. Not yet, was Moore's reply, but what was needed, particularly by 1st Battalion, were supplies; a list of which Moore communicated to Adams in descending order of priority. At the top of the list was machine gun ammunition, followed by mortar ammunition, then rockets for the Bazookas, and then grenades. Water was in short supply, and blankets and food were also noted. With radio communication poor and the time needed to relay orders too long, with the need for reorganization acute, and especially with the presence of enemy strength in a position to frustrate any move by 1st Battalion toward Hill 907, it was resolved that the attack be postponed until the next morning.

Meanwhile, Second's officers carried out a detailed reconnaissance to select jump-off locations and covered routes by which the men could get to them so as to be in position to attack when the signal was given early on the 4th.[2]

Colonel Frederick and his advance party had, during the morning of D-day, reached the area near the base of the escarpment and had soon after established radio contact with the troops atop Hill 960. From this position Frederick would be able to monitor the battle above, as well as attend to the movement of supplies from below. To move supplies up la Difensa would require Third Regiment and Service Battalion packers to endure a back-breaking six hour trip up narrow mountain trails too steep even for mules. It should be noted that the trails over which the carrying parties traveled were well within range of the enemy's mortars and artillery, and shellfire would account for many casualties among these men. Meanwhile, the men of Second Regiment, with only their ponchos as protection against the cold and dampness, would have to hunker down in whatever shelter they could make for themselves atop the scarred peak and wait. None were more miserable than the wounded awaiting evacuation.[3]

Throughout the remaining hours of daylight on 3 December, patrols were dispatched across the saddle towards Hill 907 to capture prisoners and to eliminate the snipers whose increasing volume of fire was cutting into the Second Regiment on Hill 960. II Corps forward artillery observers had by 1040 hours set up observation posts atop Monte la Difensa. Sections were posted in front of the approach from Hill 907, and on the left before the saddle separating Hill 960 from Monte Camino to warn against counterattack. Brief messages recorded in the 36th Division's G-3 Journal tell part of the story, "1255 [hours] to HQ/36th Division: Considerable mopping up now in progress. Large number of enemy snipers active. Estimate 30 or 40 PWs taken. . . . 1550 [hours] to HQ/36th Division: Snipers, machine pistols. Positions fairly well coordinated. Higher than anticipated. About 30 prisoners." Sunset came at 1700 hours, and its passing marked the arrival of the first of the Third Regiment and Service Battalion supply-packers atop la Difensa. Along

with blankets, rations, water, and ammunition, they brought the message that the British on the left, though having captured Hill 963 during the previous night, had been thrown off that morning by a strong counterattack. The attack of 142nd Infantry on the Force's right, below Difensa, had made early progress, but was now held up by considerable German artillery fire.[4]

Temperatures hovered at a few degrees above freezing. Rain had fallen intermittently throughout the day and would continue into the night. At 2100 hours the rainfall was again joined by a heavy storm of German mortar and artillery fire. During the night, the Germans began to direct *Nebelwerfer* fire – rocket propelled artillery – against the Forcemen on 960 as well. The unearthly sound of the rockets as they were launched from their tubes, produced by organ reeds mounted in their tail fins, was far more demoralizing than their actual effect. Allied soldiers nicknamed them *moaning minis* and *screaming meemies*.[5]

After waiting out most of D-day in bivouac on the southeast side Ridge 368, near the 36th Division's forward command post, First Regiment received word from General Wilbur to move west to the place that in code was called "Leggin Laces," otherwise known as Hill 907. The reason for this move is subject to speculation and the results of it would prove costly. Confused and contradictory reports arriving throughout 3 December, and recorded in the G-3 Journal of the 36th Infantry Division, may have caused Wilbur to wrongly believe that 1st Battalion, Second Regiment was firmly on Hill 907. It is also entirely possible that Wilbur was relocating the First Regiment toward Hill 907 in order to screen the advance of his 142nd Infantry across the Vallevona Plateau. An excerpt from the diary of Gerald W. McFadden, then a Captain commanding First Regiment's 4th Company, tells what followed:

> "It had been raining all the time and we were wet to the skin and miserable. At 5:30PM we were ordered to move out on a trail and get up beside the 142nd in the valley, near a hill, on the front line. Our movement was slow and we were in the center of the battalion with the 1st Battalion behind us. As soon as we turned the corner of the hill, the trail was under fire. We had to move single file, as the going was rough and rugged. Again, it began to rain. At about 6:30PM we had to stop, as the area we were about to go into, was under fire. After some delay, we did move ahead and each company spread out, up the hill from the trail. Shells were now falling near the trail. First re-

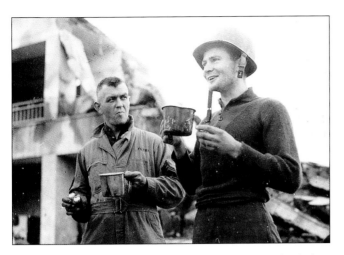

Coffee and doughnuts are welcomed by Forcemen having just returned from action at Monte la Difensa and la Remetanea, December 1943. (Lew Merrim)

Red Cross field representative, Getty Page, serves coffee to "Chief Scout" Frank Wright at the Force's Santa Maria base camp. Captain Charles B. Rimmer, Colonel Frederick's pilot, stands to the left of Wright. (Lew Merrim)

ports came in that two men from our 6th Company had been wounded. We had just settled in our positions and were digging in, when the first real shelling began. The first shell landed in my 3rd Platoon and immediately the cry went up for the First Aid medics. The next shell hit about ten feet from the foxhole where my Reconnaissance Sergeant and I were crouched, digging in the rocky shale. Two more men were hit and their groans were agonizing to hear. The shells now came so fast that there was a continual outcry all the time. The din and shocks were nerve wracking and seemed more than human nerves could stand. Men were crouching in half-dug slit-trenches and every shell that came over seemed to be aimed at you particularly. Jars and thumps would shake every bone in your body and shrapnel would whine over your head. This lasted two hours. Then a lull; the order came to move out and go further up the hill to see if we could get out of the fire. Some moved, but many were dead or wounded and couldn't move. I moved up the hill with Sergeant Tilley [Luther A. Tilley, Jr.] and we dug in, again, just as the shelling commenced. One of us had to dig while the other listened. Shells were still landing in the areas we had just left and I thought of those who were laying there wounded and dead and being riddled by shrapnel. But there was no use adding more to the injured by going down to help them. Just as we had finished digging and [had made] some half decent shelter the shelling shifted and started falling on our positions. More nerve-wracking suspense as we listed for each whine to see if it was going to hit us. But we had, fortunately, reached an overhang in the hill, over which

they were firing and none landed closer than fifteen feet from where we crouched. It was now about 3:00AM and the shelling was gradually diminishing. Likely, the Germans' shell supply was being quickly exhausted. In place of the noise, we could hear cries of the wounded, below, some of whom were delirious by now with the intense pain."[6]

1st Battalion, First Regiment Forcemen tell much the same story. The move commenced at 1730 hours, the fading light having been just enough bare the maneuvering regiment to German artillery observers on the adjacent heights. But the Germans held their fire save for several "marker" shells which landed near the regiment as the enemy gunners found the range. Soon, "it was so dark that each man held onto the bayonet scabbard of the man in front of him to keep contact."[8] Before long, the whole regiment was stretched out along the open north slope of Ridge 368, and then a seething cauldron of enemy shells erupted. Against the den of the explosions could be heard the screams of the wounded and dying. The order was passed to dig in, but the ground was so hard and rocky that this was almost impossible. After the barrage spent itself, those who could under their own power, or others who could be carried, were ordered by Colonel Marshall to queue up and to retrace their path back down the trail. Scuttlebutt of the time maintains that as the first of Marshall's men passed the 36th Division forward command post, perched near the trail, they were met by a furious General Wilbur who, while venturing not more than a few feet from the doorway of his thickly sandbagged bunker, demanded they 'get back up the hill.' The account goes on to say

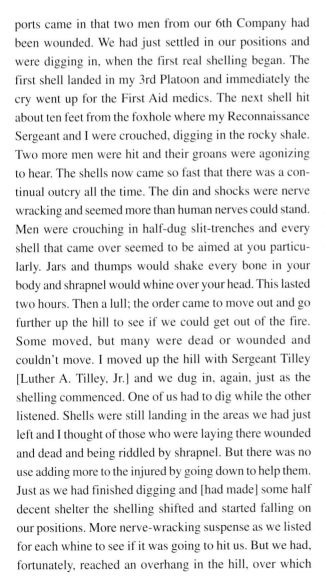

that the men ignored Wilbur, but soon after reported the episode to Colonel Frederick.[8]

At dawn on 4 December, volunteers took up the grim task of returning up the trail to help carry down the dead and wounded. Gerald McFadden's account continues:

"Dawn broke on a horrible scene. First light came through a dripping fog, which was a God-send for us. I tried to get in touch with other officers of the company, and rally their platoons. They were scattered all over. At 6:00AM an order came down to move out as quickly as possible while the fog hid us and to take as many wounded as we could. Contacted as many men as we could and sent them out back the trail. Then, with Colonel Akehurst, started out to search the area for wounded and dead. It was a horrible sight. Some men were simply mangled. Wounded had been patched up by the medics or buddies, but were now bleeding badly. Got them moving, however. Had, also, the horrible task of searching the ground for bodies and taking off one Dog-Tag. It was, perhaps, the hardest thing I ever did, up to this time, especially the friends I had known for a year and half. John Richardson, a 5th Company platoon Lieutenant was lying under Staff Sergeant Knight, who was wounded and Staff Sergeant Bargett, who was dead. Knight also had a broken leg and was delirious; two men dead and one wounded seriously, all by a direct hit. I counted about thirty dead and twelve wounded men still remaining in that death-trap, when the Colonel ordered us to clear out. I helped carry one of my own wounded men out the trail and ended up completely exhausted, when we arrived back at the area bivouac. After relaxing and some food, I had found out my company, fortunately, had lost one dead and fourteen wounded, three seriously. We stayed there until 3:00PM in the rain and then were moved back to our original place, picked up our bed-rolls and got into our sleeping bags by 6:00PM after walking bodily, with clothes on into a nearby creek to wash off the blood, mud and slime of battle. Immediately asleep."[9]

Events suggest that subsequent to General Wilbur's handling of the First Regiment SSF, it was relieved immediately from the 36th Division's control. A message from General Keyes to General Walker on the morning of 4 December, recorded in the 36th Division's G-3 Journal states: "Regiment of the 1st SSF shall not be committed to action without prior ap-

Troops take in USO entertainer, Joe E. Brown at the Capua compound after the Difensa operation, December 1943. (Lew Merrim)

proval of HQ II Corps." What is certainly true is that from this moment forward Frederick would seek that the Force never again be subject to anything lower than Corps control.[10]

By nightfall on 3 December, Colonel D.D. Williamson had rejoined his Regimental Headquarters Detachment, having come up with the supply train. Moving onto the mountain top, he now administered Second Regiment from the cave turned command post in Difensa's bowl. Lt. Colonel Moore had met Williamson upon his arrival at the top of la Difensa, had briefed him on the current situation, and had shown him to the CP. For the remainder of the operation, Williamson kept closely to his CP, informed as to what was happening around the mountainhead by reports from his subordinate officers. Before dawn on 4 December, Williamson decided to again postpone 1st Battalion's attack onto Hill 907. The prospect of an enemy counterattack, and the problem of near-zero visibility due to thick cloud cover were the chief reasons. After sunrise, 1-3, on orders from Colonel Frederick, arrived to reinforce Second Regiment atop Difensa. Frederick, meanwhile, ordered the remaining two companies of the Force's reserve battalion to join in supply packing. More reinforcements were now on the way as well, as Frederick had called for 1st Battalion, First Regiment to move onto la Difensa.

Since shortly after sunrise the previous day, persistent hostile shellfire on Difensa had caused a steady steam of casualties. During the afternoon of 4 December, Major Thomas, while scrambling for cover from a sudden enemy mortar barrage was seriously wounded in the leg. Captain Stan Waters then became the senior Company Commander in 1st Battalion, and as such, Lt. Colonel Moore appointed Waters to take over 1st Battalion until further orders.[11]

The British as yet had not captured Hill 963. Until they did so, the positions held by the Force on 960 would continue to be uncomfortable. Enemy pockets on the northern slopes of Monte Camino and southwest of Hill 907 in the draw leading to the village of Rocca d'Evandro menaced both the Force and the British. It was obvious to Frederick that the reduction of the enemy in the area of the saddle, as well as the capture of Hill 907, would have the effect of relieving pressure on the British right and thus ease their way onto Hill 963. To keep in contact with the enemy, Force patrols undertook the nerve wracking job of scouring the surrounding terrain. One patrol, whose mission it was to scout as far as the crest of Hill 907 had made the objective meeting no opposition. Working its way back later in the day, the rain slackened and the cloud cover broke. Caught in the open, it was badly shot up. Another patrol discovered a concentration of German mortars and machine guns around Hill 790 in the area of the saddle between Monte la Difensa and Monte Camino. Upon the patrol's return, the enemy's map location was furnished to artillery forward observers from the 1st Armored Division who, in turn, relayed the information to the eager gunners down below. The results of this fire mission, due to thick fog, were necessarily unobserved. However, in another instance II Corps artillery did account for breaking up a counterattack forming against Hill 960 that, according to German PW statements, was scheduled to commence at 0300 hours on 5 December.[12]

On the evening of 4 December the supply packers brought up two items that had been ordered directly by Colonel Frederick, and the procurement of which had been personally attended to by Force S-3, Colonel Wickham. Wickham remembers, "Colonel Frederick told me to go to Fifth Army with a special requisition for several dozen gross of condoms and at least ten or twelve cases of whiskey. The G-4 of Fifth Army sneered at the request and wondered what the hell they [the FSSF] were doing on the mountain. I asked that he go to General Clark, the Fifth Army Commander, for a decision. General Clark said he didn't care what they were doing on top of the mountain, that they were the only people who had ever gotten up there, and if that is what they wanted, why, send it to them."[13]

That night the men broke out the whiskey. Mere ounces per man, it was remembered by one Forceman as being, "the most welcomed sight he'd seen in his life up to that point."[14] The condoms, borrowing a page out of the lessons learned during the Kiska operation, were put over the muzzles of the Forcemen's weapons to keep them dry and free of dirt, and to keep their extra socks and personal items dry. This was a morale building coupe that only Frederick could have pulled off; and his men knew this and loved him for it.[15]

The morning of 5 December saw the survivors of First Regiment moved onto la Difensa with the manifold mission of occupying the mountaintop and assisting Second Regiment in

Memorial service at Capua-Vetere to honor the 73 Forcemen killed during the battle of Monte la Difensa-Monte la Remetanea, 12 December 1943. (Lew Merrim)

forthcoming offensive action. Frederick came up to the top that morning as well. Without further delay, he planned to attack Hill 907 as well as the enemy outposts contained in the saddle between la Difensa and Camino. This day, no counterattack by the enemy seemed likely. Allied artillery and the flooded conditions in the enemy's rear areas had made the logistics of such an attempt difficult at best. Frederick placed Major Walter S. Gray in command of 1st Battalion, Second Regiment, and with 1-3 attached, ordered him to make for 907 with all four companies defiladed on the northern side of the ridge, save for a screening force shadowing the attack on the south side of the ridge. Halfway to their objective, their movement was spotted by the enemy and, under the resulting heavy concentration of German mortar fire, Gray's men were forced to dig in. 2nd Battalion, Second Regiment reinforced by 2-1 started their attack to the south along the saddle between la Difensa and Camino in the afternoon. Two strong pockets of German troops defended a pair of knobs around Hill 790, roughly in the middle of this saddle. In all out frontal assault, aggressive leadership and bravery overcame the obstacles of scant cover and enemy machine guns to carry these two "warts." Lt. Colonel Moore's battalion occupied their newly won real estate and set up for an all around defense to wait out the night.[16]

Come late morning on 6 December, Major Gray's battalion closed the final distance onto Hill 907. This time opposition was decidedly light and the hill was captured with relative ease. Patrols were dispatched to investigate the draw to the southwest and down the spur running west from the peak of Hill 907. Gray also ordered a patrol to move down the slopes to the north of 907 with the goal of linking up with elements of the 142nd Infantry on the Vallevona Plateau.[17] A message from Colonel Frederick to Colonel Adams, recorded in the 36th Division G-3 Journal, summed up the situation at present.

"We have troops down to our left boundary at 958-087 and have consolidated for defense of the area south of la Difensa. Our attack to the west against Hill 907 has progressed so that we have passed the crest of 907. We are receiving much machine gun and mortar fire from several directions, principally from the draw running southwest from la Difensa, from western foothills of Maggiore and from northern slopes of CAMINO. We are endeavoring to place artillery supporting fire on the troublesome areas, but it is difficult due to very low visibility and the British restrictions on our artillery fire.

"I shall push the attack to the west past Hill 907 as far as condition of men will permit.

"Men are getting in bad shape from fatigue, exposure, and cold. Much sickness from a batch of bad K-ration.

"In accordance with last word, I have stopped burying dead and am collecting them for Graves Registration Service.

"German snipers are giving us hell and it is extremely difficult to catch them. They are hidden all through the area and shoot bursts at any target.

"Please press relief of troops from this position, as every additional day here will mean two more days necessary for recuperation before next mission. They are willing and eager but they are becoming exhausted. A few officers are talking too much about bad condition of men and I am combating such attitude.

"Communications are heartbreaking. Mortar fire (and travel on trail) knock out lines faster than we can repair them.

"Every time we transmit by radio enemy drops mortar fire on location.

"German reinforcements approach up draw southwest of CAMINO but I am unable to tell whether they are reinforcing or attempting to organize a counterattack.

"In my opinion, unless British take CAMINO before dark today it should be promptly attacked from the north. The locations we hold are going to be untenable as long as enemy holds north slopes of CAMINO.

"If supplies have been dropped to us, they have all landed too far west, behind Hill 907 and behind German lines.

"Do not worry about me or dry clothes for me. I am OK, just uncomfortable and tired. Signed: FREDERICK. Time Signed: 1200."

Fortunately, an attack by the British against Monte Camino on the night of 6/7 December finally succeeded in dislodging the stubborn Germans once and for all, and, by sunrise on 7 December, Force patrols from Lt. Colonel Moore's 2nd Battalion, Second had linked up with British forces who were even by that time pushing down into the valley toward Rocca d'Evandro. Organized German resistance in the Camino area was beginning to crumble. Those enemy who could were pulling back across the Garigliano River. However there were still isolated pockets of snipers to be rubbed out. Groups from First

Regiment's 2nd, 3rd, and 4th Companies combed the southeastern and southwestern slopes of Difensa with the result of eliminating the sniping on Hill 960. Acting as rear guard protection, one particularly tough pocket of approximately fifty heavily armed enemy soldiers were disposed on Hill 604, a knob on the spur that ran west from Major Gray's holdings atop 907. At 2200 hours, a rolling barrage followed closely by a sharp three-company attack by Gray cleared all accounts in the Force's area of responsibility. On the evening of 8 December, the Force, relieved in place by elements of the 142nd Infantry, filed down the mountain to board waiting trucks.[18]

In quickly sweeping the Germans from the summit of Monte la Difensa, the Force had accomplished in a few hours what Fifth Army planners had estimated would take three days.

Yet what satisfaction resonated from the dynamic manner with which they had accomplished their initial objective, was, for the time being, absent in consideration of the loss of so many friends and comrades. None of the Force's elements had walked away unscathed. The subsequent six-day battle had cost the Force dearly. On 12 December a memorial service was held at Capua-Vetere to honor the First Special Service Force's dead. In all, Frederick's command had suffered some 511 casualties: seventy-three dead, nine missing in action, 313 wounded or injured, and 116 exhaustion cases. After the ceremony, General Clark paid a visit to Colonel Frederick and his men. For the next ten days, the Force rested; and to prepare for its next assignment the men re-equipped and underwent light training.[19]

Special Feature #3

The Force's "Tough War": Photographs by Robert Capa

Legendary combat photographer, Robert Capa, arrived at Forcella del Moscoso early in the morning on 4 January 1944. He had come to this spot to catch up to forward elements of the First Special Service Force, lured both by their reputation as fearsome mountain fighters, and by the prospect of a good story. At that moment, the Force was in the process of occupying Radicosa. This small, desolate village would serve as the springboard from which the Force would launch its next series of attacks deeper into the mountains before Cassino. Capa accompanied a Force patrol into Radicosa a few hours later, and then spent the rest of the day documenting the activity he saw in and around the village. Satisfied with his efforts, and with a leaden sky threatening heavy snowfall, Capa left for Naples the next morning.

Some of the photographs taken by Robert Capa of the First Special Service Force appeared in a 1944 edition of *Life* magazine in an article titled, "It's A Tough War." Described as being "grim and unsentimental," Capa's stark images tell a story of combat, not in sweeping geopolitical terms, but in ones human and personal. On the faces of the Forcemen hang expressions that are the inevitable result of privation and fatigue. Yet in their collective countenance is borne a brand of strength inherent in men whose very nature it is to endure.[1]

L-r: combat photographer, Robert Capa; Lieutenant Finn Roll, Assistant Intelligence Officer; C.B. Grey (5-2); Rafael D. Martinez, Force Headquarters Detachment, 4 January 1944. (Lew Merrim)

Force patrol cautiously enters the village of Radicosa. Mines and booby-traps are plentiful. (Robert Capa/Magnum Photos, Inc.)

"The wife of the old Italian shepherd watched as the Germans laid their mines and now she points them out to the soldiers who are carefully removing them." (Robert Capa/Magnum Photos, Inc.)

Italian Shepherd greets litter bearers in Radicosa. (Robert Capa/Magnum Photos, Inc.)

OPPOSITE: Forceman with Thompson submachine gun surveys the mountain village of Radicosa. (Robert Capa/Magnum Photos, Inc.)

Third Regiment, led by Colonel Edwin A. Walker, enters Radicosa. (Robert Capa/Magnum Photos, Inc.)

Pack train, led by Italian muleteers bring supplies forward through a mountain pass. (Robert Capa/Magnum Photos, Inc.)

Group of Forcemen bring up bedding materials including wool blankets, shelter halves, and tent poles. (Robert Capa/Magnum Photos, Inc.)

German prisoners carrying wounded from Radicosa. (Robert Capa/Magnum Photos, Inc.)

Lashed to the stretcher, medical company aidmen carry a wounded man down a trail in mountain pass. Telephone wire is strung along the side of the narrow track. (Robert Capa/Magnum Photos, Inc.)

As Forcemen watch from higher up, II Corps aidmen remove a wounded man by litter. (Robert Capa/Magnum Photos, Inc.)

Special Feature #3

Casualties are brought out of the mountains on jeep trails to places where ambulances can remove them to field hospitals. (Robert Capa/Magnum Photos, Inc.)

Special Feature #3

Casualty is carefully lifted from jeep into the rear of a waiting ambulance. (Robert Capa/Magnum Photos, Inc.)

Special Feature #3

Forcemen pile stones to provide cover in the barren mountains. (Robert Capa/Magnum Photos, Inc.)

Outpost protects the advance of a patrol that has just been sent out. (Robert Capa/Magnum Photos, Inc.)

Special Feature #3

Standing within a rocky parapet, a Forceman uses binoculars to scan the surrounding hills. (Robert Capa/Magnum Photos, Inc.)

Special Feature #3

Canned rations are taken against mountain backdrop. (Robert Capa/Magnum Photos, Inc.)

Special Feature #3

Forceman hunkers down into the safety of his slit trench to consume cold C-rations. (Robert Capa/Magnum Photos, Inc.)

German prisoners, captured by previous night's patrol, appear relieved that their struggle is over. (Robert Capa/Magnum Photos, Inc.)

Forceman bandages an old Italian whose feet were wounded by shrapnel. (Robert Capa/Magnum Photos, Inc.)

Bombs from U.S. Army Air Force A-36As explode on a nearby hillside. (Robert Capa/Magnum Photos, Inc.)

OPPOSITE: Forcemen look skyward as North American A-36As pass overhead on their way to the target. (Robert Capa/Magnum Photos, Inc.)

Artillery forward observer with range finder and radio relays targeting information to gunners in the rear. (Robert Capa/Magnum Photos, Inc.)

Fatigue shows on the face of Colonel Edwin A. Walker, Commanding Officer Third Regiment, in a Radicosa doorway. (Robert Capa/Magnum Photos, Inc.)

Special Feature #3

Leonard G. Chatham, a Forceman from MacAdams, Ontario, with a captured German MG-42 machine gun on his shoulder. (Robert Capa/Magnum Photos, Inc.)

Forceman with walking stick talks with aidman, Kenneth D. Wilson, Headquarters Detachment, First Regiment. (Robert Capa/Magnum Photos, Inc.)

Special Feature #3

Weary pause as snow begins to fall. (Robert Capa/Magnum Photos, Inc.)

Heavily laden Technician 4th Grade of the First Special Service Force. Known to each other as "Freddy's Freighters," the Forcemen routinely man-packed loads in excess of 100 pounds into the high mountains along trails too steep even for mules. (Robert Capa/Magnum Photos, Inc.)

Men make ready to move forward. Spools of telephone wire rest in the foreground. (Robert Capa/Magnum Photos, Inc.)

Special Feature #3

Forceman stoops to fasten the buckles of his overshoes while another looks on. (Robert Capa/Magnum Photos, Inc.)

Heavily laden with food, weapons, radio equipment, and ammunition these Forcemen are about to move off to attack a high mountain several miles away. (Robert Capa/Magnum Photos, Inc.)

CHAPTER 6

Bled White

Without waiting for the completion of Operation RAINCOAT, Fifth Army began the task of reducing the enemy defenses in the valley and those strung across the rough tableland on the right side of the Mignano Gap. As a preliminary measure, 10 Corps troops assumed holding positions on Mounts Maggiori, la Difensa, and la Remetanea, freeing the whole of II Corps for this, the second phase of attacks in the Mignano Gap sector. Further north of the Gap, VI Corps exerted pressure along its front in an effort to keep the Germans off balance. II Corps was to point this new attack west along the course of Highway 6, and in the process would have to overcome elaborate and well-conceived enemy defenses – a maze of mines, barbed wire, and mutually supporting strongpoints – that stretched across the narrow valley, nowhere stronger than within the stone houses of the fortified village of San Pietro. Elements of the 36th Division launched their first attack against San Pietro on night of 7/8 December 1943, however this initial push was bitterly resisted, and the attack recoiled with heavy casualties. In order to move up the valley, the enemy positions on the adjacent hills would first have to be reduced.[1]

Rising just to the north of the Camino Hills was German-held Mount Lungo (Hill 343). North of San Pietro, standing as the right shoulder of the Mignano Gap, stood Mount Sammucro (Hill 1205). On the night of 7/8 December, the 1st Battalion, 143rd Infantry captured the summit of 1205. However, a simultaneous attempt by the 1st Italian Motorized Group (Italy having now re-entered the war on the Allied side) to gain the summit of Mount Lungo failed. Early on the morning of 10 December, the U.S. 3rd Ranger Battalion captured a northern spur of Mount Sammucro, Hill 950. Both 1205 and 950 were repeatedly counterattacked by the Germans until their loss was finally conceded on 13 December. II Corps artillery was instrumental in the successful defense of both peaks. But German artillery had answered in kind, and casualties were high on both sides.[2]

For nearly two weeks II Corps carried out continuous attacks against Mount Lungo, San Pietro, and Hill 720 (the western knob of Mount Sammucro, also known as Hill 730 on some old Italian and U.S. Army maps). By 19 December Mount Lungo and San Pietro had finally fallen into American hands, yet, the Germans tenaciously clung to their holdings on Hill 720, as well as to positions on the south facing slopes of Mount Sammucro which, on the right, flanked the length of Highway 6 and which had a commanding view of "Death Valley."[3]

Having made inroads along its front, II Corps set its sights on capturing San Vittore del Lazio, approximately two miles west of San Pietro. Two attacks toward the village by elements of the 36th Division, on the 19th and 20th of December were broken up. The German redoubt contained on Hill 720 remained the chief stumbling block. If San Vittore and the stubborn western ridges of Monte Sammucro could be brought under control, II Corps could then secure the line of departure that it needed to launch the final phase of present operations – the closing to the line formed by the Rapido River, which, incidentally, marked the front gate of Kesselring's third and most impressive defensive belt, the Gustav Line. On 22 December, the First Special Service Force was ordered to attack and eliminate the enemy defenses on Hill 720. Colonel Marshall's First Regiment got the nod. That day Force Headquarters, the regiments, and a contingent of Service Battalion moved up into the mountains to the village of Ceppagna and there opened camp amidst its terraced olive groves. Lt. Colonel Robert S. Moore now commanded Second Regiment replacing D.D. Williamson, who had been discretely relieved of command after his unsatisfactory performance on la Difensa. Lt. Colonel J.F.R. Akehurst became the senior officer of the 1st Canadian Special Service Battalion. Other changes in command, made necessary due to battle casualties, had been effected. The bloodletting of the Force which had begun while it held out on Monte la Difensa and la Remetanea was set to resume. It would continue for several grueling weeks to come.[4]

The U.S. 504th Parachute Infantry Regiment, which had taken part in earlier fighting on Mount Sammucro and which now held defensive positions across part of that mountain, was put under Frederick's command and would take part in the forthcoming attack. The paratroopers were to attack Hills 687 and 580 at H-hour. The Force's attack on 720 would be assisted by fires from the 6th Armored Field Artillery Group, the 376th and 456th Parachute Field Artillery Battalions, as well as the heavy machine guns and heavy mortars of the 1st Battalion, 141st Infantry. After tying in sufficient communications between the separate units, Frederick, with Corps approval, set H-hour for the attack as midnight, Christmas eve. Supplies, as before, were packed forward on the backs of the men. Mules had been promised but as yet had not arrived. In this event, two companies from the much depleted Second Regiment would serve as supply packers and litter bearers for First Regiment.[5]

Lt. Colonel Jack Akehurst's 2nd Battalion, First Regiment, a mere 186 men, would lead the attack, with Major Ed Pearce's 1st Battalion, First Regiment, in reserve. Having been held up so that last minute preparations could be effected, H-hour was changed to 0300 hours on Christmas morning. The American artillery barrage commenced against the German positions in a wide arc from Hill 687 across 720 and beyond to points nearby San Vittore just after 0200 hours. Enemy artillery fire countered effectively. By 0300, Akehurst's battalion was pinned squarely under heavy fire and was unable to move off on time. Akehurst himself was wounded, and communications were temporarily shot out. Colonel Marshall rushed forward to take over 1st Battalion. By 0500 hours the attack started off with Captain McCall's 5th Company on the left and Lieutenant Omar Smith's 6th Company on the right. Moving down the naked, rock strewn slope, there was little cover for the attackers save for scattered shell holes which were barely deep enough to suit the purpose. Under a blanket of protective fire provided by artillery and machine guns as well as their own light mortars,

Sand table of Mount Sammucro and Hill 720. (Lew Merrim)

Force bivouac near Radicosa, January 1944. (Lew Merrim)

the attackers made it onto 720 and wrest the Germans from their hardened pits and shelters. By 0700 hours Hill 720 had been cleared, and, the attack by the 504th's paratroopers on the right had also prevailed. 1st Battalion now moved up to 720 to consolidate the gains there while 2nd Battalion expanded the "mountain-head" in the direction of San Vittore.[6]

At 1330 hours, the 1st Battalion, 141st Infantry relieved the First Regiment which, save for a patrolling force led by Lieutenant Gus Heilman of 2nd Company, then withdrew down the mountainside through San Pietro to its newly established supply point at Ceppagna. It had been a most cruel Christmas day. "Dead and wounded in the regiment totaled 65 with another 12 out of Second Regiment's 4th Company."[7]

Though San Vittore was yet to fall, with the capture of Hill 720, the line had moved forward. This new line was now the springboard for Fifth Army as it began the next phase of attacks. "The Final Phase of the Winter Line campaign [would open] on 5 January. Fifth Army was to complete its task of destroying German positions east of the Rapido and of forcing the enemy back into his principal defensive system at the mouth of the Liri Valley."[8] Orders of 1 January 1944, prescribed that the Force was to move west investing the high mountains, and by doing so protect II Corps' right flank. Principally, Frederick's objective was to capture Mount Majo, Mount Vischiataro (Hill 1109) and their surrounding peaks. Partners in the II Corps attack, the veteran U.S. 34th Infantry Division (which relieved the 36th Division in the line on 30 December) would sweep along the lower hills to the right of Highway 6, and the U.S. 1st Armored Division would advance guiding on the main road. Further to the left, British 10 Corps' northernmost elements were to keep pace with II Corps' advance. On the right, VI Corps was to do the same, until 9 January, when it would turn over its frontage to General Alphonse P. Juin's French Expeditionary Corps. For their part, the enemy had withdrawn the weight of his forces to his next defensive line running north to south across a string of peaks including Majo, Hill 1270, Vischiataro, la Chiaia, Porchia, Trocchio, and Cedro. In the wake of his withdrawal the enemy had seeded the roads and trails with mines and booby traps. These impersonal devises lay waiting in the hundreds to maim or to deliver indifferent death to anyone who might recklessly, or perhaps unwittingly, stumble upon them.[9]

As the offensive resumed, Third Regiment, with 1-2 and 3-2 attached as supply and litter bearers, was ordered to carry out a sweeping end run across the rugged hills on the Force's right, that was to culminate in an attack on the peaks overlooking Mount Vischiataro. First Regiment, with 2-2 likewise attached, would drive for the Moscoso notch, a narrow pass through the mountains at Forcella del Moscoso (Height 708). The remainder of Second Regiment, now functioning as a single combat battalion, was to attack and capture Hill 724, west of and overlooking the tiny mountain village of Radicosa, thereby securing this cluster of six stone dwellings for use as an advance command and supply point. The Service Battalion, its presence more vital than ever on the front, would carry out supply and evacuation duties in support of the regiments. The Force supply effort now enjoyed the assistance of pack trains, led by Sardinian muleteers, that by 11 January would number almost 700 mules. The Force would also have the direct support of five battalions of artillery from the 6th Field Artillery Group, and Company B-19th Engineer Combat Regiment would accompany the striking elements to clear mines and improve trails. Trailing the Force's initial advances, the 142nd Infantry Regiment, temporarily detached from the 36th Division, would occupy and defend the lines of communication.[10]

The leading elements of Colonel Edwin A. Walker's Third Regiment set off on their long march after nightfall on 1 January. On the night of 3 January 1944, First Regiment and Second Regiment (less a small detachment) moved out three miles from Ceppagna, passing through Le Noci, and into assembly areas northwest of Mount Sammucro. Beginning their attacks at 2120 hours that night, First and Second Regiments had by the following evening captured heights 670, 724, and 775. With the capture of the heights around Radicosa, the village was secured for use as a base from which to launch attacks further

Colonel Frederick (facing away from camera) goes over plans with a group of his officers, Radicosa area, January 1944. (Author's Collection)

Forcemen gather around a map prior to breaking camp and continuing the advance, Radicosa area, January 1944. (Author's Collection)

into the high mountains that lay to the west and northwest. Opposition had been limited to mainly mortar and machine gun fire. Colonel Frederick, with the Force Headquarters Detachment personnel in tow, took up residence to oversee the next succession of attacks. On the 4th as well, Third Regiment's two pronged advance to the north swept German outposts off the outskirts of Hill 950 and netted Mount Arcalone (Hill 1027). Patrols by Third Regiment, probing along the approaches to Mount Majo drew mortar fire.[11]

By the end of the first week of January, enemy action and the increasingly difficult conditions of weather were extracting a heavy toll on the Force. First Regiment manpower had been cut by half, as had been Second Regiment's number. Third Regiment stood at about two-thirds authorized strength. In order that the drive on its right flank not be hampered, II Corps released several reserve units to augment the Force. Over the period of 6-8 January, Colonel Frederick took command of this ad hoc collection of units comprised of the 133rd Infantry Regi-

Frederick and other officers consult maps. (Lew Merrim)

BELOW: With his headquarters group, Colonel Frederick leaves his Radicosa command post for the front. (Lew Merrim)

Men of Third Regiment are briefed before starting out toward a new objective. (Lew Merrim)

Forcemen pause outside of the Radicosa chapel. (Lew Merrim)

ment, the 36th Division Artillery, Company A of the 19th Engineer Combat Regiment, Company A of the 109th Medical Battalion, as well as his own First Special Service Force. Designated as Task Force B, Frederick would be able to continue the drive across the same broad front as before and, as intended, establish "a base in the vicinity of Hill 1109, advancing southwest toward Mount Trocchio, and protecting the II Corps right flank. . . . On 10 January 1944, the Bonjour Groupment was assigned to . . . Task Force B for tactical purposes to protect the right flank of Task Force B by operating in the VI Corps zone of action."[12]

Meanwhile, by 6 January, First Regiment patrols began to probe the approach to Hill 1109. Ahead of the First and Third Regiment lines of march, it was ascertained that the enemy had withdrawn all but a few scattered outposts, preferring to make his decisive stand from positions atop high ridges. Above

1109 loomed towering Mount Majo to the northeast and Hill 1270 to the north. To leave either of these two heights in the hands of the enemy would make any foothold atop 1109 untenable, so Frederick ordered that First Regiment would time its attack to coincide with an attack on Mount Majo by Third Regiment.[13]

Starting off just after dark on 6 January, Third Regiment began the attack on Mount Majo (Hill 1259). Infiltrating silently up the lower slopes of the mountain went Lt. Colonel Gilday's 1st Battalion – his 3rd Company on the left and his 2nd Company on the right. 1st Company followed close behind in reserve. German machine gun emplacements barring the way were quietly dispatched. 2nd Battalion trailing and to the left, was to envelopment the enemy positions from the west. As the regiment crept forward nervous enemy mortarmen occasionally dropped harassing fire in on the area. The attack

Major Arthur C. Neeseman's First Regiment aid station near the Moscoso Gap, Italy. (Lew Merrim)

First aid post in the mountains. Note Geneva cross draped on roof of stone house. (Lew Merrim)

was progressing well until shortly after 2200 hours when, with the leading elements of 2nd Company only some "fifty yards from the crest of the hill,"[14] it was discovered and came under intense fire. Enemy machine guns crackled from Majo's ridgeline and the belches of mortars, firing at targets pointed out for them by the tracer-fire of snipers, were followed by the crashing of the incoming bombs.

By 0520 hours the next morning the enemy's guns directly atop Majo had been silenced. By 0900 hours considerable mopping up of Majo's western knobs had been effected. But only a few short hours later the first of the inevitable enemy counterattacks was felt. Appreciative of Majo's strategic nature, the Germans rushed what reserves were on hand into the battle for the hill. The fighting was desperate, confused, and nearly nerve shattering at times. Many Forcemen, scattered and alone on the hill fought personal battles for survival. When the Forcemen's own ammunition began running out – most of it had been expended during the initial assault – they used the weapons that had been left behind by the enemy when he had been ejected from the hill. The Forcemen had been trained in the use of enemy weapons and their official history notes: "One secret in the swift consolidation had been the capture intact with heavy ammunition supply of numerous German machine guns. These were turned around on the Germans. As each successive counterattack came over the lip of Majo the enemy fell in front of his own captured guns. Throughout the day 27 enemy counterattacks were launched, repulsed, and the dead lay in piles on the hill, while enemy shelling pulverized the hill." In total, an estimated forty-two enemy counterattacks were sent against Majo over a two-day period. The fires from the guns of the 93rd Armored Field Artillery, more than 8,500 rounds over

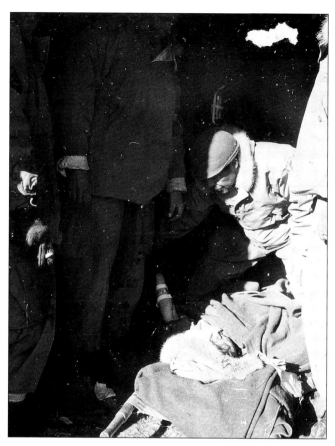

Wounded man made ready for evacuation. (Lew Merrim)

the 7-10 January period, were instrumental in helping to finally break the enemy's resolve.[15]

First Regiment jumped off on its attack at 2130 hours and moved west across the foothills of Mount Majo with Hill 1109 as its goal. Strong counterattacks, coming from three directions, stopped the regiment short of its objective. Making its

Forcemen look on as wounded are evacuated from forward aid post in the mountains. (Lew Merrim)

Italian civilians fleeing from the fighting in the mountains are questioned by Forcemen, vic. Radicosa, January 1944. (Lew Merrim)

next move during the 7th, the regiment joined the Third on top of Majo. Attached to the First was the 3rd Battalion, 133rd Infantry (Companies I, L and K), part of the newly formed Task Force B. I Company would remain on Majo to outpost the hill, relieving the Third Regiment of this task. Departing Majo at dusk on the 7th, First Regiment, with Companies L and K in tow, struck out west to clear and occupy Hill 1270, and then attack from the north, downhill, onto 1109. For the job on 1270, Colonel Marshall decided to let L Company, fresher, carry the ball. While Marshall's men, wearing their ski parkas white-side out, hunkered down in the foot-deep snow that lay in the valley, L Company above, well versed in their trade, carried the hill by 0200 hours on the morning of the 8th after clashing briefly with the enemy outpost. With its rear secure, and using the lower slopes of Hill 1270 as a jumping off point, First Regiment began moving again toward 1109. This time all was quiet as First Regiment moved onto Mount Vischiataro. The enemy who had thwarted Marshall's regiment so successfully the evening before had abandoned the position. Come morning, the outposting of 1109 was left to Company K and First Regiment moved back to join the other Force elements at Radicosa.[16]

In the valley, through which coursed Highway 6, the rest of II Corps' progress was steady if not just as grueling as in the neighboring mountains. The last of the enemy had been driven from San Vittore on 4 January, and Mount la Chiaia and Hill 342 were captured on the 7th. "Task Force A, an armor and mechanized infantry team from the 1st Armored Division, . . ." took Mount Porchia on the 7th as well, and with high casualties. British 10 Corps, operating to the southwest, claimed Cedro Hill, rounding out Allied gains in the upper valley.[17]

At Radicosa on the 8th, the Force counted the week's cost in killed, wounded and incapacitated. Effective strength among the Combat Echelon stood at 53 officers and some 450 enlisted men, not including those 1st Battalion, Second Regiment men, almost 200 strong, detailed to supply and evacuation duties. That evening First Regiment closed from Radicosa to take up positions on top of Hill 1270. Third Regiment also returned to the front taking up its now familiar position on Mount Majo. No direct enemy attacks would be leveled against these hills over the next two days but the regiments would not be spared casualties, many caused by the constant artillery harassment, others due to the dampness and bitter cold. The war diary of the 1st Canadian Special Service Battalion recounts the somber situation:

Although suffering from frozen feet and a shrapnel wound in his hand, Private Norton L. Shaver (6-3) brings in a German prisoner, vic. Venafro, Italy, January 1944. (National Archives of Canada)

A German prisoner arrives under escort of Warrant Officer JG, Samuel Wolsborn of Force Headquarters Company, vic. Venafro, Italy, January 1944. (National Archives of Canada)

"SANTA MARIA: 2 January. A bright cold day. Parkas are being sent forward as there is about 5 inches of snow in the hills and quite cold.

"7 January. Bright and cool. Casualty returns from the front include a number of frost-bitten feet.

"8 January. Continues bright and cold. Today's casualty return from the R.A.P. lists nearly 100 names, half of them frost bite and exposure, the rest battle casualties. The weather in the hills is very cold, high wind and snow. German resistance is quite severe, artillery and mortar fire still taking its toll.

"9 January. Today's Force casualty return has 122 names. Again nearly half are frost bite and exposure. There won't be much left of the Force if casualties keep at this rate.

"10 January. Mild and damp. News from the front is bad. The Force is being thrown into one action after another with only a handful of able-bodied men left and no sign of their being relieved; 73 names on today's casualty report, 40 frost-bitten feet. Those returning to camp on light duty say it is really rugged and they are all played out. Three weeks tomorrow since they left here."[18]

Relieved from holding the Majo and 1270 peaks, Companies L and I of the 133rd were sent to rejoin the rest of their regiment now assembled on Hill 1109. Timely Intelligence, supplied by the steady stream of fresh prisoners, suggested to Frederick that the enemy before him was growing weaker by the day, so he decided to maintain the pressure along his front by attacking to the west without delay to capture Hills 1030 and 780, and southwest, across Capraro Hill (698), to a line which incorporated the villages of San Michele and San Antonino. The 1st and 100th Battalions of the 133rd Infantry led off on the attack at 0500 hours on 9 January. By noon both battalions were receiving heavy flanking fire and were bogged down. At 1330 hours the 3rd Battalion, in Task Force B reserve atop Hill 1109, received a strong counterattack from the north. By the morning of the 10th, however, the enemy counterattacks had been beaten back and the advancing battalions again continued to make progress. That night, Frederick withdrew the 100th Battalion from the attack back to 1109 and replaced them with the 3rd Battalion, which continued the effort. Despite the fact that the enemy was growing weary of the

Forcemen, Corps troops, and German PWs mill about together in front of the Force clearing station at Le Noci, Italy, January 1944. (National Archives of Canada)

Two officers from 1-3 rest near the Force clearing station at Le Noci, Italy. Left is Lieutenant J. Kostelec of Calgary, Alberta; right is First Lieutenant Howard C. Wilson of Olympia, Washington. (National Archives of Canada)

Lieutenant J. Kostelec of Calgary, showing the "U.S.-CANADA" shoulder sleeve insignia worn by all members of the First Special Service Force. On 4 March 1944, Kostelec went missing in action and is now presumed dead. (National Archives of Canada)

fight for the valley, a tough pocket of enemy hold-outs, well dug in on Capraro Hill, defied further advance throughout 11-12 January.[19]

During the night 9/10 January, the First and Third Regiments SSF were joined on the Majo-Hill 1270 mass by an element of the French Expeditionary Corps, the 3rd Spahi Regiment, Algerian troops commanded by Colonel Bonjour. Those who were left of First Regiment made their way back to bivouac near Radicosa. The Third Regiment stayed on, but moved their location some 500 yards back of Majo's crest. The major elements of the FEC were in the process of relieving the U.S. VI Corps to the north, which was to go into training for the impending amphibious operation at Anzio scheduled for the end of the month. Frederick ordered that patrols from the Bonjour Groupment, now assigned to Task Force B, move immediately west to Hills 875 and 473 in order to maintain contact with the retreating Germans.[20]

Meanwhile in a bold stroke designed to aid the advance of the 133rd, on 13 January Frederick ordered Lt. Colonel Moore's reduced Second Regiment to move southwest from Hill 1109 to capture Hill 302 in the enemy's rear. Accompanying the regi-

ment were artillery forward observers and communications personnel. Once on their objective, Moore's men were to dig in for an all around defense and, from the left flank, assist by fire the advance of the 133rd. It was not until 0800 hours that the Germans discovered the Second Regiment Forcemen on 302, who were by that time calling heavy concentrations down upon packs of Germans retreating from Cervaro along paths that took them south and west of the hill. Moore's maneuver had been excellently accomplished – his command had received but one dead and one wounded. Yet the 133rd Infantry, whose forward progress remained slow, took no advantage from this stroke. The 168th Infantry had captured the village of Cervaro on the afternoon of the 11th. Subsequently relieved by E Company of the 168th Infantry, Second Regiment returned to bivouac near Radicosa.[21]

By now, Third Regiment's manpower had been reduced to what amounted to two combat companies. 1st Battalion, currently under Lt. T.M. Radcliffe, was now organized provisionally as A Company. 2nd Battalion's men, under Captain S.L. Dymond, was organized as B Company. Upon Frederick's orders, the two companies moved off – A to Hill 1030, B to

Hill 780 – there relieving elements of the 133rd Regiment. Regimental Headquarters took up a position in the saddle between the two heights. Over the next three days the regiment proceeded to mop up what resistance remained in the surrounding territory.[22]

At midnight on January 12th, the Bonjour Groupment was relieved of its assignment to Task Force B, and continued its advance toward Sant' Elia. By the evening of the next day, the 133rd Regiment reverted back to the control of the U.S. 34th Division, and Task Force B was thus dissolved. However, the Japanese-American 100th Battalion, and Company A of the 109th Engineer Combat Battalion (part of the 34th Division) were released to Colonel Frederick on II Corps orders that directed him to take this force into the village of San Michele and then to push beyond to Le Voglio (Hill 130), the last remaining high ground before the Rapido River. Frederick completed this mission by the afternoon of the 15th. That same day Mount Trocchio fell without a fight to elements of the 34th and 36th Divisions. Force patrols spent the next two days tying in the fronts of the French on the right with the U.S. 133rd Infantry Regiment on the left. Accomplishing this job by midday, "the First Special Service Force returned to bivouac vicinity Santa Maria by truck on the afternoon 17 January in the order First Regiment, Second Regiment, Third Regiment, Supply personnel. Last elements of First Special Service Force closed from Ceppagna at 172345A January."[23]

"It had been a cold and wearing struggle in the mountains. Of the Force's 1,800 combat strength, approximately 1,400 men were either dead or hospitalized. Service battalion packers and litter men were reduced 50% by fatigue and wound cases."[24] Moreover, after nearly two months of combat the Canadian

Lieutenant W. H. Langdon, carrying full kit, is about to go forward to join his unit north of Venafro, Italy, January 1944. (National Archives of Canada)

presence within the Force, proportionate with the overall casualty rate, had been drastically reduced. As the month of January 1944 came to a close, this fact prompted the First Canadian Army Commander, General Kenneth Stuart, to suggest to the U.S. and Canadian Governments that the Canadian element be withdrawn from the Force. Asserting Canada's policy of non-reinforcement of the 1st Canadian Special Service Battalion in

A close call. The German bullet only pierced the steel shell of the helmet and passed through. (Lew Merrim)

Force dead are prepared for removal from the field, Radicosa area, January 1944. (Lew Merrim)

Private Ralph Leonard, Headquarters Detachment First Regiment, adjusts the load to be carried by Medic Kenneth D. Wilson, Radicosa area, 15 January 1944. (National Archives)

Sergeant Lewis J. Merrim leads pack mule near Radicosa, Italy, January 1944. The mule carries spools of communications wire on its back. (Lew Merrim)

Supply packers, led by Harlan S. Morgan (3-2), pass a mule relay point and a French medical aid station, near Cervaro, Italy, 14 January 1944. Men of the regiments routinely stacked their rifles and donned Geneva crosses to help move medical supplies forward and wounded to safety. (National Archives)

the combat theatre, he held that Canada's contribution to the Force, in light of the administrative burden that it caused, was now somewhat questionable. But before this matter could be settled, the Force was to again be called to action. With the timely intervention of General Eisenhower, Stuart was persuaded to withdraw his recommendation for the moment. Further, Stuart allowed that normal Canadian infantry replacements – not trained parachutists as would have been ideal – would be permitted. However, even the first of these would not arrive before April.[25]

On the morning of 20 January, Colonel Frederick was called to attend a staff meeting at the II Corps command post concerned with last minute details for the attack across the Rapido River by elements of the 36th Division. Frederick offered that he would ask for volunteers from among his men to drive their T-24s to help move supplies forward in support of the attack, as they had proven in the Aleutians to be excellent over muddy terrain.[26] Later, accompanying his men to the crossing sights for the attack he was nonplused by the conspicuous absence of principal officers of the division at the front; commenting afterwards that they had done "a poor job." After the conclusion of the operation, Colonel Paul D. Adams, Force Executive Officer, was summoned to Fifth Army Headquarters in Caserta. Interviewed by General Alfred Gruenther, and then General Mark Clark, Adams was told that he was being transferred to the 36th Division to take command of the 143rd Infantry Regiment. The 143rd, whose two attempts – on 20

January and then again on 21 January – to establish a bridgehead on the western bank of the Rapido River near Sant'Angelo, were thrown back in disarray. It would be Adams' job to introduce a steady hand to the regiment and to instill in it same aggressive spirit and professional attitude that he had helped to imbue in the First Special Service Force. Lt. Colonel Kenneth Wickham, then Force Adjutant, became Executive Officer.[27]

For the next week, the Force "reorganized, re-equipped, and rested. From 24-31 January, the First Special Service Force absorbed 250 replacements [all U.S. volunteers] and conducted reorganization training to prepare for the next operation." Forcemen returning from hospital were welcomed back. But on 29 January 1944, while in the midst of planning for future operations in the Winter Line, the Frederick received orders to promptly prepare the Force for movement to the Anzio Beachhead. Proceeding to concentration Area No. 3 at Pozzuoli on 30 January, the Force, 68 officers and 1,165 other ranks, with the 456th Parachute Field Artillery Battalion (minus C and D Batteries) attached, loaded aboard waiting LSTs and LCIs. As well that day came official word of Frederick's confirmation to the rank of Brigadier General, a promotion that had been recommended by General Clark and that was allowed for by the Force's original table of organization. Departing at 1800 hours on 31 January the ships began their hundred-mile trip north. The Force arrived at Anzio on 1 February and debarked at the main pier at 1000 hours.[28]

A group of Forcemen, wearing fur-ruffed parkas and ski mittens, heat rations and warm themselves around a fire, Radicosa area, January 1944. (National Archives)

Service Company men prepare to serve a hot meal brought up in M-1941 meramite insulated food containers. (Lew Merrim)

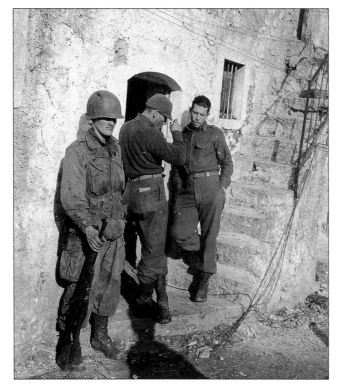

Lt. Colonel Tom Gilday and Colonel Paul D. Adams (right) discuss the recent operation on Mount Majo. (Lew Merrim)

Regimental Commanders. Colonel Edwin Walker (left) Third Regiment, and Colonel Alfred "Cookie" Marshall, First Regiment, after nearly three weeks of continuous action in the Winter Line. (Lew Merrim)

Headquarters personnel. L-r: "Chief Scout" Francis Wright, D.M.M. Hill, an unidentified Signal Corps photographer, Force photographer Lewis Merrim, and Rapheal Martinez. (Lew Merrim)

Forceman looks down the sights of his Johnny Gun, Radicosa area, January 1944. (National Archives)

Third Regiment Forcemen rest roadside near Cervaro, Italy, January 1944. (National Archives)

ABOVE AND BELOW: L-r: Headquarters scouts Hill and Wright defuse a German booby-trap, Radicosa area, 1944. (Lew Merrim)

Coffee and doughnuts for haggard Forcemen who pass through a Red Cross line at base camp Santa Maria, Italy, after having concluded operations in the Winter Line, 19 January 1944. (National Archives)

OPPOSITE:
ABOVE: Force Headquarters Detachment patrol enters the sniper filled town of Cervaro, 12 January 1944. Patrol members include Charles N. Russell, F.B. Wright, D.M.M. Hill and a Signal Corps photographer. (National Archives)

BELOW: Charles N. Russell (near left) covers the advance of scouts F.B. Wright and D.M.M. Hill. Shortly after this picture was taken German fire forced the patrol to take shelter in one of the battered houses. There, under intense fire, they held the enemy off until nightfall, at which time Russell and Signal Corps photographer Gallegher withdrew. Hill and Wright stayed behind to provide cover but were both killed. (National Archives)

LEFT: Men of the First Special Service Force move their T-24 light cargo carrier out of the zone that was under mortar fire. All volunteered to be first across the Rapido River with medical supplies and food to support the attack of the 143rd Infantry Regiment, 23 January 1944. (National Archives)

BELOW: Crouching behind rocks near Hill 780, Third Regiment Forcemen peer across the valley toward the Rapido River and Cassino, 17 January 1944. (National Archives)

BELOW: Using a shrub for cover, a Force observer snaps reconnaissance photographs of "Death Valley" terrain. (National Archives)

Raiders of the Beachhead

The landing on the west coast of Italy at Anzio, Operation SHINGLE, had gotten underway on 22 January 1944, and had been carried out by Anglo-American forces of the U.S. VI Corps, commanded by Major General John P. Lucas. The success of the operation hinged on the presumption that the presence of a large force in the enemy's rear that threatened Rome, would oblige him to draw away units then defending the Gustav Line in order to contain this new crisis. With the enemy's southern front thus weakened, Fifth Army planned, with an ensuing offensive, to cross the Rapido River, pierce the Gustav Line, and then attack northward up the Liri Valley. Not entirely out of the question was the prospect that Kesselring, fearing that his forces might become trapped, would order a withdrawal from the Gustav Line altogether. Virtually unopposed, the landing at Anzio came as a complete surprise to the Germans, and initially the beachhead was quickly expanded.

Kesselring's reaction, however, was anything but what the Allies had expected. Throwing antiaircraft personnel into the fight as infantry, and stripping small, highly mobile forces from divisions all over Italy, Kesselring had, by D+2, surrounded the Anzio Beachhead with nearly 40,000 troops. Moreover, German divisions from as far away as the Balkans and France were, in spite of Allied air harassment, sped to Anzio. Making matters worse, the attempted crossing of the Rapido River had ended in complete failure, and that meant that there would be no timely link-up with the beachhead from the south as had been anticipated. With little more than dismal prospects looming in the immediate future, Lucas had, by 1 February, called a halt to further offensive actions in order that VI Corps might consolidate its gains, and in order to build up sufficient reserves of men and of supplies to break through the tight ring that the Germans had suddenly closed around the beachhead.[1]

The First Special Service Force, once disembarked, moved at the double-quick through Anzio to an assembly area on the west side of the city. At this time it had not yet been decided as where best to employ the unit within the beachhead area. What was decided was that as per Frederick's wishes, the Force would act independently under VI Corps orders; rather than be attached to an infantry division. Next day the entire Force moved to a new concentration area about one and one-half miles south of Le Ferriere, a small village somewhat in the middle of the beachhead. By mid afternoon, Frederick learned that the Force's new mission would be to defend a frontage on the right flank of the beachhead and that the Force was to relieve units currently occupying that line. At nightfall on 2 February the Combat Echelon moved to the eastern sector of the beachhead. There, under the cover of darkness, the Forcemen relieved the 39th Combat Engineer Regiment, taking over its defensive positions on the western bank of the Mussolini Canal. The Service Battalion remained in place near Le Ferriere to await further orders. 5-3 lost two of its company officers that night. Lieutenant C.R. Scoggin, while attempting a reconnaissance of his company's sector, was killed by a German S-mine. Lieutenant David W. Cuddy, who had been accompanying Scoggin, fell mortally wounded by the blast and died the next morning.[2]

Emptying into the Tyrrhenian Sea some five miles east of Nettuno, the Mussolini Canal traced an uneven course northward, fed by a system of shallow drainage ditches that creased the Littoria Plain. The canal was built in 1926 during one of Benito Mussolini's fascist work programs. As a result, the adjoining countryside, now predominantly flat, sandy farmland,

LCIs moored at Anzio, Italy. (Lew Merrim)

Service Battalion 6x6 truck emerges from the cargo hold of an LST at Anzio. (Lew Merrim)

had been reclaimed from the once malarial Pontine Marshes. Lately the canal offered a very strong defensive position as it was an impassable barrier to all types of enemy armored vehicles. Its depth, eight to ten feet in most places, its width, sixty yards at its widest point, and its treacherous current, combined to make it equally as challenging an impediment to attacking infantry. The network of roads that cut across the predominantly flat terrain of the eastern beachhead was ample, but practically all motor traffic was restricted to those roads, the open fields being too soft to support vehicle traffic. Sprinkled throughout the neighboring countryside were farmhouses offering excellent points for observation as well as for ambush. Apart from shallow drainage ditches, ravines, and "fringes of trees along the roadside," the terrain offered practically no cover whatsoever, and all daytime movement, except during times of poor weather, could be easily observed.[3]

Though the Mussolini Canal could be counted as a defensive advantage, the Force's front, some 12,000 yards, was equal to one-quarter of the entire beachhead perimeter. This being the case, Frederick's men would be spread out very thinly. Having not had time to fully recover the losses sustained while fighting in the mountains, upon its arrival at Anzio, First Regiment stood at only half strength. Second Regiment was in similar shape. Third Regiment, having received all of the replacements taken on in late January was at near full strength. First Regiment took over one-third of the Force's front; five kilometers that stretched from the mouth of the canal northward. Third Regiment's frontage, the remaining two-thirds, began on First's left flank and extended along the canal's western bank to a point some eight kilometers distant (inclusive of a bridge referred to as "Bridge 5") where it tied in to the right flank of the U.S. 504th Parachute Infantry Regiment. This

Force equipment, carried aboard 6x6 trucks, is unloaded at Anzio, February 1944. (Lew Merrim)

Aerial view of Force front line positions behind the Mussolini Canal, probably in Third Regiment zone, 19 February 1944. (National Archives)

boundary, incidentally, was moved south some 1,500 meters on 6 April. Second Regiment went into position a short distance behind the canal line as Force reserve ready to counterattack if the Germans made a breakthrough, and to carry out patrols.[4]

During their short stay on the canal the 39th Engineers, whom the Force relieved, had been constantly harassed by the Germans whose outpost line occupied positions and buildings just across the waterway. The Germans certainly had heard the stirrings of the engineers being relieved. During the Force's first night on the canal, a German combat patrol decided to test what their new neighbors were made of by spraying small arms fire and throwing grenades across the canal into First Regiment's area. This sparked a hot but brief fight ending when the Germans decided to withdraw. Incensed by the brazenness of the enemy, the Force immediately set about rectifying the situation. The Germans had blown most of the pre-existing bridges, so on the night of 3 February Force combat patrols crossed the canal over improvised footbridges to probe the German outpost positions and to generally raise hell.[5]

Anzio offered an entirely different environment than that which Force had been accustom to while operating in the mountains. Chiefly, this highly trained and aggressive unit now found itself assuming a static, defensive posture. Early in February, Frederick urged Lucas that the Force be used to seize Mount Arrestino, a crest in the Lepini Hills "that gave the enemy the dominant observation on Highway 7."[6] But the defensive-minded Lucas had turned Frederick down, preferring to sit on his current holdings. However it was anything but Frederick's intention to merely lay behind the canal and wait for something to happen, though he would have to settle for more localized action in the form of constant patrolling. The Force's patrolling was quite effective as an entry in the Summary of Operations Report of the First Special Service Force for February 1944, states: "It is certain that the enemy acquired a distinct dislike for the aggressiveness of [our] numerous patrols which knifed into his positions each night."[7]

By 7 February, Force patrols had pushed the German outpost line back nearly 1,500 yards. This resulted in there coming into existence a sort of no-man's land between the two opposing forces. "During daylight this no-man's land looked like a peaceful Italian countryside. As soon as darkness fell, the area became a place of maneuver for the numerous patrols sent out by both the enemy and ourselves."[8] Indeed, the one characteristic the branded Force operations at Anzio was the fact that they were, for the most part, carried out at night. The Force's

Force bivouac on back side of Mussolini Canal berme. (Lew Merrim)

The steeple of the village chapel at Borgo Sabotino, First Regiment zone, Anzio. (Lew Merrim)

copious night training and its previous combat experience on the southern front would be used to the fullest. These operations would not involve the whole of the Force at any time, but rather would be limited primarily to section, platoon, and company level forays. Larger raids, carried out by whole battalions or regiments were less frequent.[9]

In no time, the order of day to day activity began to take on a familiar pattern. During the day, the men of the regiments holding the front line improved their defenses by deepening their excavations, constructing mortar pits, and automatic rifle and light machine gun positions. In fact, most gun pits were outfitted with numerous captured enemy automatic weapons in addition to the Forcemen's own weapons. In this fashion, the men would be well prepared to meet what enemy might dare an approach on the canal, and be well sheltered from the intermittent enemy artillery and mortar fire. Come night, however, the Forcemen blackened their faces and hands, and, melting into the darkness, slipped across the canal to run amok

Peering out into no-man's land from First Regiment positions. (Lew Merrim)

through the German positions. Demolition patrols using RS cratered roads and blasted away culverts to block the path of enemy armor. They also demolished buildings to deny their use by the enemy for observation, as listening posts, and as strong points. Reconnaissance patrols scoured no-man's land registering the whereabouts of enemy positions for future patrols or slating them as targets for a coming day's artillery shoot. Ambush patrols laid traps for wandering bands of Germans, and combat patrols confronted the enemy at close quarters in sharp, shocking raids. Mines, enemy artillery, and clashes with opposing patrols were commonplace and sometimes costly, but from this constant contact with the enemy the Force was able to draw a fairly complete picture of enemy strength arrayed against it.[10]

As a passive measure to keep the Germans from getting too close to the canal, by the end of March the Force's front had, with the help of engineer troops, been "completely wired and protected by a network of minefields. Approximately 13,702 AP [antipersonnel mines] and 490 AT [antitank mines] have been laid."[11] Initially there had been only one intact bridge by which to cross over the canal. Crossings at other locations were effected by the use of rubber boats set up on a rope and pulley system. However, "by the close of the [February-March] period 15 footbridges and 5 vehicular bridges had been constructed across the Canal. Four of the latter bridges [being] of Class 40 construction, suitable for medium tanks, one treadway and three semi-permanent."[12]

During the months of February, March and April, and into the first week of May, company-level patrols from the regiments, particularly Second, repeatedly raided the villages of Sessuno, Borgo Piave, and Littoria, all of which lay east of the Mussolini Canal in no-man's land. In the case of an early

Sessuno action, one company attacked the village overwhelming its defenders. The company then proceeded to hold the village for some three hours. In the interim, when German reinforcements arrived to drive the Forcemen out, they too were overcome. The Forcemen then withdrew across the canal leaving behind an estimated eighty German dead and taking with them seven prisoners of war. Second Regiment companies twice raided the enemy outpost line during February. Another village, Borgo Sabotino, lay immediately across the canal from First Regiment's positions. Captain Gus Heilman led his company into the village and secured it, effectively moving the front line forward in this area. The village was renamed "Gusville" in honor of Heilman. During the night of 28/29 February a reinforced platoon from 2nd Company, First Regiment led by Lieutenant George Krasevac discovered a pocket of Germans apparently forming for an attack in the courtyard

Forcemen examine abandoned enemy field piece near Cabbage Castle, First Regiment sector, Anzio. (Lew Merrim)

of a farmstead just beyond Gusville. Krasevac, having the element of surprise, quickly attacked, killing several enemy and taking the rest prisoner. As Krasevac's men waited in the yard several more groups of Germans blundered in and were promptly taken prisoner. Compelled to withdraw by the coming dawn, amazingly Krasevac's trap had netted 111 German prisoners during this single evening.[13]

Nighttime listening posts and observation posts, usually occupied by three men (two facing forward and the other to the rear), secluded themselves well-forward of the main line of resistance and often times right under the enemy's nose. Linked to friendly lines by means of sound power telephones and wire, these outposts plotted enemy positions and activity in no-man's land. One particularly daring Forceman was twenty-eight year old native-Canadian Sergeant Tom Prince. Preferring to undertake his risky beachhead work alone, Prince's courageous exploits of 8 February were enough to earn him Canada's Military Medal.[14]

"Creeping across the canal after dark, paying out telephone line as [he] went, Prince slipped into a deserted farmhouse two hundred yards from the enemy lines. Here, he patiently waited for daylight. From this vantage point he could clearly pinpoint German tanks as they rumbled back and forth, constantly changing position in order to avoid American shells. That morning, Prince spotted a pair of tanks and called down accurate artillery fire that destroyed both. The enemy did not realize that he was in the ruined house, but about noon some mortar bombs fell behind it, cutting Prince's telephone line. The quick-witted sergeant donned a black hat and jacket which he found lying in the house and, imitating an excitable Italian, rushed outside. He darted about, waving his arms, all the time searching for the break in the cable. He found it, [and pretending to tie his shoelace] made the necessary repairs, then went out front and performed 'another little dervish dance' for the benefit of any Germans who happened to be watching. He went back in the house, and called down shell fire that destroyed two more tanks before nightfall."[15]

The Force's modest size was offset by the overt boldness with which it carried out its defense. A German officer captured by the Force on 29 February stated that, "we have great trouble finding definite information of the First Special Service Force. The prisoners we have taken do not talk. The best view in the *Hermann Göring Division* [then in the line opposite the Force] is that you are a division, by the frontage you hold and by having three regiments."[16] To further this notion, Frederick ordered that traffic on the hard surfaced roads some

Beach west of Cabbage Castle in First Regiment sector, Anzio. (Lew Merrim)

Force machine gun position covering a stretch of the front line along the Mussolini Canal, Anzio. (Lew Merrim)

distance behind the canal be superficially increased to lead the Germans to believe that a much larger force was being supplied.[17]

But the enemy forces were well-motivated. Numbering among them several units from the elite *Hermann Göring Panzer and Parachute Division*, they would continue to fight hard despite being bested in most encounters with the Force. During February, First and Third Regiments repulsed at least four direct attacks on the canal line. These attacks ranged in size from thirty troops to as many as a whole German infantry battalion supported by tanks. However, as the months wore on and in light of their ineffectiveness, the frequency of these direct attacks against the canal line diminished. In April, however, the Germans tried a new type of attack on the Force in the form of one of Hitler's new secret weapons. Called the *Goliath*, it was a remote controlled tankette steered by a control box that was connected to the vehicle by wires that, as it drove, payed out from a spool mounted on its back. The Goliath was a perfect small-scale replica of a tank chassis and packed a 300 pound charge of blasting gelatin. Force outposts spotted several of these one day crawling across no-man's land heading in their direction. The first clambered into a house and was detonated. A second rolled up to an outbuilding with the same result. Coming to life, the Forcemen fired at a third with a heavy machine gun setting it ablaze. That night a Force patrol undertook to recover the burned out hulk for the eager Intelligence people who wished to examine it. It took nearly a dozen Forcemen to hoist it up and carry it back. The job was excellently accomplished as the vehicle was retrieved from within 150 yards of the German lines.[18]

In late February VI Corps had felt the worst of the German counterattacks against the beachhead. But the Allies had held, and after that point, action overall on the beachhead settled down to stalemate. No major actions were provoked by either side, both apparently too worn out. By April the buildup of supplies and men inside of the beachhead was beginning to tip the balance of power in Allied favor. Intelligence gathered by Force patrols on the right flank revealed that in this sector "the enemy was shoring up against the inevitable Allied break-out."[19] Aerial photos confirmed this. Houses were being fortified with

General Frederick (right) is greeted by Major General John P. Lucas in front of his VI Corps Headquarters at the Anzio Beachhead. (National Archives)

Mortar pit covers ruins of Bridge 2 in the Third Regiment zone. The peaks of the Lepini Mountains loom in the background. (Lew Merrim)

INSET TOP: The Forceman on the right pushes another eight-round *en bloc* clip into his M-1 rifle as white chemical smoke envelops the farmhouse. (National Archives)

INSET BOTTOM: Kneeling in the tall grass, rifleman pour fire into the windows and doorways. (National Archives)

A Force patrol passes a wire barrier as it moves toward no-man's land along one of the beachhead's interior roads. (National Archives)

Launching an attack on an enemy outpost. While riflemen lay down suppressing fire, a Forceman prepares to fire a 2.36" high explosive rocket into the house, Anzio Beachhead, 1944. (National Archives)

timbers and sandbags. New diggings, new minefields, and more wire. To deal with this recent development, Frederick decided that a change of tactics was in order. The Force would, supported by armor, initiate a number of punishing daylight attacks aimed at softening these new enemy defenses.[20]

During the early morning hours of 15 April 1944, Lt. Colonel Moore's Second Regiment (minus one company) raided German defensive works in the area from Cerreto Alto to the sea, and along the Strada Litoranea. Supporting Moore were Company H of the 1st Armored Regiment, elements of the 81st Reconnaissance Battalion (A and D Companies attached on 7 February), and one platoon from Company B of the 701st Tank Destroyer Battalion. The raid was most successful, netting one officer and 43 men of the German *2nd Battalion*, *735th Grenadier Regiment*, and 17 men of the Italian *Barbarigo Battalion (Light)* of the *San Marco Marine Regiment*. U.S. losses in personnel and equipment totaled one man slightly wounded, two medium tanks destroyed, and two tank destroyers and one armored car damaged.[21]

Another tank-infantry raid carried out on 18 April on the northern flank of the Force's frontage caught the Germans there napping, and also yielded successful results. But a subsequent attack on the southern flank, this time on 1 May, showed the Germans there had quickly recovered from their earlier lassitude by strengthening their positions and alertly meeting the new attack with a tenacious defense.[22]

When not engaged in combat the Forcemen spent whatever time they could making their situation on the beachhead more livable. Some men took interest in collecting the racy German propaganda leaflets, while others took to fabricating "foxhole" radios made with battery carbons, a razor blade, a length of wire, lead from a pencil, and the crystals from a sound power telephone. With these improvised radios the men "could pick up a girl broadcaster in Rome putting out propaganda programs. [They] referred to her as the 'Berlin Bitch'."[23] Juxtaposed against the backdrop of war, Anzio's pastoral setting was, with the approach of spring, one that could reveal tranquil beauty as one Forceman described. "The pretty little white farmhouses had their barns attached so that they formed one building. They had been long since vacated, and their inhabitants evacuated to safety. The fields, and the flat land, were covered with gently blowing poppies. They looked like huge undulating carpets. The size of the poppies amazed me; some were as large as my hand!"[24] As many as 17,000 civilians had been removed from the beachhead by VI Corps. Left behind were a great variety of livestock and household belongings. Cows, horses, pigs, chickens, eggs and whatever useful items that could be carted or carried away were brought back from night patrols and put to use by the Forcemen either to supplement their 5-in-1 and 10-in-1 rations, or to furnish their dugouts and living quarters.[25]

Leaping a ditch, other Forcemen move in on the flank. Shock and aggressiveness were cornerstones of Force tactics. (National Archives)

Force Johnny gunner, spare magazine in hand, hustles down the length of a barbed wire fence to a point where he can support the attack. (National Archives)

In March a Force patrol on their way to collect the morning's eggs from one particular hen house surprised and captured three enemy soldiers who, with baskets in hand, apparently had the same intention. They were soon identified as Italians. Under questioning it was found that the leader of this trio, an immaculately uniformed Sergeant Major, spoke English quite well. Further interrogation revealed that he had been the prisoner of the British in North Africa and had been paroled with the promise that he would not again take up arms against the Allies. Once his transgression was known to his captors, he was more than willing to cooperate and divulged that his unit was the *Barbarigo Battalion* of the *San Marco Marine Regiment*. This formation represented "the first Fascist unit employed as an entity since the Armistice."[26]

When the Force arrived at Anzio, its reduced strength necessitated a provisional reorganization of First and Second Regiments; First being constituted of three companies and Second being constituted of four companies. Initially, new volunteers (and old Forcemen returning from hospital) to fill the gaps torn in the regiments were slow in coming; during the month of February the regiments receiving but ten enlisted personnel. On the other hand, the Service Battalion, drawing on the normal replacement system, was able to procure fifty-one new men as replacements during the month of February. Some of these men, in point of fact, were Force combat men who had been wounded and having recovered were then assigned to the Service Battalion. The shortage of replacements changed on 25 March when the Force received a large number of men from the 4th U.S. Ranger Battalion.[27]

Elements of two battalions from Colonel William O. Darby's Ranger organization, the 1st and 3rd, had, on the night of 29/30 January, set out on the mission of capturing the im-

Under covering fire, men close the final yards to the house and move in to clear it. (National Archives)

From within the farmhouse, Forcemen armed with Thompson submachine guns fire at the retreating enemy. (National Archives)

portant crossroads town of Cisterna di Littoria, which lay astride Highway 7 (the Appian Way), one of the principal arteries leading to Rome. Infiltrating toward the town up the deep irrigation ditches, the Rangers were to seize the town in advance of a heavier follow-up force from the U.S. 3rd Division. Disaster struck when at dawn on the 30th, the Rangers ran headlong into fresh troops of a panzer grenadier division that had just arrived on the front. Out gunned, surrounded, and eventually overwhelmed, of the 767 Rangers who attacked Cisterna, only six infiltrated back to friendly lines.[28]

Less than two months after the Cisterna disaster, Darby's 6615th Ranger Force (Provisional) was disbanded. On 25 March, the Force received all 4th Ranger Battalion personnel, less those veterans with more than two years' service. "The largest portion of the 4th Ranger Battalion group [eventually some 400 men] was assigned to the First Regiment, resulting in its reorganization to regimental size. This reorganization took place while the unit was holding a sector on the front line."[29] In all for March, six officers and 298 enlisted replacements were assigned to the Force. Beginning in April, another 150 replacements were assigned to the Force from 1st, 3rd, and 4th Ranger Battalion personnel who had either been in hospital or had otherwise been left behind during the attack on Cisterna. These men were assigned to the regiments for orientation and training. The Rangers, themselves well-trained and possessing a high *esprit* were a welcome addition to the Force. Second Regiment was restructured to its customary six companies on 15 April and remained in Force reserve. Moreover, Frederick received the Rangers' Cannon Company of four self-propelled 75mm guns, and had them moved to dug-in positions on the west bank of the Mussolini Canal to offer supporting fire to the regiments.[30]

On 27 April 1944, the Force received the first Canadian replacements as yet to replace combat losses. These 15 officers and 240 other ranks, many veteran soldiers, had been intensively trained for three weeks at Santa Maria di Capua-Vetere under the watchful eyes of Captain O'Neill and Lt. Colonel Akehurst (who was at that time recovering from wounds received during the attack on Monte Sammucro). These men were evenly distributed amongst the three regiments. By the end of April the Force had absorbed 21 officers and 515 enlisted men. In May, another large influx of replacements was absorbed by the Force when 16 officers and 325 enlisted men joined the unit. At Anzio the Force suffered a total of 54 killed in action, 51 missing in action, and 279 wounded in action. In all it received 53 officers and 1408 replacements, inclusive of those Forcemen returning from hospital. Numbers alone give no description of the Force's operations during the 98 days it spent on the Mussolini Canal, yet they do illustrate the fact that the Force was somewhat able to rebuild itself, though largely not with men who had received the high degree of training as the original Helena lot.[31]

Throughout the month of February, Force Service Battalion, less a detachment left behind at Capua-Vetere to operate the base camp, remained at the position established on 2 February. However, contingents of Service Battalion personnel had immediately gone forward to prepare a forward supply dump that they incorporated into the side of the embankment made by the spoils excavated from the canal ditch. Some distance in back of the canal, other Service Battalion men excavated a hole, that when covered over with a tarpaulin, was large enough to serve as a temporary dispensary. In March, Medical Detachment personnel relocated to a two story house that could more adequately serve the needs of all three regiments. The second

LEFT: Forcemen at work deepening their beachhead shelters behind the Mussolini Canal dike. Left to right: Sergeant R. Stevenson (4-2), Private W.J. Robinson (5-2), and Staff Sergeant J.A. Playford (5-2). Anzio, Italy, c. 20-27 April 1944. (National Archives of Canada) RIGHT: Force defensive position, reminiscent of WWI trenchment, incorporated into the levee of the Mussolini Canal, Anzio. (Lew Merrim)

floor of this building served as the dental clinic. Other buildings were utilized by the Service Battalion. Within a mile of its CP, a three story building was taken over by the personnel and administrative sections who shared it with men of the finance disbursing section. A nearby outbuilding was taken over by the Communications Detachment to house the switchboard for the Force's telephone network. Another building, nearer to the CP, was occupied by the forward message center, and the Intelligence and Publications sections. In addition to their normal duties, thirty-six men from Service and Maintenance Companies formed litter-bearing parties that accompanied Second Regiment's nightly forays into no-man's land. Others manned 57mm antitank guns and took part in security and wire patrols along the beachhead's interior roads in back of the Canal as a second line of defense.[32]

On the night of 17 February twenty-four of Service Battalion's litter bearers accompanied a 6-2 combat patrol across the Canal. The mission of the patrol was to investigate a possible enemy artillery position in an abandoned quarry that lay to the south of Sessuno. The litter bearers, being non-combatants, were unarmed as per the Geneva Convention. Creeping forward through the moonless night, a Forceman in the leading element of the patrol spotted a German half-track. A rocket from his bazooka made a direct hit on the half-track and, as it must have been completely loaded with ammunition, made a terrific explosion on impact that lit up the surrounding area "brighter than Broadway on a Saturday night."[33] Unarmed and in the middle of a plowed field, the Service Battalion men could do little but hug the ground. An ensuing thirty-minute fire fight, including an exchange of grenades, mortars, and machine gun fire, left two of the litter bearers dead and another four wounded, not to mention causing like casualties amongst 6th Company. From this time forward, orders were that no non-combatants would accompany the patrols across the Canal, instead they were to wait at the Canal's edge to assist returning patrols with casualties.[34]

Throughout the first half of the campaign, the entirety of the beachhead, particularly those areas around the ports of Anzio and Nettuno were frequently shelled as they were under constant German observation from the Lepini and Laziali Hills. To thwart this, VI Corps engineers set about using special generators and burning smudge pots that during the day produced oily smoke screens that hung over the beachhead area in an attempt to obscure the movement of soldiers and vehicles from the vigilant Germans. This condition notwithstanding, movement during daylight in the Force's sector of the beachhead

Forcemen man an M-1917 Browning medium machine gun from a dugout overlooking the Mussolini Canal. The M-1917 was a water-cooled weapon, and, as such, had a higher sustained rate of fire than that of the air-cooled M-1919A4 model. Though the M-1917 was a very reliable weapon, it was cumbersome, and was therefore relegated almost exclusively to defensive use. (National Archives of Canada)

Force machine gun emplacement guards an Anzio crossroads. (Lew Merrim)

Captured enemy machine guns were widely put to use. This man has plenty of ammunition on hand as well, Anzio. (Lew Merrim)

was restricted to that of small groups of men, less they draw a reaction from the Germans. Hidden in tunnels near the hill towns of Cori and Velletri, two German 280mm railroad guns would at odd intervals crawl from their hollows to cast enormous shells into the beachhead area. The Allied soldiers nicknamed one gun *Anzio Annie*, and the other was called the *Anzio Express*. One American soldier described their colossal 562-pound projectiles by saying they, "sounded like a boxcar coming in sideways."[35] The harbors were also subject to enemy air attacks. The Germans carried out these raids primarily at night as Allied fighter cover, coupled with the fire from the Allies' newly introduction radar-tracked antiaircraft batteries around the ports soon made daylight incursions too costly for the *Luftwaffe*. However, the enemy's nighttime attacks routinely ran the gauntlet and caused much damage. Preceded by pathfinder aircraft (dubbed *Maytag*s by the Forcemen as their small motor reminded them of a washing machine's) that dropped flares to mark the intended target, enemy bombers would soon arrive overhead to drop their deadly payloads.[36]

Yet, neither were the Germans spared the punishment of artillery shelling or aerial bombardment. American and British howitzers, and in some instances Naval artillery, this fire directed from aerial observation, pounded the German positions relentlessly. Operation STRANGLE, an aerial interdiction campaign carried out in a 500 mile ring around the beachhead would, by April, shift the balance of air superiority over the beachhead peremptorily in Allied favor as well as serve to choke off the flow of supplies to the enemy both at Anzio and further south at the Gustav Line.[37]

The artillery groupment in support of the First Special Service Force was made up of the 160th Field Artillery Battalion (relieved by the 69th Armored Field Artillery Battalion on 12 February), Company B of the 645th Tank Destroyer Battalion, and the 456th Parachute Field Artillery Battalion – approximately eighty guns in all. This artillery conglomerate found itself taking under fire targets, typically enemy tanks, infantry, and strongpoints, designated for it by Force patrols as well as its own forward observers in support of the front line units. It also engaged in counter-battery fire missions and unobserved harassing fire against the right flank of the beachhead. The laying of smoke screens between enemy units and Force patrols was also a common practice. Occasionally the batteries would shoot Allied propaganda leaflets over to the enemy side which resulted in the capture of a number of enemy deserters by Force patrols.[38]

Man of the 39th Engineer Combat Regiment prepares M-1A1 anti-tank mines to be laid before the First Special Service Force front at Anzio. (National Archives)

Troops of the 39th Engineer Combat Regiment build a foot bridge across the Mussolini Canal to be used by the First Special Service Force. (National Archives)

The Parachute Artillerymen's close association with Force is worthy of further note. The 456th Parachute Field Artillery Battalion (minus C and D Batteries) had first been banded to the Force at Santa Maria di Capua-Vetere on 14 December 1943, and had supported the Force during the Christmas day attack on Monte Sammucro and in subsequent actions in the Winter Line. On 2 February, the airborne artillerymen joined the Force behind the Mussolini Canal. That day C and D Batteries along with the 456th PFAB designation were assigned officially to the U.S. 82nd Airborne Division. On 16 February, "by General Order No.20, the 5th Army, the 456th PFAB less personnel and equipment, was transferred to the European Theatre of Op-

Group from 5-2, with faces and hands blackened, wait for darkness to begin their patrol. Left to right: Private Dan Lemaire, Private First Class Richard Stealy, Sergeant Charles Shepard, Lieutenant H.H. Raynor, and Private First Class James A. Jones. Anzio Beachhead, Italy, c. 20-27 April 1944. (National Archives of Canada)

erations. In the same order, the 463rd PFAB (less [Batteries] C and D) was organized with the personnel and equipment of the 456th. At this time the [463rd PFA] Battalion was required to furnish a cadre of 6 officers and 61 enlisted men." Remaining with the 463rd at Anzio were twenty-seven officers and 309 enlisted men.[39]

Under normal circumstances the battalion would have consisted of a Headquarters and Service Battery; A, B, and C Batteries of four gun crews each; and D Battery, a machine gun battery to furnish antiaircraft and antitank protection to the battalion. The guns, M-1A1 75mm pack howitzers, had been originally designed to be broken down and borne as nine separate loads on the backs of mules, hence the "pack" label. The 1,268 pound guns could fire their thirteen pound shells to a maximum range of 9,500 yards. Throughout February and March 1944, the battalion operated two batteries, A and B, of six guns apiece. During the month of April, enough replacements were received to build the battalion back up to its normal strength. However, D Battery was never reconstituted; its personnel and equipment being assimilated into the other batteries.[40]

Throughout April and beyond, physical conditioning and refresher training in all weapons was carried out by the Second Regiment and by companies, platoons, and sections from First and Third Regiments that "could be relieved from the line during daylight hours. Emphasis was placed on unit training to effect the integration of replacements received during the month. Other subjects were covered, including training in Tank-Infantry cooperation, the assault of strong points, village clearing, and small unit tactics. The 1st Armored Regiment and 81st Reconnaissance Battalion cooperated in every way with the training program. Fifteen Infantry-Tank exercises [the first on 10 April] were undertaken."[41]

On 9 May, after ninety-eight days of continuous combat, the First Special Service Force was relieved of its front along the Mussolini Canal by the U.S. 36th Engineer Combat Regiment. The long awaited breakout of the Anzio Beachhead was now close at hand. By the first of May, the ranks of the Force had swollen to include 159 officers and 2,585 enlisted men. It would need every man in the coming operation. As yet the Force had no replacement pool as did the infantry divisions of Fifth Army. Frederick, in any event, had no plans to attempt integration of replacements into the rifle companies once the fighting began.[42]

Front left view of the German Goliath tankette picked up by the Force at Anzio on 11 April 1944. In this view can be seen one of the tankette's two battery driven electric motors. Instead of blowing up, this Goliath burned up after being hit by machine gun fire and was carried away on a hospital stretcher. (National Archives)

BELOW: Camouflaged M-10 Tank Destroyers of the 1st Armored Division's 701st Tank Destroyer Battalion. Vehicles from this battalion gave supporting fire to the First Special Service Force, and on several occasions accompanied Force raids into Anzio's no-man's land. (National Archives)

VI Corps Ordnance man shows control wires of the tankette, also called a "Doodlebug" by the Allied troops at Anzio. (National Archives)

Forcemen move up drainage cuts during Ceretto Alto attack, April 1944. (National Archives)

Private Edward J. Wall, formerly a member of the U.S. 4th Ranger Infantry Battalion, pauses for a cigarette near a knocked-out Sherman tank during the attack along the Strada Litoranea, Italy, 15 April 1944. (National Archives)

Staff Sergeant Cyril V. Krotzer, Headquarters Detachment, Second Regiment, during closing stages of Ceretto Alto raid, 15 April 1944. (National Archives)

RIGHT: Brigadier General Frederick (left) and Second Regiment Commander, Lt. Colonel Robert S. Moore confer during the raid on Ceretto Alto, 15 January 1944. (National Archives)

Sergeant Maurice Parker, Headquarters Detachment, 2d Battalion, Second Regiment, with two prisoners captured during the 15 April raid along the Strada Litoranea. (National Archives)

With dawn, the withdrawal back across the Canal begins. German prisoners carrying their wounded are escorted by members of Second Regiment, 15 April 1944. (National Archives)

Procession of German and Italian PWs netted by Force raid. (Author's Collection)

Forceman Bill Spalding with German prisoner captured on raid, 15 April 1944. (National Archives)

German and Italian prisoners, outside of Force Headquarters, await interrogation by Force S-2 personnel. Seated, the German PWs have made themselves comfortable, while their Italian Fascist comrades lay on the ground. (National Archives)

Forcemen gather to view the contents of a parcel from home. Left to right: Lieutenant H.M. "Doc" Savage (1-3), Sergeant Al Sproule (5-2), "Moe" Lazarus (5-2), Tom F. O'Brien (5-2) with V-42 knife, and Sergeant D.J. Stonehouse (5-2). Anzio Beachhead, Italy, c. 20-27 April 1944. (National Archives of Canada)

LEFT: German prisoners captured on Force raid share straw with one of the Force's pet cows. (National Archives)

Reading mail from home is Captain G.H. Baker of Chase, British Columbia. Anzio Beachhead, Italy, c. 20-27 April 1944. (National Archives of Canada)

Captain W.M.W. Wilson, left, and Sergeant D.J. Henderson feeding candy to their 4-2 company mascot, Nero, a two-month-old colt. (National Archives of Canada)

Forcemen cart useful items scrounged from around the beachhead back to their bivouac, Anzio. (Lew Merrim)

Two Forcemen milk a cow somewhere in the Anzio Beachhead, April 1944. (National Archives of Canada)

Winning horse and rider of the Force Rodeo, Peaceful Valley, Anzio. (Lew Merrim)

Members of Force Service Battalion operate a field kitchen, Anzio Beachhead, Italy, April 1944. (National Archives of Canada)

Gathering eggs from an Anzio farmstead. (National Archives of Canada)

Standing in front of Force Headquarters, General Frederick welcomes Lt. General Mark W. Clark (middle), Fifth Army Commander; and Maj. General Lucian K. Truscott, Jr., VI Corps Commander (in jeep). (Lew Merrim)

90mm antiaircraft gun of the 216th Antiaircraft Battalion, Anzio Beachhead, Italy. (National Archives)

Billowing smoke generated by the 179th Chemical Smoke Company obscures the front line near Cabbage Castle in the First Regiment area. (National Archives) INSET: Closeup of smoke generator in operation at Anzio.

ABOVE: Casings from German butterfly bombs are inspected by Force Intelligence personnel, Anzio. (Lew Merrim)

ABOVE RIGHT: M-7 self-propelled 105mm howitzer of the 69th Armored Field Artillery Battalion in support of the First Special Service Force, Anzio. (National Archives)

RIGHT: Members of the 463d Parachute Field Artillery Battalion prepare to fire a round from their 75mm pack howitzer. The 463d supported the First Special Service Force during its entire time at Anzio and subsequently during the drive on Rome, and along the Franco-Italian border. (National Archives)

BELOW: Force company gathered for training lecture, Anzio Beachhead, Italy, April 1944. (National Archives of Canada)

INSET LEFT: Battle Drill. A 6-2 section practicing patrol duties. From right to left are Staff Sergeant K.S. Chapman with Thompson submachine gun, Sergeant T.C. Potenza carrying the Johnny gun (DOW 2 November 1944), Sergeant N.J. Overall with a Bazooka, Sergeant T.F. Olynyk carrying the SCR-536 handie-talkie radio, Sergeant H.W. McCarthy with a Thompson (KIA 6 June 1944), and others. Anzio Beachhead, Italy, c. 20-27 April 1944. (National Archives of Canada)

INSET RIGHT: Captain (later Major) S.L. Dymond (with helmet under arm) and Lieutenant J.D. Mitchell, both of 4-3. Anzio Beachhead, Italy, April 1944. (National Archives of Canada)

Map #3

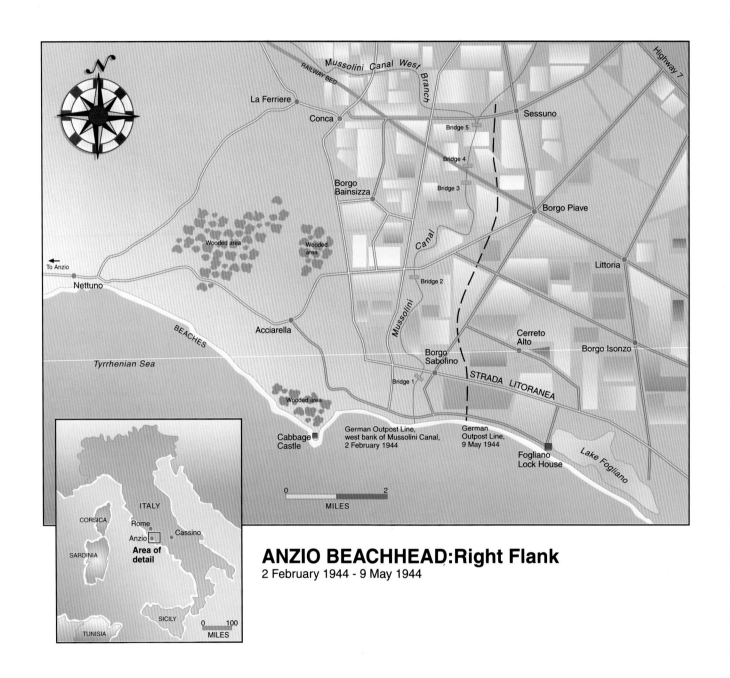

ANZIO BEACHHEAD:Right Flank
2 February 1944 - 9 May 1944

RESTRICTED

FIRST SPECIAL SERVICE FORCE

APO 4994,
New York, N.Y.,
14 April 1944.

MEMORANDUM

LESSONS FROM THE ITALIAN CAMPAIGN

1. INTRODUCTION.

The material contained in this memorandum is not to be considered as tactical doctrine. It represents a resume of the main lessons and observations of the officers and enlisted men of this Force digested from reports and verbal comments made during the operations of the Force in the Italian Campaign.

The observations serve to confirm the soundness of basic principles found in the American and Canadian training literature and in the standard and specialized phases of the training of this Force. There are few "new" tactical lessons but the importance of these observations lies in their confirmation, under battle conditions, of these principles, and in their illustration of the need of judgment and flexibility in the application of the principles learned. We see the application and modification of basic doctrine to meet effectively the peculiar characteristics of the Italian campaign.

2. TERRAIN.

The missions of this Force have been over practically all types of terrain with the exception of desert and jungle. Of particular interest to us are the limitations and peculiarities of high, rugged, mountainous country. In such country terrain alone affects almost every phase of operations, e.g. routes of approach, flank security, tactics, supply, care and evacuation of wounded, and communications. All must be studied, adapted and executed with flexibility and adroitness as demanded by the terrain. To this must be added the limitations imposed by severe weather conditions where rain, mud, and cold added to the difficulties of movement, supply, and health.

The most important single lesson learned from the terrain covered was that without exception high ground must be taken and held. Key terrain features must be seized to give us dominant observation, to deny that observation to the enemy, and to give us all the tactical advantages of field of fire and maneuverability accrued to the force which sits on top of its enemy.

We soon found that whenever the enemy held the ground above, whenever he had as much as one observer who was located on a dominant feature, we suffered from his mortar and artillery fire.

In seizing and operating on this high ground we found it best to make all movements as high on the ridge slopes as possible without using the crests and ridges themselves. In occupation of temporary defensive positions the military crests were occupied, but apart from the occasional hidden observer, the physical crests were avoided. Often it became advisable to occupy reverse slopes with outposts on the forward slope and flanks. This practice seemed to be the rule with the enemy and

RESTRICTED
-1-

RESTRICTED

care had always to be taken when attacking ridges not to be caught by enemy fire from the reverse slope when the ridge was reached.

It was also found that owing to the existence of many adjacent peaks on one mountain mass, it was often possible for the enemy to have observation of your approach to another ridge from your flank or rear even though you might be above him. Because of the lack of cover and concealment on these slopes, this necessitated careful selection of routes of advance and almost constant use of darkness for advance, supply, and evacuation.

A further reason for the use of high ground lies in the fact that covered approaches on roads in valleys and in river beds, were found to be mined. The higher rugged slopes were generally clear of mines, although were too well-worn trails were dangerous in country where the enemy had had time to prepare his defenses.

We learned beyond any shadow of doubt that fighting in this mountainous terrain required the highest degree of physical fitness for all ranks. Not only the combat soldier, but supply train personnel, stretcher bearers, staff officers, and runner, all required great physical stamina. Ground and weather combine to exhaust every one involved. This need required constant surveillance on the part of all commanders and was rendered all the more difficult by the cramped wet foxholes in which the men were forced to remain for long periods. The only answer appears to be the constant utilization of rest periods for physical strengthening and the constant daily care of body and feet whenever and wherever the opportunity offers. Cases occurred where two companies were fighting on the same high ground under extreme weather conditions. One company commander made it a personal task to see that every man removed his boots and rubbed his feet at least once per day no matter how intense the action, another company commander did not take the same precaution. The cases of "trench foot" in the former company were negligible, in the latter company high casualties from this cause resulted.

Mountain warfare requires a high degree of junior leadership and opportunity for subordinate commanders to exercise initiative. It was often found that the terrain in the vicinity of the objective afforded enemy observation and fire which called for action beyond that originally contemplated. The subordinate must be willing to assume this responsibility and must be given opportunity to do so.

3. ATTACK.

a. Command:

The necessity for good leaders, well-trained, willing to accept responsibility, and prepared to lead their men in a real and active sense is self-evident. It was confirmed every day of our fighting. We found that our men will perform as they are led and will follow their leader into any situation no matter how hazardous. We found, too, that this leadership does not commence on the field. It must always be present, and is expressed in the day by day confidence of his men, the discipline and bearing of his unit, the constant surveillance by the commander, and his careful preparation prior to action.

One of the commander's most difficult problems in our engagements lies in his decision as to where he himself will operate. It is a question of effectiveness and control, and he is ever faced with the questions: "Will I bee too far out or too far in?" "Can I obtain the best results by being with my forward elements or should I remain where

RESTRICTED
-2-

RESTRICTED

the reserves may more readily be controlled?" There is, of course, no standard answer - one situation may require the frontline leadership of the commander even at the expense of considerable control, another may demand his operating well in the rear where control of both supporting and reserve troops is facilitated. And the answer is not always a compromise.

We have had commanders too far forward, and possibly on occasion too far in rear to appreciate effectively the rapidly changing situation were communication is poor. But our commanders very soon learned to appreciate the particular situation and to operate accordingly. They found that in rugged mountainous country where maneuverability was limited, approaches long and time consuming and communications sometimes unreliable, it was generally advisable to be with the forward troops.

We have found too that even on flat terrain, large patrols and raiding parties require the presence of the commander well forward, and often in front of the party.

One of the principal functions of command is preparation for action. It has been observed that results often vary in direct ratio to the reconnaissance and prior preparation of the commander. On the other hand, the commander must be careful to see that during his preparation, he makes allowance in his time-table for adequate and complete briefing of his subordinates and all participants in the action. A comment from 3d Regiment reads:

"Senior officers take too much time for reconnaissance and leave little time or no time for the people who have to fight."

The Company Commander, 4th Company, 2d Regiment has this to say:

"Plan: (a) It is paramount that each man knows the situation, what to expect and what to do both before and at the time the action starts.

"(b) Pre-arranged plan - (1) Formation most advantageous, i.e., for daylight, bright and dark nights. (ii) Estimate number and kind of weapons to be carried and ammunition loads for certain missions. Close attention should be paid before the operation to exact choice of weapons required for the accomplishment of the mission and more especially to the amount of ammunition required. Standard loads often result in unnecessary quantities of ammunition, with resultant loss of equipment or diminishing of mobility. For example, mortars are of little value on night operations, but are often carried. A company raid, seldom if ever calls for the expenditure of 9000 rounds of 6 LMG's, when Johnson guns are carried. But the standard load is usually carried even if the task is to clear two or three houses."

b. Orders:

There were a number of comments submitted with reference to orders.

RESTRICTED
-3-

RESTRICTED

The Company Commander, 6th Company 2d Regiment, advocates that future training include a review of field orders so that such orders may be clear, concise, complete, and without ambiguity.

Our engagements revealed a definite need for constant care in the issuance of orders. Probably the two main faults observed were a failure to give a concise clear definition of the object of the mission and ambiguous wording in the detail of the plan. This occurred for the most part only in hasty verbal orders. Because of this danger a lesson learned is, that where time permits and the operation contains any complexity or difficulty, written orders should be issued. This insures a much stricter relaying of the order to lower echelons and also gives the commander the opportunity to see his full order and to eliminate extraneous and ambiguous phraseology.

A real difficulty in mountain fighting and in large raids lies in the transmission of rapid verbal orders. Often reliance has to be made on the passage of an order down a line of troops. Very often the order either fails to reach its destination or arrives in such altered form as to be useless or even dangerous. In one case an important troop movement was seriously delayed by such a failure. The best answer would appear to be the steady reminder by the platoon commander to his men of the vital importance of passing on such messages and of passing them accurately, and also the limitation of such instances to cases of extreme necessity. Where this form of transmission is inevitable, a careful appreciation and check has to be made by all subordinate commanders, particularly if the order so transmitted varies or cancels the original order. The failure to do so has resulted in some confusion and delay.

c. Reconnaissance:

Before any attack can be made and any night patrol sent out, reconnaissance is essential to its complete success.

Important information can also be obtained from outposts and earlier patrols. Sometimes these sources are neglected. For other remarks on reconnaissance, see "a. Command".

The Company Commander of 3d Company, 2d Regiment (Prov) advocates this inclusion in training programs:

"One or more groups of five men in each organization trained for straight reconnaissance missions, emphasizing stealth and patience to complete the mission, with additional training in the use of shadows and terrain to conceal movement. This training should include crawling over all types of terrain, stressing silence in doing so." (Ed Note: One important training aim in this Force, which is near complete achievement, is that all combat ranks be fully trained for this work.)

A section leader of 2d Regiment states:

"Positions to be attacked cannot be scouted out too well. Give the scouts more time."

d. Formations:

RESTRICTED
-4-

Historical Document #4: Lessons Learned from Italian Campaign

Page -5-

R E S T R I C T E D

Experience has confirmed that formations must be adopted as terrain, mission, and enemy activity require. Observations on this point have been varied.

A section leader of 2d Regiment remarks:

"The wedge formation with automatic weapon on either flank is the best, every man can fire instantly."

Another section leader of the same regiment states:

"When using the arrow head formation at night, the ends of the formation have a tendency to close in. Therefore, if they come under fire, it takes some time to build up a skirmish line to the front."

A number of observations were submitted showing the ever-present tendency of even veteran troops to bunch. These observations all confirm the obvious result of bunching - heavy casualties from mortar, nebelwerfer and artillery fire. Another result has been the presentation of a target to enemy MG positions.

    e. Field and Small-Group Tactics:

Something has been said already on this subject as it affects mountain fighting, under the head "Terrain," and other phases will be discussed.

The Company Commander of 4th Company, 2d Regiment has submitted the following comments:

"(c) Carrying Out Plan with Speed:

    "(1) Each section must have its job, i.e. covering or assault. Each man knows his position and job in the section... Jerries are prone to withdraw from outposts, be watchful for that and be prepare to pursue by fire and cut off by maneuver."

An officer of the 3d Company, 2d Regiment has this to say:

"Hit him hard and move in where our hand grenades are effective. He dislikes them. Night patrols into new enemy positions are very good as long as he hasn't had time to set out wire and mines. If a position is wired and mined, daylight assault with preparatory artillery barrage and armor support is better than night attack. (Ed Note: This statement appears to be too sweeping. Many tactical conditions must be taken into consideration, i.e. terrain, enemy strength, friendly supporting arms, and subsequent action planned.) At night, once his fixed line of fire is ascertained, it is easy to move in on his flanks."

A section leader of 2d Regiment writes:

"Aggressiveness and fast maneuvering to the flanks and, if possible, the rear, we find the best policy for taking out machine gun nests. With our machine gun giving covering fire the men with light weapons will creep in on the assault with grenades (fragmentation).....Like all battles, surprise is

R E S T R I C T E D
-5-

Page -6-

R E S T R I C T E D

important, get the drop on them and aggressiveness will carry you through with very few casualties. Don't be pinned down by fire. Fast maneuvering at night will usually break up Jerry's show.....We are fighting on strange ground, the enemy knows every rock and ditch. Quick thinking, maneuver fast is our policy. When we are not shooting we are digging. When we are not digging we are shooting. When we take up a position, we dig and dig deep. It pays."

The Company Commander of 1st Company, 1st Regiment brings out this point:

"I feel that we have not made all the use of smoke that we should have. Smoke would eliminate certain casualties in the attack."

One officer, the Company Commander of 6th Company, 2d Regiment, emphasizes the need for continued combat training by stating:

"Review of battle training, fire, and movement. The use of sections and platoons upon different objectives, under different conditions to stimulate decisions and action under battle conditions."

All our engagements have confirmed the most important single principle of infantry combat - the effective use of fire and movement.

    f. The following of artillery fires and concentrations:

This Force learned early in its combat experience of the advantage and necessity of following closely the line of impact of its supporting artillery concentrations and barrages. Terrain and other conditions affect this considerably. Where the attack is up the steep slope of a high mountain mass as at la Difensa, it is almost impossible to employ anything in the nature of a creeping barrage and any barrage laid down has to be either on the ridge or plateau at the top or on the slopes well forward of the advancing troops, inasmuch as their rate of progress over such difficult ground cannot be estimated accurately. This has resulted in very heavy barrages being laid on the ridges some considerable time before the assaulting troops were in position to attack. The enemy were little effected by the barrage because of their bunkers and defensive positions and were found to be alert and active again by the time the assault went in.

Over more level terrain this difficulty is not so great and every effort is made to keep our assault wave close up to the line of impact.

    g. Employment of our infantry supporting weapons:

We have learned from experience, sometimes slightly bitter, a lesson of the utmost importance to infantry units and of particular importance to a force such as ours - the lesson of "self-reliance" by the employment of our own supporting weapons.

It is very easy for subordinate commanders charged with the responsibility of the attack to overlook at certain phases of the attack the full employment of their own supporting weapons. Calls for artillery support are sometimes made where the task is one for the unit's mortars or heavy machine guns, if such are available. The rocket launcher and rifle grenade are not always fully exploited.

R E S T R I C T E D
-6-

Page -7-

R E S T R I C T E D

The control and coordination of the supporting arms and careful constant coordinated planning is of the first importance to both offensive and defensive operations.

    h. Consolidation:

Our experience has been that enemy forces launch an immediate counterattack whenever possible in order to regain ground lost, and precede this attack with mortar and artillery fire. Very often this fire proved to be extremely accurate and of heavy concentration and would fall on the vacated enemy positions and on the ridge lines, both good targets for registered fire. Consequently, the need for immediate and efficient consolidation is obvious.

The Company Commander of 6th Company, 2d Regiment in discussing training recommends:

"In the consolidation include the disposition of the men, the ammunition expended, casualties to your own men and their positions."

4. DEFENSE.

Until recently the Force has not had much combat experience on the defense. Consequently, this subject did not take a prominent place in the observations submitted. The question of outposts, however, did receive a number of interesting comments.

    3d Regiment submitted the following statements:

(i) "Houses are not death traps but give protection from artillery and mortar fire and patrols will not be surprised in them if they are properly outposted."

(ii) "If you set up in a house or shed, don't forget there are three directions you can't fire or hear from - you are handicapped to start with."

(iii) "If your intention is to secure a house, you do not get in it. Place your fields of fire to cover it. Basically you were probably not given the mission of holding the house but of engaging the enemy in that vicinity. The house has or possibly will attract the enemy. That is all the value the house has to your operation 90% of the time."

(iv) "A patrol from a neighboring infantry outfit, 13 strong, was sent out to outpost a house. Nothing happened for two nights. They assumed that nothing would. They relaxed. All members of the patrol were taken PW. A subsequent patrol went out to search for them, found all their weapons neatly stacked. Not one weapon had been fired or a grenade used. The enemy patrol apparently was not even large enough to carry off the captured weapons. Never get in a house at night."

It will be noted that in the above reports opinion varies on the use of houses for outposting. All are quoted in order to show the arguments involved and the reactions of those directly concerned with outposting missions. The lesson learned would appear to be that all houses are suspect. Their use for outposts must be carefully considered

R E S T R I C T E D
-7-

Page -8-

R E S T R I C T E D

with reference to the usual battle conditions and will depend on these. They draw fire and present targets. They sometimes lull the outposting troops into a false sense of security and they limit fields of fire and maneuverability. On the other hand, they often provide excellent observation, protection from small arms fire, and concealment from view.

    An officer of 2d Regiment states:

"Hasty fortifications, men do not dig foxholes or gun positions deep enough. When not under fire they should be dug."

"Camouflaging positions should be stressed in training. Some men in shallow holes build their camouflage material too high above the line of the ground, giving the position away."

The Company Commander of 3d Company, 2d Regiment in discussing training submits:

"Defense: Suggest more training in the use of camouflage, the setting of automatic weapons, construction of obstacles and outposting of defensive line, stressing the necessity of changing location of outposts. An outpost known to the enemy has not much value in gaining surprise."

    3d Regiment emphasizes that:

"Wire and mines are not an obstacle if not covered by fire."

5. PATROLS.

Many varied and interesting observations were made on the subject of patrols. Certain points were given emphasis. The need for "singleness of object," clear definite orders beforehand, the full knowledge of these orders by all members of the patrol, and clear concise reports by the patrol leader on return, are all stressed. A number emphasize the need for daylight reconnaissance before night patrols go out.

    1st Regiment submits the following:

(i) "Security of positions and patrols cannot be stressed enough. Further emphasis on each man having a definite sector to observe while on patrol must be made."

(ii) "Each organization should have a few selected men trained in individual or small team scouting. The value of our reconnaissance depends on the training that these men have had." (Ed Note: The objective of this Force is to have all combat personnel highly trained in both individual and team scouting.)

(iii) "On patrolling - Combat patrols should rarely be less than a platoon strength. Careful attention should be paid to the relation between the strength of the patrol and the mission selected. Reconnaissance patrols - Adequate time should always

R E S T R I C T E D
-8-

Historical Document #4: Lessons Learned from Italian Campaign

be given the patrol leader for daylight
reconnaissance of routes and positions."

The Company Commander of 4th Company, 2d Regiment makes the
following "general remarks."

(1) "Men are becoming careless about making noise."

(ii) "On all stops be in a position to repel any
attacks, all around defense."

(iii) "Hit the ground on flares."

(iv) "The Germans soldier if outnumbered likes to lie
'Doggo' and let the opposition pass. Be alert to pick
up small numbers through searching the logical
positions in the vicinity of houses and adjacent
ground."

(v) "The German in night fighting seldom fires at a
definite target. He merely covers ground. Observe and
assault accordingly."

(vi) "Dark nights best for reconnaissance patrols and
small combat patrols. Bright nights best for platoon
or company raids, i.e. aids control immensely; men
seem to have more confidence in themselves and
weapons." (Ed Note: Conditions peculiar to certain
situations will affect this decision.)

The Company Commander of 3d Company, 2d Regiment states:

"Scouting and patrolling should be stressed more;
particularly formation for all types of patrols.
Patrols should be given one task only, either
fighting, or reconnaissance, or standing. Their
mission should be clearly defined. The continued use
of one point or route for consecutive patrols should
be discouraged since it ultimately leads to ambush by
some form of the enemy's defense."

3d Regiment submits:

(i) "The distance a patrol can operate from its lines
is limited. If it must penetrate enemy territory very
deeply, an intermediate strong point must be
established."

(ii) "Movement by night should be off roads but close
enough to observe. Enemy patrols use roads and
natural approaches."

(iii) "Reconnaissance patrols should be 6-8 men with
JAR, 2 TSMGs, and the remainder carry rifles. Every
man should carry a couple of hand grenades.

"Fighting patrol about 15 men, with two JAR, lot of
TSMGs, and grenades." (Ed Note: This will depend on
the mission.)

(iv) "Our patrols complain about the indiscriminate
use of flares by own troops when a patrol is out.

When a flare goes up freezing is not the solution.
You can't look like a tree where there are none."

(v) "Helmets should not be worn by night patrols...."
(Ed Note: The may be exceptions to this.)

A section leader of 2d Regiment has submitted a very interesting
memorandum which has genuine value, particularly from the point of view
from which it is written and from its realistic form of expression:

"When the times comes for your first fur-rubbing with
the enemy, you will perhaps be imagining all sorts of
possible awful things that are just about to happen,
and so will your men with you. So, when the hidden
enemy opens up on you, it is small wonder if you
don't have plenty of ideas on just what would be the
best thing to do and just how you will do it. This is
all right; use good judgment, but use it fast. Don't
try and use the whole "Soldiers Handbook" and other
field manuals all at once. Instead you can grab hold
of yourself and shout to your automatic weapon team
to open fire at where you think the enemy is, or, of
course, if someone else has spotted him, tell your
men beforehand not to keep silent but speak up and
tell you they saw where the fire came from so you can
get your fire where it will do the trick. Don't be
afraid to talk loud if it is in the daytime, because
your voice is a real tonic at this time, both to
yourself and the men with you. Don't worry too much
how your men will conduct themselves when they get
under fire, just keep yourself cool and your men will
be right there acting like they had been under that
stuff lots of times before. But don't get strung out
too far or when the enemy hits you, especially if its
from close quarters, you will find you have lost
almost all your control. Each man will be taking
himself a little private cover wherever it's handy
and you will have a time trying to get lined up for
business because each man may have to be told just
what to do for a minute or two so you don't want them
hidden away all over hell's half acre. When you are
all used to being fired at, you can take greater
intervals between men because sooner or later mortar
bombs from the enemy will catch you unexpectedly and
they often times kill people, sometimes three or four
if you bunch up. After you have your automatic
weapons working on your target, you can start
shifting your men into desired positions because it's
then the enemy who is pinned down, and if you draw
fire from another place get some of your weapons on
it at once. Let each man be bold and expose his head
or more if need be to have useful fire from your
group. I have seen men get down behind a large rock
and bang away straight in the air just to be
shooting. I can't see that this serves any useful
purpose and it certainly doesn't help your supply of
ammunition. Don't do like an infantry squad I once
witnessed who happened to run into an enemy sniper.
This squad leader at once called for his BAR and
promptly started keeping all the ammunition bearers
in the country busy bringing ammunition but they
moved nowhere. The sniper probably sneaked out to the

---

rear since it was among rocks large enough to
maneuver around easily. Instead when you pin down
your quarry, get in there with your grenades at once
and destroy him. I don't know if this squad got their
man or not, chances are they did, and chances are
they are still laying there burning up that BAR, and
the sniper probably is home in Berlin on furlough by
now."

6. NIGHT OPERATIONS.

This Force received constant training in night operations which
has stood it in good stead in action. Many of the principles and
expedients studied and practiced have been confirmed. The problems of
control, direction, security and surprise are all intensified a
hundredfold in night fighting.

The value and necessity of night operations showed themselves
clearly time and time again. By such operations the essential element
of surprise was often obtained where it could be obtained in no other
way, because of dominant observation on the part of the enemy. Often,
too, it provided the only means for troop movements without having
losses from enemy artillery fire.

The problem of control, as always, was found to be particularly
acute. Part of the answer at least lies in the simple plan, the
knowledge of this plan by all, the constant supervision by all leaders
and subordinate commanders and a sound communications system familiar
to all.

The problem of direction at night is also serious. Terrain often
becomes unrecognizable at night, prominent terrain features disappear
and perspective is lost. Under combat conditions time does not always
permit daylight reconnaissance. Guides are not available at all times,
and it was also found that guides cannot always be relied on. Several
units relying on guides found themselves temporarily lost. It was not
long before all commanders learned that, guide or no guide, a constant
use of the compass and prior map study were the surest ways of
guaranteeing the discharge of the responsibility that was theirs - of
getting their troops to the appointed place at the appointed time.

Security at night presents special problems. Advance guards and
flank guards are easily separated from the main body if great care is
not taken. Ambush by the enemy is always a hazard.

Surprise, one of the touchstones of victory in any action, is
often said to be achieved by the combination of speed with good
tactics. In night operations particularly the element of silence must
be added. And the achievement of silence over rough terrain in darkness
has been found to result only from strict discipline, good training,
and constant supervision.

An officer of 3d Company, 2d Regiment has this to say:

"At night it has been found that every move must be
simple due to difficulty in keeping control. Our set
up is well adapted for night work, because the
section has enough fire power to tackle a single
position while the other section prepares to handle
any other situation that may arise. We found the SOP
for the section in attacking positions at night very
beneficial."

While discussing training, the Company Commander of 3d Company,
2d Regiment recommends:

"Night training in greater proportions, stressing
coordination of movement, formation, and
communications. Greater stress laid on night firing
and quick engagement of enemy positions. Continual
training on handling weapons in the darkness
stressing alternative firing positions for all
weapons and speed in moving to alternative
positions."

A section leader of 2d Regiment states:

"We have learned a great deal in night fighting since
we have been in Italy. Never charge a prepared
position before you are certain of the exact
position. Then charge with all your firepower, give
it everything you have......keeping contact with
everyone is very difficult on dark nights. But it is
very important. Men have a tendency to bunch up at
night."

7. WEAPONS.

Certain comments were received with regard to our weapons and
their employment.

"A line cannot be defended by MGs alone.......The
rifle is still the more accurate weapon and its use
in defense should not be overlooked. Mere amount of
ammunition thrown out is not sufficient. A lack of
understanding of the purpose and methods of final
defensive fire has been found among the men.
Concentration on one type of tactics, e.g. the
attack, means that all get rusty on the principles
and methods of defense."

The Company Commander of 4th Company, 2d Regiment points out:

"On recent patrols when we have contacted the enemy,
the riflemen did not take full advantage of the
fire-power of the M-1."

"In night work when in close contact with the enemy,
TSMGs and hand grenades are chief weapons. JAR clips
are still causing trouble." (Ed Note: Clip dents
easily thus blocking the feeding of rounds.)

A Section leader of 2d Regiment remarks:

"We carry too many heavy weapons for an assault. I
think the Johnson gun is a very maneuverable weapon
and is much better for assaults, patrols, and
night-fighting, because one man carries the complete
weapon and doesn't have to wait so long for the No 2
man to get into action. The LMG is a very good weapon
but is not the gun for assaults, and patrols. (Ed
Note: The writer is obviously considering assaults by
small groups; even here the LMG may be an excellent
weapon.) There should be more Johnson guns and Tommy
guns in an outfit like this (Ed Note: This result is

Historical Document #4: Lessons Learned from Italian Campaign

achieved by the selection and distribution of weapons for the particular mission.) With any automatic weapon you should never fire too long in one position before you move unless you are dug in.....Our bayonet has never been any use......The Bazooka should never be left behind at any time regardless of the mission. The best weapon we have for knocking out tanks, it serves the purpose of breaking the Jerries' morale. They hate it. A very good weapon for clearing houses, also machine gun emplacements. Every section should have a Bazooka. No patrol should be without one of these.

"The Jerries are also afraid of our hand grenade and rifle-grenade. Our mortars and machine guns are too heavy for our kind of work we have been doing. Our M-1 rifles can't be beaten but I believe the German machine gun has ours topped a bit because one man is sufficient and it takes at least two to man ours." (Ed Note: This section leader raises several points on which there is a difference of opinion; but his opinions, based on his experience, are well worth noting.)

8. ENEMY TACTICS AND WEAPONS.

Some valuable lessons have been learned of the enemy's tactics and the employment of his weapons.

An officer of the 1st Regiment who saw action on Mount la Difensa noted from his observation of enemy outposts and snipers that they sited their outposts, usually manned by two men with a MG or MP, with an additional sniper in a well-concealed position some 50-100 yards to the _left_ of the outpost. The reason for this appeared to be that when the outposts fired their automatic weapons (often simply into the air to attract our fire) our riflemen would show themselves always to the right of their own cover, because their natural body-position for firing is that of fire from the right shoulder. This exposed our riflemen to the lone enemy sniper located on the left of the enemy outpost.

3d Regiment makes a somewhat similar observation:

"Due to early training, the German soldier expects every American to emerge from the right hand side of his cover. He seldom watches the left side."

1st Regiment also submitted the following observation:

"An enemy defended outpost of approximately 30 men......was the object of one attack by one of our patrols. The patrol was misled as to the strength of the outpost and the enemy gained the advantage of surprise. This was caused by:

"(1) The enemy did not disclose the strength of the outpost by constructing obvious defensive obstacles. Trip wires and AP mines served the purposed desired by the enemy without giving the show away.......(2) Good discipline of the enemy in position prevented disclosure to previous reconnaissance. Hasty minefields proved their value. Previous

---

reconnaissance had perhaps lulled the suspicions of constant mining activity by the enemy and our men ran into mines where none had been found before."

An officer of 2d Regiment states:

"The German soldier is generally well-disciplined but his is not the soldier of earlier war years. He dislikes fighting at night and fighting at close range, (Ed Note: The enemy is not consistent in this respect.) preferring to keep us at a distance and use his mortar, at which the Germans are well-trained. He sets up good defensive positions, well-camouflaged and protected by wire and mines. His positions, however, are placed to cover a certain front and are very vulnerable from the flanks, especially at night when he fires on fixed lines."

A section leader of 2d Regiment makes the following contribution:

"German small arms: Don't underestimate their small arms fire. Jerry snipers are crack shots. Their machine gunners still play the old waiting game. He uses the machine pistol a lot to direct mortar fire. Don't let that fool you, it is still a very effective weapon for close in fighting - resembles our Tommy gun. We find the German soldier sticks pretty close to the book rules. His machine gun will have a fixed line of fire not easily changed."

The following interesting note was submitted by another section leader of 2d Regiment:

"The German soldier as we have come to know him is a well-trained, well-disciplined and able fighter. Years of training, plus years of actual combat are factors which prove themselves an obstacle to any opposing force.

"In the field we find that Jerry knows his stuff. Positions are strategically located and well-camouflaged on all types of terrain. His cross-fires are effective and he knows how to get the maximum results.

"The machine gun and machine pistol are the primary assault weapons of German foot troops and both are capable of tremendous fire-power. These weapons definitely have a faster rate of fire than our own, which has evidenced no particular advantage.

"Our first engagement with the German proved him to be a master with the mortar and he continues to maintain our respect. The hand grenades employed are far inferior to ours, but in the hands of a good man they serve their purpose.

"In conclusion I might say that we have come to respect the German soldier as a worthy opponent. Thus far we have kicked the pants off Jerry in most instances; however, we know he still packs a good wollop. We have and we can beat him at his own game."

Another section leader of 2d Regiment writes:

"The Germans very seldom ever put out any flank protection and seem to have five or six men in one emplacement. In most cases the Jerries have one machine gun to cover the other. They have had much more time to conceal their positions. They carry their dirt away from their emplacements and make it very tough to find at night."

3d Regiment reports:

(1) "For night work, the enemy fires on fixed lines along likely routes of approach, ditches, draws, the obvious approach on a hill, etc.; he generally depends on cross-fire and does not search with his fire. When fired upon the average enemy MG operator ducks into his hole and sticks up his hand to fire. This does not apply to German paratroops.

(2) "Enemy fire is sudden and destructive, his observation is good. Move from cover to cover."

9. COMMUNICATIONS.

The Force Communications Officer reports:

"(1) Radio:

In the first operation of this Force in the Italian theater, a mortar bomb made a direct hit on a SCR 694 which had just gone on the air. This, combined with other factors, led to the discontinuance of the use of AM radio sets and the procurement of the SCR 509. Some of the factors governing the change were the susceptibility of the SCR 694 to moisture, the necessity of having trained operators to handle the set, and the heavy weight of the 694. Several set failures were experienced due to the heavy rain which fell during the major part of the operation. The 509 has given excellent service within its range, and was not unduly affected by moisture.

"(2) Comments on German Radio Direction Finding:

Throughout the operation of this Force the Force Hq has operated a 100 watt radio transmitter and, over a period of several months, the following conclusions were reached. Although the radio station was at times heavily shelled, it is not believed that the shelling necessarily resulted from the operation of the station. Other areas, where no radio stations were working, were just as heavily shelled. While the location of a radio station can be accurately plotted, it appears that the operation of the station alone is not sufficient to provoke an undue amount of shellfire. As a safety factor, radio stations have been set up three or four hundred yards from the CP or troop concentrations, and on the flank.

"(3) Radio Security:

There has been a noticeable lack of security on both AM and FM radio transmission. Some has been the fault of carelessness of CW operators, but the bulk of the trouble has been while using voice. Officers who use voice radio should bear in mind the necessity of having their transmissions planned before they begin to speak, preferably written out, and that reference material is at hand before they begin transmission. I have seen several cases where the secrecy of codes was nullified when transmission given in code were repeated immediately afterward in clear text, and the location of future friendly activity was clearly disclosed to the enemy. It is also obvious that too little thought is given to the composition of radio messages. They are too lengthy and the same information could be expressed in a fraction of the words usually used. Lengthy transmissions are excellent insurance that the radio station sending them will be picked up by enemy intercept, its location plotted, and its traffic copied from that time on.

"(4) Wire - Mountain Operation:

One of the chief obstacles to wire operations in the rugged terrain found in the south Italian campaign was the difficulty of transporting sufficient wire to install the necessary circuits. Owing to the circuitous and roundabout routes necessitated by the terrain it would frequently take six or seven miles of wire to cover one mile on the map. The employment of mules and reel unit RL24 helped immeasurably in solving this problem. One defect noted in the construction of the RL24 was the lack of a lock nut and washer on the end of the axle. The wire drums would often roll a considerable distance downhill when the mule from which the wire was being laid lost its footing. Larger wire crews are necessary when operating in the mountainous country as mules are sometimes unable to negotiate the steeper slopes and the amount of wire carried per man is necessarily small. Almost all wire laid from Force to regiments was W110 but it was found advisable to carry W130 as wire routes forward into enemy territory could not be reconnoitered and when terracing or other terrain obstacle prevented the use of mules, W130 could be used to continue the wirelaying by hand. For this purpose a German back reel, which included a bobbin arrangement for evenly winding the wire on the drum, was found to be satisfactory. To save weight, a ten drop switchboard, consisting of the RL24 units, a ringing circuit, and a sound power phone, was built. Considerable difficulty was experienced due to the tendency of troops and mule trains to reach an objective by following the wire, while traveling at night. This would sometimes lead to the forming of a trail along the wire route and consequent damage to the wire by the traffic. Careful consideration must be given to the adequate supply of clothing and food for wire-laying personnel. Required to work, without rest, for long periods in rain and snow, the

proportion of men who become casualties through
sickness, is great unless forethought is given in
supplying adequate food, clothing and bedding. It was
found necessary to carry sleeping bags, ground
sheets, and Coleman gasoline stoves. The K-Ration is
not adequate for more than two days."

Further observations on communication received from commanders
stress the need for combat personnel trained in field communications,
telephone wiring parties, the use of sound power phone, the use of the
message book, and the recognition of enemy field communications. We
have learned that the combat troops must often be self-reliant on the
maintenance of its communications.

10. MISCELLANEOUS.

a. Infantry - Artillery Cooperation:

This Force has had the good fortune to observe and participate in
some excellent infantry-artillery cooperation. A choice example of
close cooperation occurred when a German company was repulsed and
captured on the Anzio front by a combination of accurate artillery fire
and a skillful ambush by a platoon and section of 1st Regiment. With
forward observers maintaining their regular front line posts in a
position to bring immediate and accurate artillery fire on the enemy
company located in a group of houses, it was possible to slip a small
group of our troops in rear and to a flank of the enemy position.
Before the enemy was aware that he was under observation the trap was
set, heavy artillery fire was brought down on the buildings and the
whole company was driven into the arms of the waiting patrols. The
success of this action resulted from an efficient combination of a
sound appreciation of the tactical situation, a good plan executed with
speed and precision, good observation positions by forward observers
and accurate artillery firing.

Several observations and recommendations have been made relative
to the need of training infantry officers in the basic elements of
forward observing. In many cases where advance is rapid, and
particularly in mountainous country where sudden situations develop
without warning, accurate forward observing on the part of the infantry
has been of immediate benefit; and, conversely, lack of it has
sometimes delayed operations or prevented the taking advantage of
short-lived target opportunities. In making the observation it must be
clearly understood that infantry officers are not and should never be
considered as Artillery Forward Observers. They have their own job
calling for their full attention and should undertake artillery
observation only in real emergency. It is for such an emergency that
this recommendation is intended.

1st Regiment has made the following observation:

"The men have a good idea of the effect of enemy s/a
fire but initially are surprised by the effects of
enemy artillery fire. Perhaps a closer liaison
between the artillery and the infantry in training
would correct this. Regarding our own artillery, it
was observed that observation training for the
infantry might well include some artillery
observation training in methods and selection of
targets, as well as giving the men a better idea of
just what the artillery can do and how it can support
them.

b. Medical Evacuation.

In our engagements in rugged mountainous country we rapidly
learned the necessity of departing from the normal in the situating of
aid posts. The extreme difficulty in evacuating wounded over
precipitous trails, in darkness and under fire, with the delay
involved, rendered it necessary to put aid stations almost as far to
the front as the forward troops, if adequate medical aid was to be
rendered in sufficient time. This practice was adopted very early in
our engagements. The difficulties of terrain also required many more
stretcher-bearers than are normally employed, and it often became
necessary to use reserve combat troops to the point of exhaustion in
order to accomplish efficient evacuation of the wounded.

c. Physical Fitness.

The need for physical fitness of the highest order by all
personnel has been stressed in the discussion of mountain warfare. It
cannot be over emphasized. Demands much above accepted peak performance
are made suddenly and without warning. Will and determination alone are
not enough. The necessary physical strength must be there. And it was
soon found that it must be there in every man in the command not alone
in the combat soldier.

d. Morale.

The all-important driving force of morale is an elusive quality.
Its fluctuation in fighting troops is difficult to gauge. Being
entirely comparative in its quality the point of lowest morale in one
organization may be higher than the point of highest morale in another.
But both measurements are important. The commander strives not only to
achieve a morale equal or higher than that of other units, but he
strives to prevent relative depression in the morale of his own unit.
Such depressions, if they occur, have a bad effect on the proficient
performance in the field. The best antidotes found in our combat
experience appear to be aggressive action however limited in scope, new
combat tasks whenever and wherever possible, opportunity to rest at
regular intervals, hot food at every available opportunity and sound
unit discipline with its resultant pride in appearance of personnel and
lines.

The most important single factor in morale is victory in battle.
It matters little how small the battle is. It is the simple fact that
victory over his enemy is what counts with every man. And it need not
be his own, personal victory; that of any member of his unit is his,
and he rightly so considers it.

An observation received from the Company Commander of 4th
Company, 2d Regiment deals with one specific question of morale. This
officer points out that "a man who has been hit usually upsets the men
around him." An effect of this nature rapidly diminishes in importance
as the troops become veterans but there is little doubt that even
seasoned men are sometimes influenced by casualties in their midst,
particularly where, as in the case of many small patrols, their whole
attention is not absorbed by the enemy. The lesson learned is that the
answer to the problem lies in psychological hardening training by all
commanders, and the efforts of the leader on the spot to transfer any
feelings of confusion and alarm into immediate aggressiveness and
revenge. The casualty should be removed at the earliest possible
moment.

Special Feature #4

The Black Devils of Anzio

The origins for much of the mystique that surrounds the First Special Service Force can be traced to its exploits on the Anzio Beachhead. With faces blackened against the night, the Forcemen would glide out across no-man's land to materialize, seemingly out of thin air, in the midst of the enemy works. Striking the Germans with great speed and agility, the raiders would then, just as suddenly, melt back into the night returning to their own lines. In less than two weeks from the time it arrived at Anzio, the Germans had grown wary of the First Special Service Force. Illustrating this fact was a diary recovered from the body of a German Lieutenant of the *3rd Platoon Hermann Göring Alarm Company Pauke* by a Force patrol on 14 February 1944. An entry on 11 February: "Reports from Sessuno of Black Devil raid last night." The

Lieutenant's last entry, on 13 February: "Sharp attacks on *Vesuv* (another Alarm Company). We never hear these devils when they come."[1] The diary and its contents soon became common knowledge on the beachhead, and it was at this moment that the "Black Devils" nickname became forever linked with the First Special Service Force.

The enemy's growing dread of the First Special Service Force was furthermore indicated by the statements of his prisoners. One German PW attested that he had been "told by his superiors that he was 'fighting an elite Canadian-American Force. They are treacherous, unmerciful and clever. You cannot afford to relax.' A ten-day furlough, he said, would be granted to any German soldier who could capture a member of the Force."[2]

Behind an Anzio haystack, First Lieutenant H.H. Raynor briefs his platoon of 5-2 prior to setting out on a night patrol into no-man's land. Note blackened faces and hands. Anzio Beachhead, Italy, 20 April 1944. (National Archives of Canada)

Special Feature #4

Forcemen, with faces blackened and cradling Thompson submachine guns, about to set out on a night patrol. Left to right: Sergeant Charles Shepard, Lieutenant H.H. Raynor, and Private First Class James A. Jones. Anzio Beachhead, Italy, c. 20-27 April 1944. (National Archives of Canada)

General Frederick wished to further the enemy's uneasiness by initiating some type of psychological warfare. He handed the job over to the First Special Service Force's Assistant Intelligence Officer, Finn Roll, a Norwegian-born American citizen who spoke Norwegian, French, German, Italian and English. It was Roll who came up with the idea for a menacing brand of calling cards. General Frederick later recalls that, "When we were at Anzio, I got a radio message from the War Department to notify Lieutenant Finn Roll that his father, who was then in Oslo [working with the resistance, had been picked up by the Nazis.] . . . Apparently the Germans had found out that Finn Roll was in the United States Army, so they took his father out and shot him."[3]

Henceforth 'calling cards' in the form of stickers branded with the Force's spearhead insignia accompanied Force patrols into no-man's land. Mounting lighting raids as before, the Forcemen now, as well, plastered these stickers on stobs, doors, and on the helmets and foreheads of the enemy they killed. A second, more intimidating version of these stickers included a warning in German: *Das Dicke Ende Kommt Noch!* Translation: The Worst Is Yet To Come! While being one of the Force's more highly publicized activities, the actual number of occasions a red spearhead came to adorn a German corpse is perhaps less than that celebrated in legend. However, what is undeniable is that although Frederick's relatively small numbers defended a length of Anzio's perimeter that under normal circumstances would have been allotted to a whole division, the aggressive attitude of the *Black Devils* more than compensated. This spirit of boldness and determination rippled across the beachhead and helped to sustain the Allies through some of Anzio's darkest days.[4]

Special Feature #4

The Worst Is Yet To Come! Forcemen pasted stickers like these onto doors, fence posts, and even on the bodies of enemy dead as a method of conducting psychological warfare. (Courtesy Hayes Otoupalik/Author's Collection)

Enemy soldier from the *Hermann Göring Panzer and Parachute Division* lays dead in no-man's land in front of Force lines. For many enemy troops the "worst" often came in the form of the Force's violent nighttime raids and ambushes. (National Archives)

Forcemen Paul E. Novembre (left) and Baptista Piccolomini, both of Third Regiment, inter the remains of a German soldier. According to Novembre, German bodies had lain in no-man's land across from the Force's front since February. By April the bodies had begun to "smell so much that we couldn't eat our food." (National Archives)

For others, the "worst" came as a result of futile frontal attacks. These dead Germans lay sprawled in a shallow irrigation ditch, killed during an incursion against Force front line positions along the Mussolini Canal, Anzio Beachhead, Italy. (National Archives)

Special Feature #5

Field Uniforms & Equipment of the First Special Service Force

M-1941 wool knit cap. (Author's Collection)

The Force's version of Bermuda shorts. Rather than being of the same style as Canadian summer issue, what arrived from the Quartermaster Corps were simply "suntan" cotton trousers that had been cut off and hemmed "at what someone thought was the knees." Though not exactly what had been requested, the men made do by rolling them up. The short sleeve shirts, however, were well-liked. (Author's Collection)

RIGHT: The basic training outfit worn by all members of the First Special Service Force at all stations consisted of jump boots, an OD wool flannel shirt, and green herringbone twill mechanic's coveralls. (Reconstruction)

Special Feature #5

LEFT: Leather A-2 flight jacket belonging to a member of the First Special Service Force's Combat Echelon. Note Force's red spearhead insignia has been painted on the left breast of the jacket. In the event that a man either left the Force, or was transferred from the Combat Echelon to the Service Battalion, his leather A-2 jacket was to be turned in to the Force Supply Officer. (Courtesy Hayes Otoupalik)

Cowboy and Canuck pass off-duty time at Fort Harrison by engaging one another in checkers. The American wears the Force's standard overseas cap with red, white, and blue piping, while the Canadian dons a non-regulation tam-o'-shanter with the regimental crest of his previous unit. Both wear A-2 leather jackets. (National Archives)

ABOVE: M-1941 field jacket, referred to as the "bum freezer" by men of the Force. This jacket was a common fixture of Force uniform during the early training days at Helena. The M-1941 field jacket also saw field use by Forcemen. (Courtesy Ken Bennett)

LEFT: Lt. Colonel Gerald E. Rodehaver, Commanding Officer Service Battalion, wearing an M-1941 field jacket during ski training in Blossburg, Montana in 1942. Rodehaver commanded the Service Battalion until 1 October 1943 when he was replaced by Major Richard W. Whitney. (Thomas W. Hope)

Special Feature #5

The Framed Rucksack. Based on the Norwegian Bergen design, the main feature of the rucksack was its large canvas cargo compartment with a drawstring closure at its top, over which was secured the flap by means of two web straps. There was a zippered pocket incorporated into the interior of the flap, and three large storage pouches on the exterior of the main compartment. The means to carry a rifle on the right side of the pack was provided by a metal clip that hung from the frame and that fastened to the sling swivel on the butt of the rifle, and a hanger strap that, being attached to the top of the rucksack through a large eyelet, was twice wrapped around the rifle and then secured to a hook built into the left packstrap. On the left side of the rucksack were several tabs with eyelets that allowed equipment to be fastened. The mountain carrier for the M-1910 entrenching tool had its belt hanger stitched at the opposite end of the blade as was that of the standard carrier, by this allowing the end of the E-tool's handle to ride flush with the bottom of the rucksack. The pack was secured around the waist by an adjustable web strap. (Reconstruction)

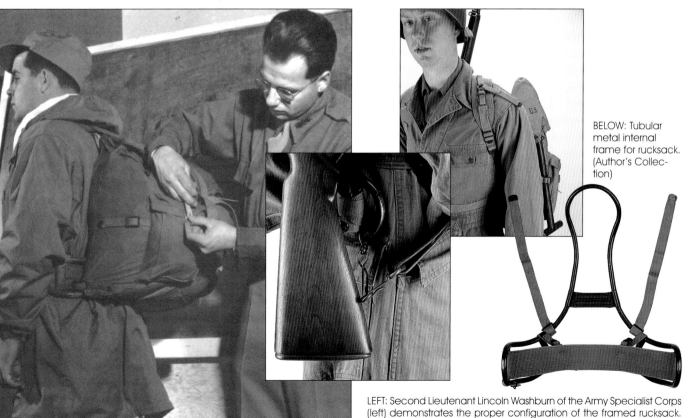

BELOW: Tubular metal internal frame for rucksack. (Author's Collection)

LEFT: Second Lieutenant Lincoln Washburn of the Army Specialist Corps (left) demonstrates the proper configuration of the framed rucksack. (National Archives)

191

Special Feature #5

BELOW: Reversible ski parka, with zippered neck and front slash pockets, and gathered cuffs. This item was worn by the Force throughout much of the cold-weather training it conducted in Montana. (Courtesy W. Michael Myers)

RIGHT: Forceman with skis and ski poles in hand, and wearing the reversible ski parka and white overtrousers. The skis have been strapped together to make them easier to carry. (Thomas W. Hope)

Special Feature #5

First Regiment man pauses to light his cigarette before entrucking for Amchitka harbor to board the APD U.S.S. *Kane* on the eve of Operation COTTAGE, 14 August 1943. Like all members of the Combat Echelon taking part in the operation, this man wears jump boots, mountain trousers, Arctic field jacket, and M-1C helmet which he carries in his hand. He also wears the M-1941 wool knit cap – a very popular item with the Force; and on his hands are wool knit wristlets. Items of equipment include a nine-pocket mounted cartridge belt to which has been attached an M-1918 double web magazine pocket holding two clips for his issue M-1911A1 automatic pistol. The man is armed additionally with an M-1 rifle and an M-1942 bayonet. Over his shoulder he wears a bandoleer containing six eight-round *en bloc* clips for the rifle. The normal combat load for a rifleman was between 128 and 224 rounds of ammunition depending on the discretion of his company commander. (Reconstruction)

Special Feature #5

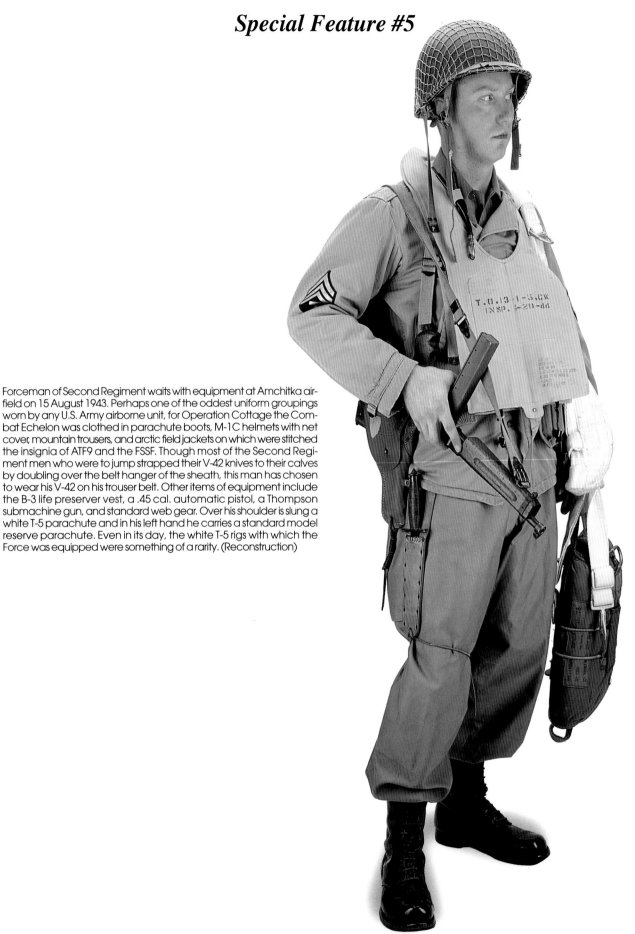

Forceman of Second Regiment waits with equipment at Amchitka airfield on 15 August 1943. Perhaps one of the oddest uniform groupings worn by any U.S. Army airborne unit, for Operation Cottage the Combat Echelon was clothed in parachute boots, M-1C helmets with net cover, mountain trousers, and arctic field jackets on which were stitched the insignia of ATF9 and the FSSF. Though most of the Second Regiment men who were to jump strapped their V-42 knives to their calves by doubling over the belt hanger of the sheath, this man has chosen to wear his V-42 on his trouser belt. Other items of equipment include the B-3 life preserver vest, a .45 cal. automatic pistol, a Thompson submachine gun, and standard web gear. Over his shoulder is slung a white T-5 parachute and in his left hand he carries a standard model reserve parachute. Even in its day, the white T-5 rigs with which the Force was equipped were something of a rarity. (Reconstruction)

ABOVE: Front view of one of the Force's white T-5 parachute rigs. (Courtesy Hayes Otoupalik)

Interior view of M-1C steel helmet designed specifically for wear by airborne troops. The steel shell was coupled to the plastic liner by means of snaps at the ends of the web chinstraps. A leather chincup was fastened to the liner suspension by means of two metal buckles. Also pictured is a U.S. issue helmet net with neoprene foliage band, and a parachute inspection card signed by Sergeant Thomas M. Sellers of Force Service Company's Parachute Platoon. (Courtesy K. Ross/Hayes Otoupalik/Author's Collection)

Medic's M-1C helmet with Geneva cross painted on both sides. (Courtesy G. Piselli)

M-1C helmet with chincup and chinstraps fastened. (Courtesy J. Ranoia)

As the Force was designated an airborne unit, the M-1C helmet was standard issue. This example is shown in conjunction with a neoprene foliage band, another standard item of issue to the First Special Service Force. (Courtesy K. Ross)

Special Feature #5

Gloves including leather palm olive drab wool gloves, unlined horsehide riding gloves, wool inserts for trigger finger mittens, and wool knit wristlets. Other items include an olive drab wool muffler, phrase books, and Italian occupation script. (Courtesy J. Ranoia/Author's Collection)

Two examples of the Dual-Type Life Preserver flank an Army Air Force B-3 Life Preserver Vest, known more commonly as the "Mae West." (Courtesy J. Ranoia/P. Johnston)

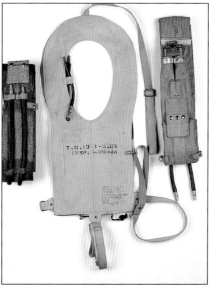

Special Feature #5

OPPOSITE: Platoon Leader of Third Regiment attempts to make radio contact with his company commander northwest of Mount Sammucro, Italy, 3 January 1944. The SCR-536 handie-talkie radio was the standard at the platoon and company level. It often gave poor service in mountainous terrain and under heavy fog conditions; a deficiency brought out all too clearly during the Force's first operation in Italy. Clothing includes an M-1941 wool knit toque, a first pattern parka, mountain trousers, leather palm OD wool gloves, and jump boots. The tail of the parka has been rolled up so as to give easy access to the trouser pockets. Over his jump boots this man will soon slip on a pair of arctic overshoes – a fancy name for rubber goulashes whose rubber uppers have been traded for black felt due to wartime shortages. Equipment includes an M-1910 entrenching tool with mountain carrier, and carbine magazine pockets. The ever-handy mountain pocket knife hangs from the man's neck by a length of OD suspension line, and he is armed with an M-1A1 carbine. (Reconstruction)

BELOW: First pattern reversible parka ruffed with wolf fur at both cuffs and around the hood. A drawstring for the hood is located at the neck, and drawstrings are located at each cuff. This model has simple slash front pockets and is was quite long, its tail reaching to about the knees.
RIGHT: First pattern parka reversed to white side. (Author's Collection)

RIGHT: The Second pattern reversible parka, seen here, is shorter than the first pattern, and has a drawstring built-in in its tail. The cuffs have adjustable button closures, and the front slash pockets are closed by buttons as well. The hood is trimmed with wolf fur and can be tightened by a drawstring as in the earlier model. This pattern has a three button neck that can be opened for ventilation. (Author's Collection)

Special Feature #5

ABOVE: M-1941 wool knit toque. (Author's Collection)

RIGHT: Wool high-neck sweaters such as this example were a common item of issue to the Force. (Author's Collection)

Boots and shoes including (l-r) cap-toe and ruff-out field service shoes, parachute jumper's boots, M-1943 combat boots, and arctic overshoes. It appears that the field service shoe saw little use by the Force beyond its early Helena days. The M-1943 began to make an appearance with the Force during its time at Anzio. By the time of the southern France campaign, it had almost completely supplanted the jump boot for field work. (Courtesy J. Ranoia/Author's Collection)

Special Feature #5

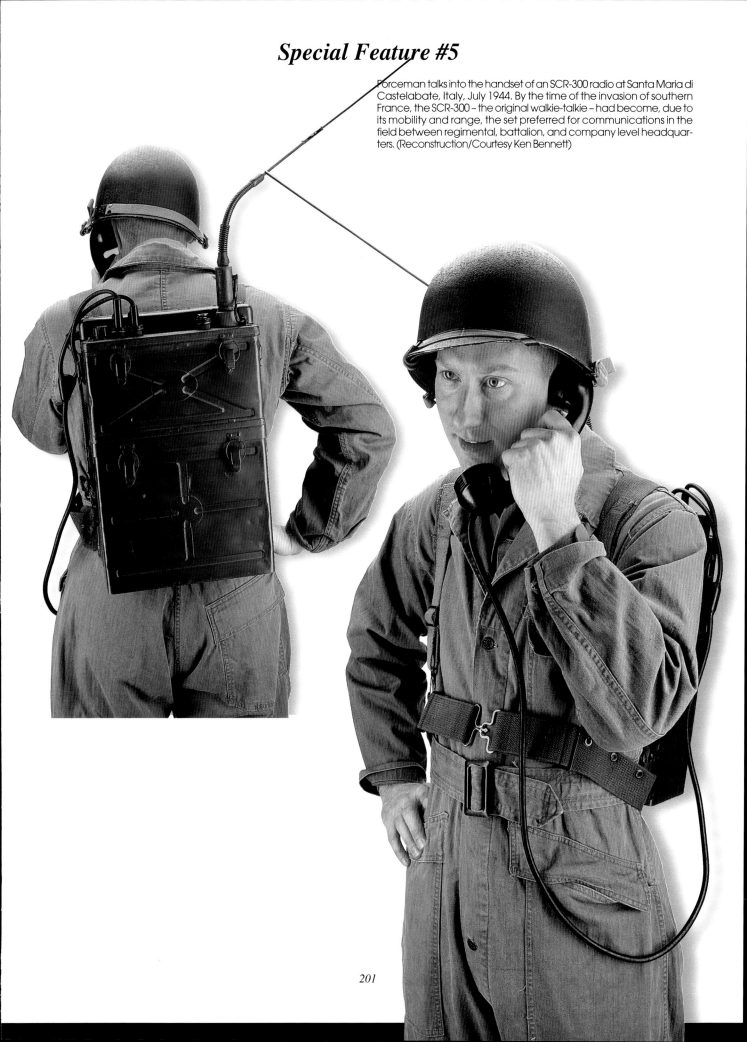

Forceman talks into the handset of an SCR-300 radio at Santa Maria di Castelabate, Italy, July 1944. By the time of the invasion of southern France, the SCR-300 – the original walkie-talkie – had become, due to its mobility and range, the set preferred for communications in the field between regimental, battalion, and company level headquarters. (Reconstruction/Courtesy Ken Bennett)

Special Feature #5

Signal Equipment including SE-11 (M-227) signal lamp with canvas case; SCR-536 handie-talkie radio with padded case, spare crystals, vacuum tube and mouthpiece cover; M-3 binoculars (left) with M-17 case; Bausch & Lomb manufactured 6 power binoculars with russet leather case; TL-122A, B, and C flashlights; very pistol with verys; and M-1938 dispatch case with message book. (Courtesy J. Ranoia/C. Nesbitt/G. Piselli/ Author's Collection)

OPPOSITE: Communications and Signal equipment including AL-141-B yellow aerial recognition panel in its canvas carrying case; two examples of the EE-8 battery powered field telephone, one in early leather carrier, the other in wartime economy canvas carrier; field telephone switchboard; DR-8A wire spool with RL-39 hand assembly and ST-35 neck strap; and field message book. (Courtesy J. Ranoia/Ken Bennett)

Special Feature #5

The Yukon packboard was extensively used by the First Special Service Force to manpack large quantities of supplies to places where access by both mule and vehicle were restricted. (Reconstruction/Courtesy W. Michael Myers)

Special Feature #5

LEFT: Formed plywood packboards such as this example began to see regular use by the First Special Service Force during the southern France campaign. However photo evidence shows formed plywood boards being used in training by the Force as early as May 1943, perhaps only to test them. (Courtesy Ken Bennett)

TOP: Load consisting of wool blanket, ammunition box, and mountain sleeping bag, is secured to formed plywood packboard with lashing ropes and, in the case of the ammo tin, by means of a metal shelf and quick release strap. (Author's Collection)

ABOVE: Quick-release feature of the formed plywood packboard as well as issue shoulder pads that slipped on over the packstraps. (Author's Collection)

Special Feature #5

This Section Leader from Second Regiment will wait for full darkness before blackening his face and setting out with his patrol across the Mussolini Canal into no-man's land at Anzio, Italy. The straps of his M-1C helmet have been quietly secured under the foliage band that is stretched over his steel pot. He is armed with an M-1 Thompson submachine gun and has stuffed five 30-round magazines into pockets meant to hold 20-rounders, having secured the flaps around each. In the loops of his M-1936 field suspenders hang two Mk-IIA1 fragmentation grenades. (Reconstruction)

M-1943 field jacket. The Force had the luxury of being able to acquire almost any item of clothing and equipment deemed needed. The selections made by the Force Supply Officer resulted in the Force having a most unique uniform. The Force utilized the M-1943 field jacket but opted not to adopt the matching M-1943 trousers. Instead the Force secured stocks of U.S. Army mountain trousers that were found to be more suitable. As with the M-1943 trousers, the Force never adopted the Army's mountain jacket as part of its uniform. (Author's Collection)

Special Feature #5

M-1936 belt suspenders. Left, standard pattern in light shade olive drab. Right, variation in darker shade olive drab with padded shoulder straps. Both dated 1943. (Courtesy J. Ranoia/Author's Collection)

Clothing including olive drab flannel shirt with FSSF shoulder sleeve insignia, M-1937 web waist belt, olive drab wool trousers, Mountain trousers with various Army Air Corps trouser suspenders, cotton drawers, light wool socks, and oatmeal-colored winter drawers and undershirt. (Courtesy G. Piselli/Author's Collection)

M-1936 canvas field bag or "musette" was issued to all men of the Combat Echelon and was carried either by securing it to the M-1936 field suspenders, or by an adjustable web strap. This pack saw use most often as a part of the Force's light raiding order. (Author's Collection)

The M-1928 haversack saw service with the Force in training at Castelabate and, subsequently, during the southern France campaign. (Author's Collection)

Special Feature #5

OPPOSITE: OD wool flannel shirt and trousers along with standard jump boots, was an often seen uniform combination, especially at Anzio. This man wears a standard M-1 helmet, and carries an M-1 rifle with fixed M-1 bayonet, as well as an automatic pistol on his hip. On his belt are the M-1924 first aid pouch containing the Carlisle field dressing, and an M-1910 canteen with cover. In his right hand he carries a pair of M-1938 wire cutters, and affixed to his field suspenders an M-1910 entrenching tool – having known better than to leave behind this indispensable tool, even though he has run out of room to hang it on his cartridge belt. (Reconstruction)

M-1910 "T-handled" entrenching shovel with rucksack carrier (marked B.B.S. Co. 1942), and standard M-1910 carrier, M-1938 wire cutters with carrier, M-1910 entrenching pickmattock with carrier, M-1910 entrenching ax with carrier, M-1943 entrenching shovel (folding) with M-1943 carrier. (Courtesy G. Piselli/Hayes Otoupalik/K. Ross/Author's Collection)

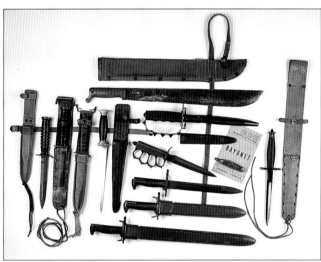

Edged Weapons and Tools. M-1942 machete with case; M-3 fighting knife with plastic M-8 scabbard and leather M-6 sheath, M-1 bayonet with scabbard, M-1942 bayonet with scabbard, mountain pocket knife, V-42 fighting knife with horse hide sheath, knuckle knives, and privately manufactured stiletto. (Courtesy J. Ranoia/G. Piselli/K. Ross/Hayes Otoupalik/Author's Collection)

RIGHT: Time and Direction. Lensatic compass with luminous dial and waterproof case, pocket compasses, watch compass, wrist watch, whistles. (Courtesy J. Ranoia/G. Piselli/K. Ross/Author's Collection)

During cold weather survival training, a Forceman, huddling under improvised shelter, prepares his rations with his mountain cookset and single burner gasoline stove, c. January 1943. (National Archives)

RIGHT; Individual equipment including mountain cookset; 1-burner gasoline stove; M-1932 meat can with M-1926 knife, fork, and spoon; aluminum and enameled versions of the M-1910 canteen and cup with cover; shelter half with guy lines, folding tent pole, and five wooden pegs; OD cotton bath towel; K-ration dinner and emergency D-bar ration. (Courtesy J. Ranoia/G. Piselli/ K. Bennett/Author's Collection)

Special Feature #5

Typical personal items carried by both officers and enlisted men including soap, sewing kit, shaving kit, shaving cream, comb, toothbrush, tooth powder, medicated chewing gum, malted milk tablets, aspirin, "pro" kit, cigarettes, matchbook, cigarette lighter, playing cards, and Force-made V-mail letters and postcards. (Courtesy G. Piselli/August C. Erdbrink)

Special Feature #5

An alarm is sounded during a defense against chemicals exercise at Fort William Henry Harrison. (Author's Collection)

BELOW: Chemical equipment including a lightweight service gas mask and M1A1 training gas mask with waterproofing kit, M-1 eye protectors, and a package containing a clear plastic gas cape designated as the individual protective cover. (Courtesy J. Ranoia/G. Piselli/Author's Collection)

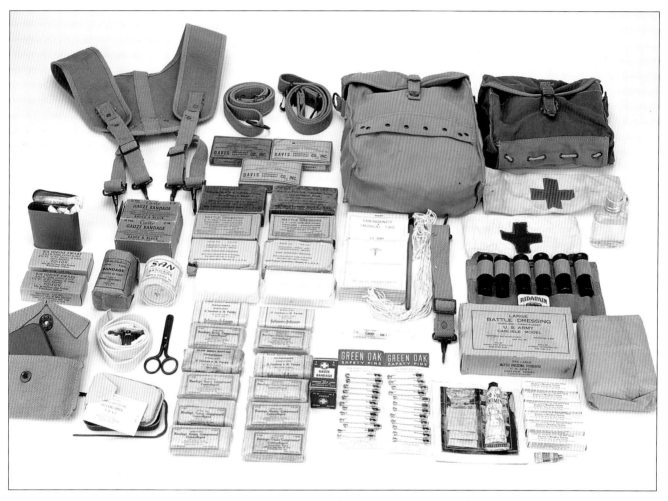

Airborne medic's kit display. (Courtesy G. Piselli)

CHAPTER 8

To Rome from the South

"My own feeling was that nothing was going to stop us on our push toward the Italian capital. Not only did we intend to become the first army in fifteen centuries to seize Rome from the south, but we intended to see that the people back home knew that it was the Fifth Army that did the job and knew the price that had been paid for it" – Mark Wayne Clark[1]

For two months preceding 11 May, the Mediterranean Allied Air Forces (MAAF) carried out Operation STRANGLE, an air campaign south of the Pisa-Rimini line aimed at choking off the flow of supplies to the German *Tenth Army* around Cassino and the *Fourteenth Army* encircling the Anzio Beachhead. Though the operation did not entirely deny the enemy the means to resupply himself, it did diminish his capacity enough in that respect to reduce his overall ability to withstand the Allied offensive that was planned for that Spring. Code-named DIADEM, the May offensive was to be a coordinated attack by Allied forces against the Cassino and Anzio fronts. In the south, the British 13 Corps and the Polish 2 Corps were poised to cross the Rapido River. Once across they were to capture Monte Cassino and Cassino village, and then push northward through the Liri Valley toward Rome with Fifth Army units screening the left flank of the advance along the coastal plain. As those forces neared the Anzio Beachhead, General Alexander, Allied 15th Army Group commander, proposed that VI Corps launch a coordinated attack north-by-northeast up the Velletri Gap to capture Valmontone which lay astride Highway 6. Alexander pointed out that the capture of Valmontone would cut German *Tenth Army's* line of retreat from the Cassino front and could perhaps result in destroying that army south of Rome. The disposition of Allied forces from that point on would likely put British Eighth Army – not Clark's Fifth U.S. – on the likely axis to capture Rome.[2]

"Although General Alexander clearly intended the [British] Eighth Army to play the major role in DIADEM, General Clark wanted to ensure that the Americans, not the British, took Rome, and he actively sought to have the

Fifth Army's role increased to bring about this aim. Although he was rebuffed in his efforts during a tense 1 May meeting with Alexander, the latter was aware that Clark's views differed from his own. To maintain cordial relations with his ally, Alexander provided only the most general orders to Clark, thus allowing him great flexibility in determining Fifth Army deployments during the coming weeks."[3]

Preceded by a devastating artillery preparation, DIADEM commenced at 2300 hours on 11 May 1944, with the attack of twenty-five Allied divisions against the Gustav Line. After five days of bitter fighting the Allies pierced the German line in several places causing the enemy to begin a fighting withdrawal northward up the Liri Valley. However by 19 May, Eighth Army's advance up the corridor began to stall against a stiffening German defense. Rather than throw his full weight into supporting the attack of the embattled Eighth Army, Clark used this opportunity to spur ahead his II Corps towards Fondi and Terracina. Beyond these two villages, II Corps had but a short distance to cover before it would link up with Fifth Army forces at the Anzio Beachhead. Once this event took place, Clark might then be in a position to mount a drive on Rome.[4]

By May VI Corps strength at Anzio stood at 90,000 troops – 20,000 more than had the opposing *Fourteenth Army*. Now in command of Allied forces at Anzio was General Lucian K. Truscott, Jr., who had taken over VI Corps on 23 February 1944. Clark had relieved Truscott's predecessor, General Lucas, later commenting that the latter was unable to continue at that post, apparently "ill – tired physically and mentally – from the long responsibilities of command in battle. . . ."[5] During April

Large sand table depicts terrain of the Lepini Mountains and Force objectives for the breakout. (Lew Merrim)

and early May, four plans of attack out of the Anzio Beachhead were formulated by Truscott's staff, those being codenamed BUFFALO, CRAWDAD, GRASSHOPPER, and TURTLE. The one which particularly suited Alexander's overall strategy was Operation BUFFALO aimed toward Valmontone. However, Clark instructed the VI Corps commander that once the breakout was underway, he should be prepared within a day's notice to change the direction of VI Corps' thrust toward Rome.[6]

On 5 May, General Clark gave official word that Truscott was to implement Operation BUFFALO in accordance with Alexander's wishes. BUFFALO, itself, called for the VI Corps launch the breakout from the Cisterna front along two axes: the first aimed in the direction of Velletri at the base of the Colli Laziali (Alban Hills), and the second toward Cori and the Lepini Mountains. VI Corps' available forces included the U.S. 1st Armored Division, the U.S. 3rd, 34th, 36th, and 45th Infantry Divisions, two British infantry divisions, and the First Special Service Force (Reinforced). The 3rd Infantry Division was given the mission of capturing Cisterna by attacking with all three of its infantry regiments at once: the 7th frontally, and the 15th and 30th to envelop the town from the right and left respectively. To the left of the 3rd Division, the 45th Division would launch a supporting attack toward Carano. The 1st Armored Division, organized into two combat commands (CCs), CCA and CCB, would attack into the open country to the west of Cisterna. The Force's job was to screen the Corps' right flank along the Mussolini Canal. The 34th and 36th Divisions would remain in Corps reserve to exploit any breakthrough or to move on Velletri. On the far left of VI Corps, a diversionary demonstration by the British 1 and 5 Divisions was to be made on the night prior to D-day. The Mediterranean Allied Air Forces

would also assist the breakout by bombing targets ahead of the ground force's planned routes of advance. As Allied forces from the south ground their way toward Anzio, D-day for Operation BUFFALO was set for 23 May 1944.[7]

When the Force was relieved from its front line positions along the Mussolini Canal, the morale was high among the men of the regiments. "There [had been] a great zest to be in on patrols and get in some hard blows against the Germans."[8] On the other hand, after so long in static positions it was necessary that the Force spend a good deal of time undergoing intensive physical training in order to bring the men back to peak condition. Far enough to the 'rear' as to be safe from small arms fire, the Force still did not escape casualties resulting from enemy shelling as well as from the occasional air

2nd Battalion, Second Regiment officers: Lt. Colonel Robert S. Moore (wearing helmet), Battalion CO; and Major Stan C. Waters (with shirt off). With them are Major George Evashwick (left), and T/4 J.W. Peebles (behind jeep), Anzio Beachhead, Italy, 14 May 1944. (Herb Langdon) Moore, who had led Second Regiment since 29 December 1943, was moved over to 2nd Battalion so that Lt. Colonel J.F.R. Akehurst could be placed in command of the Second Regiment. However, it was largely on Moore whom Frederick was relying; the latter stating that Moore was, "... so good that he would carry the 2nd Regiment along."

Forcemen move out across a wheat field during Operation BUFFALO, the breakout of the Anzio Beachhead, 23 May 1944. (National Archives)

raids. It was planned that the Force's attack out of the beachhead be supported by several armored elements. So that the men might gain further experience in working with armor, the Force carried out extensive tank-infantry training with troops of the U.S. 1st and 13th Armored Regiments (Light), and the 191st Tank and 645th Tank Destroyer Battalions. So effective was this training program that it was adopted by other units at Anzio. As was always the case, the men studied maps and were briefed thoroughly on tactical plans and initial objectives.[9]

Service Battalion's role in the upcoming offensive, as always, would be an important one. If the attack progressed as expected, the battalion's supply and medical functions would be taxed to the utmost. To more adequately cope with what was anticipated to be a costly fight, 150 litter bearers were drawn from Service and Maintenance Companies and given first aid lessons by the Force's medical officers. Each regiment was to have fifty of these litter bearers attached to it during the coming operation. Collecting stations would be set up as close to the fighting as was practicable. As well, the battalion would see to it that the flow of rations, supplies, and ammunition to the regiments was continuous once the fighting commenced.[10]

At night, between 9 and 21 May, Second Regiment patrols into no-man's land were maintained along the Mussolini Canal front so that the Germans might be fooled into thinking that the Force, not the 36th Engineer Combat Regiment, was still holding that line. On Corps orders, two companies of Second Regiment undertook separate combat patrols on 21 May to make contact with the enemy. The principal aim of these particular patrols was to capture prisoners, and from them to find out if the enemy was aware of Allied preparations for the coming offensive. One of the companies made its way to the vicinity of a familiar abandoned quarry, while the other struck off in the direction of Borgo Piave. Both raiding parties were hotly resisted by enemy artillery and small arms fire, but their task was accomplished. In all the Force snared seventeen prisoners (one an officer), and left behind thirty-nine known enemy dead. The Force's losses were heavy: eleven dead, two missing, and twenty wounded.[11]

On D-1, the Forcemen closed camp, boarded trucks and moved toward the front. After covering several miles, the trucks

Three Force litter bearers bring in a wounded Forceman from the front by means of a hand cart, 23 May 1944. (National Archives)

stopped. At this point the men debussed and formed up. They would march the rest of the way. After two hours they reached the place that was to be that morning's line of departure, arriving there at 0300 hours on 23 May. The jumping-off spot was a shallow gully some 150 yards behind the main line of resistance, the south bank of the Fosso di Cisterna. Weighted down with weapons and ammunition, and tired from the march, the men sank into the ditch to wait for the signal to go. That same night, Frederick's supporting armor, comprised of Company A of the 191st Tank Battalion, and two companies of the 645th Tank Destroyer Battalion, moved into forward assembly areas some distance behind the Force. Attached to the Force as well were Company D of the 39th Engineer Combat Regiment, Company D of the 84th Chemical Battalion, and Collecting Company A of the 52nd Medical Battalion. In direct support of the Force were five battalions of light and medium artillery, among these the 463rd Parachute Field Artillery Battalion. Also included in that number was the 3rd Pack Field Artillery Battalion (Provisional) which on 2 May had been assigned to Frederick who attached it operationally to the 463rd.[12]

The Force was to attack northeast out of the beachhead, on the Corps' extreme right, across a 2,100 yard front that was bounded on the right by the west bank of the Mussolini Canal. The Force's principal mission was to protect the right flank of VI Corps as it moved up the Velletri gap and onto the Valmontone plain. Frederick's first goal was to breach the German main line of resistance, advance to cut Highway 7, and then consolidate on a line just north of the Cisterna railroad. Then, during the next phase of the offensive, the Force would attack to capture Mount Arrestino in the Lepini Mountains, and the village of Cori, on its way to cutting Highway 6 – Via Casilina – at Valmontone.[13]

At H-hour on D-day, First Regiment SSF, reinforced by 1st Battalion of Second Regiment, would pass through the 168th Infantry (34th Infantry Division) along the main line of resistance, cross the Fosso di Cisterna, and move into the attack. From left to right would be 2nd Battalion, First; 1st Battalion, First; and 1st Battalion, Second. On the Force's right, the flank would be open to the Germans who remained active within the all too familiar no-man's land of the last four months; a flank that might become even more exposed as the attack progressed. Frederick felt that neither the 168th Infantry or the 36th Engineer Combat Regiment would provide adequate protection on this flank. Resultantly Third Regiment SSF was ordered to advance from the line of departure following the advance of First, but along the eastern side of the Mussolini Canal. The

L-r: Sergeant Rogan, Private Josefski, and Lieutenant Smithers of the 463rd Parachute Field Artillery Battalion call for artillery support, 23 May 1944. (National Archives)

100th Infantry Battalion (Nesei) would push out, following in Third's wake, in the direction of Littoria to cover Third Regiment's right flank. Second Regiment (-) would follow First ready to repel German counterattacks from either of the flanks or the front. Jumping off at H-hour on the Force's immediate left, Pollack Force, a provisional tank-infantry formation from the 3rd Division, was to move forward abreast of the First Special Service Force and cover the Force's left flank. Once the Force had advanced as far as the Cisterna railroad line, it was

24 May 1944, 1300 hours. Casualty evacuation by litter jeep. (Herb Langdon)

to consolidate, and then be relieved by elements of the 34th Division. Once this was accomplished, the regiments were to regroup, and then carry on with the next phase of the attack.[14]

As an interesting sideline to the breakout, on the eve of D-day, approximately fifteen Forcemen were organized into two radio teams under Major Becket. Herb Peppard (1-1), one of those fifteen, recalls that the 'volunteers' who had been assigned to this mission had been drawn from all three regiments. The men were astonished to learn that they would be making a parachute drop that night onto a hill between Highways 6 and 7. Once on the ground the men were to report by radio whatever enemy activity was within observation. That day, the group left Anzio on a ship and sailed south to Salerno. There they strapped on their parachutes and loaded aboard a C-47 Dakota. After dark, they took off for their hilltop drop zone (DZ). Nearing the DZ, German antiaircraft fire became incredibly intense. One Forceman remarked that the flare from the bursting ack-ack was so constant that one could 'read the paper by it.' Prevented by this heavy barrage from reaching the designated hill, Major Becket decided it best to turn back and try again the next night. This they did, but once again, heavy enemy fire crisscrossed the sky around the aircraft forcing it to turn back from this, the second and final attempt.[15]

D-day for Operation BUFFALO, 23 May, dawned clear and sunny. H-hour was set for 0630 hours. Preceding H-hour, combined II Corps artillery laid down a thunderous ninety-minute barrage along the length of the German front line. H-hour arrived, but the attack was held up briefly as only a small number of the armored vehicles that were to support Fredrick's infantry had come up to the start line. As the covering barrage "walked" forward, Colonel A.C. Marshall, First Regiment's commander, decided to wait no longer and gave the word to jump off without lingering for rest of the tanks. On First Regiment's left wing, 6-1 was the assault company and led the 2nd Battalion's attack. Their job would be to punch a hole in the German's main line of resistance and then consolidate their gains. 5-1 would then pass through and continue the attack. 4-1, attacking on the battalion's left, was to stay abreast of 5th Company. As a preliminary effort, at H-minus 15, one platoon of 4-1 advanced and cleared an enemy-held house immediately in front of 6th Company's line of march. When zero hour arrived, 6th Company, supported by a handful of tanks, took to their feet and advanced. Fifteen minutes later 4th and 5th Companies followed.[16]

U.S. medium tanks move to the front to join the northerly attack of the First Special Service from the beachhead, 24 May 1944. (National Archives)

The 1st Battalion of First Regiment had gotten its attack off on time. Within half an hour of starting out two medium tanks and two tank destroyers joined the leading elements of the battalion and were assisting its advance by fire. 500 yards were quickly gained, though the battalion had been constantly engaged in firefights. A short time later the remainder of First Regiment's supporting armor crossed the Fosso di Cisterna on improvised bridges, but as the armor closed within several hundred yards of the enemy's MLR it ran headlong into extensive minefields. A number of tanks and tank destroyers were put out of commission, and the further threat of mines halted the rest, effectively robbing the regiment of its heavy support. 1st Battalion's commanding officer, Lt. Colonel Walter S. Gray, who had insisted on accompanying the assault platoon from his battalion's lead company was killed by machine gun fire during the early moments of the attack. The battalion was taken over by Major Jerry McFadden.[17]

Several hundred yards northeast of the Fosso di Cisterna, First Regiment's 2nd Battalion broke through the German main line of resistance. Rows of skirmishers advanced across the ditches and fields of tall wheat cleaning out pockets of resisters along the way. However, as the battalion neared the Boschetto di Mosca woods, a hornet's nest of German fire suddenly came to life. Over the staccato beat of the enemy's machine guns could be heard the throaty cough of German mortars followed moments later by the crash of their shells. Under the weight of this heavy enemy fire, the battalion's advance bogged down. Task Force Pollack, whose attack was to have by now traversed this tangle, was conspicuously absent on the Force's left. Heavy small arms fire from German outposts had stopped TF Pollack at the Fosso di Cisterna.[18]

25 May 1944, 1900 hours. Personnel of Headquarters Detachment 2nd Battalion, Second Regiment and Italian partisans on Mount Arrestino overlooking former beachhead. (Herb Langdon)

German Mark VI tank knocked out by artillery. This Tiger was one of 17 that attacked leading elements of the First Special Service Force when they reached Highway 7 on 23 May 1944. (National Archives)

Forcemen move along railroad tracks as they make their approach to Mount Arrestino. (National Archives)

By 1000 hours forward elements of First Regiment, mainly from 1st Battalion had cut Highway 7 and, moving another 200 yards north, had crossed the Cisterna railroad line and had begun to dig in. Elements of 1st Battalion, Second, advancing along the west bank of the canal had moved up as well; 3-2 having taken up a position to guard the Ponte Mussolini, the Highway 7 road bridge that spanned the Mussolini Canal. Meanwhile, other elements of that battalion were moving beyond Highway 7 toward the Ponte Marchi, the canal railroad bridge. On the eastern side of the Mussolini Canal, Third Regiment's screening maneuver was making measured progress against stiff resistance.[19]

By 1200 hours the enemy artillery fire that had harassed the Force's attack throughout the morning redoubled itself with ferocious intensity. German heavy artillery firing from positions both in Littoria to the east and Cisterna to the west blanketed the Force sector, making movement of supplies and reinforcements forward along the Ninfa road – the only road in the area suitable for that purpose – all but impossible. It also caused casualties among the Force units dug in along the Cisterna railroad. Counter-battery fire from VI Corps artillery was called upon at this point. Moments later forward artillery observers spotted a concentration of German infantry and armor, plainly forming for a counterattack, sheltering in a ten acre stand of trees 1,000 yards east of the Ponte Mussolini. Seven battalions of VI Corps artillery were put to work on the woods. Their twenty minute time-on-target barrage, added to by a payload of bombs dropped by a flight of dive-bombers, tore deep gaps in the enemy infantry, but did little to phase the armor. After pausing to regroup, the German tanks and an estimated battalion of infantry moved out of the woods to attack the Force.[20]

Dark clouds that had gathered overhead began to pour rain. For the soon drenched Forcemen, who had been engaged in constant fighting all day with no resupply, ammunition was running dangerously low. Even more critical, the lightly equipped Forcemen, having outpaced most of their supporting armor, had little on hand to deal with tanks. Bearing down the Ninfa road toward the railroad bed, and advancing along Highway 7 toward the canal from the east, were an estimated company of German Mark VI Tanks – Tigers. Shortly after 1500 hours, the Tigers had taken up positions and began shelling First Regiment's forward-most positions near the Ninfa road overpass and along the railroad bed. All that the Forcemen had to use against the tanks were their 2.36" Bazookas, but even direct hits by the antitank rockets did little more than scorch the paint of these fifty-six ton behemoths. As German armor and infantry exerted pressure from the front and right flank, and with heavy small arms fire coming from the left, the Force's forward positions were quickly becoming untenable. With casualties mounting, the men were directed to begin an orderly

26 May 1944, 1300 hours. Looking south at Cori. (Herb Langdon)

In the shade of some trees a Force section takes ten near Cori. (Lew Merrim)

withdrawal to an ephemeral line running along the south side of Highway 7 where they were to dig-in in a shallow ditch.[21]

At this point Frederick demanded that his attached tanks and tank destroyers at once make every effort to move forward into positions to support the infantry. So far that day only two platoons of light tanks had made appreciable gains. These had, by midday, posed themselves approximately 200 yards south of Highway 7. By 1530 hours, and at long last, two platoons of M-4 medium tanks and one company of M-10 tank destroyers

26 May 1944, 1500 hours. Rocca Massima. (Herb Langdon)

27 May 1944, 1130 hours. Second Regiment approaches Artena. Valmontone lies hidden by hills in right background. (Herb Langdon)

29 May 1944, 1330 hours. Looking south from 3-2's headquarters at Artena under shellfire. (Herb Langdon)

Firefight for Staz di Artena railroad station as seen from a tower inside of Artena. (Lew Merrim)

rolled north across Highway 7 to meet the enemy armor. Immediately the American tanks went into action. Their 3-inch and 75mm shells succeeded in knocking out two Tigers and disabling three others. But the Tigers were more than a match for the relatively thin-clad American vehicles. With terrible efficiency the Tigers brought their 88mm main guns to bear on the American armor, and in short order as many as fourteen Shermans and all but two of the M-10 Tank Destroyers were lost, forcing the rest to withdraw. Frederick asked II Corps for the immediate transfer of another battalion of tank destroyers to his command. Truscott allowed this, but these vehicles would not arrive on the Force front before nightfall and by then they would be too late to influence the current situation.[22]

As 88mm shells, mortar and machine gun fire erupted on every side, all that the Forcemen could do was keep their heads down and call for artillery support. Wisely, the order was passed for the out-gunned First Regiment to withdraw south a further 600 yards to a more defensible line parallel to the Boschetto di Mosca woods where it could tie in with the Pollack Task Force that had by this time come up on the left. Meanwhile II Corps, Force Cannon Company and all attached artillery, concentrated

their fires on the enemy's armor and infantry dissuading him from attempting any further gains.[23]

As darkness began to fall, the First Regiment got the word that it was to move back to the morning's jumping-off spot just as soon as relief could be effected. On the right wing, Third Regiment was relieved on its position along the Mussolini Canal at 1800 hours by the 100th Battalion (Separate) and moved to the rear for rest and reorganization. Later that night, the 1st Battalion of the 34th Division's 133rd Infantry moved up to relieve the First Regiment SSF along its line west of the Mussolini Canal, accomplishing this by 2200 hours. However, 3-2 held on at its position, cut off at the Ponte Mussolini, until it was contacted by Force patrols early the next morning. Part of what had made the first day of the attack so trying for the First Special Service Force was the fact that the unit attacking on its immediate left, 3rd Division's Pollack Force, was unable keep pace. Indeed, the Force had outdistanced even its own armored support. The 3rd Division, attacking on the left towards Cisterna, had, on the whole, faired badly, suffering 1,626 casualties on the first day of the breakout alone. Extensive mine fields, and two enemy divisions, well-entrenched

A Force company approaches Colle Ferro across an oat field. (Lew Merrim)

and with orders to hold the vital crossroads village at all cost, had put up a most tenacious defense.[24]

During the hours of darkness on 23/24 May elements of the 34th Infantry Division passed through the First Special Service Force to continue the attack against the Germans who by now were beginning to withdraw to prepared positions to the north and northeast. However, at first light on the 24th another, albeit limited, counterattack began to materialize. As this small rear guard force of enemy tanks began to move into position, they drew a hail of fire from Force Cannon Company and the 463rd Parachute Field Artillery Battalion. This accurate fire succeeded in destroying one and setting another on fire while forcing the remaining vehicles to retire. The Force spent the remainder of the 24th resting, re-equipping and reorganizing without further contact with the enemy, save for air burst and other assorted artillery fire which, although causing several casualties, began to peter as the day wore on. Celebrated in other quarters that day, the 125-day isolation of the beachhead was ended when a motorized force from the U.S. 85th Infantry Division met a VI Corps engineer patrol moving south from Anzio.[25]

Advancing through 24 May and into the early hours of the following morning, the 34th Division had moved the front to a line along the south bank of the Teppia Canal. The Germans had by now all but abandoned the area that had been the scene of the last two days' fighting, and as the Forcemen made their approach march to the next line of departure they took in the devastation that had been left in its wake. After two days of fighting the German main line of resistance had collapsed and his forces had begun to retire "in ineffective retrograde" across the Lepini Mountains to Highway 6. At 0640 hours that morning Third Regiment, with Second Regiment following on the right flank, passed through the 133rd Infantry and again went into the attack. The Force's next mission was to move up into the hills to capture Mount Arrestino, a wooded height about two miles south of Cori. First Regiment moved off last, screening the advance on the left. The maneuver progressed well against light opposition. As the men climbed into the mountains they could view the extent of their former bastion at Anzio as had the Germans until only recently. So frail did it seem that many wondered how the enemy had failed in his attempts to drive the beachhead into the sea. Now, as countless flights of Allied fighters and bombers hummed busily overhead, small disorganized bands of enemy soldiers, beyond the range of small arms, were glimpsed at through field glasses as they fled northward. By 1400 hours Mount Arrestino was captured by Third

Jeeps, armored cars, and tank destroyers in the village of Colle Ferro. (Lew Merrim)

Regiment overcoming one enemy self-propelled gun and three machine guns as the only resistance. To the west and east, First and Second Regiments invested the lower slopes.[26]

On 26 and 27 May the Force, now in its element, moved rapidly through the mountains, pausing to reorganize and re-equip in Cori, and then moving on through the village of Rocca Massima on its way to its next objective, Artena. To aid in the trek over the winding mountain trails the Force was assigned a Sardinian mule train which hearkened back to earlier operations in the Winter Line. The way was unopposed save for an exchange with one platoon of Germans who when challenged quickly withdrew.[27]

By 1100 hours on the 27th, the Force column halted on the hillsides overlooking Artena, where it waited until the 3rd Infantry Division finished mopping up the pockets of resistance that remained inside of the town. Two days earlier, Cisterna, one of the initial objectives of the Anzio campaign, had finally fallen to troops of the 3rd Division. After that hard-won victory, the division had continued its attack northward up the Velletri Gap with its right flank screened by the First Special Service Force. Originally the Force was to have swept through the mountains on a more easterly route, but only days before Clark had decided to materially alter Operation BUFFALO by diverting most of the VI Corps toward a new objective, Rome. Frederick now found the Force temporarily attached to the 3rd Division with Valmontone their common objective. That night, from 1800 to 2200 hours, Force elements moved into bivouac along the high ground flanking Artena, there relieving the 3rd Division's 15th Infantry along the hillsides. Force Headquarters and 2nd Battalion of Second Regiment occupied the village itself relieving the 7th Infantry.[28]

The village of Artena sprawled across a north-facing hillside just a few miles south of Valmontone, and from the hills surrounding the village the Forcemen could look across the valley and observe enemy traffic on Highway 6. "Convoys, hurrying to escape from the Liri Valley, were pouring northwest by day and night. Allied fighters and bombers punished moving columns at will, claiming 645 vehicles destroyed and 446 damaged [on the 25th alone]." Through the day and into night hostile shellfire fell in the Force's area. Adding its weight to the enemy defense, the *Hermann Göring Panzer and Parachute Division*, which had been withdrawn from the Anzio front several months earlier, and which until days before had been rebuilding in Leghorn, had just arrived on the front. Now it was thrown into the battle to check the Allied advance toward Highway 6.[29]

On the morning of 28 May the First Special Service Force, with attached engineers and artillery, as well as one platoon from the 601st Tank Destroyer Battalion and one platoon of medium tanks from the 751st Tank Battalion, swept down from Artena to establish a new front line along high ground that at one point straddled the Valmontone-Artena road, parallel to and south of the railroad line. The 3rd Division launched a simultaneous attack on the Force's left. Enemy tanks, artillery, and machine guns laid down a heavy curtain of fire. The Germans had also brought up flack wagons and depressing their guns were using them in a highly effective antipersonnel role. Against this fire, by 1900 hours the attack had gained its objective, that being a crescent-shaped line around Artena. Yet, for advancing a few hundred yards, the Force had paid a relatively high price in casualties. Moreover, resistance continued from snipers and other small arms fire emanating from within a cluster fortified houses and strongpoints to the west of the Artena-Valmontone road. However, by midnight, this fire had abated somewhat. The attack of the 3rd Division had made progress, having moved into a position from which to launch a drive on Valmontone. But before that could happen, the enemy tanks and artillery dug in between the railroad and the village would first have to be reduced.[30]

The 29th of May showed an increase in enemy artillery and tank fire that caused damage and a number of casualties, particularly in the Force's rear area. Part of the cause, it was soon discovered, was due to a Fascist civilian who was inside of Artena directing enemy fire by light signals, and who in addition to this had been cutting every telephone wire he could get his hands on. The man was soon apprehended, but the artillery continued. In light of this, all Force units continued to

harden their defensive positions during the day. During the night the Force line was intermittently shelled. Counter battery fire from Allied artillery, provided in large part by heavy guns of the 6th Field Artillery Group which had just been attached to the Force, crossed the German fire overhead. To bolster the Force's front line, a platoon of tanks and another of tank destroyers, having been attached to Frederick on the afternoon of the previous day, moved in behind the crest of the ridge and were dug-in in "hull down" positions.[31]

To try to gain a more accurate picture of what enemy forces lay before them, the Force sent out several patrols after dark on the 29th. A demolition patrol led by Lieutenant Jim Pringle of Second Regiment infiltrated behind enemy lines with the objective of destroying both a road bridge on Highway 6, and a railroad bridge that was immediately south of it. At both locations a preponderance of enemy troops blocked the patrol from carrying out its plan. A reconnaissance patrol also set out to ascertain information about the enemy. That patrol returned before sunup on the 30th to confirm that large numbers of enemy troops were occupying positions in and around Valmontone.[32]

On 30 May at 0115 hours, the enemy undertook a reconnaissance in strength aimed down the Artena-Valmontone road against the Force front. Covering fire from German artillery, tanks and Nebelwerfers fell in a steady stream. The attack was estimated to be at battalion strength and was supported by tanks. Force artillery countered and halted the advance of the enemy armor near the Staz di Artena railroad station. The battle lasted for almost four hours. In the end, small arms fire from First and Third Regiments generated casualties enough among the enemy's infantry to cause him to break off the attack. But though the German infantry had retired, his armor stayed on to occupy the railroad station. Throughout the remainder of the day, the Force's attached artillery raked enemy targets north of Artena and even engaged a German truck convoy moving west on Highway 6 north of Colle Ferro. Force patrols cautiously probed the front to check on enemy activity and to locate the positions of his guns. Entrenched enemy tanks and self-propelled guns posed a perpetual problem. Meanwhile all Force units continued to consolidate their current holdings against what was expected to be a full-scale counterattack.[33]

By 1830 hours that evening the inevitable counterattack was sighted, approaching down the Valmontone-Artena road. The first blow against the German thrust, a preemptive artillery strike, was landed when fires from Force Cannon Company and the 463rd Parachute Field Artillery succeeded in halting the armored column and dispersing its accompanying infantry as it passed through the area of the Staz di Artena railroad station. Within the station the enemy attempted to conceal a number of his tanks and self propelled guns, and before long forward observers spotted a cluster of enemy infantry apparently reforming in a draw near Colli di Barigliano, some 2,000 meters south of Valmontone. With these lucrative targets, the artillery of II Corps and of the 6th Armored Field Artillery Group made ready to land the knock out punch. Commencing fire with a time-on-target attack, their devastating barrage flattened the railroad station and annihilated the German infantry. The remainder of the night passed more quietly.[34]

During the last day of the month the front had begun to settle down as, thanks to effective counter-battery work, enemy self-propelled artillery fire slackened. Though the enemy gave no ground, the initiative had swung to the Allied side as units of the II Corps – the 85th and 88th Infantry Divisions – had moved into the line on the left of the 3rd Division. With these newly arrived troops, the time had come to jump off on the attack to capture Valmontone. The 3rd Division would attack early the following morning and was to advance on Valmontone directly, while the 85th and 88th Divisions would screen the left flank widening the wedge. The Force, with a limited objective attack, would be jumping off on the right.[35]

At 0430 hours on 1 June Frederick's attached artillery commenced with a heavy barrage on the German line. At 0500 hours Colonel Akehurst's Second Regiment, supported by tanks and tank destroyers, stepped off on an attack which succeeded in gaining its objective, a wooded high-ground overlooking the Artena railroad line one mile east of the Staz di Artena, by 0800 hours. On Second's right, Third Regiment pushed out to the east in the direction of Colle Ferro. Its attack progressed against stiff enemy resistance which developed into a counter-attack against the regiment's right flank. This was turned leaving and estimated forty enemy dead, and by 0830, Third Regiment, too, was on its objective and digging in. At 1400 hours on 1 June the First Special Service Force was relieved of its attachment to VI Corps and found itself back under the command of General Keyes' II Corps. First Regiment, which in the wake of the 3rd Division's attack had been relieved in place the previous morning, was ordered in the wee hours of 2 June to send a patrol, accompanied by armor, to reconnoiter the road leading eastward to the village of Colle Ferro, some three miles southeast of Artena.[36]

By 2 June the situation for the Germans, attempting to stem the onrushing tide of Allied forces from the south and east had become most desperate. On the night of 27/28 May, units of the U.S. 36th Infantry Division, which had been landed at Anzio on 19 May, had discovered an undefended gap in the German lines at Mount Artemisio, just to the east of Velletri. As Allied units began to pour into the breach, Field Marshall Albert Kesselring, commander of German forces in Italy, was compelled to order his units to "break off contact" and begin a retreat through Rome to the north.[37]

At 1000 hours on 2 June the Force was relieved in its sector by the 15th Infantry. Three hours later the First Special Service Force, with the help of the 752nd Tank Battalion and elements of the 117th Reconnaissance Squadron, attacked and captured Colle Ferro, netting 425 German prisoners – the entire German garrison – in the process. But, as usual, the enemy made the Force pay for its gains. Throughout the remainder of the day sporadic hostile shellfire, some of it as large as 170mm, fell in and around the town causing a number of casualties. Of potentially greater danger, Italian civilians notified Forcemen about the presence of fuzed demolitions on several local bridges and in a munitions factory located within the town. U.S. Engineers, with the assistance of a German prisoner who had been one of those who had planted the charges, succeeded in neu-

Wine for the liberators, vic. Colle Ferro, Italy. (ECPA/France)

tralizing all of the explosives before any were detonated. Later that day the Force made contact with the 3rd Algerian Division, part of the French Expeditionary Corps coming up from the Cassino front. By evening the Force released Colle Ferro to the Algerians, and received orders to return to bivouac in the vicinity of Artena.[38]

By 3 June Fifth Army was pursuing the retreating enemy northwest along Highway 7 and, after the 3rd Division's capture of Valmontone, west along Highway 6. At this point the Howze Task Force (TF), a provisional armor and infantry groupment, was attached to the First Special Service Force at 0915 hours. II Corps orders planned that Frederick would use the Howze Task Force to attack by day, and his own Force to attack by night. Closing from its bivouac at Artena, the First Special Service Force, for the moment riding in trucks, moved down Highway 6 toward Rome, hurrying to meet TF Howze. Tanks equipped as bulldozers had hastily cleared the roads. For mile after mile the shoulders were littered with the burnt and mangled wreckage of enemy vehicles and equipment, dead men and dead horses. Practically unopposed in the sky, Allied air power had rained Hellish destruction down upon the fleeing Germans.[39]

Before 1800 hours the Force moved into assembly areas in the vicinity of Colle del Finocchio on Highway 6 scarcely seven miles from the Rome city limits. While this maneuver was taking place the Force column was mistakenly strafed by several American P-38 fighter aircraft. Orange smoke grenades were set off – the signal for friendly troops – and the fighters disengaged. After some reorganization Second and Third Regiments again moved west. With their objective being a phase line running through Tor Sapienza, at 2155 hours Second and Third Regiments passed through the Howze TF and continued the attack. First Regiment, so reduced by casualties as to be reorganized into a single battalion, was placed in Force reserve.[40]

By midnight Frederick had established his command post in a Finocchio farmhouse. There he received a message from Clark which read:

"Fifth Army forces are rapidly approaching the city of Rome. The intentions of the enemy are not known; he may decide to fight within the city or he may withdraw to the North. It is my most urgent desire that Fifth Army troops protect both public and private property in the city of Rome. However, the deciding factor is the enemy's disposition and actions. If the Germans oppose our advance – battalion and all higher commanders are authorized to take private action without delay to defeat the opposing enemy."[41]

His helmet festooned with flowers, a Forceman exchanges candy for a rose from an Italian child. (ECPA/France)

Johnny gunner takes a respite in the company of an Italian femmina. (ECPA/France)

Certainly if Fifth Army was to maintain the enemy rout beyond Rome, it could not afford the Germans the luxury of an unmolested retreat through the city. Despite Hitler's 3 June announcement declaring Rome an open city, the necessity for U.S. forces to immediately secure intact the many bridges over the Tiber River would certainly force a confrontation with the Germans, who, if allowed enough time, would likely blow the bridges. To that end, shortly after 0100 hours on 4 June General Frederick received a radio message from General Keyes, II Corps commander that read, "Secure bridges over the Tiber River above the 68 Northing within the City of Rome."[42]

Other American outfits, the 3rd, 85th and 88th Infantry Divisions, were closing on the city as well, and as one Colonel on the II Corps staff put it, "There was a horse race on to Rome." The mission to capture six of the Tiber bridges was given to Frederick not only in recognition of the fact that his command possessed the ability to get the job done in the way that was required, but also as a gesture on the part of II Corps to ensure that when the "great day" arrived the First Special Service Force would have the honor of sharing in "the kill." Frederick, while not being unaware of historical significance of the moment, was far more impressed by the urgency of his duty, and wasted no time implementing the Corps' order.[43]

At 0400 hours on 4 June, 2nd and 4th Companies of First Regiment were given the mission of securing the Tiber bridges in Rome. To carry out the mission, these Forcemen climbed onto the backs of tanks from Colonel Hamilton Howze's 13th Armored Infantry and by 0500 hours had started rolling westward down Highway 6. Behind the Force-Howze groupment followed elements of the 351st Infantry Regiment and eight armored cars of Company A of the 81st Armored Reconnaissance Battalion. By 0620 hours the head of the column had pierced the Rome city limits. At 0630 hours two leading tanks were suddenly hit by German antitank fire and put out of action. At this point the column stopped and the infantry dismounted and deployed. Immediately a hot firefight developed. A sizable force of German infantry supported by self-propelled

guns had taken up positions along a salient between Highway 6 and Via Pronestina. Ordered by Kesselring to win as much time as possible so that the remnants of his armies could escape through the city, these Germans clung to their lodgment tenaciously.[44]

At 0945 hours a five-man patrol was sent from Captain Gus M. Heilman's 2nd Company to see if a way for the tanks could be found around the impasse. At 1100 hours the rest of 2nd Company, supported by tanks, began to push out to the north in an effort to outflank the Germans. Come 1300 hours the whole of First Regiment, pivoting 90 degrees, jumped off on a northward thrust toward Acque Bollicante. Meanwhile Second and Third Regiments were advancing west from Tor Sapienza, a Roman suburb, and down Highway 5. By 1500 hours First Regiment had succeeded in turning the enemy position and had linked up with elements of Third Regiment. With that, Third Regiment was ordered to take over the advance to the Tiber Bridges. From this point on, Colonel Howze characterized the armor-infantry attack into the heart of Rome as, "smooth, a knockout." After spending the rest of the day clean-

Pause in the advance toward Rome. Forcemen rest on the roadside in the shade of an M-10 Tank Destroyer of the 601st Tank Destroy Battalion's Company C. (ECPA/France)

ing out the nests of snipers that were discovered remaining in and around the Acque Bollicante district, First and Second Regiments, with attached armor, were directed back to rear assembly areas for rest.[45]

Earlier that afternoon, while the battle on Highway 6 was still in full swing, General Clark with his staff called a meeting between Generals Keyes and Frederick and himself to find out what was holding up the advance. The episode, recounted in Adleman and Walton's, *Rome Fell Today*, bears particular mention:

"Impatiently, he [Clark] asked General Keyes and General Frederick for the reason. Frederick answered that he did not want to use artillery to blast the German block loose because of the number of civilians in the area. Clark refused to consider this much of a reason. 'I wouldn't hold up too long,' he told Frederick. 'We've got to get in there.' Just then one of the photographers accompanying Clark suggested that the three generals pose in front of a pole upon which was nailed a directional sign reading, Roma. After the photograph was taken, Clark said, 'Golly, Bob – I'd like to have that sign in my command post.'

"Frederick went up the pole himself after the sign, but, at that moment, a hidden German sniper, evidently unable to resist a target consisting of a trio of generals, cut loose with his Schmeisser. The three men dove into a nearby ditch and, before they crawled back to a safer position, Frederick surrendered to an irresistible urge. 'That,' he told Clark, 'is what's holding up the First Special Service Force!'"[46]

Cleaning out pockets of resistance as they were met, troops of Third Regiment were making their way toward the Tiber River as were small groups of Forcemen from the other regiments who had not received the order to stand down. Meanwhile throngs of jubilant Romans, somewhat prematurely celebrating their liberation, began flooding into every major thoroughfare and *piazza*. As the swelling humanity began to slow the forward progress of his troops, General Frederick decided to see for himself what was happening at the bridges. Utilizing a half-track for the purpose, Frederick, accompanied by Captain Newt McCall, two enlisted men and a driver broke away from the main advance and sped along the quiet side streets. Reaching the southern-most bridge in the Force zone the group dismounted and began searching for what demolition charges might be placed on the bridge. Alone, and well ahead of even

Howze Task Force armor rolls past Forcemen and Italian civilians. (ECPA/France)

Lt. Colonel J.F.R. Akehurst, senior Canadian officer, on the road to Rome. Akehurst was given command of Second Regiment on 1 May 1944, prior to the commencement of Operation BUFFALO, in order to maintain the command ratio – U.S. to Canadian – within the FSSF. (Lew Merrim)

Forcemen move up Highway 6 toward Rome in trucks. (ECPA/France)

Recent German prisoners are herded into the Force's temporary command post at Finocchio for interrogation. (Lew Merrim)

Hugging the ground, Forcemen lay fire upon the suspected position of an enemy sniper. A brick electrical transformer station stands in the background. (ECPA/France)

Surrounded by newsmen, Brigadier General Frederick (right); Lieutenant General Mark W. Clark, Fifth Army Commander (second from right); Brigadier General Donald W. Brann; and Major General Geoffrey Keyes study situation maps on the outskirts of Rome. General Frederick wears one of three original prototype V-42 knives delivered to the Force, distinguishable from the standard pattern by its bright stainless steel hilt and fittings. (National Archives)

On the outskirts of Rome, a Forceman prepares to fire his Bazooka. This man is additionally armed with an M-1 carbine and a V-42 fighting knife. Note the extra missiles that are carried in the canvas bag normally intended for the light weight gas mask. (ECPA/France)

Tanks and jeeps of the Howze Task Force race along Highway 6 into Rome. Riding on the rear decks of the tanks are Forcemen of Major G.W. McFadden's Provisional Battalion of First Regiment, 4 June 1944. (National Archives)

Members of Major Ed Thomas' Headquarters Detachment, 2nd Battalion, Second Regiment, race past a burning German Mark VI tank during the capture of Rome, 4 July 1944. (National Archives)

the most forward elements of his command, Frederick's party suddenly found itself being approached by a sizable number of enemy who themselves had designs on holding the bridge. Knowing not what else to do, Frederick commanded the Germans to, "Halt!" When the Germans kept coming, Frederick and his men opened fire. Three of the enemy were killed, twelve were captured. The rest fled. Frederick was hit twice, in the arm and in the leg, making three (he had been hit by a shell fragment earlier) his total number of wounds for the day. The driver of the half-track was killed in the exchange. Not wishing to temp fate a second time, Frederick and his group made contact with Force units then coming up. Taking some of these men along, Frederick then continued with further reconnaissances.[47]

By 2300 hours Force units held a total of eight of Rome's Tiber bridges. Luckily, through the rapid advance of the First Special Service Force and armored units of the Howze Task Force the enemy had been denied the time to prepare demolitions at any of the crossings. While Lt. Colonel John G. Bourne's 2nd Battalion of Third Regiment, with supporting armor, remained in Rome to guard the Tiber River bridges, the balance of the Force was directed to muster in Tor Sapienza.[48]

That evening, Frederick, at the insistence of Force medical officer, Major Arthur Neeseman, turned himself into a field hospital outside of the city. "Frederick had been hit three times that day. Added to his six previous wounds, he could now lay undisputed claim to being the most-shot-at-and-hit general in American history and he was finally willing to concede his mortality."[49] Impatient for his own recovery, Frederick stayed in the hospital only one night. The next morning he returned to Rome, there to stay with his Force until it was ordered to stand down.

On the morning of 5 June, the 91st Reconnaissance Squadron was attached to Frederick's command with the mission of screening the II Corps right flank. Later that morning the Howze Task Force was relieved of its attachment to Frederick. By the morning of the 6th, the FEC had moved into position north of Rome, and with that the 91st Reconnaissance Squadron was relieved of its screening duty and as well its attachment to the First Special Service Force. With 6 June, also came the announcement that the long-awaited landing of Allied forces on the occupied coast of France had begun. That evening, elements of the 3rd Division came up to relieve Lt. Colonel Bourne's battalion from its security duty along the Tiber River. Quickly the fighting moved north of Rome. During the night the Force began movement to bivouac near Lago Albano to await further orders.[50]

Force medics load a casualty into a half-track, Rome, evening of 4 June 1944. (National Archives)

Force casualty receives plasma before being loaded aboard an ambulance. (Lew Merrim)

U.S. Infantrymen file into Rome (right), as Forcemen leave the city passing under Porta Maggiore on their way to Tor Sapienza, c. 5 June 1944. (ECPA/France)

The evening of liberation. With German prisoners in tow, Leutenant Pringle leads his 4-2 platoon out of the Italian Capital down streets lined with jubilant Roman citizens. Porta Maggiore is in the background. (ECPA/France)

Map #4

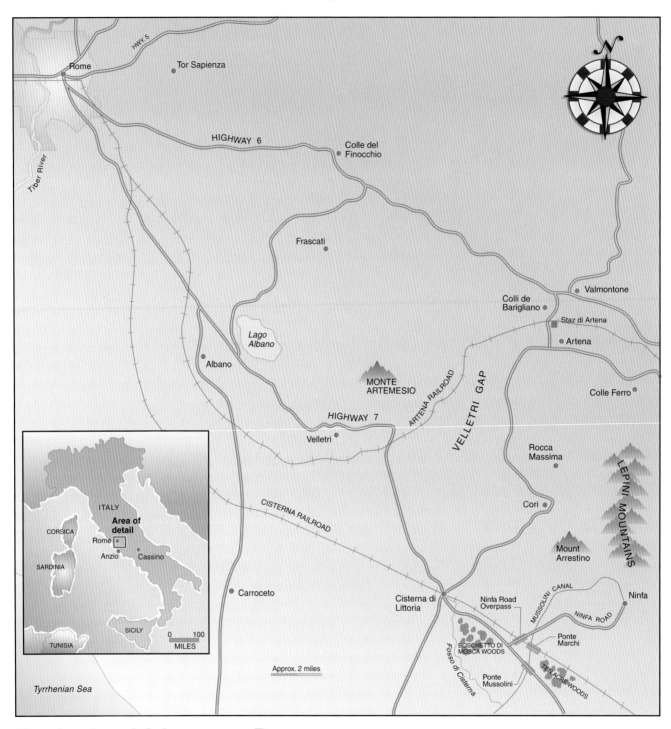

Breakout and Advance on Rome
23 May 1944 - 4 June 1944

Special Feature #6: Reports from Rome

Though an 88th Division reconnaissance platoon was given official wartime credit for having been first into Rome, modern historians concur that it was Frederick's North Americans who led the way into the city proper. After the war, the 88th Division's commander, Major General John E. Sloan, admitted that "the platoon wasn't strong enough to maintain its position inside the city limits . . ." and that ". . . the First Special Service Force beat us in strength. However, we followed them very closely, and in our race there with the Special Service Force, we actually collided and had a little fire fight due to a misunderstanding between the two forces."[1] Sworn statements by key officers and men who were among the leading Force elements, were prepared and submitted to Fifth Army historians shortly after the fall of Rome. The facsimiles of these reports that appear on the following pages, prepared from the original documents, illustrate well the hectic sequence of events. (Continued on page 317.)

SUBJECT: Patrol to Rome

TO: Robert T. Frederick, Brigadier General, USA
          Commanding, First Special Service Force

On the morning of 2 June 1944 while the 3rd Regiment First Special Service Force was pushing from Artena, Italy Southwest toward Colle Ferro, 3rd Regiment Commander, Colonel Edwin Walker received a call from General Robert Frederick about 0730 hours requesting I report to Force Headquarters for a special mission.

I was instructed to report to Major General Keyes, II Corps Commander for a secret mission, taking with me one special picked enlisted man from each Regiment of the Force. These men were Sgt. T. W. Phillips of Seguin, Texas from the 1st Regiment, S/Sgt. K. R. S. Mieklejohn of Edmonton, Alberta Canada from the 2nd Regiment, and Sgt. J. E. Brannon of Princeton, New Jersey from the 3rd Regiment. Upon reporting to II Corps Headquarters, I was informed I was to lead a patrol of picked men from each unit within II Corps, with an Officer from the 91st Reconnaissance Squadron as my second in command. These men were to come from II Corps Infantry, Artillery, AAA, Engineers, MPs, etc., and were all picked for their outstanding performance and courage. I was told the reason that an Officer from the Force had been selected to lead the mission, was because of the Force's ability to get the job done in the way that he wanted it conducted, and that it was only fitting that the Officer should come from one of his best units.

The enemy had been fighting a strong rear guard action for two days astride Highway 6 and Via Tuscolana guarding the way to Rome, and had beaten off all attempts of our troops to push [them] off the Alban Hills until the morning of 2 June 1944, when they started withdrawing to the North.

Our mission was to leave II Corps with 60 men, 18 jeeps, and 2 M-8s and in any way possible get into Rome ahead of other Allied forces, send back the enemy situation within the City, and at the same time post II Corps route signs along prominent streets and in public squares. Our mission organization included one movie camera man, two still camera men, and a news reporter, attached for media coverage on the patrol.

We departed II Corps Headquarters at 1400 hours, 3 June, 1944 after organizing and forming elaborate plans as none of the assigned personnel had ever worked together before. Our convoy headed for Frascati, Italy where we were to pass through the 338th Infantry and join the Ellis Task Force from the 91st Reconnaissance Squadron, which was spearheading the drive on Rome in our assigned sector. We were to accompany this unit as far as possible as they had tanks and tank destroyers attached and could provide us needed support until we could break away and swing ahead. They were to help us also in case we were cut off in any way or got into so much trouble we couldn't handle it. Upon arriving in the vicinity of Frascati we were informed by the C.O. 2nd Battalion 338th Infantry that the Ellis Task Force had passed through them about an hour ago. In about 15 minutes we found a long convoy of troops and tanks stalled on the road by fire from snipers. We proceed to pass the convoy as we had been given first priority passes on all roads within II Corps Sector by General Keyes. As we passed the lead tank of the convoy, I noticed a bewildered look on the tank commander's face, but thought nothing of it at the time.

We proceeded at about 15 MPH thinking all the time that the area was clear except for snipers because when we asked members of the convoy who they were, they said that they were from the 88th Division. In about 5 minutes we were fired on by snipers from a group of houses which held us up until we could deploy and clear them. We captured 2 and killed 2 enemy at this point. Proceeding again we were fired on by

- 2 -

---

2 Jerry self-propelled guns and an unknown number of snipers with machine guns. We immediately deployed and prepared to fight. Upon hearing the firefight, lead tanks of the convoy came forward and engaged the SPs knocking out 1 and causing the other to withdraw. We then advanced with one platoon of infantry from the convoy and found a road block in the form of a bridge out, covered by enemy infantry with machine guns. We forced them to withdraw killing 2, wounding 2, and taking 4 prisoners. A bulldozer then came forward and constructed a bypass.

During the delay, I went back to the convoy that had pulled up behind us and started a conversation with the lead tank captain. His first words were, 'What in hell are you doing here, are you crazy or lost?' I told him that we were trying to catch the Ellis Task Force. He said, 'Hell man that's us!' We had been leading the main task Force for the last 7 miles without knowing it.

When the bypass was completed we dropped behind the lead tanks and TDs and proceeded on our way to Rome. Twice we were held up by fire from our front and flanks, and once by an enemy counter attack consisting of tanks and infantry which destroyed one TD and one tank before we could continue.

At night fall we were stalled south of the city near some large radio towers by enemy tanks. After a short fight, we were able to advance to an area near the movie studios south of Rome on Via Tuscolana, where by dawn the Ellis Task Force had forced the enemy to start withdrawing. During this period we took 10 prisoners and killed one enemy. Up to this time the Task Force had lost 2 tanks, 1 TD and 5 killed. My group had one slightly wounded assigned to us from the 3rd Division Battle Patrol Group.

Receiving information that the Force was closing in on Rome to our right we swung out in front of the Task Force to complete our mission. All morning another group of camera men and news reporters were reported trying to pull ahead of us but lost their ambition when fired on by snipers. At the city limits we found an overpass prepared for demolition but due to our rapid advance the enemy didn't have time to blow it. We cut the wires before the charges could cause any damage and crossed into Rome at 0600 hours passing under the gate at Via Tuscolana while our camera men took documenting pictures. At this time we came under intense machine gun fire which forced us back across the overpass. From 0600 until 1100 hours we fought with the Task Force in the overpass area and at 1200 hours we decided to try it again. We passed under the gate the second time and proceeded about 500 yards into the apartment area of Rome where we were stopped by Italian civilians informing us that just around the corner was a Tiger tank. Our scouts reported the tank also.

By this time the Germans realized that we were bringing in no heavy stuff so they moved in another tank to cover our escape route and one about two blocks up the street on our main route into the city. We had a 12 foot wall to our rear and a bank in front of us which was our only advantage. They had us completely cut off. The enemy then sent in two platoons of infantry to eliminate us but we drove them off with fire from our M-8s and 50 Cal MGs mounted on some of our jeeps. One of our M-8s parked just around the corner from the Tiger tank waited for him to advance. This would have been about like a bee against an elephant. The tank advanced about 200 feet and then for some reason stopped. Two of the crew got out and our men cut them down. The remaining crew then opened up blasting everything in sight. Fortunately for us we were behind the bank and all shells went over our head and all air burst were too high and far away. I radioed back for TD or tank support as they could cross the overpass without danger from the machine guns and snipers. They only sent us 2 more jeeps and 2 more M-8s. We were running low on ammo and decided that we had better get out if possible. We had a lot of close ones but no patrol member was

---

hit except for approximately 10 Italian Partisans who had joined us and tried to charge the tanks with only Thompson submachine guns. They were all killed.

We had been sweating out mortars but learned that the Force was cutting in to our right taking away any advantage the Jerries had. In one place where the Jerries tried to place a mortar, other Italians dropped grenades on them from 2nd story locations forcing them to give it up.

The tank to our rear had us cut off but could do no damage where we were. I sent a bazooka team to try and disable him. They fired two rounds hitting him in the tracks and causing him to swing his gun around leaving our escape temporarily free. Why he didn't fire at our reinforcements when they came up isn't known. This was the chance we had been waiting for so we loaded and went like hell back to the overpass.

Before we all got out the enemy tank had covered the street again and made a direct hit on the jeep in front of me killing all passengers including 2 Italians and one Frenchman that had joined us. Before he could reload our last two jeeps passed through his field of fire. On returning I gave enemy locations to Colonel Ellis and then went back to the movie studios to rest, reload and eat.

At 1830 hours we went back to the same area and found the 88th Division and some tanks in a fire fight which had been going on for the last few hours. The infantry in our area was all confused because they couldn't destroy some machine guns that were causing their problems. S/Sgt. Miecklejohn took a patrol of our men to knock them out but the Jerries withdrew when he realized that positive action was starting against them. The tankers had taken considerable casualties but due to the strength caused the enemy infantry to withdraw. The enemy tankers then surrendered or withdrew leaving the rest of the way into Rome clear.

During the entire period our camera men had been taking pictures and posting our II Corps signs [which read "Follow the Blue To Speedy II"]. They were also the first reporters and cameramen into Rome. As soon as the forward convoys started to move again we went back to the movie studios and spent the night planning to return the next day and complete our picture mission. The M-8 tank commander that parked his vehicle to stop the Tiger received a Silver Star, all killed received the Silver Star, and all other personnel received the Bronze Star for their heroic action on this mission.

                                    T. M. Radcliffe
                                    Capt. First Special Service Force
                                    Patrol Commander

- 3 -

Special Feature #6: Reports from Rome

HEADQUARTERS FIRST SPECIAL SERVICE FORCE
APO 4994, U.S. ARMY

10 July 1944

SUBJECT: Entry of First Special Service Force
           Into City of Rome.

TO: Commanding General, Fifth Army,
           APO 464, U.S. Army.

1.   Reference is made to message number 485, Headquarters Invasion Training Center, 6 July 1944, requesting authentication report as to time and place of entry of elements of this command into the City of Rome.

2.   Attached are the affidavits of Captain Gus M. Heilman and Sergeant Frank D. Welch of this command, stating the facts concerning the entry into the City of Rome for the leading elements of this command. The foremost elements of this command in the approach on Rome on 4 June 1944 were the 2d and 4th companies of the First Regiment. These companies formed the infantry component of an infantry-tank column approaching the city along Highway 6. The tanks of this column were provided by the 13th Armored Regiment. The column arrived at what is presumed to be the city boundary at 0630 hours. At this point there was a large sign on Highway 6, stating in one word, ROMA. This point is located on Map ITALY, 1:50,000, Sheet 150 IV ROMA, at the point 809644. The two leading tanks were put out of action at this point by anti-tank fire and the infantry deployed. Heavy fighting at the locality of this road junction prevented further movement until 1100 hours, at which time Captain Heilman's company attacked to the northwest. His attack reached a street intersection at 790664 at 1700 hours. At 1800 hours this company was passed through and relieved by the second Regiment of the First Special Service Force which had approached the city generally along the road and railroad from Tor Sapienza.

3.   At about 0945 hours, Captain Heilman sent a patrol under the command of Sergeant Welch to enter Rome, approaching from the south of Highway 6, to reconnoiter tank approaches into the city which would bypass the resistance the unit had encountered at 0600 and was still fighting. This patrol moved south from Highway 6 to the main road lying between Highway 6 and 7. The patrol moved into the city and reached a street intersection near 788638 at 1230 hours. It then retraced its steps and encountered the special column of selected troops from all units on this same road at a point near 605625.

4.   The Second Regiment of this command by-passed the First Regiment and turning south, continued into the city as far as the Railroad Station. The Third Regiment passed through the First Regiment and continued through the northern section of the city to the Piazza di Popolo, arriving there at 2100 hours and occupied the northern eight bridges across the Tiber. These bridges were secured by 2300 hours.

5.   At the time of the attack on Rome I was in command of the Third Regiment of this force.

EDWIN A. WALKER
Colonel, 1st Special Service Force,
Commanding.

APO 4994
New York, New York
10 July 1944

Statement of Captain Gus M. Heilman concerning entry of First Special Service Force Troops into the City of Rome on 4 June 1944.

Reference Map: ITALY, 1:50,000 - Sheet 150 IV Roma.

On 4 June 1944 I was commanding Second Company, First Regiment, First Special Service Force in the drive on the City of Rome. At about 0500 hours a column of tanks with infantry mounted on top of tanks was formed to push rapidly into the center of Rome with the mission of taking the bridges over the Tiber River. The tanks in this column formed one battalion of the 13th Armored Regiment. This battalion of medium tanks and tank destroyers was commanded by Lieutenant Colonel Kairns. Fourth Company, First Regiment, commanded by Captain Jennings, rode astride the leading tanks of this column. My company rode on the tanks immediately in the rear of Captain Jenning's company. At approximately 0630 hours the head of the column arrived at a large sign marked, "Roma", located on Highway 6 at 809644. At this point the two leading tanks of the column were knocked out by German anti-tank weapons. The infantry deployed, and heavy fighting continued throughout the morning. At 1100 hours my company moved forward from its deployed positions in an attack to clear the enemy from the sector north and west of the road junction (8085644). Our attack, supported by tanks, arrived at the next phase line at approximately 1500 hours. This phase line is the street 791657-796658. At about 1530 hours I was ordered to continue the attack forward from my deployed position and arrived at 1700 hours along the road Via Pronestina, east of point 789644. At 1800 hours the Second Regiment, First Special Service Force, approaching Rome along Via Pronestina, made contact with my company, relieved me, and carried the attack on through the City. In support of my attack and in rear of me was one company from the 88th Division. I am sure that no troops were able to enter Rome on Highway 6 until after my attack had cleared out the resistance north of Highway 6. Some time after my attack had cleared out this resistance, the Fourth Company, First Regiment, Then commanded by Major McFadden, proceeded from the Roma sign forward into the city along Highway 6. I do not know the exact time of movement of this column but it was some time after my company had moved forward.

GUS M. HEILMAN
Captain, 1st Special Service Force.

Sworn and subscribed to before me this 10th day of July 1944.

RICHARD W. WHITNEY,
Major, 1st Special Service Force,
Adjutant.

A F F I D A V I T

APO   )
                 : SS
New York N.Y.   )

Before me, the undersigned, authorized to administer oaths in cases of this character, appeared Frank D. Welch, 39176613, Sergeant, Second Company, First Regiment, First Special Service Force, who being duly sworn states:

"On the morning of 4 June 1944, as a member of the Second Company, First Regiment, First Special Service Force, I was proceeding into the City of Rome along Highway 6 as part of an assault column of tanks and infantry. At 0630 hours the head of the column arrived at a large sign on the highway reading, "Roma." This sign is located at approximately 809644. Heavy fighting developed in this sector. At about 0945 hours, Captain Heilman, my company commander, sent me in command of a patrol of five men to move south from our position on Highway 6 and reconnoiter other routes on which the armor and infantry could proceed further into Rome. I proceeded back along Highway 6 to the road junction at 825638, then turned south to the road junction at 817615. At this point I captured a number of German vehicles and three prisoners. Because of the density of enemy fire I decided to send back three members of my patrol with the prisoners and equipment. Private Ferretti, Third Company, First Regiment, and I then proceeded further into Rome, moving along the road RJ-817615 - street intersection 787638. Moving along this road, we crossed the railroad tracks and arrived at the street intersection at 1230 hours. Returning along my original route, I met a reconnaissance unit of armored cars and jeeps and personnel from all units attacking Rome. I met this column on the road at a point about 605625, where I stopped and talked to Staff Sergeant T.W. Phillips, a member of my company who had been assigned to enter Rome with this column. I then returned cross-country to the road intersection near the Roma sign to render my report. I arrived at this road intersection at about 1530 and found that only the aid station of my regiment remained at this point."

FRANK D. WELCH, 39176613
Sergeant, 2d Co, 1st Regt,
1st Special Service Force.

Sworn and subscribed to before me this 10th day of July 1944.

RICHARD W. WHITNEY,
Major, 1st Special Service Force,
Adjutant.

HEADQUARTERS
FIRST REGIMENT
FIRST SPECIAL SERVICE FORCE

A.P.O. 4994, c/o P.M.,
New York, N.Y.
12 July 1944

SUBJECT: Entry of Second Regiment into Rome.

TO: Commanding Officer, First Special Service Force.

1.   At the time of the First Special Service Force's entry into ROME on 4 June 1944 I was in command of the Second Regiment.

2.   At 0400; hours, 4 June, the Second Regiment reached its objective, namely the road running due SOUTH from TOR SAPIENZA to HIGHWAY 6. At that time, accompanied by S Sgt. Riggs and Tec 4 Delcamp, I reached 3 KM post on the road entering ROME from the EAST parallel to and immediately NORTH of HIGHWAY 6, where we watched 3d Co. under Capt. Dogherty come up into position.

3.   At 1530 hours the Second Regiment left TOR SAPIENZA having been given orders to advance on ROME astride the railroad line running into the CENTRAL STATION from the NE. In this operation it was supported by two companies of tanks from Col. Howze's regiment of the First Armored Division.

4.   At 1915 hours, 4 June, 4th Co. under Capt. W. M. W. Wilson, and 5th Co. under Lt. H. M. Savage, accompanied by Major S. C. Waters, O.C. Second Bn., reached PONTE MAGGIORE, and at 2000 hours entered the CENTRAL RY. STATION.

5.   At 1915 hours, 4 June, 6th Co. under Lt. W. H. Langdon entered PLAZA VENIZZA where for approximately half an hour they were engaged in a fire fight with at least one armored car and to mechanized vehicles carrying enemy troops. In this fight Lt. Langdon lost three men killed and eight wounded.

J. F. R. Akehurst,
Lt. Col., 1st Sp Sv Force,
Commanding.

Special Feature #7: Cannon Company - Darby's Ace in the Hole Joins the Force

Along with the large number of former Darby's Rangers that either volunteered or who were assigned as replacements, the First Special Service Force inherited the Ranger organization's Cannon Company. The Cannon Company consisted of four White Motor Company M-3 Gun Motor Carriages – vehicles that mated an M-1897A 75mm field gun (also known as a "French 75") to the chassis of an M-3 half-track. Colonel William O. Darby called Cannon Company his "ace in the hole." In due course aces appeared on the four half-tracks, painted on the gunshields and elsewhere, uniquely identifying each as either *Hearts*, *Diamonds*, *Clubs*, or *Spades*.[1]

Each half-track's six-man crew consisted of a commander/radio operator, a driver, a gunner, an assistant gunner, a loader, and an assistant loader. Up to 200 rounds of 75mm high explosive, armor piercing, and white phosphorous ammunition could be stored aboard each vehicle in both factory-made and improvised bins. In addition to the main gun, each half-track was typically armed with a .30 caliber M-1919A4 light machine gun at the 'track commander's position and a .50 caliber M-2HB machine gun mounted in the rear bed of the 'track. 81mm and 60mm mortars with ammunition were also carried aboard each vehicle but were used in the normal ground mode. Extra rations, supplies, and personal items were carried in the field expedient open stowage compartments that were welded to, and which extended the width of and eighteen inches beyond the rear of each 'track.[2]

The Cannon Company (or *Platoon* as it was often called by other Forcemen referring to the small scale of this adjunct) was commanded by a First Lieutenant and had a Second Lieutenant as his executive. The company headquarters further contained a clerk, a scout/messenger, a radio operator, and a medic. Rounding out the company was a small motor pool section headed by a motor pool Sergeant, a mess Sergeant and some cooks, and – as one member described them – *other hangers on*.[3]

Fully motorized, the company was additionally equipped with two motorcycles (one most often used by the company commander, the other by his messenger) and several Willy's jeeps to carry its motor pool and other personnel. To fill its further needs for transportation in southern France, several civilian luxury cars were commandeered on an unofficial basis. As the Force lacked organic artillery, the Cannon Company filled a practical need. As had been the case with Darby and his Rangers, Frederick relied on the M-3 Gun Motor Carriages to provide his fast moving Force available artillery support when and where it was needed. In southern France, the half-track's guns, augmenting attached howitzers, provided effective fire against point targets well forward and were often used for armored reconnaissance. Because the guns were self-propelled, they could fire and then quickly shift to a new position, thus confusing the enemy's counter battery fire.[4] (Continued on page 318.)

Cannon Company's "Hearts" M-3 gun motor carriage with crew in front of stone house in which they took up temporary residence, southern France, 1944. L-r: Nelson E. Rice, Assistant Gunner; David L. Bens, 'track Commander; Frank J. Cleary, Loader; and Balcom, Driver. (David L. Bens)

W.E. Ketchens stands in front of the Force Cannon Company's "Diamond" 'track in Castellar, southern France, 1944. (Note the black diamond edged in white painted on the left front fender of the M-3 gun motor carriage. Ketchens joined the Force from Darby's Rangers and his Ranger scroll is stitched above the spearhead on his left shoulder. (David L. Bens)

CHAPTER 9

The Last Campaign

On the night of 6/7 June, the Force was relieved of its screening job on the II Corps right flank, and assembled in Tor Sapienza in preparation for movement to Lago Albano. There the Force would reorganize and recover from its exertions of the last few weeks in anticipation for whatever new mission Fifth Army commanded.

The Force moved into bivouac at Lago Albano on 7 June. That evening a German soldier, apparently a straggler, wandered into Third Regiment's area and was snared. Civilians reported that other enemy soldiers, some possibly deserters, were hiding out in the vicinity. These Germans, separated from their fleeing countrymen either by accident or on purpose, were, as individuals or small bands, raiding the local farms for food, and were generally stirring up trouble. The next day, three companies, one from each regiment, were dispatched into the surrounding hills to search for "enemy stragglers, documents and equipment, minefields and bridges prepared for demolition." However, in this instance the rumors turned out to be just that, with all patrols netting negative results.[1]

Sixteen miles from Rome, Lago Albano was a large, circular lake that filled the cone of a long-extinct volcano. On the shore of the lake was nestled the resort, Castel Gandolfo, that since the 17th century had been the summer retreat of the popes as it incorporated a papal residency, Villa Barberini, and its surrounding gardens. For most of the first week there, the Force shared the lake with throngs of French *Goumier*, who, like pilgrims of a gentler time, came to the lake to swim and recreate. Passes to both Rome and Naples were granted, and the men spent them taking in the sights and indulging other sundry pleasures. However, on 12 June, the Force got back down to business.[2]

No doubt the abrupt change of signals was due to an alert by Fifth Army that the Force be "prepared to make an assault landing in the rear of the current enemy front lines to assist the advance of the Fifth Army."[3] Until further notice training resumed on a fixed schedule: from 0800-1130 hours, then a lunch break, and then picking up in the afternoon from 1300-1600 hours. Shake down, resupply and re-equipping was made a priority. Canadian and U.S. replacements that the Force had just received, four officers and 213 enlisted men in all, were to as quickly as possible be assimilated into units. Stressing marksmanship, refresher training on all weapons was carried out on improvised ranges located on the northern shore of the lake. Bayonet drill was practiced, and physical conditioning in the form of calisthenics and marching was applied. Other military subjects were mixed in as well – map reading and use of the compass, personal hygiene, first aid, and construction of field fortifications. Scouting and patrolling exercises were carried out in an area southwest of the lake. Meanwhile, a tennis court near the Force command post was commandeered by Captain D.M. O'Neill and put to use as a classroom for teaching his hand-to-hand combat techniques. In all courses, the acclimation of Canadian replacements was given precedence.[4]

While the Forcemen trained, Force headquarters personnel busily drafted and redrafted assault landing plans based on the rapidly changing enemy front lines. Soon, however, the need for an amphibious operation by the Force passed altogether, as the weak German resistance of the moment obviated the need for such a landing. Yet training now continued as a matter of course.[5]

On 23 June 1944, the First Special Service Force paraded in a ceremony where a number of men were awarded the Sil-

Parade for awards earned during the breakout and capture of Rome, Castelabate, Italy, 23 June 1944. (Lew Merrim)

ver Star by General Frederick. Upon the conclusion of that ceremony Frederick addressed his men. "One of a general's pleasant jobs is to decorate soldiers with the medals they have so richly earned, . . . and one of the toughest jobs for a general is to say good-bye to an outfit he loves."[6] Stunned by the news most of the Forcemen stood speechless in wide-eyed disbelief, as though their family was being split up.

It was perhaps Frederick's nimble handling of the array of units at his disposal during action in the Winter Line or during the drive on Rome that had marked him for higher command. Shortly after the Force arrived at Lago Albano, the prospect had cropped up that General Frederick take over the reins of the 36th Infantry Division. This course seemed very likely, but only a few days before the transfer was to take effect, Frederick received new orders countermanding his move to the 36th, instead, assigning him the job of creating and leading a provi-

sional airborne division in the invasion of southern France, Operation DRAGOON. Upon assuming command, Frederick would receive his second star – a promotion to Major General. The 1st Airborne Task Force, Frederick's new unit, would be cobbled together from British and American airborne outfits currently in the Mediterranean, or that would soon be arriving. Among those units being seconded to Frederick's new command was the 463rd Parachute Field Artillery Battalion, it being relieved of its attachment to the Force on 30 June 1944, so ending the two units' long association.[7]

Ground forces for Operation DRAGOON were being organized under the control of Lt. General Alexander M. Patch, who had been named commander of the U.S. Seventh Army in March 1944. Patch had been given his choice of Fifth Army units from which to flesh out his Seventh. He selected the U.S. VI Corps, comprised of several veteran U.S. infantry divisions,

General Frederick address the Force at Castelabate, Italy, announcing his reassignment to the 1st Airborne Task Force. (Lew Merrim)

Trading good-byes with his officers; here General Frederick extends a firm handshake to Lt. William S. Story. (Lew Merrim)

including the 3rd, 36th, and 45th; and, not surprisingly, he requested and secured the transfer of the First Special Service Force.[8]

After an emotional farewell, General Frederick departed Lago Albano to take command of the 1st Airborne Task Force. Colonel Kenneth G. Wickham would, soon after, leave the Force as well, to join Frederick as his executive officer. Replacing Frederick as Commander of the First Special Service Force was Colonel Edwin A. Walker, formerly Third Regiment Commander.[9] Canadian, Lt. Colonel R.W. 'Bill' Becket was given command of Third Regiment. Lt. Colonel Robert S. Moore had Second Regiment, and Lt. Colonel J.F.R. Akehurst, senior Canadian, was placed in command of First Regiment.

As July opened, the Force made preparations for movement south to a new training area. However, a small segment of the Service Battalion would remain behind at Santa Maria di Capua-Vetere until after the invasion, when a permanent base on the French mainland – eventually it would be located in Nice – could be established. In addition to the vehicles organic to the Force, some 140 trucks were secured from Transportation Section, PBS, for movement of supplies and personnel to the new training area. At the same time, two quarter-ton trucks and five half-tracks equipped with SCR-193 and SCR-284 radios were secured for use in future operations. When all was ready, the Force moved overland from Lago Albano to the port of Anzio. There the men boarded transports that took them by sea to Salerno where the Force debarked and once again took to the roads to cover the final leg of the trip. On 4 July 1944, the Force opened camp at its new training station at Santa Maria di Castelabate, Italy. Immediately it received 48 enlisted personnel as replacements. After settling in to its new surroundings, the Force commenced with amphibious training in earnest, carried out jointly with the resources of the Invasion Training Center. To this was added the specialized training that was customary to the Force – save for parachute training as a scarcity of equipment and available aircraft made this impossible.[10]

Amphibious training emphasized "rubber boat landings using APDs and LCIs for Naval transports. The LCIs proved to be unsatisfactory for this type of operation and were released. The Naval transports lying off about 7,000 yards; debarking personnel into rubber boats; landing craft towing rubber boats to 1,000 yards from shore and then paddling rubber boats to shore, landing on cliffy shores. Physical condition, night operations, and military discipline were also stressed. . . . Naval beach marking parties and Naval Shore Fire Control parties were attached to the Force for training during the entire training period."[11]

After the formal ceremony, Frederick exchanges farewells with Force Senior officers, and then departs. (Lew Merrim)

Training at Castelabate came nearer to completion with field exercises undertaken separately by each regiment. Each exercise comprised all phases of an amphibious operation of the type that the Force had been preparing for over the last nine weeks. "Beach marking, assault landing at night on rocky beaches from rubber boats, scaling cliffs with full combat load, attacking rapidly inland to secure objectives and prepare for counterattack, and selection and preparation of beach for landing of supplies."[12]

The Force's preparation had been rigorous. The personnel roster reflected this, recording the loss of some 688 officers and enlisted men as non-battle casualties and two enlisted men as killed during the nine-week period. One of those killed was the victim of the Mediterranean's strong undertow, while the other fatality was due to a house cave-in unrelated to training.

Second Regiment officers aboard the U.S.S. *John Cropper* en route from Anzio to Salerno, 2 July 1944. Left to right: First Lieutenant Clifford Cook, First Lieutenant James Stevenson, Captain Adna H. Underhill, and Major George Evashwick. (Herb Langdon)

Lost to the Force as well were another 255 officers and men who were transferred from the regiments and the Service Battalion. Yet these losses were offset by the return to active duty of some 663 officers and men who had either been on light duty or in hospital. By the close of July the Force numbered 159 officers and 2,356 enlisted men.[13]

By the beginning of August, 1944, plans were being finalized for a combined training exercise by the Force, with all attached Naval personnel, against the islands of Isola di Ponza and Zannone, which lay approximately fifty miles west of Naples in the Gulf of Gaeta. This would be the dress rehearsal for the Force's upcoming mission, and would be carried out in an identical fashion as was foreseen for the actual combat operation. As would be the case, plans were coordinated with the Naval personnel concerned, and all Force personnel were briefed in detail as to their individual responsibilities and objectives. From 7-9 August the practice mission was conducted. Leaving Castelabate at 1300 hours on the 7th, the Force, minus administrative and Service Battalion personnel sailed aboard APDs and troopships to the waters off the coast of the islands. At H-hour, First Regiment landed on Zannone, while Second and Third Regiments landed simultaneously on Ponza.

Left to right: Captain Sheldon C. Sommers, Medical Detachment, Service Battalion, (formerly Surgeon of the 1st Ranger Infantry Battalion) and Lt. Colonel Bill Becket aboard the U.S.S. *John Cropper*. (Herb Langdon)

By 0630 the following morning, both islands were 'reduced,' and the regiments set about securing the islands against a hypothetical counterattack. By 1300 hours the Force and attachments were all back aboard their transports and on their way back to Castelabate. Next day, Force officers and headquarters personnel with participating Naval commanders gathered at

Captain Preston R. Thaxton of Force Headquarters Detachment lectures on demolition techniques to men of 1st Battalion, Second Regiment, Castelabate, Italy. (Herb Langdon)

Castelabate where the results of the training mission were dissected and critiqued. In all but a few respects the practiced procedures were, with only minor adjustment, found to be adequate for the actual invasion.[14]

Now the countdown for the invasion of southern France began. The Force's combat regiments, along with elements of the Service Battalion, attached Naval shore fire control parties, and Naval beach marking parties embarked onto five American transports: the U.S.S. *Green*, U.S.S. *Barry*, U.S.S. *Osmond Ingram*, APD U.S.S. *Tattnall*, and U.S.S. *Roper*, and two Canadian LSIMs: the H.M.C.S. *Prince Baudouin*, and the H.M.C.S. *Prince Henry*. At 1245 hours on 11 August, in convoy with Naval escort, the Force departed Castelabate and sailed to Propriano, Corsica to stage. In addition to the troopships, the convoy contained the battleship H.M.S. *Ramilles*, the heavy cruiser U.S.S. *Augusta*, five light cruisers, three destroyers including the H.M.S. *Lookout*, sixteen PT boats, and fifteen small craft.[15]

Dropping anchor in Corsica's Gulf of Valencio, all Force personnel moved to shore and from 12-13 August took up temporary bivouac on Corsica where the men were allowed the opportunity to rest, clean weapons and equipment, and relax. More importantly, the men were now let in on their exact target for the invasion and were given detailed final instructions. The Force was part of the SITKA Task Force under the overall command of Rear Admiral Lyal A. Davidson, whose flagship was the U.S.S. *Augusta*. On the morning of 14 August, Force and other personnel again boarded their assigned ships. Aside from the First Special Service Force, the convoy also carried the 700 men of Lt. Colonel Georges-Regis Bouvet's African Commandos, who would undertake a separate landing near

Platoon of 3-2 trains in wire-breaching techniques, Castelabate, Italy 6 July 1944. (Herb Langdon)

Cavaliere le Lavandou on the French mainland. At 1000 hours the SITKA Task Force weighed anchor and steamed toward southern France.[16]

Briefing revealed to the men that they were to attack and take control of the Isle du Levant and the Isle de Port-Cros, two islands in the d'Hyeres group situated several miles off the coast of France on the left flank of the invasion beaches. The regiments, with elements of the Service Battalion and attached Naval personnel, would land on the islands before daylight. Ashore, they were to wipe out the islands' defenders and destroy a strategic gun battery on the eastern tip of Levant before the landings on the mainland occurred. Reconnaissance photographs indicated the presence of a battery of four 6.5-inch guns located near the Phare du Titan lighthouse on Ile de Levant. This battery was well within range of the western zones of the thirty-seven-mile-long stretch of Riviera coastline that

A group from First Lieutenant Percy M. Crichlow's 1st Platoon (3-2), gets acquainted with the SCR-625 mine detector, Castelabate, Italy, 13 July 1944. (Herb Langdon)

Lieutenant Boyd A. Humphrey (standing, center) oversees the training of his 2nd Platoon (3-2) in mine removal. Castelabate, Italy, 13 July 1944. (Herb Langdon)

Men of 3 Company, Second Regiment in rubber assault boats being towed by LCVPs, Castelabate, Italy, 15 July, 1944. (Herb Langdon)

Men of 3 Company, Second Regiment seated in rubber assault boats practice being towed by LCVPs. Cliff scaling area can be seen in background. Castelabate, Italy 15 July 1944. (Herb Langdon)

had been selected as the place for the U.S. VI Corps to land. In fact, plans for the U.S. 3rd Infantry Division to come ashore at Cavalaire-sur-Mer were only agreed to on the condition that the Titan battery be attacked and destroyed before H-hour.[17]

Colonel Walker's plan of attack called for landing his three regiment's simultaneously on the two islands – First on Port-Cros, Second and Third on Levant – by the seaward approach, up steep cliffs. Walker reasoned, and rightly so, that all prob-

able landing sights had been heavily wired and mined. Undoubtedly these beaches would be defended. The cliffs became his natural choice. Besides, the Forcemen were well suited to such a challenge. Many on Seventh Army's staff doubted the wisdom in Walker's choice of landing areas. From reconnaissance photographs, it appeared that the sheer cliffs might prove difficult to scale and thus lead to disaster. Walker shot back: "'But that's why I want it!' . . . 'Don't you realize that the Germans have figured it out exactly the same way? In other words, there are ninety-nine chances out of a hundred that this area of the island is the most weakly defended – precisely because it's the hardest to attack!'"[18]

Three islands make up the Iles d'Hyeres which lie approximately twenty-five miles east of Toulon, and some seven miles offshore. Ile de Port-Cros, the middle of the trio, is approximately three miles long at its longest point. Ile du Levant is just under six miles long. Proper beaches were few and meager at best. Movement inland would be difficult through wild tangles of scrub-pine and Myrtle, an incredibly dense foliage called *maqui* by the natives. There were few roads, and only scattered patches under cultivation. Added to First Regiment's list of obstacles to overcome, "Port-Cros contained three small forts dating from the seventeenth and nineteenth centuries."[19] The third island in the group, Porquerolles, lay roughly ten miles to the west of Port Cros. Though the island contained a number of shore batteries and a German garrison of over 200 troops, it, because of its distance from the landing beaches, posed no threat and so would be bypassed. Once Levant and

LEFT: Major Robert B. Holt (seated, foreground), Major Edward H. Thomas (standing), Captain Adna H. Underhill (behind Thomas), and First Lieutenant James Stevenson (standing at rail), aboard destroyer during amphibious training offshore of Castelabate, Italy, 15 July 1944. (Herb Langdon)

Port-Cros were secured French troops would move in to garrison the islands. On Port-Cros the French would also guard a large radar station that was to be immediately established on the island. This radar was considered an urgently needed asset to future operations.[20]

In terms of intelligence, most of the information about the islands and the Titan battery gathered thus far had been the result of aerial inspections. Agents in the French Underground had also reported the existence of the battery. But at least one person, French Naval officer, Commander Yann Le Hagre, had raised doubt, asserting that the guns had been destroyed in November 1942, the same month as had seen the scuttling of the French Fleet. Le Hagre then related to Patch's staff an account that lent credence to his view. On 8 June 1944, the French submarine *Casabianca*, while running on the surface under a full moon, had engaged a German patrol boat in the waters under the very nose of the Titan battery. Throughout the thirteen minute exchange, silence had been the only response registered by the Titan guns. To Le Hagre, there could only be one reason. Yet to General Patch's staff, evidence contained in aerial reconnaissance photographs spoke more loudly than the opinion of one French officer.[21]

In order to gain a clearer picture of just what was happening on the Iles d'Hyeres, the U.S. Navy offered that a submarine be used to carry out a pre-attack periscope reconnaissance. If the results of this were inconclusive, then the Navy suggested that scouts in kayaks be launched from the submarine onto the island to take an even closer look. Lt. Colonel Robert Burhans, Force S-2, accompanied by Third Regiment Reconnaissance Sergeant Jim Kurtzhal, flew to Corsica where they

Force officers chat during respite on Corsica prior to Operation DRAGOON. Left to right: Lieutenant John G. Simms, First Lieutenant Clifford Cook, First Lieutenant James R. Stevenson, Captain Adna H. Underhill, Captain Frank W. Erickson, and Lieutenant James F. Pringle. 13 August 1944. (Herb Langdon)

met with a Royal Navy officer and a man from the British Commando's Special Boat Section. They practiced at becoming acquainted with folbots, folding kayaks used by the SBS, and then put out to sea in a small submarine, the H.M.S. *Untiring*, to reconnoiter Ile de Levant and Ile du Port-Cros. An offshore reconnaissance confirmed, largely, what had been shown by the aerial photographs. The risky business of landing scouts on the island was not attempted.[22]

During approximately the same period as had seen Lt. Colonel Burhans' reconnaissance party carrying out its assignment, so too to Corsica had been detailed a separate party of Forcemen, tasked with an entirely different mission. Master

Landing craft and rubber boats crowd the shoreline at Yellow Beach, Ile du Levant, 16 August 1944. (Herb Langdon)

Sergeant Thomas M. Sellers was sent to Corsica along with five other Forcemen from the Parachute Platoon. There they helped prepare an A-20 Havoc to use aerial delivery containers for the purpose of dropping supplies to an OSS Detachment in southern France. Sellers and the other men carefully packed the containers, which were filled predominantly with 9mm ammunition, but other supplies as well. The containers were then hoisted into the Havoc's bomb bay. Sellers went along on the mission and the supplies were crash-delivered without the aid of parachutes to a spot designated by the OSS with aerial recognition panels – Sellers becoming perhaps the first Forceman to 'enter' southern France, if only briefly by air.

At 2200 hours on 14 August, SITKA Task Force reached the transport area approximately four and one-half miles from their island objectives. The ships carrying the First Special Service Force moved into position and then shut off their engines. Ahead of them the silhouettes of Levant and Port-Cros loomed as black hulks against the night sky. The Forcemen, their faces smudged with burnt cork and their equipment silenced with friction tape, stood waiting for the signal to haul themselves over the sides of the transports, down the scramble nets and into their rubber boats. For the assault troops, assembled in boat parties, that signal came at approximately 2300 hours. The entire landing force was en route to the landing beaches by 2350 hours. Attached by lines to the landing craft, the rubber boats bearing the assault sections were towed at a speed of four knots to a point approximately 1,000 yards offshore of their respective landing areas. PT boats took up posi-

Typical of the hastily erected German roadblocks confronted by the Force in southern France. This wire entanglement near Villeneuve-Loubet has been booby-trapped with mines, 28 August 1944. (Herb Langdon)

tions along the course between the transport ships and the rendezvous areas as sentinels for the landing craft coxswains to guide on. Casting off in the small hours of 15 August, one year almost to the hour from the landing on Kiska, the assault waves made their way toward the rocky scrambles. Seated upon GORPs (two-man electric surfboards), Naval beach marking parties equipped with signal lamps (an emerald-colored light for Emerald Beach, and so on) had taken up positions just offshore of each of the landing beaches. From Levant, the bright beacon of the Phare du Titan lighthouse briefly flickered on and then went black again.[23]

All was quiet as the first rubber boats, those of the security platoon, found purchase on Ile du Levant at 0135 hours and the Forcemen began to swarm up narrow ravines to the

Guarding the harbor of Toulon, Fort l'Eminence, one of Ile de Port-Cros' trio of Napoleonic-era star fortresses as seen from the air, 17 August 1944. Its thick stone walls and surrounding dry moat allowed the occupiers of l'Eminence to stand off repeated attacks by small arms fire for several days. (National Archives).

Moments after receiving a direct hit from a salvo of 15-inch shells from the battleship H.M.S. *Ramilles*, the first of forty-eight German soldiers emerge from the cracked Fort l'Eminence to surrender, Ile de Port-Cros, 17 August 1944. (National Archives)

rocky heights. The climb was not as difficult as it had been expected to be. There were no sentries where the Force came ashore, and as such, surprise was complete. Both Second and Third Regiments had been put ashore by 0200 hours. Atop the cliffs, the Forcemen proceeded to their respective assembly areas, quickly reorganized, then immediately moved toward their objectives. Second Regiment's 2nd Battalion began to push out to the northwest toward the ruins of Fort Arbousier while 1st Battalion made for Port del Avis. Meanwhile, Lt. Colonel Bill Becket's Third Regiment swung right, his 1st Battalion, led by Major Raymond T. Hufft, making for the eastern end of the island, toward the Titan lighthouse and its namesake gun battery – the Force's principal objective on Levant – and his 2nd Battalion moving to assault from the rear the enemy position defending Yellow Beach near Point du Liserot just to the north-northeast. Along the way to their objective, 1st Battalion, Third had a brief scrape with a small German force. 2nd Battalion, Third quickly smashed the fifteen-man enemy position behind Yellow Beach and then set about clearing the beach area for the landing of supplies, and for the evacuation of wounded and prisoners.[24]

As men from Major Hufft's 1st Battalion neared the big guns, there was no firing – all remained quiet. Hufft's attack went in and what he and his men discovered quickly brought back shades of Kiska. "'Another goddamned dry run!' a Black Devil called out in the darkness, reflecting the sentiment of most men."[25] What was supposed to have been a gun battery housing three or four 164mm guns threatening the landings on the French mainland was discovered to nothing more than a shrewd mock-up, elaborately constructed from corrugated metal, wooden segments and drain pipes, cleverly painted and camouflaged, and guarded by straw dummies. However, no sooner had the Titan objective been 'seized' when enemy mortar shells began falling around the lighthouse.[26]

Making its approach to Port del Avis, a group from Lt. Colonel Moore's 1st Battalion ran up against an enemy pillbox

Gustave A. Lindholm and Laddie Palasch, 3-2, clean weapons and organize their equipment at Cavalaire, southern France, 17 August 1944. (Herb Langdon)

Forceman displays captured German Schu-Mine 42s. The body of the mine was constructed either of impregnated plywood or hardened compressed cardboard, so as to evade mine detectors. The charge consisted of seven ounces of cast TNT. The mine's other components included the Z.Z. 42 pull igniter and a No. 8 detonator (shown held in this man's right hand). (Author's Collection)

manned by and handful vigilant defenders. The pillbox was quickly crushed, but the firefight had apparently alerted the remainder of Levant's garrison to the Force's presence. At this point about twenty enemy soldiers escaped the island in a small boat, however the bulk of the enemy on Levant moved into well-prepared defenses in the area of Port del Avis, particularly the area of the Grand Avis jail ruins, there to make a final, determined stand. From the enemy's sheltered positions, Lt. Colonel Moore's 1st Battalion began to receive heavy machine gun and mortar fire. In light of this, the battalion consolidated and dug in along a line to the northeast of Port del Avis preliminary to a concerted attack to be carried out with Moore's 2nd Battalion, that was now on its way from the southwest after sweeping aside an enemy outpost within the crumbling walls of Fort Arbousier. Colonel Walker, whose Force Headquarters Detachment had come ashore moments after the regiments, ordered the 2nd Battalion from Lt. Colonel Becket's Third Regiment committed to the attack as well. While the three battalions got into position, fire from the destroyer H.M.S. *Lookout* was called upon to keep a lid on the Port del Avis defenders. Within their concrete gun pits and pillboxes, the last of Levant's defenders endured a bone-jarring barrage while awaiting the final showdown. By evening, Lt. Colonel Moore's 2nd Regiment (reinforced) had surrounded Port del Avis on three sides. The attack was ordered and the battalions closed in pouring on a fusillade of small arms fire. Fragmentation grenades and high explosive rockets quickly overwhelmed Levant's holdouts ending the battle at 2034 hours on D-day. The island yielded some 110 prisoners.[27]

Landing at the same time as had the two other regiments on Levant, Lt. Colonel Akehurst's First Regiment came ashore on Ile de Port-Cros between Cap du Tuf and Port-Man. Here too the landing was unopposed, Akehurst's men having gained complete surprise. The first men ashore quickly made their way up cliffs and then hung ropes to assist those who followed. Once above the bluffs, the regiment advanced to take control of Port-Man meeting only token resistance; and then, with 1st Battalion on the right and 2nd Battalion to the left, swept westward to occupy dominating positions along the island's central ridgeline where the regiment consolidated its positions preparatory to pressing the attack forward. By 0630 hours most of the eastern half of Port-Cros was firmly in the hands of Akehurst who reported his progress to Colonel Walker on Levant.[28]

In order to secure the left of the line that First Regiment had established, Lieutenant Herb Goodwin's 6th Company was dispatched to the southwest to reduce Fortin de la Vigie, one of

Closeup of German Schu-Mine 42 components. (National Archives)

Section of 5-3 moving east through terraced countryside, southern France, c. November 1944. (Author's Collection)

Port-Cros' three forts, and a suspected enemy strongpoint. Goodwin's men found the trail leading to Vigie, and following it they quickly converged on their objective. After an exchange of small arms fire, the Forcemen crossed the bridge spanning the dry moat that surrounded the fort, and entered into the central compound to attack the small garrison. The lone German sentry came forward and was fired upon and wounded. Two more Germans appeared carrying a machine gun, but quickly decided that the odds were against them so fled over the wall toward some nearby trees. They were gunned down before reaching the bracken. Other defenders surrendered. The first of the enemy's fortified positions on Port-Cros had been rapidly taken. However, most of Vigie's garrison had escaped through a tunnel.[29]

Assault on a Maginot Line pillbox. One Forceman moves in close while another covers him from below. Reaching the structure, a fragmentation grenade is tossed through the aperture. (Author's Collection)

The Germans that had been captured were first interrogated, and were then herded down to a beach that had been cleared for the purpose of landing supplies. A search of Vigie uncovered a telephone setup with an open line to Fort l'Eminence that, it had been learned, was the largest and most formidable of Port-Cros' forts, and which contained the German company headquarters. Using the telephone, an interpreter made contact with the commander of the l'Eminence garrison, calling for his surrender. This was refused. No contact could be made with the Germans holding out within Fort l'Estissac, the island's other ancient citadel. Its defenders, as was the case with the enemy holed up in Fort l'Eminence, would have to be forced out.[30]

While 6th Company had been dealing with Fortin de la Vigie, Akehurst had dispatched numerous patrols from his 2nd Battalion westward to make contact with the enemy who, as it had now been confirmed, had withdrawn into the two ancient battlements located in the northwest quarter of the island. Early prisoners stated that Port-Cros and Levant were each defended by roughly one company of German infantry from the *1st Battalion* of the *917th Regiment*, a part of the 'limited-employment' *242nd Infantry Division*. The Germans on Levant and Port-Cros, while battle experienced, had previously suffered from maladies such as frozen feet on the Russian Front rendering them somewhat immobile. However, the relative mobility of troops fighting from within fortified static positions was hardly a factor.[31]

Given the construction of the two remaining forts, overcoming the enemy's positions would be no mean task. "The walls were twelve feet thick, and twenty feet of hard packed earth topped the ceilings. Over the decades, tangles of wild greenery had covered the forts so that they were nearly invis-

ible to the casual observer."[32] From Fort l'Eminence, the enemy's single 76mm gun was put into action sending shells into and around Port-Man, causing several casualties. By 0815 hours 4th Company began its first attack against l'Eminence only to stir up a hornet's nest. The enemy's reaction, an impenetrable wall of machine gun fire and hand grenades, caused 4th Company to withdraw with casualties to the safety of Fortin de la Vigie.[33]

Third Regiment officers move within Maginot Line fortifications, near Franco-Italian Border, c. November 1944. (Author's Collection)

At 1600 hours, naval shore fire control parties radioed a request to the heavy cruiser *Augusta* to train her guns on Forts l'Estissac and l'Eminence, as well as on the village located on the northern shoulder of the port facility. Shell upon shell from the *Augusta's* eight-inch guns fell upon the enemy redoubts, but were unable to penetrate the forts' thick walls. After this attempt to shake the Germans loose failed, Akehurst decided to try a different approach, dispatching Major Gus Heilman's 1st Battalion to clear Port-Cros village before attempting to once again make an advance on either fort. By nightfall, Heilman's men moved in to occupy the village. There they discovered a fortified German position that came to be known as the Chateau. No attempt to attack the Chateau was made during the night. Rather, 1st Battalion patrols bottled up the Chateau, as well as the two forts to keep the enemy from escaping.[34]

Come daylight on 16 August, a telephone line to the Chateau was tapped by Sergeant Bernard E. Helming who invited the German Lieutenant in commanded to surrender his position. The German officer did not believed that the American on the other end of the telephone was anything other than a member of a small raiding party, and because the Port-Cros defenders had had no contact with the French mainland, the German Lieutenant was ignorant of the general Allied land-ings that had been made the previous morning. The telephone line remained open as Helming continued in his attempt to wear down the Lieutenant. But instead of waiting for the German to make up his mind, Major Heilman decided, "Oh, the hell with it, . . . let's go on in."[35] At 1120 hours 3-1 stormed the Chateau. The battle lasted little more than thirty minutes, ending with three enemy dead and nineteen taken prisoner. 3rd Company took seven casualties: one dead and six wounded.[36]

Colonel Walker transferred from Levant to Port-Cros during the afternoon of 16 August. Now he and Akehurst were about to raise the stakes for the Germans inside of l'Estissac and l'Eminence. Earlier, a request had been made for bombing of the two forts. At 1600 hours 1st Battalion was ordered to withdraw from the area of the forts and the village back to Fortin de la Vigie. The aerial assault against the two old forts commenced during the afternoon of 16 August in the form of sixteen Allied dive-bombers. From his vantage atop the walls of Fortin de la Vigie, Forceman Peter Cottingham remembered the aerial attack against l'Eminence, just over a mile away, northwest of and in a valley below his position.[37]

"The sun was high in the southeastern sky as the first wave of dive bombers appeared to materialize from it. . . . My first glimpse of the bombers gave us a real jolt as they appeared to be headed directly for our fort. . . . As the leader of the first

First Lieutenant Robert R. Smith (5-3) amidst wrecked Maginot Line fortification, near Franco-Italian border, c. November 1944. (Author's Collection)

Force aid station incorporated into a Maginot Line fortification, southern France, c. November 1944. (Author's Collection)

wave opened up his cannons it became clear that he had the right target. All of his opening burst went well over our heads, impacting on the fort below us." After the first wave of four planes had fired their rockets into the fort, "so much dust and smoke rose into the air that it was impossible for the following waves to hit the target with any degree of accuracy. . . . When the smoke and dust settled we expected to see a white flag raised or at least we expected a phone call to tell of their surrender. Such was not to be."[38]

With no change in the situation, Akehurst made plans to send a company from his 1st Battalion against l'Estissac. 2nd Company, under covering smoke, moved to take up residence once again in Port-Cros village. Meanwhile, Captain William H. Merritt's 3rd Company took up positions along the ridges that flanked the star-shaped Fort l'Estissac. 1st Company was in battalion reserve. Once darkness was complete, Merritt's men moved in closer to surround the fort. Launching the attack at 2030 hours, 3rd Company was met by a hail of machine gun bullets and hand grenades. High explosive rockets fired from the Forcemen's Bazookas were used to batter down the main gate. With Captain Merritt leading the way an assault group rushed headlong into the fort's central courtyard. A savage battle erupted and continued until 3rd Company was finally able to bring enough men and firepower within the fort to overcome the tenacious German defense. In the end the storming of the fort yielded twenty-three prisoners, but had cost the lives of four Forcemen, including Captain Merrit.[39]

Ruins of Castillon, near Franco-Italian border, c. November 1944. (Author's Collection)

Shortly after 3rd Company had begun its attack against l'Estissac, 6th Company attempted to crack the defenses of Fort l'Eminence. The company came under exceedingly strong enemy defensive fires. Elements of two platoons pressed in closer, Bazooka teams making an attempt to blast open the fort's main gate. However, this portal would not budge, so the attempt to take the fort was called back. The fighting on Port-Cros had entered its third day when, on 17 August, Rear Admiral Davidson arrived on the island to confer with Walker and Akehurst on the progress of the battle. In light of the ineffectiveness of both aerial bombardment and Naval artillery efforts thus far, Akehurst asked Davidson if he had anything larger

Supplies en route from the beaches to the front. Typically, as seen in the trailer of this jeep, bread was carried in white mattress covers, southern France, c. November 1944. (Author's Collection)

Water bladder shouldered by sweater-clad Forceman, southern France, c. November 1944. (Author's Collection)

Staff Sergeant John Marshall, Headquarters Detachment, Second Battalion, Third Regiment, one of the supply packers near the Franco-Italian border, southern France, c. November 1944. (Author's Collection)

Supplies moving up by mule and by man, near Franco-Italian border, c. November 1944. (Author's Collection)

Forcemen carry supplies up to their mountain outposts using formed-plywood packboards, near Franco-Italian border, c. November 1944. (Author's collection)

he could hurl at the fortress. Davidson offered one last resort. He would bring the 15-inch guns of the battleship H.M.S. *Ramilles* to within six-mile range of Port-Cros. At 1100 hours First Regiment personnel drew back a safe distance from the target. By 1300 hours, shells from the *Ramilles* split the air overhead. The first salvo landed harmlessly beyond the fort. The second salvo fell short. Corrections were hastily computed and the third volley landed squarely on target. Smoke and earth erupted from l'Eminence, and almost immediately white flags were observed through the pall, at 1315 hours, marking the end of the struggle. Dazed, two German officers and forty-six enlisted men either staggered out of, or were carried from the pulverized redoubt to be taken prisoner.[40]

The previous day, Second and Third Regiments had been relieved on Ile du Levant by French troops, Second boarding LCIs to make the short trip to the mainland near St. Michel, France. Third had remained on Levant, close by in case it became necessary to commit the regiment on Port-Cros. Now, on the afternoon of 17 August, First Regiment departed Port-Cros, and Third Regiment departed Levant to join the rest of the Force at bivouac on the mainland at Sylvabelle. Once there the Force reorganized and re-equipped for future operations. On 19 Au-

gust the Force was alerted to move to St. Raphael to join Maj. General Frederick's 1st Airborne Task Force then sweeping east along the coast toward the Franco-Italian Border. The Force arrived at St. Raphael and bivouacked around Chateau Aurelian from 20-21 August.[41]

On 21 August the Force's First and Third Regiments moved onto the front line, relieving the British 2 Parachute Brigade of

Members of 5-3 pose for the camera, near Franco-Italian border, c. November 1944. (Author's Collection)

Force front line outpost, Franco-Italian border, c. November 1944. (Author's Collection)

Marino J. Bianco (5-3) stands in front of his hut, Franco-Italian border, c. November 1944. (Author's Collection)

Forceman Jake H. Wright operates his small-scale distillery, while Bill Zilkie, left, and another, monitor his progress, southern France, c. November 1944. (Author's Collection)

its attachment to the 1st ABTF. Second Regiment was in Force reserve. From this starting line the Force began an eastward drive along the Mediterranean Coast. On the whole, resistance encountered was fleeting. For his part, the enemy hampered the Force's advance by blowing bridges and culverts, and cratering roads. Roads, and their verges too, were heavily mined. Small pockets of rear guards engaged leading Force elements only long enough to allow larger bodies of enemy troops to slip away.[42]

As a measure to replace combat losses and to otherwise maintain organization strength once the southern France campaign was underway, a replacement training pool had been set up at Santa Maria di Capua-Vetere under veteran Force officers and enlisted men who, due to wounds received, were not physically fit for combat. The first group of 191 Americans and 60 Canadians had begun a four week course in July with "weapons instruction, physical conditioning, scouting and patrolling, and night operations."[43] This first batch of replacements to cycle through the program had completed its training by 22 August and was then sent to join the regiments in southern France. Immediately, "a second replacement training group of 225 Americans was secured from Seventh Army replacement centers and was immediately started on the Force's special replacement training program."[44]

During its drive, the Force reduced or liberated numerous villages and towns including Les Veyans, Tanneron, Grasse, St. Marc, St. Ann, Valbonne, Opio, Biot, Mougins, La Colle, Villeneuve-Loubet, Vence, St. Paul, St. Laurent, St. Jeannet, La Gaude, Colomars, La Begude, Aspremont, Chateauneuf, Contes, and St. Thomas. More than 330 enemy soldiers were taken prisoner during this continuous effort. Additionally, an unknown number of enemy were killed and wounded, and a large quantity of enemy materiel and equipment was either captured or destroyed. By 2 September the Force had taken up positions in the vicinity of Nice. Six days later, less than three weeks since it began and after covering more than 45 miles, the First Special Service Force reached the French-Italian border and took up defensive positions, receiving orders not to advance beyond.[45]

During the drive, "each day brought its quota of two or three towns occupied, a number of machine gun positions destroyed, a score or so of PWs taken, a mined road crater filled or a bridge replaced by the Engineers. Casualties . . . were slight. . . . The greatest hardship on officers and men alike was the strain of being almost continually on the move, with no opportunity for rest or relaxation. . . . It was not until November, when positions became stabilized on the frontier, that it was found possible to withdraw units into reserve."[46]

Map #5

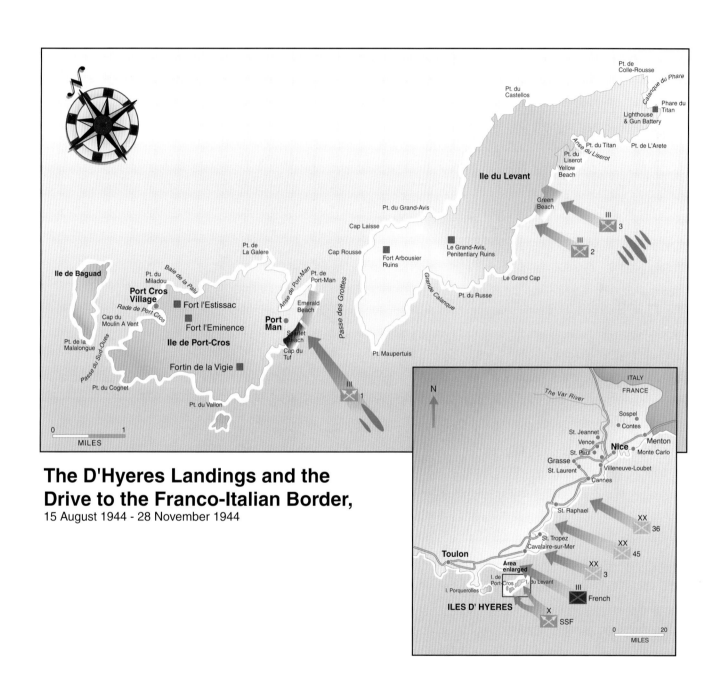

**The D'Hyeres Landings and the
Drive to the Franco-Italian Border,**
15 August 1944 - 28 November 1944

Historical Document #5: Lessons Learned from French Campaign

FIRST SPECIAL SERVICE FORCE

N.Y.,
1944.

APO 4994,
New York,

2 November

MEMORANDUM:

LESSONS LEARNED FROM THE FRENCH CAMPAIGN
Since 15 August 1944

1. INTRODUCTION.

In many ways the part played by this Force in the action in South France since 15 August has been similar to our experience in previous campaigns. However, certain aspects of the problems involved this far have been vastly different and new to our experience in combat. Herein lies an opportunity to learn and we have learned often time the hard way. It is with the purpose of passing on to all concerned the benefits of conclusions drawn from these experiences that this memorandum is prepared.

To point out some of the outstanding differences between the problems encountered in this and previous campaigns:

a. Our landing on KISKA, 15 August 1943, one year to the day before our amphibious operation against the Islands of LEVANT and PORT CROS was executed in northern waters in which no man could live more than a few minutes as opposed to the warm Mediterranean and mild weather conditions prevailing in this area on 15 August of this year. KISKA is a mountainous mass of formidable proportions in comparison with the lower altitudes and lesser area of the HYERES group with the vast difference entailed in the problems of supply and evacuation, communications, and the tactical employment of troops.

b. The pursuit of the enemy across Southern France to the Italian border was conducted under very different circumstances from those surrounding his flight from ANZIO to ROME and beyond the Tiber River. In Italy the enemy's withdrawal was hasty to a degree bordering on route. He was hard-pressed to remove as much heavy equipment as possible and remain far enough ahead of his pursuers to keep his rear guard from being overrun. Our Air offensive harassed his columns day and night with telling effect as witness the roadside littered with destroyed German materiel.

In France the enemy virtually set the pace in his orderly withdrawal to defensive positions along the Italian border. None of the roadside litter of Italy was in evidence in Southern France. Always our forces arrived in cities and towns only to find the enemy had departed in good order, taking everything with him only a few hours earlier. With the exception of rear guard engagements fought in all instances on terrain favoring the enemy's defense and withdrawal, and of his own choosing, it was never necessary to drive him out of cities or from key terrain features by weight of a major engagement. At times the pressure maintained by our armored reconnaissance patrols did cause him to depart in some haste but in nearly all cases he was able to

-1-

---

salvage or to deny to our use the major part of his equipment and transport.

How different, this, from ARTENA, VALMONTONE, VELLETRI and CISTERNA.

c. Our defensive operation along the French-Italian border differ mainly from our activities on ANZIO in regard to terrain. Mountain warfare is not new to us, but whereas in previous campaigns we have retained the offensive, we now find ourselves in one involving neither offense nor defense. The situation has resolved itself into one wherein both sides seem to be content on either side of the French-Italian border and maintain contact by combat and reconnaissance patrols while supporting artillery on both sides conduct a series of duels directed from OPs on the high peaks.

Although or present positions are thoroughly prepared for defensive action the enemy seems reluctant to attack and we are denied offensive action except for minor raids and patrols, by restraining orders which limit our advance to positions along the Italian border.

This resume of Lessons Learned in France is compiled, for the main part, from the comments and opinions turned in by our leaders in combat echelon and represent the thought of the people most entitled to definite opinions based on first-hand information.

Our part in the action in South France is divided into three distinct phases.

(1) AMPHIBIOUS OPERATIONS AGAINST ISLANDS OFFSHORE.

(2) RAPID PURSUIT OF AN ENEMY IN ORDERLY RETREAT.

(3) HOLDING OPERATIONS ON THE ITALIAN BORDER.

Ed. Note:

The material contained in this report in most cases represents the consensus of many opinions and for this reason alone few attempts can be made to credit the source unless the observation derives from a specialized group, for example, Cannon Co, Medical Detachments, Communications, etc.

2. PHASE 1. - AMPHIBIOUS OPERATIONS AGAINST ISLANDS OFFSHORE.

a. Lessons learned in training for Amphibious Operations.

Prior to the actual operation, it was found that there were many obstacles to be overcome to ensure a successful rubber boat landing. Working on strange ships at night can easily result in confusion and can only be avoided after many days of constant training and rehearsals. Initially, it is necessary to have the same boat crews working constantly together. This leads to a mutual confidence among the men and does much to raise the morale.

Once training for ship-to-shore operations commences, it is to be desired that the units train, if possible, from the actual

-2-

---

ship that will ultimately be used during the actual landing. This enables all personnel to become thoroughly acquainted with the super structure, net stations, nets and deck fixtures. In these respects, all ships differ and unless the men are given the opportunity to become thoroughly acquainted with such, moving about a strange ship at night causes confusion.

b. Conduct of Troops on Landing.

Once the troops providing security are in position it is necessary for an immediate, quick reconnaissance of the area to locate trails or roads leading toward objectives. Guides can then be stationed to orient successive troops without loss of time. When several companies are landing almost simultaneously, predesignated rendezvous must be used to allow reorganization.

Where terrain is difficult, there is a tendency for troops to lighten their combat load. This has to be avoided or it will result in the unit lacking sufficient heavy weapons ammunition at a time when it may be needed.

Daybreak may prove to be a critical time because of the possibility of counterattacks once our presence is known. At this time, the troops are tired and need rest which they are unable to get. Officers and NCO's will find it necessary to drive troops during this phase or momentum will be lost.

Continued reconnaissance is very necessary to allow a commander to have necessary last-minute information available to be incorporated in his plan of attack.

In any landing, the initial surprise should be exploited in full, the enemy should never have the opportunity to re-group before the final exterminating blow. On both island the enemy put to good use the cover of darkness after the first day's fighting to fall back to previously prepared positions in old fortifications where he could easily have withstood a siege of some duration, had we not resorted to dive-bombing and Naval bombardment followed by infantry assault.

So much depends upon the unforeseen incident in this type of operation that it seems impossible to lay out detailed plans for the tactical employment of troops. Once the attacking waves leave the ship, control is difficult at best and sometimes impossible. For this reason it is highly necessary that each small unit leader be thoroughly acquainted with the general plan and be prepared to set with decision and promptness to get his part of the job done.

The comments of the Company Commander of 3rd Company, 2d Regiment are presented here, not as tactical doctrine, but as food for thought.

"The landing on LEVANT proved that a successful rubber boat landing can be made in the face of an alert enemy force. The type of terrain on the Island brought out several interesting points, as did certain other conditions encountered there.

"In the initial landing the formation of platoon waves rather than company waves would save a good deal of congestion and confusion. The beach-marking platoon should go ashore in single file, since in their case,

-3-

---

the speed factor is eclipsed by that of silence and security. The consecutive waves should be spaced at least 100 yards apart otherwise the beach will become jammed. This means that each wave will not be able to maintain visual contact with its predecessor but will have to guide in on the beach-marking lights.

"The only feasible formation for movement over ground as densely wooded as was LEVANT, is single file. For that reason no attempt should be made to move units of over company strength in one body, and the plan, where possible, should be broken down into company objectives from the original landing."

c. Medical, Evacuation of Wounded.

Initially, during darkness, aid stations can only be set up near the beach and until daylight arrives or the tactical situation will permit light, only a very limited amount of surgery can be done. Combat surgical teams did excellent work both ashore (after daylight) and aboard the hospital ship.

As the troops move forward, evacuation is generally over rough terrain and additional litter teams are necessary. It was found that at least two teams per company were required. In addition, it was under some circumstances necessary to employ enemy prisoners as litter teams.

We soon learned that at least two landing craft must be available at all times and reserved for no other purpose than to evacuate wounded to the hospital ship or the surgery ship. Cases requiring transportation to these ships admitted no delay as only the more seriously wounded were sent to them.

d. Problems of Supply.

During the amphibious phase of the current operation careful consideration had to be given to supply problems. It was found that sufficient regimental supplies (food, water and ammunition) could be loaded in the landing craft to carry through the first 48 hours. Subsequent supplies were unloaded from the ship as soon as the tactical situation allowed and by daylight of D-day we had sufficient supplies ashore to last four days.

The water situation on the islands became acute after the first day. The supply and resupply of water from our landing ships proved inadequate to our needs and had we not found the little fresh water on the islands to be usable, emergency supply would have become necessary.

On the Island of LEVANT one beach alone was found to be suited to the landing of supplies. Some tendency was noted to pile up supplies on this beach faster than could be consumed or transported to inland dumps. This resulted in unnecessary concentrations of ammo and other supplies on the beach.

After the first day of fighting, POW's were very useful in handling supplies.

e. Comments concerning Naval activities.

-4-

Historical Document #5: Lessons Learned from French Campaign

During the operation, the employment of naval shore parties as beach markers proved highly satisfactory. In addition to the actual shore party, the use of a Group approximately 300 yards off shore, indicating beach direction by means of a predetermined colored light was found to be very helpful. It is necessary, however, that boat crews do not depend entirely on shore parties to guide them to their target. It is imperative that each crew be given an initial bearing to follow on leaving the ship and a second one when released from the landing craft. It is suggested that an Army officer ride in the landing craft until such time as the rubber boats are released. He is then able to coordinate the desired release point with the landing craft coxswain.

It was found that the L.C.A. (Br) type was far superior to the L.C.V.P. as a towing craft. This type of craft makes practically no noise and enables the rubber boats to be towed much closer to shore, the only limitation being the distance off shore that the craft might be silhouetted.

Once the rubber boats were released, the landing craft rendezvoused approximately 1,500 yards off shore and called in in a predetermined priority, by means of colored lights. This worked exceedingly well and is recommended for use in all such operations.

In some instances it was noted that towing craft showed a marked reluctance to approach the shore to within the predetermined 1,000 yards. This resulted in releasing the rubber boats too soon which adversely affected the landing of scheduled waves of rubber boats on the beach.

3. PHASE II. - RAPID PURSUIT OF AN ENEMY IN ORDERLY RETREAT.

a. The Tactics of Pursuit.

Ed. Note:

The opinions and conclusions of this sub-title
are those of the Commanding Officer, Third Regiment and
are herein set forth in their entirety as they embody or
at lease reflect the thoughts and observations of many
others.

"Until the enemy made his stand in the vicinity of the Italian border the tactical problems confronting us were, with few exceptions, those involved in the steady and rapid pursuit of a retreating enemy. These problems were silhouetted by the peculiar nature of our forces and the entire Task Force - both were specialized, both were lightly equipped and lacking in adequate artillery and transportation.

"The pursuit was made on foot. Contact was not always easy to maintain. Roads were blown, trails were mined in many cases. The enemy was confused and poorly led. He did not fight a time-delaying action but, rather, made long disjointed withdrawals, fighting where he could gather his strength and with widely varying determination. His opposition was sporadic, unexpected, and difficult to foretell.

"Our lack of transportation made it impossible to keep the close contact and pressure at all times that would have prevented

this opposition and would have hampered his demolitions, mining and road-cratering activities.

"One lesson learned was that motorized patrols made up in some degree for the fact that the infantry was not motorized, and enabled the infantry to move as rapidly as possible under the cover of these patrols. At CONTES a company was motorized in two half-tracks and two jeeps and sent forward to TOUET de L'ESCARENE where it made contact with the enemy.

"Another lesson learned was that early reconnaissance yields important results not later obtainable. Reconnaissance made while a position to the rear is being occupied catches the enemy before he has been alerted, and his positions and strength are easily determined. If patrols are sent out after a position is occupied the enemy is found to be alerted and under cover.

"Excellent results were obtained from aggressive long-distance patrols, many of which were sent out prepared to spend several days in the enemy lines. These patrols were for the most part very small in size and composed of seasoned scouts.

"A lesson noted several times was that on occasion it pays, in pursuit, to "over-commit" your strength. A show of strength on a lightly-held objective often carried the objective with little or no opposition. Had the strength committed been in the amount considered tactically sufficient to take the objective in these cases there might well have been much stiffer opposition with a consequent increase in casualties before the mission was accomplished.

"It was learned at TOUET de L'ESCARENE that a sudden surprise attack with heavy fire power on a more or less impregnable position may result in the abandonment of the position even though it cannot be captured at the time. In this case the objective was a narrow railway tunnel entrance with two blockhouses built into its construction. A 77mm gun lay in the entrance and at least two MGs were firing from the blockhouse. The tunnel mouth was set deep in a ravine with sheer cliff on either side. The blockhouse had side ports. The only approach was down the railroad track itself or over a twenty-foot drop in front of the side ports. The position, as long as it could be manned, was to all intent and purposes impregnable to infantry attack.

"The attack was launched by a platoon of Third Regiment supported by a 75mm cannon mounted in a half-track. The approach had been made swiftly and under cover so that good surprise was achieved although the enemy were already alerted and firing on French Patriots. The cannon was run into position 150 yards from the tunnel mouth and some 90 rounds were fired into the tunnel and on the blockhouse ports. During the fire all platoon weapons engaged the same targets. When fire was lifted and the platoon closed in the cries of the enemy wounded could be heard. However, as the leading elements reached the entrance one enemy machine gun opened fire at point blank range and light casualties were suffered. Although heavy machine gun fire was once more brought to bear on the blockhouse the enemy MG could not be silenced and the attack was abandoned for eight hours. On reconnaissance at this time it was found that the enemy had abandoned the position--an extremely important one as it was his escape route to SOSPEL.

"Important lessons were learned in the use of civilian information and intelligence. Such information was plentiful, colored and covered every conceivable branch of enemy activity. It was, however, highly inaccurate at times and misleading, and care had to be taken that information was not accepted from enemy agents.

"It became evident that the best manner for handling such information in order to make immediate beneficial use of it was to have your intelligence personnel right with the forward elements of the advance guard. This information was passed on, as obtained, to the advance guard and to the commands. In this fashion tactical decisions could be made on the run and valuable time and ground saved.

"In pursuit the rapid repair of routes of advance is of extreme importance. Where the enemy had had sufficient time to crater the best roads in numerous places the Engineers were often taxed beyond capacity. We found that our advance elements could obtain excellent cooperation from the civilian population in the repair of roads and reconstruction of bridges, and much use was made of this labor. On several occasions were Engineer aid could not be obtained immediately we were able by means of large volunteer groups of civilian laborers to keep our attack moving and our vehicles and supplies moving up.

"One well-known tactical difficulty became well-illustrated on at least one occasion. Where flanking and encircling movements are attempted with large units the element of timing is extremely difficult. Difficulties of terrain, enemy minefields and other unexpected obstacles may delay one of the large units employed to such an extent that the timing is so far thrown out as to necessitate a complete change in the tactical plan as the action proceeds. This is further emphasized by the difficulty of communication and control where two cooperating units are to converge over a wide area. Consequently broad enveloping movements employing large units were closely synchronized before being attempted and envelopment tactics using smaller units up to and including companies were ordered wherever possible."

b. Conduct of Troops in Towns and Cities.

The Commanding Officer of our 2nd Regiment has some interesting and helpful observations on the problems contingent to the advance of a Liberating Army in pursuit of a well-hated enemy. They have a definite bearing on tactical and security problems arising from the desire of a joyous civilian population to demonstrate its gratitude to the soldiers responsible for its deliverance and from the manifold effects upon the daily conduct of civil affairs in a liberated community.

He fells that it is highly undesirable to halt and attempt to bivouac troops within cities and town which the enemy has recently evacuated, for the following reasons:

The inhabitants of the community are wildly hospitable to all soldiers. They are deeply hurt if their proffered advances are not accepted with the resulting adverse effect upon public relations. Another angle of this intermingling of civilians and soldiers under these circumstances is the opportunity for the enemy to plant his agents in public places such as barrooms, hotels and other places frequented by soldiers. Loose talk is

impossible to control. The soldier is willing to talk of his experiences and there are many ears eager to listen to every word he says. In the confusion following upon the heels of German withdrawal one person in civilian clothes looks and acts very like another.

In case of counterattack it would be next to impossible to regain control of scattered troops in time to take adequate counter measures unless sufficient reserve is posted to cover the approaches to the town.

The civilian population has been in dire need for four years of certain items of clothing, cigarettes, sweets, coffee and any kind of food. The spirit of camaraderie which prevails between the French people and the American soldier makes it very hard for him to withhold these things from them when they are so plentiful for him and he knows he can be resupplied. This inherent generosity of the American soldier results in a supply problem of no mean proportions. There is also the temptation to trade these issue items for wine, souvenirs, etc. The black market is eager to pay the soldier huge prices for almost anything he has to sell and this temptation proves too great for many of our men.

Command Posts in towns, even though the troops may be bivouacked outside, present problems of their own. The unit commander is looked upon as the deliverer of the populace and consequently embodies all the concepts of "The Great White Father." He is immediately deluged with all sorts of civil affairs from local politics to settling claims. In short, when the Army moves into a town, the Commander of troops assumes responsibility for everything in the eyes of the inhabitants. His time can very easily be occupied with every conceivable diversion from his real concern - that of fighting a war. He suggests that, should it become necessary to set up in a city, a French speaking Civil Affairs Officer be appointed to screen all contacts with the townspeople and allow only the most urgent cases or those of a military nature to come to his attention.

Ed. Note:

From these observations, in which other commanders concur, it would appear that for purposes of security and expediency it is better to push on through a town or city than to stop, even overnight, while in pursuit of the enemy.

c. Use of Special Units and Problems of a Specialized Nature

The Cannon Company

Ed. Note:

The remarks of our Cannon Company Commander lend to verify opinions presented in other reports. Therefore his verbatim account represents a digest of many opinions submitted by other leaders, on the use or lack of use of his weapon.

"The first lesson we learned in France was on our first operation. Our gun, 75mm half-track mount, could have been used to great advantage on the Isle de LEVANT where we found fortified positions and had no artillery available to engage them. The enemy

Historical Document #5: Lessons Learned from French Campaign

had only mortar and machine gun strongpoints which our cannon fire could have reduced easily with minimum casualties among our troops. The vehicles can be handled with ease by the Navy, and after the infantry have secured a beachhead they can be landed and be under cover in a few minutes. It may be noted that this vehicle is very maneuverable in heavy sand.

"The 75mm half-track mount is very mobile and can and has been used as an armored reconnaissance vehicle with infantry to the VAR RIVER. The distance and area covered by the reconnaissance is, of course, governed by terrain.

"We have also used the half-track to force enemy arty to fire at inconvenient times thus enabling our artillery to fire effective counterbattery. The half-track is very fast and can be some distance away before enemy artillery can register.

"When in a defensive position, we have learned that the gun can be profitably used for close-in support of the infantry. They should be placed so that they can move to any forward position rapidly. Several counterattacks have been broken up before the enemy had advanced into effective small arms range of our troops.

"We have managed to trap the enemy on several occasions in tunnels and have inflicted heavy casualties on them. Our troops should be warned of the danger of being caught in the same manner. Shrapnel will travel for several hundred yards down a tunnel and the concussion is terrific. Then, too, troops in the tunnel are unable to return fire.

"Our gun has also been used for close-in support of the advancing infantry; for example, advance on GRASSE. They should be employed with the forward company in groups of not less than two tracks.

"Also, when towed artillery is unable to move forward with troops the gun can be used as an indirect fire weapon to engage enemy artillery with counterbattery fire."

Communications

This paragraph contains material submitted by both command and communications personnel and represent the conclusions of both the user and those charged with the installation and maintenance of communications channels.

A commentary on field equipment in general may prove enlightening to those most concerned. In this connection certain excerpts from the report of Communications Officer, 2nd Regiment, are presented here.

"In the mountainous, rocky terrain we have been fighting through we learned that tactical situations requiring wire to be laid called for 110 wire. If it was impossible to lay 110 wire then radio communication was more reliable than telephone communication. By using combat wire only in places where the terrain was not too mountainous and covered with soil in place of rocks would combat wire stand up for any length of time.

"Our B.D. 72 is too bulky to be used in the field. Where a switchboard is needed to maintain wire communication using less phones and providing better service by reason of having separate

lines to each phone, we found the German 10 drop switchboard to be very suitable and used it exclusively for this type of work until a permanent position was established.

"It was found that during our move across Southern France that an SCR 284 was not dependable for radio communication to Force HQ in mountainous country when operating on a broad front. An SCR 193 or larger is required.

"It is thought that the SCR 300 would be better for radio communication from regiment to battalions and from battalions to companies for these reasons: (1) The SCR 300 is more compact and weighs less than SCR 509; (2) The SCR 300 can be operated on the move, (3) The SCR 300 has nearly the same range as the SCR 509. From hilltop to hilltop it will carry almost as far, and a hill large enough to obstruct SCR 300 communication will, in most cases, obstruct SCR 509 radio as well."

All concerned expressed a desire for more communications vehicles to be used exclusively for the purpose. Resupply of batteries of all types became a major problem during our rapid movement across country.

Commander, 3rd Regiment says:

"Where forward movement is rapid and sustained, communications are a constant problem. One lesson learned was that, rather than have the normal system of radio communications fanning forward from the more powerful stations located with rear CPs to less powerful stations toward the front is was better to have a strong radio set up with the most advanced elements. This was achieved by the use of a 284 set, and later, 1 193 set, mounted in a command jeep carried well forward. In this manner information was accurately and constantly sent back to higher command as it was being received."

The old difficulty again cropped up concerning certain misuses of voice radio equipment. There is still a tendency to use voice radio as freely and openly as the telephone. This practice can result in the loss of lives.

We have found it necessary to take precautions against sabotage and tapping of our wires. This was especially true where our lines passed through towns.

One danger in using underground cable circuits (commercial) is that the circuit cannot always be cut forward of the place where the splice is made resulting in the possibility that such circuits may be tapped in enemy territory. Open wire (commercial) can easily be cut forward of the splice which precludes this danger and provides a reliable means of wire transmission.

Commercial open wire (pole line) extends the talking range of field telephone equipment an obviates the necessity of laying long trunk lines resulting in a great saving in wire and man hours.

Supply

Comments concerning problems of supply have been frequently mentioned in a general way in connection with other lessons learned. The following conclusions are of a more specific nature.

Supply Officer, 2nd Regiment submits the following observations:

"Study maps before a mission, this is an excellent source for information on routes of advance and for supply.

"When troops are on the move three items of supply will be important, ammunition, water, and rations.

"The ammunition supply should be kept mobile. Half-tracks with fire units have been found to be the best method.

"Water purification tablets should be available to troops at all times.

"K rations are the easiest ration to transport to troops in a difficult position. The C ration is about the same.

"Half-tracks are the best for transporting ammunition, 6 x 6 trucks and 4 x 4 trucks with trailer can be used for all other items."

Our supply problems during the early days of the advance across Southern France and before our rear echelon landed with our heavy transport, were much the same as those of any fast moving unit of comparable size. We traveled light and required little.

Upon arrival of our heavy supplies and transport, forward supply points were set up and moved by echelons in rear of advancing troops. Our supply setup proved adequate at all times in that supplies of all kinds were always kept within reach of Regimental Transport.

As the tactical situation became more stabilized and our troops moved into defensive positions in areas where access was found difficult, we found it necessary to use mules and packers in order to supply front line units on the higher mountain peaks where the jeeps could not go. In one instance the problem was solved by the use of a power driven cable-way, built and operated by our Engineers.

Troops in these isolated positions soon learned to conserve their supplies as every pound cost much labor and re-supply was uncertain. In some cases water was carried up on pack boards from water points. "A man who has packed a five (5) gallon can of water up a trail that a mule cannot climb, does not waste water."

In general, it may be said that any item of supply or equipment needed by our troops was received by them in good time if available in the Theater.

Naval Fire Support

Our advance along the sea coast from MONACO to MENTON and our holding operation along the Italian border in which we are now engaged, has been greatly aided by Naval gunfire especially in the coastal areas. This fire was closely coordinated with the fires of land batteries by the Naval Liaison Officer who remained in close radio contact with Naval F.O. parties in forward OPs and with the ships. Many lessons were learned regarding the correct and most

effective use of Naval support. The comments of the N.L.O. will prove of interest to all concerned.

"Naval gunfire should be used in conjunction with, not as a substitute for, supporting artillery. It has a definite use against enemy positions beyond the range of land artillery or those positions in defilade to the artillery.

"Results show what effect of Navy fire on bridges or other given point targets are of small value and should not be called for. Navy shore fire was definitely meant for neutralization of areas.

"The use of artillery forward observers to spot Navy fire was shown to be very effective. These observers may have direct communication with the supporting ships using the same radio used for artillery fire (SCR 609 FM Crystal Controlled).

"Much of the Navy fire along the coast has been direct fire. The use of artillery to spot the ships on the target was of considerable value.

"Intelligence and operations reports sent daily to the ships proved helpful to Naval Commanders. Photographs and overlays were of aid in understanding the positions and situations of ground troops."

d. General.

Certain observations of a general nature covering a wide variety of subjects have been submitted and are worthy of note. Executive Officer of our 1st Regiment has this to say:

"When the enemy are withdrawing and pursuit overland is rapid, troops are inclined to be overly excited and as a result, may become somewhat careless with respect to security while on the move. As movement is generally over good roads, flank security is sometimes essential.

"During this phase, close support by the Cannon Company proved to be invaluable. Enemy strong points, pillboxes and gun positions were rapidly done away with by these weapons up with the forward companies.

"It was found that on may occasions, unit close-support weapons (particularly 81mm mortars) would have been useful but they were not available. It is suggested that if they were kept mobile they could be of inestimable value.

"During rapid overland moves it was found that using 1/50,000 scale maps was better than using a larger scale, as to use a large scale map necessitates frequent changing and makes map supply exceedingly difficult. In static or temporary positions, however, the large scale map is to be desired.

Company Commander, 3rd Co, 2nd Regiment:

"There is no place in our combat echelon for men who are troubled with old wounds or ailments of physical kind. It is far less troublesome to keep a man in a rest area rather than in combat when you are counting heavily on him. Each man should carry two full water bottles."

Historical Document #5: Lessons Learned from French Campaign

4. PHASE III. - HOLDING OPERATIONS ON THE ITALIAN BORDER.

Our present situation finds us operating on terrain reminiscent of our experiences in the Italian campaign. There were learned many lessons regarding the use of key features both by ourselves and by the enemy. Lessons of this nature need be learned only once to be well remembered and put to good application.

We have held our present positions, with the exception of minor movements, through the late fall weather and early winter. Defensive warfare in the mountains in fair weather is one thing, and quite another matter during the rainy season and early snow.

Although the terrain, being of a mountainous nature, is familiar to our troops, this is their first experience in holding a line on high ground for an extended period of time. Always before we have had the drive and lively interest which only the spirit of the attack and movement can impart to our troops.

Our activities now can be divided into three general classes.

a. Occupation of Commanding Ground.

There is nothing new in the organization of the ground which we hold. Basic tactical principles have been applied to all our problems of defensive warfare. Although our positions may appear to be thinly held in numbers of men it will be noted that all approaches to them are outposted, covered by defensive fires which can be called on short notice, mined and booby trapped, and blocked by wire entanglements and road blocks covered by fire and observation.

b. Reconnaissance and Combat Patrols and Raiding Parties.

Our men have had ample opportunity to learn new lessons while conducting patrols and raids into enemy held territory.

Some of these lessons as reported by leaders of such patrols are listed below.

On patrols of 15 or more men there should be at least one man who can speak German fairly fluently.

Men must not be allowed to bunch up. Leader must constantly be on alert to see that men stay spread out.

If the underground forces patrol on our behalf it is advisable to send someone with them to report the findings.

The enemy has a complete and thorough military knowledge of the terrain we are fighting on, therefore our reconnaissance should be constant and accurate.

We learned again the outstanding lesson of the Italian campaign - the use of high ground and the difficult approach. As always, the high ground gave us not only the observation but the domination of the surrounding terrain. And, as always, we found that our patrols, by using the difficult and consequently unexpected approach, achieved the element of surprise which

---

enabled them to accomplish their mission more rapidly and with fewer casualties.

Another lesson is that every man should know exactly the limits of our own minefields in front of him and the pattern of the mines. Too many times only two or three men know the limits and patterns of the minefields and if they all happen to be off the hill at the same time it leaves the men on the hill with no means of getting beyond their own defenses. Promiscuous booby-trapping of individual positions is also dangerous.

c. Artillery Support.

Artillery support both direct and general is of primary importance in our present situation. It has been proven again that a preponderance of artillery can hold the enemy back at arms length. He must remain out of reach of our long range guns thus creating a wide "No Man's Land" between his lines and ours.

Harassing fires on suspected and known enemy gun positions were found to be very effective as a counter measure. The peculiar arrangement of the main road net can be described as a coastal road with primary feeder roads running at right angles away from the sea and following the stream lines back into the hills. The main supply routes roughly parallel the ridge lines which the enemy must hold. This setup offers a splendid opportunity for interdiction fire from our Naval support guns off shore firing at all points where feeder roads intersect the coast road and for our land batteries to harass the feeders farther inland.

Counter battery fire and fire placed on opportune targets observed and directed from Air OP or ground OPs has proved highly effective.

Our Cannon Company weapons have been used with telling effect as a supplement to attached howitzers. These guns being self-propelled can fire from positions well forward and work very well against point targets. By firing from one position and then rapidly shifting to another the illusion is crated that we are using more guns than we really possess and helps to confuse the enemy's counter battery fire.

Some interesting observations were made by the Commanding Officer, 3d Regiment, on the use of artillery. He says:

"It was noted early in the campaign and confirmed in the later more defensive stages that one of the best means to keep enemy artillery batteries silent was to send a cub plane into the air in their vicinity. This often proved more effective than counter battery fire itself.

"An interesting result was obtained from the use of direct fire on heavy fortifications. While the normal results of 75mm fire, at any range, against such formidable fortifications as existed at FORT CASTILLON are not expected to be great, it was found that such fire if direct and carefully placed, could have a distinct harassing and damaging effect. The main gate of the Fort, the only vehicular entrance, was put out of commission entirely after our first barrage. And it was noted that casualties were removed from the Fort after every direct fire mission. Care has to be taken that such fire missions are brief as well as

---

accurate and that all troops in the line in the vicinity of the fire are under good cover because there is always an immediate enemy artillery reaction."

5. CONCLUSIONS.

Conclusions of some of the Officers and Non-coms of 2d Regiment on subjects having a general relationship to problems arising from our present situation are listed below:

"Defensive MG and mortar positions should be chosen with more care and more time spent on improving them.

"If select troops are to maintain an aggressive spirit, a will to attack and close, they should be used for that and spared the attrition on personnel and breakdown in morale which goes with holding a line under bad weather conditions and under continual harassing fire..

"All commanders should build up their subordinates. More and more responsibility should be placed on them so they will be ready if anything should happen to their immediate commanders.

"Never assign platoons from a different company if one company can do the job. Control and teamwork are too difficult."

"Cleanliness should be stressed: Too many men are lost to the hospital from infections often resulting from not enough use of water."

"Provided that the company has communication with supporting artillery an artillery FO is not absolutely essential, although things run more smoothly when one is present. Each officer and non-com officer should be able to direct fire and adjust artillery fire. We operated for a month in our present position without a FO, and never had difficulty in getting artillery fire where and when we wanted it."

"Never depend on fog in mountainous country for concealment. You will be left in the open at the most unexpected times."

"Direct phone connections to all outposts and OPs are necessary. All outposts and OPs have their own separate sectors and many targets are only momentary. Many good targets have escaped artillery fire because of the lack of phones and the time it took to run to the nearest phone to contact the artillery."

"Combat boots are better than jump boots in mountain work. Morphine should be carried by the section leaders as well as the platoon officers. Physical conditioning should be stressed more in our future training."

"None of my three mortar commanders like the new assault or knee mortar. They feel that at close quarters it can be effectively replaced by rifle grenades, and that at other times the speed with which it can be set up does not compensate for the decrease in accuracy."

"I've learned never to underestimate the enemy. No matter what his condition he is always capable of putting up a good fight. In realizing this we are just giving the devil his due; and it might help to keep us alive and see the end of this thing."

"One thing which impressed me very much was, never give Jerry the benefit of a doubt. A gap in the line may prove disastrous, as he so well proved to us on a few occasions. Although we know he must inevitably admit defeat, he is still a soldier - I'm sure we will profit by never underestimating his possibilities."

DISTRIBUTION:

CG, 1st ABTF	5
CO, 1st ABTF Arty	1
CO, FSSP	1
S-1, "	1
S-2, "	1
S-3, "	1
S-4, "	1
Force Surgeon	1
" Signal Off	1
CO, 1st Regt	27
CO, 2d Regt	27
CO, 3d Regt	27
CO, Cannon Co	1
CO, 463d Prcht FA Bn	4
CO, Co C, 40th Engr Rgt	4
Hist File - S-3	1
Cdn Hist File	2
FSSF File	2

Tools of the Trade
Principal Weapons of the First Special Service Force

I n terms of small arms, for its size the First Special Service Force wielded an array matched by no other American infantry unit during World War II. To illustrate this point, a comparison of organizational allowances of weapons can be made between that of a Force combat company and those of other U.S. Army company-sized units. A Ranger infantry company (77 personnel as per T/O&E 7-87, 29 February 1944 – comparable in numbers to a Force combat company), while matching the Force in submachine gun strength, had but two Bazookas to the Force's six, as well as only two-thirds the number of Browning machine guns and 60mm mortars. A U.S. parachute rifle company had (at 176 men as per T/07-35T, 24 February 1944) more than twice the numbers of a Force combat company. Yet in mortars a single Force company carried an equal amount. And while the airborne company had three more Browning machine guns than did its Force counterpart, a Force combat company enjoyed twice as many Bazookas. This high ratio of organic support weapons within the companies of the Force's Combat Echelon, over and above the many other personal weapons at their disposal, gave the First Special Service Force "a withering dose of firepower to deliver on the enemy."[1]

Fighting Knife, V-42

Perhaps no article of equipment is as synonymous with the First Special Service Force as their stiletto – the V-42. The knife was designed by Colonel Frederick and Force S-4, Major Orvil Baldwin. Known to the men who used it as the *Force Knife*, each was individually hand made by W.R. Case & Sons Cutlery Company of Bradford, Pennsylvania. The 'V' in the designation stood officially for 'victory,' although some proposed that 'vengeance' was more apt. The '42' represented the vintage of its design, 1942. Three prototype knives, with polished steel finishes, were delivered by Case in August 1942. Frederick carried one of these prototypes throughout the Italian Campaign, while Baldwin retained the two others. After several modifications, general production on the standardized pattern commenced in November of that year. In total, Case produced an estimated 3,500 V-42s. The first 1,750 were procured for the First Special Service Force, and of these the first 500 were individually numbered.

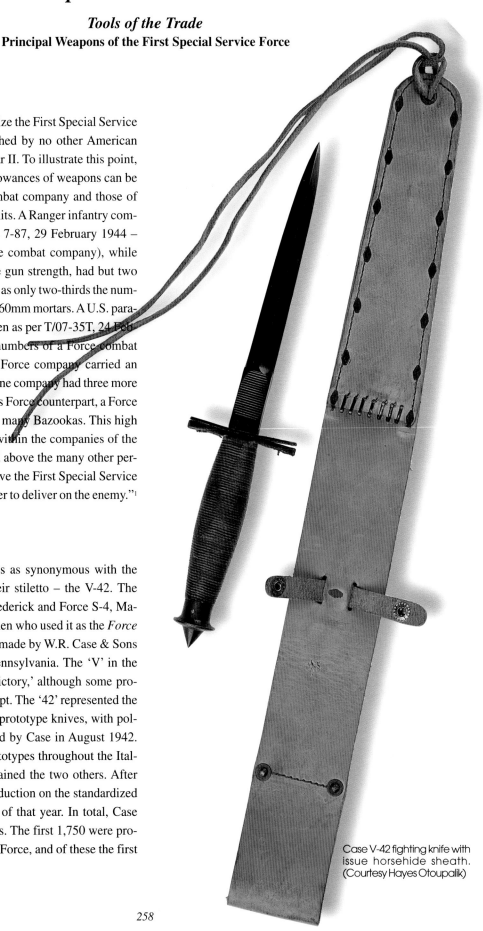

Case V-42 fighting knife with issue horsehide sheath.
(Courtesy Hayes Otoupalik)

Forcemen, Staff Sergeant Emil A. "Daddy" Bier, and Sergeant Wilmer E. Engle, both of 4-2, try their hand at milking "Blackie." Note the V-42 knife on Bier's right hip. The sheath has been modified to incorporate a wire belt hanger and an M-1916 pistol holster. Anzio Beachhead, Italy, c. 20-27 April 1944. (National Archives of Canada)

The overall length of the standard V-42 was approximately twelve and one-half inches; the blade being roughly seven and three-sixteenths inches long, double hollow-ground, and very sharp. The blades of the earliest V-42s turned out by Case were somewhat longer, but as they tended to snap at the end, the length was reduced. On the ricasso there was a grooved 'thumb-print.' With the knife positioned in the user's hand with his thumb on the ricasso this would ensure that the blade entered the intended victim's body horizontally, thus passing easily between the ribs. The hilt was fashioned from finely grooved leather washers, and a leather pad was incorporated into the back of the slightly down-turned metal crossguard thus preventing the user's fingers from freezing to it under conditions of extreme cold. Topping the hilt was a fearsome temple spike. All metal parts were blued.

Issued with each V-42 was a twenty-inch long, horsehide sheath. These sheaths were sewn together and then reinforced, seven rivets down each side. Others examples utilized staples in lieu of rivets. There was a single grommeted eyelet at the base so that the sheath could be tied down to the leg by means of a leather thong, and there was a metal staple at the throat. There was a belt loop at the top from which to hang the sheath from the web belt or pistol belt. These sheaths were necessarily long so that the knives would hang below the tail of the long ski parkas worn by members of the Force. With use, the sharp point of the V-42 tended to work its way through the back of the sheath. To prevent this, some men had the Force armorer rivet a piece tin plate to its back. Only members of the Force's Combat Echelon were issued the V-42. Characterized by one Force Canadian as being "a mean little weapon,"[2] the V-42 has attained somewhat legendary status. Yet as another put it: "If the truth were known, it probably punctured and opened more cans than it slit enemy throats."[3]

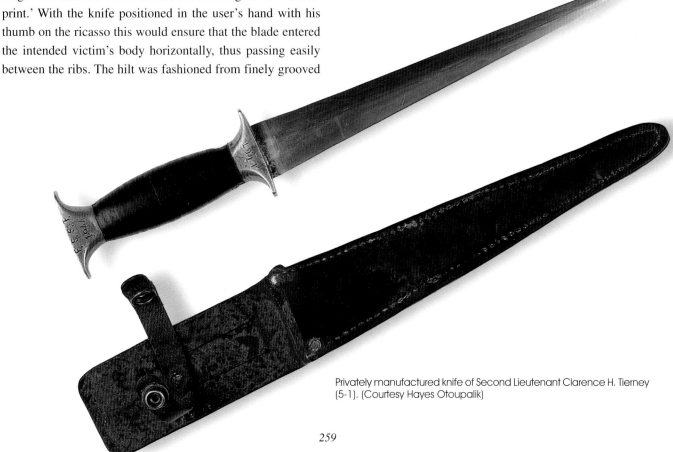

Privately manufactured knife of Second Lieutenant Clarence H. Tierney (5-1). (Courtesy Hayes Otoupalik)

Special Feature #8

Johnson Light Machine Gun, .30 Caliber, M-1941

The First Special Service Force had serious need for a light-weight machine rifle, of characteristics similar to the Browning automatic rifle, and that could be carried with airborne troops in parachute operations. The Force's Canadian officers suggested adopting their beloved Bren light machine gun, but as it was chambered in .303 caliber rather than the U.S. Army's standard .30 caliber this made that choice impractical. However, a highly successful solution was found.

Produced by the Cranston Arms Company of Providence, Rhode Island, the .30 caliber M-41 Johnson light machine gun met the qualifications. The Johnson was fitted with a folding bipod, and employed, conjointly, a conventional twenty-round detachable box magazine that fed in from the left side, with a five-round rotary internal magazine. Another of the Johnson's design innovations allowed for the magazine to be topped-off while remaining affixed to the weapon, by either loose rounds or by five-round chargers. Additionally, the weapon was fitted with a grip safety. From a closed bolt the weapon could be fire single shots. From an open bolt the weapon could be operated on full-automatic with a selective rate of fire – 300 or 900 rounds per minute. The weight of the M-41 with full magazine was approximately fourteen pounds in contrast to the approximately twenty-three pounds of the Browning automatic rifle and twenty-six pounds of the Bren gun; and it could be broken down into three pieces for a maximum length of approximately twenty-two inches permitting it to be parachuted in the same manner as the M-1 Rifle. The lightness in weight and ease of assembly (from 20-50 seconds) made it an extremely valuable parachutist's weapon. Its high volume of fire made it perfect as a small unit support weapon.

An agreement was reached whereby 125 Johnson light machine guns, complete with accessories, spare parts and barrels, and instruction manuals, were in May 1943, delivered to the First Special Service Force from those procured by the U.S. Marine Corps from the frozen stocks of the Netherlands Purchasing Commission. In return for the 'Johnny Guns,' the Marine Corps was furnished by the Force with a quantity of

RIGHT: 5-2 men field stripping the M-41 Johnson light machine gun. Left, Private W.P. Lelievre; right, Private L.E. Roussy. Anzio Beachhead, Italy, c. 20-27 April 1944. (National Archives of Canada)

Special Feature #8

the newly developed RS explosive, that the Force had on hand in abundance. Each of the Force's 108 sections was allocated one Johnson light machine gun. Within the section the 'Johnny Gunner' was supported by an assistant who carried spare magazines. As no purpose-made magazine pouches existed the clips were often carried in the leg bags of the mountain trousers or in the M-1 ammunition bag. The Service Battalion was issued no Johnsons, and instead was allocated 30 Browning automatic rifles that were distributed between Headquarters, Service, and Maintenance Companies. Though the Johnson was never officially adopted by either the Marine Corps or the U.S. Army, its reliability was undeniable.[4]

Three views of the M-41 Johnson light machine gun. (Courtesy United States Army Ordnance Museum)

Browning automatic rifle with its bipod, spare 20-shot magazine, and the M-1937 magazine belt. (Courtesy K. Bennett)

Rifle, .30 Caliber, M-1

Designed by John C. Garand, the M-1 rifle was accepted for U.S. service in 1936, replacing the M-1903 Springfield. Mass production commenced in 1939, and soon after the M-1 achieved the status of becoming the world's first general issue self-loading (semi-automatic) rifle. The M-1 was gas-operated. Chambered in .30-06 with a muzzle velocity of 2,800 feet per second, the effective range of the M-1 was approximately 500 yards, although the maximum range was up to 3,000 yards. Ammunition, loaded into the rifle's internal magazine, came in the form of eight-round *en bloc* clips. When the last round was fired both the empty shell casing and the *en bloc* clip were ejected at once. The bolt remained open as a signal to reload. The length of the weapon was forty-three and one-half inches, and, at nine and one-half pounds, the M-1 was heavy, but not appreciably more so than the Commonwealth's standard rifle, the Number 4. Furthermore, the M-1's high rate of fire, coupled with its rugged reliability, won it high regard.

In the First Special Service Force most men, whether in the Service Battalion or Combat Echelon, were armed with an

Field equipment display by Captain Edward H. Thomas of Second Regiment. (Author's Collection)

American Forceman chats with his Canadian comrade whilst running the bore of his M-1 Garand rifle, Fort William Henry Harrison, c. 1942. (Thomas W. Hope)

Rifles with associated ordnance and web gear. M-1 rifle, disassembled, atop padded Griswold bag; M-1 rifle atop green Pliofilm bag; M-7 rifle grenade launcher, M-1903 rifle; .30 caliber 8-round *en bloc* clips for the M-1 rifle; bore cleaner, M-1918 nine-pocket mounted cartridge belt; M-1923 10-pocket dismounted cartridge belt; cloth six-pocket bandoleers, web rifle sling; and numerous types of rifle grenades including M-9A1 antitank (upper left), T-2 impact fragmentation, Mk-IIA1 fragmentation grenade with grenade adapter, incendiary grenade with grenade adapter, and M-19 parachute flare. (Courtesy J. Ranoia/G. Piselli/Author's Collection)

M-1 rifle. The M-1 accepted a number of bayonets including the M-1905 and M-1942 models with their sixteen-inch blades, as well as the standard M-1 pattern with its ten-inch blade. Typically, two riflemen from each combat section were grenadiers. Using M-7 rifle grenade launchers fitted to the muzzles of their M-1s, these men could project a number of pieces of ordnance including M-9A1 antitank rifle grenades, T-2 impact fragmentation rifle grenades, as well as standard MkII fragmentation grenades that had been married to M-1A2 grenade projection adapters.[5]

Rocket Launcher, 2.36 Inch, M-1

The First Special Service Force was among the first units in the American Army to take delivery of this new weapon. In fact, some of the earliest examples were shipped to Helena where the Force conducted initial trials, the results of which established procedures that became part of the original field manual. The M-1 *Bazooka*, so named because of its resemblance to "a comic wind instrument played by a well-known American entertainer," was the very first truly portable anti-tank weapon introduced into the U.S. Army. It was the first modern rocket launcher, and the first launcher to employ shaped charge antitank rockets. The weapon's primary component was its 61" smooth bore tube into the rear of which was inserted the rocket. Typically the Bazooka was operated by a two-man team – one man to load, the other to fire. The rocket was ignited by means of an electrical discharge produced by a pair of flashlight batteries. The sudden ignition of the rocket's propellant produced a devastating back blast, and the end of the tube was fitted with a lightweight mesh screen to shield the firer. The Bazooka weighed approximately thirteen pounds and was sixty-one inches in length. Its M-6A1 and M-6A2 rockets weighted 3.4 pounds each and could penetrate armor up to 4.7 inches thick at a maximum range of 300 yards, though it was measurably more effective at shorter ranges. Though the rocket launcher had been designed first and foremost to be used against enemy armor, the Force found it to be highly effective against blockhouses and other hardened enemy positions.[6]

The 2.36" M-1 antitank rocket launcher. The M-1 Bazooka is the first modern rocket launcher, and the first to employ a hollow charge projectile. (Courtesy United States Army Ordnance Museum)

BELOW: Testing the M-1 Bazooka near Fort William Henry Harrison, Montana, c. Winter 1942-1943. (Author's Collection)

Special Feature #8

60mm Mortar, M-2 with Mount, M-2

The M-2 60mm mortar was the standard American light infantry mortar. It consisted of four basic parts, the barrel or *tube*, the bipod, the base plate, and the sight. This mortar was a crew-served weapon typically operated by a four man team comprised of a mortar gunner, an assistant mortar gunner, and two ammunition carriers. The weapon was aimed using its M-4 sight, that while being transported was detached and carried in its square leather case. The tube was smooth bore and mea-sured just over 28 inches. The total weight of the mortar was 42 pounds. The mortar's shells were called bombs, and most often it was the M-49A2 high explosive shell that was fired; although the M-83 illumination shell was also fired from this weapon. Mortar bombs weighed approximately three pounds. The range was from 100 yards to the maximum being just short of 2,000 yards. To fire the weapon the loader simply dropped the shell, stabilizing fins first, down the barrel. When the shell reached the bottom of the tube, the propellant would ignite sending it on its high-trajectory flight to the target. In the First Special Service Force the 60mm mortar was allocated on the basis of one per platoon.[7]

BELOW: M-2 60mm mortar with shell. Mortars were issued to the Force on the basis of one per platoon. (Courtesy United States Army Ordnance Museum) RIGHT: View of 3-1, 60mm mortar pit at Anzio. Left to right: Sergeant Leonard L. Grew, Private J.F. Ball, and Private F.A. Murphy. Note leather carrying case for the mortar's sight at right of pit. (National Archives of Canada)

Automatic Pistol, .45 Caliber, M-1911A1

Called the *Colt* after its designer, and also the *Forty-five*, the M-1911A1 was a self-loading, semi-automatic weapon that utilized a reliable recoil operation to cycle ammunition from its seven-shot magazine housed in the grip. An eighth round could be loaded in the breach. Though its .45 caliber round left the muzzle at relatively low velocity, its mass was enough to bring down almost any opponent no matter where he was struck. The weapon was approximately eight and one-half inches in length, and fully loaded it weighed nearly two and one-half pounds. This sidearm was carried in its issue M-1916 russet brown leather holster, or simply in the owner's pocket. The Force's initial table of organization, dated 5 July 1942, made no mention of the .45 automatic. However, when the Force was re-organized in early 1943, all members of the Combat Echelon were issued one of these coveted weapons. Issues for subsequent replacements were not always available.[8]

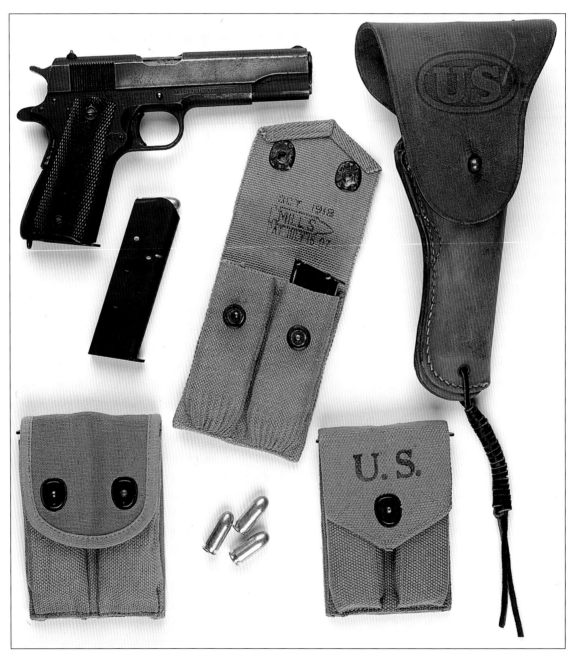

Every member of the Combat Echelon was issued the standard U.S. sidearm. Shown is the M-1911A1 automatic pistol, spare 7-round magazines, M-1916 leather holster, and, from left to right, M-1918, M-1919, and M-1923 double web magazine pockets. (Author's Collection/J. Ranoia)

Special Feature #8

Thompson Submachine Gun, .45 Caliber, M-1A1

The M-1A1 variant of the Thompson submachine gun was modified from the earlier 1928 model as it was simplified for mass production. Eliminated were the lock, actuator, breech oiler, buttstock catch, compensator and barrel fins. A straight forehand replaced the forward pistol grip, and a simple flip sight took the place of the predecessor's complex backsight. A further simplification was the M-1A1's fixed firing pin positioned on the face of the bolt. Adopted by the U.S. Army as its standard submachine gun in April 1942, the M-1A1 had a cyclic rate of 600-800 rounds per minute and chambered the same man-stopping .45 caliber ammunition as did the M-1911A1

automatic pistol. The *Tommy Sub*, as it was popularly called by Force Canadians, accepted both twenty and thirty round box-type magazines, and when fully loaded weighed in at about eleven pounds. A selector switch allowed the operator to fire either single shots or fully automatic. In the latter mode, the weapon's recoil was such that its muzzle tended to climb. Nevertheless, issued primarily to Section Leaders of the Combat Echelon, it was a tremendously popular weapon.[9]

By the close of 1944, the U.S. Army began to phase out the Thompson replacing it with the less-costly .45 cal. M-3 and M-3A1 submachine guns, the M-3 model having been introduced two years earlier. Nicknamed *Grease Gun*, the weapon

Submachine Guns: M-1A1 Thompson SMG (top), M-3A1 SMG, spare magazines for the M-3A1, five-pocket 20-round magazine pouch for the Thompson, and 30-round magazine case with shoulder strap. (Courtesy Pete Johnston)

Special Feature #8

bore a strong resemblance to that automobile repair shop tool, as it was manufactured chiefly from stamped parts, save for the barrel and the bolt. It weighed ten and one-half pounds, and instead of a wooden buttstock, the Grease Gun employed a retractable wire stock. Its cyclic rate was almost half that of the Thompson's so its designers made no provision for it to fire single shots.

Grenades

Augmenting each Forceman's individual weapons, he normally carried several hand grenades. There were a variety, but all employed the same basic mechanism and were small enough to be thrown by an individual soldier. Grenades were either filled with an explosive or some form of chemical. Each type incorporated a fuze assembly comprised of a safety pin, a handle or *spoon*, a striker, a cap, the fuze proper, and the charge. Grasping the grenade in one hand while holding the spoon in place, the soldier would next pull the pin from the fuze assembly by its ring. As long as the spoon was depressed it would prevent the striker from firing the cap and thus igniting the fuze. When either the grenade was thrown, or the spoon was released, the ventilated fuze would begin to burn down and in a few brief moments (about 4-5 seconds) detonate the charge contained in the body of the grenade.

Most often carried was the MkII fragmentation hand grenade. Weighing one and three-tenths pounds, this grenade had a deeply scored cast metal shell which caused it to be called the *pineapple*. Filled with TNT (or in some cases EC blank fire powder) it packed a devastating blast that sent jagged fragments in a 30 yard radius. Other grenades included the smooth cased MkIIIA1 offensive hand grenade, the Thermite-filled incendiary hand grenade, the white phosphorous hand grenade, as well as a variety of colored smoke grenades.[10]

Sergeant Lewis J. Merrim, Force photographer, here wielding a M-1A1 Thompson submachine gun rather than his normal camera. (Lew Merrim)

M-18 smoke grenade, incendiary hand grenade, and examples of the Mk-IIA1 fragmentation hand grenade with its cardboard shipping tube, and two-pocket web carrier. (Courtesy J. Ranoia/G. Piselli)

LEFT: Former Hot Dog stand being used as first platoon command post. Left, Private Thadeus Leszczynski; right, Staff Sergeant A.J. Ahfield, both of 3-1, Anzio Beachhead, Italy, c. April 1944. Oddly, the Mk-IIA1 fragmentation grenade hanging from the Private's shirt pocket came with a yellow paint job, a standard pre-war practice to mark live munitions, but not so for this stage of the war. (National Archives of Canada)

Carbine, .30 Caliber, M-1 and M-1A1

During World War II, the M-1 carbine filled a practical need for a lightweight weapon that could be easily wielded by troops such as vehicle drivers, engineers, and artillery and mortar crewmen, as well as being an adequate weapon for officers in the field. It was a gas operated, semi-automatic weapon that, like the M-1 rifle, was chambered in .30 caliber, but which fired a pistol-shaped cartridge. The carbine was magazine fed, accepting 15 and 30 round box-type magazines (although it seems that the late-war issue 30 round magazine never saw use by the Force). As often times happens, military arms undergo a certain evolution. In the case of the M-1 carbine, it was modified from its original form to include a folding wire stock and a wooden pistol grip. The new weapon was classified as the M-1A1 carbine. With the stock folded it was very compact making it an ideal weapon to be carried by airborne troops. Both M-1 and M-1A1 carbines were fitted with a flip site graduated to 300 yards, although the weapon was at its best at distances well inside of 100 yards.

When the First Special Service Force was originally organized it was only intended to carry out acts of sabotage. It was reckoned that, in large part, stealth, not force of arms, would be the factor contributing most to the success of its missions. Accordingly all men of the Force's Combat Echelon were armed primarily for self defense, with the M-1 carbine. If heavier fire power was needed, the Forcemen could reach for the Thompson submachine gun or the M1919A4 Browning machine gun carried aboard each Weasel.

When the Norway venture was dropped and the Force reorganized into an assault infantry formation, the M-1 carbine, as the principal individual weapon, was set aside in favor of the more powerful M-1 rifle. However the carbine, especially the M-1A1 model stayed on in the Force, it for the most part filling the role that its designers had originally intended.

Late-model M-1A1 carbine (top) with folding stock, pistol grip, and adjustable rear sight; and standard M-1 carbine. Also pictured: olive drab web slings, spare 15-round clip, and double web magazine pockets. (Courtesy J. Ranoia/K. Ross)

Special Feature #8

Browning Machine Gun, .30 Caliber HB M-1919A4

The advent of the light machine gun was the realization of the need for a portable support weapon which could be employed *by* the attacking infantry, rather than by support troops away from the point of contact. The Browning machine gun was an air-cooled weapon, with a perforated barrel jacket. It was recoil-operated and fired from an open bolt which further helped to ventilate the weapon while in operation. The gun weighed 31 pounds. In the ground mode it was used with a collapsible M-2 tripod. The tripod weighed 14 pounds. Between the rear two legs of the tripod was fixed a traversing bar. To that was attached a mounting gear incorporating a wheel that managed the elevation and depression of the gun. The gun's integral pintle mount mated it to the tripod and was latched in place.

Perfectly suited to a swift, mobile unit like the First Special Service Force, the .30 Browning M-1919A4 machine gun was an excellent close support weapon that was issued on the basis of one per section. The M-1919A4 was a crew-served weapon, manned by a machine gunner and his assistant with, in most cases, two additional men assigned as ammunition bearers. Ammunition for the weapon came in canvas belts containing 150 rounds each. These belts had a brass tab at either end to assist loading, and were transported in olive drab metal tins with hinged lids. The cyclic rate of the Browning machine gun was roughly 500 rounds per minute, while its sustained rate of fire was 150 rounds per minute.[11]

Browning M-1919A4 machine gun shown with boxes of belted ammunition, .30 cal. cleaning kit, and M-1 general purpose ammunition bag. (Courtesy J. Ranoia)

From the edge of a creek bank, Forcemen man a .30 cal. M-1919A4 Browning light machine gun. Note the improvised wooden carrying handled affixed to the weapon's perforated barrel jacket. (National Archives of Canada)

The Breakup and Beyond

Throughout the month of September the Force remained attached to the 1st Airborne Task Force and carried out a mission of guarding the Seventh Army's right flank. The Force's activity during this time was marked by aggressive patrolling, raiding, and systematic improvement of its fortifications. High ground was gained from which artillery observation could be achieved, and attached Engineers worked to strengthen the front lines by the addition of minefields and wire entanglements, as well as to improve jeep and foot trails to the mountaintop outposts. An especially effective form of artillery support was provided by Naval gun fire thanks to the Force's close proximity to the Mediterranean Sea. Enemy targets that were otherwise unattainable by land-based artillery often fell easy prey to this powerful asset. Before the Force's front line had been consolidated, the enemy (elements of the German *34th Division*) counterattacked several times, yet save for a platoon from 2-1 that, on 9 September, was temporarily pushed off its position northeast of Menton by heavy mortar and machine gun fire, enemy thrusts were repulsed inflicting heavy casualties. By the close of September enemy offensive action against the Force's front line had fizzled almost altogether; although the enemy maintained his redoubts, one of the strongest being Fort Castillon.[1]

During September as well, the Force's rear echelon was moved from Santa Maria di Capua-Vetere, Italy, to Nice, France, on Seventh Army orders. By 23 September all Force personnel and equipment had arrived in France. The establishment of the Service Battalion's supply apparatus in Nice, greatly facilitated the movement of supplies to the Force's forward-most elements. Drawing from 1st Airborne Task Force supply dumps, critical shortages in practically all types of supplies were few; all classes of supplies, generally, being adequate, if not abundant. The supply effort remained thus and so throughout the next several months.[2]

On 15 October, the 1st Airborne Task Force was relieved of its attachment to the Seventh Army and attached to the Sixth Army Group. The FSSF continued to carry out its current mission. Remaining attached to the Force, as they had been since September, were the 887th Engineer Company, elements of the 2nd Chemical Mortar Battalion, and the 602nd Field Artillery Battalion (Pack). During the latter stages of October, the 2nd Chemical Mortar Battalion was relieved from its attachment to the Force as was the 602nd FAB. But to make up for this loss, 81mm mortars were made available to Force elements, and, once more, the 463rd PFAB was attached to the Force, reuniting these old partners.[3]

Current action on the Force front was much as it had been during the latter days of September. The enemy restricted himself mainly to small scale patrols with infantry, and sporadic harassing fire with 105mm and 75mm artillery. Effective counter-battery kept the enemy's artillery fire to a minimum. Force reconnaissance and combat patrols operated along the front, and contact patrols maintained communication with the U.S. 517th Parachute Infantry Regiment that held an adjacent stretch of border-line beginning at Mount Diaurus, north of the village of Castillon.[4]

During the last few days of the month, enemy demolition crews suddenly became active busying themselves by cratering the coastal roads to the east of the Force front. Then on the night of 26 October the enemy "disposed of" approximately 300 rounds of mixed caliber ammunition by firing it across the Force front; ". . . a quantity and pattern of artillery usually

Force bivouac, Loup River flats, Villeneuve-Loubet, France, December 1944. (Author's Collection)

Shower tents, Villeneuve-Loubet, France, c. December 1944. (Author's Collection)

indicating retirement. During 27-28 October the enemy grew silent and by noon of the 29th [Force] patrols approached Sospel without contact after Mt. Razet and Fort Castillon were found deserted.

"As the month closed contact had not been regained nor had pursuit been pressed. It appeared that the *34th Division* was preparing to steal home."[5]

By November, it was apparent that the war, at least in this sector, was winding down. On 10 November, the 3rd Platoon of the 552nd Antitank Company was attached to the Force, and took up positions to cover the Force's seaward flank. A week later the 517th Parachute Infantry was pulled out of the

line, replaced by an armored infantry outfit. This also had the effect of moving the Force's left boundary somewhat further south. More reshuffling of units was effected the next day, when on 18 November the 463rd PFAB was relieved of its attachment to the FSSF and the 602nd FAB was again placed in support. On 21 November, the Force received orders relieving it from its attachment to the 1st Airborne Task Force (which was dissolved two days later), in turn assigning it to the 44th Antiaircraft Artillery Brigade. Next day the 442nd Regimental Combat Team took over the positions that had been held briefly by the armored infantrymen on the Force's left. And so it lasted for the next several days.[6]

Rations, beer, and cigarettes. Force bivouac, Loup River flats, c. December 1944. (Author's Collection)

First Sergeant James E. Tuso, 5-3, with libation in hand, Villeneuve-Loubet, France, c. December 1944. Tuso's cuts were likely to have been acquired during a bar-fight with a member of another U.S. Army unit. (Author's Collection)

Reading the Stars and Stripes, Force bivouac, Villeneuve-Loubet, France, c. December 1944. (Author's Collection)

On 28 November, the First Special Service Force was relieved from its static positions by the 100th Infantry Battalion of the 442nd RCT, and moved to bivouac near Villeneuve-Loubet, France, to await further orders, and to make preparations to begin training for future operations. But such would not be the case.[7]

The First Special Service Force was about to fall victim to what Canada called the conscription crisis of 1944. This "crisis" was the result of a gross misallocation of Canadian volunteer personnel, coupled with a current rate of infantry casualties well exceeding the figures forecast for Canadian Military Headquarters by the British at the outset of the war. These figures, in part, were the basis for Canada's National Mobilization Act of 1940. The NMA also prescribed that conscripted Canadian military personnel could only be employed for home defense. Now the suggestion that some Canada-only personnel – trained infantrymen – be employed overseas had the effect of causing all-out political panic. As Canada scrambled to tighten the tourniquet on the predicament, the First Special Service Force was caught in the squeeze.[8]

"Only the Sixth Army Group lobbied for the retention of the First Special Service Force because of its special capabilities in snow and mountain operations. Looking ahead to the advance into southern Germany, the army group envisioned the use of the FSSF in the Alps, then the French Vosges Moun-

Forceman Wendell Johnson (5-3) receives his pay. Lieutenant John Redd stands at right. Villeneuve-Loubet, France, c. December 1944. (Author's Collection)

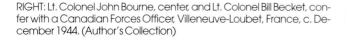

Pay day. Lt. Colonel John G. Bourne, Commanding Officer, 2d Battalion, Third Regiment (far left), presides. Villeneuve-Loubet, France, December 1944. (Author's Collection)

RIGHT: Lt. Colonel John Bourne, center, and Lt. Colonel Bill Becket, confer with a Canadian Forces Officer, Villeneuve-Loubet, France, c. December 1944. (Author's Collection)

tains, and finally in the Black Mountains. The army group's concern was heightened by its recent rejection of the War Department's offer to it of the 10th Mountain Division (the army group rejected the offer because the 10th was not scheduled to arrive in theater until March 1945 due to a shortage of shipping space for pack animals). Lacking a proven mountain unit, the Sixth wanted to hold on to the Force."[9]

Nevertheless, First Canadian Army Commander, "General Stuart had already recommended its disbandment, pointing out that, since the Force's departure from Italy for southern France in August, 'effective Canadian administrative control is quite impossible.' Stuart contended 'that this unit appears now to be submerged to such an extent with the U.S. Forces that the value to Canada of its retention is no longer apparent.' When the Americans concluded that it had, in any case, outlived its usefulness, the Force was disbanded. . . ."[10]

On December 3, 1944, Service Battalion officers received word from Colonel Walker informing them of the imminent deactivation of the Force. Canadian officers received notification that same day. The ceremony would take place on 5 December in a field nearby the Force encampment.[11]

At 1400 hours on 5 December 1944, on the Loup River Flats the Force paraded *en masse* as it had on a number of previous occasions. Only this time would be the last. After a memorial service for the Forcemen who had fallen in France, the Adjutant read the inactivation order. The colors were marched to a position in front of the assembled formation, were cased, and then marched off the field. In a brief address, Colonel Walker bid good-bye to the Canadians. Canadian senior officer, Lt. Colonel J.F.R. Akehurst had already departed France for Avellino, Italy, to make preparations for the arrival of the Force's Canadian contingent. Lt. Colonel Becket, accompanied by the Canadian color bearer, took up a post to the front left of the formation. At the command "all Canadians fall out," those men broke ranks and assembled behind Lt. Colonel Becket, forming for the first time as a separate entity the 1st

The 442d Regimental Band, on hand for the inactivation ceremony, played taps, followed by the national anthems of Canada and the United States, Villeneuve-Loubet, France, 5 December 1944. (Author's Collection)

Furling the Force Colors for the last time, Loup River Flats, 5 December 1944. (Author's Collection)

Canadian Special Service Battalion. The Americans remained at attention leaving vacant the openings left by their departing comrades. As the 442nd band struck up a march, Lt. Colonel Becket paraded his battalion across the front of the formation "in a final review."[12]

The Breakup: 1st Canadian Special Service Battalion, 37 officers and 583 other ranks, walks past, Loup River flats, Villeneuve-Loubet, France, 5 December 1944. (Author's Collection).

Force Americans salute their Canadian counterparts as they pass, Loup River flats, Villeneuve-Loubet, France, 5 December 5, 1944. (Author's Collection)

On the following evening the Canadians, 37 officers and 583 other ranks, collected their accouterments and boarded trucks that would take them to Marseille, to board ship for Naples. "The U.S. members gathered around to say a last farewell. The convoy moved off, breaking the grips of last handshakes, and disappeared down the road to the coast. . . ."[13] Once in Italy, the group reported to the Canadian Headquarters at Avellino. There, infantry replacements who had joined the Force either in Italy or southern France were sent to rejoin their former units. Parachute qualified personnel were then transferred to England. Departing from Naples aboard the liner *Arundel Castle* this batch of Canadians arrived at Victoria Barracks, Aldershot, England in January 1945. There, a number of men were assigned to duty as instructors, while others entered officer candidate training. The balance were absorbed into the 1st Canadian Parachute Battalion, from which a goodly number had volunteered for the Force some two years earlier, and with which they would last out the final days of the war.[14]

The U.S. forces that remained departed southern France on 28 December 1944 by train arriving four days later in the village of Barneville-sur-Mer, France, on the Normandy coast opposite the islands of Guernsey, Alderney, Sark, and Jersey (that, incidentally, remained occupied by German forces). There, this last remnant of the First Special Service Force was

Officer of the 474th Infantry Regiment (Separate) oversees embarkation of surrendered German forces in Norway at war's end. (Lew Merrim)

redesignated, on 6 January 1945, as the 474th Infantry Regiment (Separate) with Colonel Edwin Walker in command. That same day, a draft was received from European Theatre of Op-

Parachute qualified Canadian officers and men gather in Aldershot, England, January 1944, to hear the announcement that the 1st Canadian Special Service Battalion is to be disbanded. From l-r in the first row are Gerald W. McFadden, Stanley C. Waters, and John G. Bourne. Left of, and behind McFadden stands William S. Story. In the right of the frame, squarely facing the camera, stands Charles W. Mann. Note that as these men have reverted to the Canadian National Forces they all now wear standard Canadian Army battle dress uniforms and rank insignia. However, all wear the First Special Service Force shoulder sleeve insignia; and officers the FSSF branch of service insignia on their berets. (National Archives of Canada)

Task Force A, made up in part by the U.S. 474th Infantry Regiment (Separate), parades in Oslo, Norway, 4 July 1945.

erations Headquarters for parachutists to join the 82nd, and 101st Airborne Divisions as replacements. Three days later, 8 officers and 345 enlisted volunteers and assignees entrucked for La-Haye-du-Puits railhead and eventual assignment. The 99th Infantry Battalion (Separate) joined Walker's new regiment on 19 January 1945, as its third battalion. The 474th was made up of many disparate parts: 684 officers and men from the original FSSF; 434 officers and men from the 1st, 3rd, and 4th Ranger Battalions; 900 officers and men of the 99th Infantry Battalion; 156 officers and men of the 552nd Antitank Company; and 1,064 infantry replacements to the First Special Service Force and the 474th Regiment.[15]

After refitting and training, the 474th departed Barneville on 1 April 1945 to join the U.S. Third Army then battling its way into Germany. Following in the wake of Third Army's advance the 474th carried out security missions until V-E day, 7 May 1945. On 9 May, Colonel Walker received orders shifting the 474th to Norway as part of Task Force A to undertake the disarming and repatriation of some 300,000 German troops who had surrendered separately from the main Nazi capitulation. With the conclusion of this mission in October 1945, the 474th departed Norway aboard the Victory ship *Dominican Victory* arriving in New York on 25 October 1945.[16]

In his *Historical Prospective on Light Infantry*, Major Scott R. McMichael comments that "few units in World War II equaled the glowing reputation established by the FSSF. It never met defeat in battle. It accomplished the most difficult missions with an *élan* and a proficiency that astonished all outside observers, including the Germans. In size equal of an infantry regiment, the Force consistently accepted tasks appropriate to a regular division. Moreover, the unit remained effective even after it had sustained casualties that would have incapacitated another force."[17]

An overall maturity – the average age in the Force was 26 – and a general coolness under fire were leading factors; and, with few exceptions, officers and enlisted men alike possessed an inherent capacity for leadership. This had been one of the goals of Frederick's rigorous weeding-out process in Helena, where, as one Forceman put it, "the door swung both ways." Officers and NCOs had "*won* their slots in the chain . . ." resulting in "a loose, comfortable discipline that withstood thick fire and heavy casualties."[18] All throughout, it was Robert T. Frederick, the Force's redoubtable yet unpretentious commander, who set the standard.

Coupled with its other attributes, the Force's diverse training and its abundance of specialized equipment marked it as an elite implement of war to be used judiciously. However, "the most significant problem experienced by the Force was its misuse by corps and army commanders."[19] Squandered in the meat grinder that was the Winter Line, consumed in the costly daylight frontal attack that was the breakout of the Anzio Beachhead, and wasted in the advance across southern France,

Fort William Henry Harrison – where the Force's journey began – immediately post war. The abandoned Post Headquarters and empty company streets, once so alive with activity, are silent. The First Special Service Force is now but memories, yet the comradeship that it forged endures. (Lew Merrim)

each casualty the Force sustained represented the irreplaceable loss of not just a fighting-man, but that of a parachute jumper, a demolitionist, a saboteur, a ski-trooper, a mountain climber, and an amphibious raider.

Only during the assault on Monte la Difensa, and the amphibious operations against Kiska and the Iles d'Hyeres was the Force used in a manner purely indicative of its training. However, one could argue that no other outfit but the Force could have accomplished any of the missions allotted to it with the same aggressive manner and bold attitude. "Outsiders who witnessed their onslaughts from neighboring hills often thought Forcemen too reckless and risk-taking, but the speed and cohesion of the attack most often kept the ledger in balance."[20] Examples of this were the quick capture of both Mount Majo and Hill 720. What's more, who else but the *Black Devils* could have waged so dramatic and tenacious a defense of the Mussolini Canal line?

The reason for the Force's success, as told by Lt. General Stanley C. Waters, was that it was imbued with many strengths.

Waters (who rose to the rank of Major in the First Special Service Force) offers, "there are essentially seven elements in the make-up of any effective military force. I will list them in what I believe to be the proper order: Leaders, Men, Discipline, Training, Physical Fitness, Morale, and Equipment (although it could be argued that the first six are of equal importance and only equipment may be of lesser importance).

"You will recognize that the Force excelled in all elements with particular emphasis on Men, Physical Fitness, and Morale. In my later experience, if I was asked to compare the Force with other first class troops I served with or commanded, I would always single out the quality of the men, their superb strength and endurance plus their indomitable spirit and high morale. We would have been a formidable force equipped only with clubs."[21]

More truly glorious than its victories on the battlefield, the First Special Service Force's greatest achievement is the lasting brotherhood that it forged between its Canadians and Americans united by common purpose in war.

Special Feature #9

Campaigns, Battle Honors, and Decorations and Awards
Of the First Special Service Force

Campaigns and Battle Honors: United States
Aleutian Islands
Naples - Foggia
Rome - Arno
Southern France
Rhineland

Campaigns and Battle Honors: Canada
Monte Camino
Monte la Difensa
Monte la Remetanea
Monte Majo
Anzio
Rome
Advance to the Tiber
Italy 1943 - 1944
Southern France
Northwest Europe 1944

Casualties:
Killed By Enemy Action 401
Wounded By Enemy Action 2253
Missing In Action 124

Decorations and Awards:
Distinguished Service Cross 20
Legion of Merit 5
Silver Star Medal 121
Bronze Star Medal 140
Air Medal 1
Soldier's Medal 1
Purple Heart 1406
Good Conduct Medal 1049
Combat Infantryman's Badge 2416

FAR LEFT: Ribbons for various medals and decorations received by members of the First Special Service Force. From top to bottom: Asiatic-Pacific Campaign Medal with battle star; European-African-Middle Eastern Campaign Medal with invasion spearhead and battle star; American Campaign Medal; American Defense Medal; Distinguished Service Cross; Legion of Merit; Silver Star; Bronze Star; Soldier's Medal; Air Medal; Purple Heart with an Oak Leaf Cluster; Good Conduct Medal; and World War II Victory Medal. (Author's collection)

LEFT: The Combat Infantry Badge. (Author's collection)

Special Feature #9

Major General Geoffrey Keyes, II Corps Commander, awards the Silver Star medal to Private Richard B. Aitken of the First Special Service Force, Capua-Vetere, 20 January 1944. (National Archives)

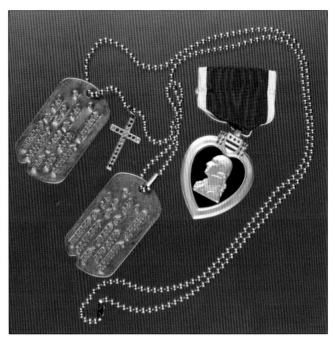

Identification tags and Purple Heart medal of Technician 5th Grade Charles E. Lay. Lay was a member of Service Company's Parachute Platoon, the members of which were all required to make the two qualifying parachute jumps – the only personnel of the Service Battalion so required. (Courtesy Hayes Otoupalik)

Forcemen parade for Silver Star awards, Anzio Beachhead, Italy. (National Archives)

Special Feature #9

For gallantry in action while undertaking operations on the Anzio Beach-head, six men of the Force are about to receive the Silver Star. These are to be presented by General Frederick. (Lew Merrim)

Lt. General Mark W. General Clark decorates Brig. General Frederick, Anzio. (Lew Merrim)

Medal of valor winners. L-r: Private R. B. Aitken (1-3), Silver Star; Sergeant John A. Rich (3-3), Distinguished Service Cross; Sergeant Camille Gagnon (2-3), Silver Star; Private Norman E. Enberg (2-3), Silver Star. Anzio, Italy, April 1944. The Distinguished Service Cross was awarded to those individuals who demonstrated, ". . . extraordinary heroism in connection with military operations against an armed enemy." (National Archives of Canada)

Special Feature #9

Parade for awards at Santa Maria di Castelabate, Italy, July 1944. (Author's Collection)

On 15 October 1944, the reconnaissance squadron that had supplied the Force with aerial photographs throughout the southern France campaign was relocated. Using this 4"x5" Speed Graphic camera and an improvised mount, Force photographer Sergeant Lewis J. Merrim then assumed aerial reconnaissance duties using a Stinson L-5 spotting plane flown by a pilot from the 463rd Parachute Field Artillery Battalion. (Lew Merrim)

BELOW: In all, Sergeant Merrim undertook 17 reconnaissance flights over enemy held terrain, accompanied by Lt. Watts, a photo interpreter on loan to the Force from the British Army, and the 463d PFAB's pilot. Flying slowly at 1,000 feet, Merrim was able to capture highly detailed and useful images. For his actions, Sergeant Merrim was awarded the Air Medal. The citation reads: "Because of the necessarily low altitude flown, the unprotected aircraft attracted much enemy antiaircraft fire, but at no time did this deter Sergeant Merrim's enthusiasm for participating in his self-appointed duty." (Lew Merrim)

Appendices

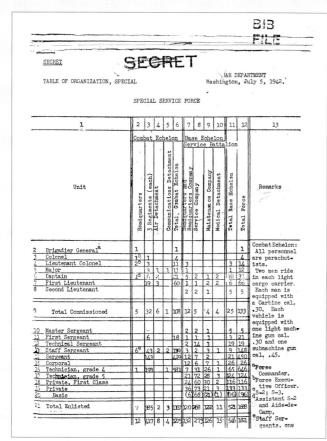

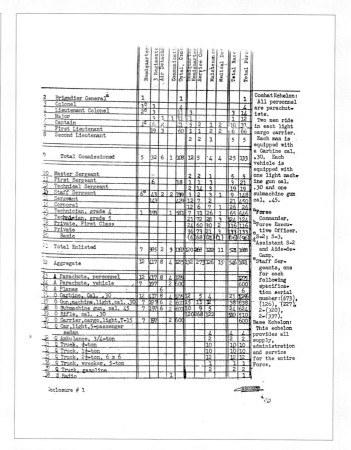

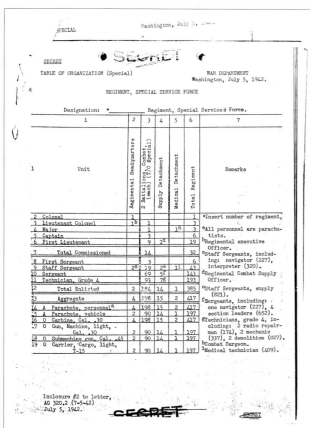

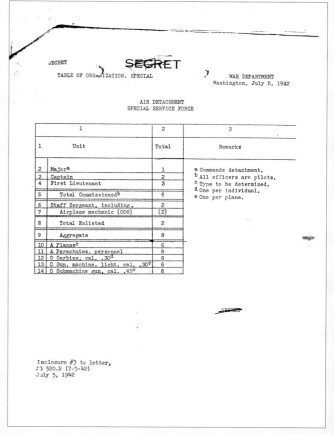

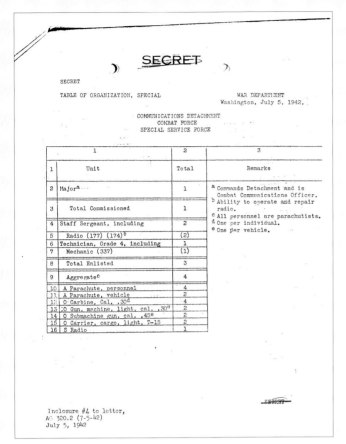

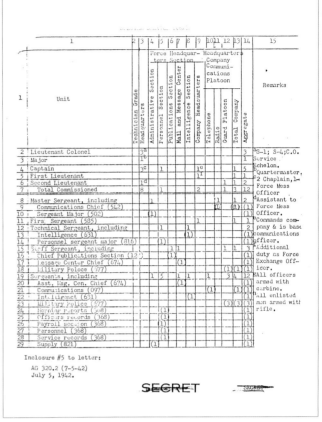

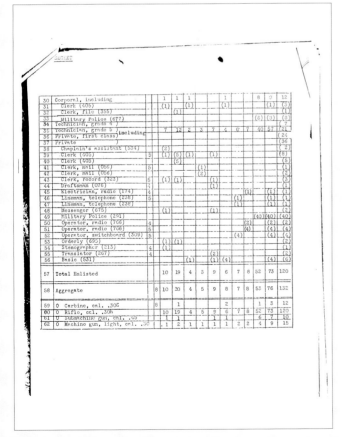

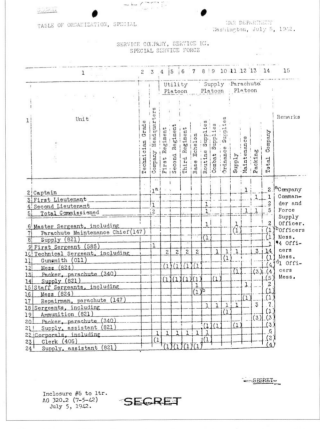

Appendix I: Historical Document #6 - Table of Organization

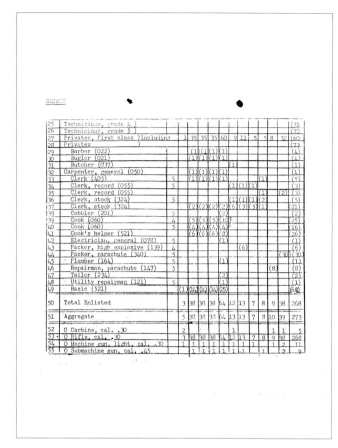

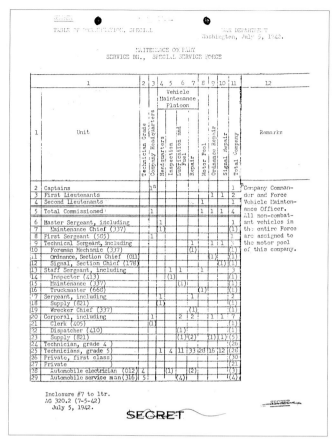

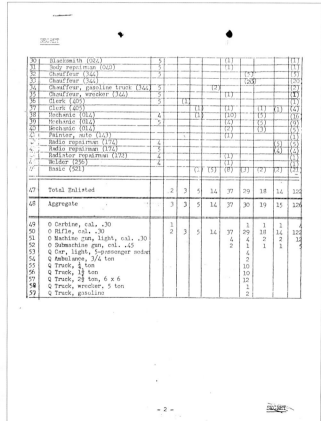

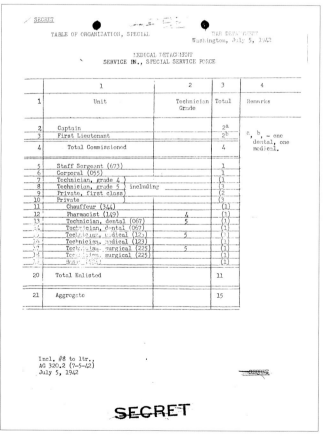

SECRET

TABLE OF ORGANIZATION (Special) WAR DEPARTMENT
Washington, July 5, 1942.

COMBAT BATTALION, SPECIAL SERVICE REGIMENT

Designation: * _____ Battalion, ** _____ Special Service Regiment

	1	2	3	4	5
	Unit	Battalion Headquarters	3 Combat Companies (Each) (T/O Spec.)	Total Battalion	Remarks
2	Lieutenant Colonel[a]	1		1	Personnel of combat units are administered, supplied and serviced by the Service Battalion, and have no duties other than training and combat.
3	Major[b]	1		1	
4	Captain		1	3	
5	First Lieutenant		3	9	
6	Total Commissioned	2	4	14	
7	First Sergeant		1	3	[a]Commanding battalion.
8	Staff Sergeant	1[c]	6	19	[b]Executive Officer.
9	Sergeant	3[d]	22	69	[c]Operations (814)
10	Technician, Grade 4		31	93	[d]Sergeants including: navigator (227), intelligence (631), and mechanic (337).
11	Total Enlisted	4	60	184	
12	Aggregate[e]	6	64	198	[e]All personnel are parachutists.
13	A Parachute, personnel	6	64	198	* Insert number of battalion.
14	A Parachute, vehicle	3	29	90	**Insert number of regiment.
15	O Carbine, Cal. .30	6	64	198	
16	O Gun, Machine, light, Cal. .30	3	29	90	
17	O Submachine gun, Cal. .45	3	29	90	
18	O Cargo Carrier, light, T-15	3	29	90	

Inclosure #9 to letter,
AG 320.2 (7-5-42)
July 5, 1942

SECRET

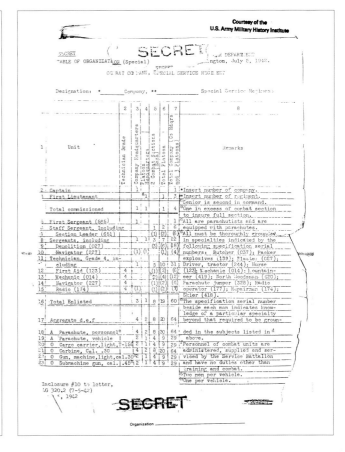

SECRET

TABLE OF ORGANIZATION (Special) WAR DEPARTMENT
Washington, July 5, 1942.

COMBAT COMPANY, SPECIAL SERVICE REGIMENT

Designation: * _____ Company, ** _____ Special Service Regiment

	1	2	3	4	5	6	7	8
	Unit	Technician Grade	Company Headquarters	Platoon Headquarters	2 Combat Sections	Total Platoon	Total Company (Co Hqrs and 3 Platoons)	Remarks
2	Captain		1				1	*Insert number of company.
1	First Lieutenant		[a]1		1		3	**Insert number of regiment.
	Total commissioned		1	1		1	4	[a]Senior is second in command. One in excess of combat section to insure full section.
3	First Sergeant (585)		1				1	[b]All are parachutists and are equipped with parachutes.
6	Staff Sergeant, including			1	2	6	[c]All must be thoroughly grounded in specialties indicated by the following specification serial numbers: Butcher (037); Packer explosives (139); Blaster (067); Driver, tractor (244); Nurse (123); Mechanic (014); Mountaineer (419); North Woodsman (420); Parachute jumper (328); Radio operator (177); Repairman (174); Skier (418).
7	Section Leader (651)				(1)	(2)	6	
8	Sergeants, including		1	3	7	22	
9	Demolition (027)			(5)	(6)	18	
10	Navigator (227)	(1)		(1)	(4)	
11	Technician, Grade 4, including		5	10	31	
12	First Aid (123)	4		(1)	(2)	(6)	
13	Mechanic (014)	4			(2)	(4)	(12)	
14	Navigator (227)	4		(1)	(2)	(6)	
15	Radio (174)	4	(1)		(2)	(2)	(7)	
16	Total Enlisted		3	1	8	19	60	[d]The specification serial number beside each man indicates knowledge of a particular specialty beyond that required to be grounded in the subjects listed in [d] above.
17	Aggregate d,e,f		4	2	8	20	64	
18	A Parachute, personnel[c]		4	2	8	20	64	[e]Personnel of combat units are administered, supplied and serviced by the Service Battalion and have no duties other than training and combat.
19	A Parachute, vehicle		2	1	4	9	29	
20	O Cargo carrier, light, T-15	2	1	8	20	64	
21	O Carbine, Cal. .30		4	2	8	20	64	
22	O Gun, machine, light, Cal. .30		1	4	9	29	[f]Two men per vehicle.
23	O Submachine gun, cal. .45		2	1	4	9	29	[g]One per vehicle.

Inclosure #10 to letter,
AG 320.2 (7-5-42)
... , 1942

SECRET

Organization _____

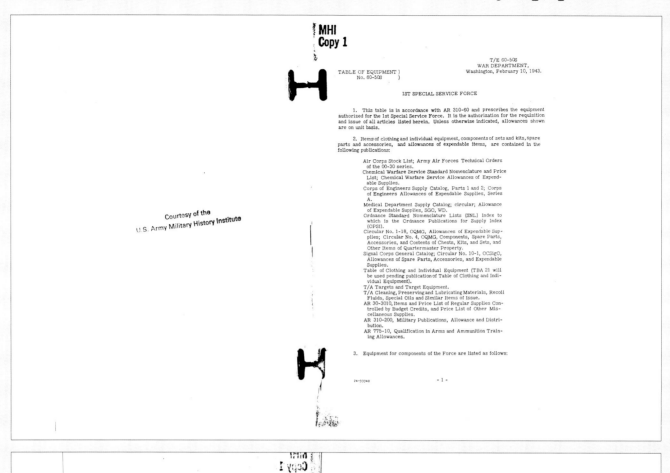

MHI Copy 1

T/E 60-503
WAR DEPARTMENT,
Washington, February 10, 1943.

TABLE OF EQUIPMENT)
No. 60-503   )

1ST SPECIAL SERVICE FORCE

1. This table is in accordance with AR 310-60 and prescribes the equipment authorized for the 1st Special Service Force. It is the authorization for the requisition and issue of all articles listed herein. Unless otherwise indicated, allowances shown are on unit basis.

2. Items of clothing and individual equipment, components of sets and kits, spare parts and accessories, and allowances of expendable items, are contained in the following publications:

Air Corps Stock List; Army Air Forces Technical Orders of the 00-30 series.

Chemical Warfare Service Standard Nomenclature and Price List; Chemical Warfare Service Allowances of Expendable Supplies.

Corps of Engineers Supply Catalog, Parts 1 and 2; Corps of Engineers Allowances of Expendable Supplies, Series A.

Medical Department Supply Catalog; circular; Allowance of Expendable Supplies, SGO, WD.

Ordnance Standard Nomenclature Lists (SNL) Index to which is the Ordnance Publications for Supply Index (OPSI).

Circular No. 1-18, OQMG, Allowances of Expendable Supplies; Circular No. 4, OQMG, Components, Spare Parts, Accessories, and Contents of Chests, Kits, and Sets, and Other Items of Quartermaster Property.

Signal Corps General Catalog; Circular No. 10-1, OCSigO, Allowances of Spare Parts, Accessories, and Expendable Supplies.

Table of Clothing and Individual Equipment (TBA 21 will be used pending publication of Table of Clothing and Individual Equipment).

T/A Targets and Target Equipment.

T/A Cleaning, Preserving and Lubricating Materials, Recoil Fluids, Special Oils and Similar Items of Issue.

AR 30-3010, Items and Price List of Regular Supplies Controlled by Budget Credits, and Price List of Other Miscellaneous Supplies.

AR 310-200, Military Publications, Allowance and Distribution.

AR 775-10, Qualification in Arms and Ammunition Training Allowances.

3. Equipment for components of the Force are listed as follows:

- 1 -

	Page
Force Headquarters Detachment, Combat Echelon	2
Regimental Headquarters Detachment, Combat Echelon	7
Regimental Medical Detachment, Combat Echelon	11
Regimental Supply Detachment, Combat Echelon	13
Battalion Headquarters Detachment, Combat Echelon	17
Company, Combat Echelon	20
Air Detachment, Combat Echelon	24
Communications Detachment, Combat Echelon	28
Headquarters and Headquarters Company, Service Battalion	31
Service Company, Service Battalion	37
Maintenance Company, Service Battalion	44
Medical Detachment, Service Battalion	52

T/E Special

FORCE HEADQUARTERS DETACHMENT, COMBAT ECHELON
FIRST SPECIAL SERVICE FORCE

AIR FORCE EQUIPMENT

1	2	3	4
Item	Allowances	For Computation	Basis of Issue and Remarks
Kit, interpreter, photo type F-2	2		

CHEMICAL EQUIPMENT

Curtain, gas-proof, M1	2		

- 2 -

ENGINEER EQUIPMENT

1	2	3	4
Item	Allowances	For Computation	Basis of Issue and Remarks
Compass, lensatic, luminous dial with case	16		1 per indiv.
Glass, magnifying, self-illuminating	1		
Glass, reading, 4 1/2, with case	3		
Sketching equipment	1		
Stereoscope, magnifying, mirror, w/binoculars and case	1		
Stereoscope, magnifying pocket	1		
Tube, tin, map-storage, water-proof, 4" x 39"	5		

ORDNANCE EQUIPMENT
a. Organizational Equipment

Bayonet, M1905 and Scabbard, bayonet, M3	9		1 per EM.
Binoculars, M3	16		1 per indiv.
Carbine, cal. .30, M1A1	7		1 per O. (See SNL B-28.)
Knife, fighting, type V-42, with sheath	16		1 per indiv.
Pistol, automatic, cal. .45, M1911A1	16		1 per indiv. (See SNL B-6.)
Projector, signal, ground, M4	4		See SNL B-24.
Rifle, U S, Cal. .30, M1	9		See SNL B-21.
Watch, wrist, 7 or more jewel	9		1 per EM.

- 3 -

ORDNANCE EQUIPMENT
a. Organizational Equipment (Cont'd)

1 Item	2 Allow-ances	3 For Compu-tation	4 Basis of Issue and Remarks
Watch, wrist, 15 or more jewel	7		1 per O.

b. Motor Transport Equipment

Carrier, cargo, light, T-15, complete with tools and equipment.	8		
Tool Set, Motor vehicle mechanics, complete with tools.	1		1 per mech. mtr.
Tube, flexible, nozzle, for refillable gasoline drums	8		1 per cargo carrier, T-15.

QUARTERMASTER EQUIPMENT

Axe, ice, mountain	8		
Axe, intrenching, M1910	1		
Bucket, Water, canvas, 18-qt	8		1 per cargo carrier, T-15.
Carrier, axe, intrenching, M1910	1		1 per axe, intrenching, M1910.
Carrier, cutter, wire, M1938	1		1 per cutter, wire, M1938
Carrier, pickmattock, intrenching M1910	2		1 per pickmattock, intrenching M1910.
Carrier, shovel, intrenching, rucksack	6		1 per shovel, intrenching, M1910
Case, canvas, dispatch, M1938	13		1 per O; EM, first 3 gr.
Case, flag, duck, cotton, colors	3		

24-33340   - 4 -

QUARTERMASTER EQUIPMENT (Cont'd)

1 Item	2 Allow-ances	3 For Compu-tation	4 Basis of Issue and Remarks
Case, flag, duck, cotton, standards	2		
Case, magazine, 30-round, with shoulder strap	8		1 per cargo carrier, T-15.
Clipper, hair	1		When authorized by CO.
Container, fuel, 1-qt	16		2 per stove, cooking, gasoline, 1-burner, M1941.
Cookset, mountain	8		1 per 2 indiv.
Crampons, mountain pr	8		
Cutter, wire, M1938	1		
Drum, inflammable liquid (gasoline), steel, w/carrying handle, capacity 5-gal.	32		4 per cargo carrier, T-15
Flag, aircraft and auto, Brig. Gen.	1		See AR 260-10.
Flag, boat and field, Brig. Gen.	1		Do.
Flag, color, organization (silk)	1		Do.
Flag, distinguishing, bunting	1		Do.
Flag, national colors (silk)	1		Do.
Flagstaff, colors	5		
Hammer, piton, mountain	6		
Kit, repair, ski	8		1 per 2 indiv.
Lantern, electric, portable	8		
Lantern, gasoline, w/mantle and pump	4		
Machete, 18" M1942	1		

24-33340   - 5 -

QUARTERMASTER EQUIPMENT (Cont'd)

1 Items	2 Allow-ances	3 For Compu-tation	4 Basis of Issue and Remarks
Pickmattock, intrenching, M1910	2		
Ropes, climbing set	6		
Saw, buck, light-weight	2		
Sheath, machete, leather, 18"	1		1 per machete, 18", M1942.
Shovel, intrenching, M1910	6		
Sling, color, web, OD	3		
Snaplink, mountain	12		
Stove, cooking, gasoline, 1-burner, M1941	8		1 per 2 indiv.
Tent, mountain, 2-man, complete with pins and poles	12		1 per O; 1 per 2 EM.
Whistle, Thunderer	16		1 per indiv.

SIGNAL EQUIPMENT

Camera, PH-324	1		
Camera, PH-430	1		
Converter, M-209, or cipher devise, M-94	1		
Exposure meter, PH-77-C	1		
Flag set, M-133	1		
Flashlight, TL-122-A	16		1 per indiv.
Panel set, AP-30-C	1		
Panel set, AP-30-D	1		

24-33340   - 6 -

SIGNAL EQUIPMENT (Cont'd)

1 Item	2 Allow-ances	3 For Compu-tation	4 Basis of Issue and Remarks
Radio set, SCR-536	6		
Radio set, SCR-694	8		Installed in cargo carrier, T-15.
Signal Lamp equipment, SE-11	1		

REGIMENTAL HEADQUARTERS DETACHMENT; COMBAT ECHELON
FIRST SPECIAL SERVICE FORCE

ENGINEER EQUIPMENT

1	2	3	4
Compass, lensatic, luminous dial, with case	6		1 per indiv.
Glass, magnifying, self-illuminated	1		
Glass, reading, 4 1/2", with case	1		
Sketching equipment	1		
Stereoscope, magnifying, pocket	1		
Tube, tin, map-storage, water-proof, 4" x 39"	1		

ORDNANCE EQUIPMENT
a. Organizational Equipment

Bayonet, M1905 and Scabbard, bayonet, M3	3		1 per EM.
Binoculars, M3	6		1 per indiv.
Carbine, cal. .30, M1A1	3		1 per O; See SNL B-28.

24-33340   - 7 -

Appendix II: Historical Document #7 - Table of Equipment

ORDNANCE EQUIPMENT (Cont'd)
a. Organizational Equipment (Cont'd)

1 Item	2 Allow-ances	3 For Compu-tation	4 Basis of Issue and Remarks
Knife, fighting, type V-42 with sheath	6		1 per indiv.
Pistol, automatic, cal. .45, M1911A1	6		1 per indiv; see SNL B-6.
Projector, signal, ground, M4	1		See SNL B-24.
Rifle, U S, cal. .30, M1	3		1 per EM; see SNL B-21.
Watch, wrist, 7 or more jewels	3		1 per EM.
Watch, wrist, 15 or more jewels	3		1 per O.

b. Motor transport equipment

1 Item	2 Allow-ances	3 For Compu-tation	4 Basis of Issue and Remarks
Carrier, Cargo, light, T-15, complete with tools and equipment	3		
Tube, flexible nozzle, for refillable gasoline drums	3		1 per cargo carrier, T-15.

QUARTERMASTER EQUIPMENT

1 Item	2 Allow-ances	3 For Compu-tation	4 Basis of Issue and Remarks
Axe, ice, mountain	2		
Bucket, water, canvas, 18-qt.	3		1 per cargo carrier, T-15.
Carrier, cutter, wire, M1938	1		
Carrier, pickmattock, in-trenching	1		1 per pickmattock, intrench-ing, M1910.
Carrier, shovel, intrenching, rucksack	2		1 per shovel, intrenching, M1910.
Case, canvas, dispatch, M1938	4		1 per O; opns sgt.

24-33340   - 8 -

QUARTERMASTER EQUIPMENT (Cont'd)

1 Item	2 Allow-ances	3 For Compu-tation	4 Basis of Issue and Remarks
Case, magazine, 30 rounds, with shoulder strap	3		1 per cargo carrier, T-15.
Container, fuel, 1-qt.	6		2 per stove, cooking, gaso-line, 1-burner, M1941.
Cookset, mountain	3		1 per 2 indiv.
Crampons, mountain pair	2		
Cutter, wire, M1938	1		
Desk, field, empty, fiber, company	1		
Drums, inflammable liquid (gasoline), steel, w/ carrying handle, capacity 5-gal.	12		4 per cargo carrier, T-15.
Hammer, piton, mountain	1		
Kit, repair, ski	3		1 per 2 indiv.
Lantern, electric, portable	2		
Lantern, gasoline, w/mantle and pump	1		
Pickmattock, intrenching, M1910	1		
Ropes, climbing set	1		
Saw, buck, light-weight	1		
Shovels, intrenching, M1910	2		
Snaplink, mountain	2		
Stoves, cooking, gasoline, mountain, 1-burner, M1941	3		1 per 2 indiv.
Stoves, tent, (complete w/equip-ment)	1		

24-33340   - 9 -

QUARTERMASTER EQUIPMENT (Cont'd)

1 Items	2 Allow-ances	3 For Compu-tation	4 Basis of Issue and Remarks
Tent, command post, complete w/pins and poles	1		
Tent, mountain, 2-man, complete w/pins and poles	5		1 per O; 1 per 2 EM.
Typewriter, portable, elite type, standard keyboard, w/carrying case	1		
Whistles, Thunderer	6		1 per indiv.

SIGNAL EQUIPMENT

1 Item	2 Allow-ances	3 For Compu-tation	4 Basis of Issue and Remarks
Camera, PH-324	1		
Camera, PH-431	1		
Converter, M-209, or cipher device, M-94	1		
Exposure meter, PH-77-C	1		
Flag set, M133	1		
Flashlight, TL-122-A	6		1 per indiv.
Frequency meter set, SCR-211	1		
Panel set, AP-30-C	1		
Panel set, AP-30-D	1		
Radio set, SCR-536	2		
Radio set, SCR-694	2		Installed in cargo carrier, T-15.
Radio set, SCR-714	1		Installed in cargo carrier, T-15.
Signal lamp equipment, SE-11	1		

24-33340   - 10 -

REGIMENTAL MEDICAL DETACHMENT, COMBAT ECHELON
FIRST SPECIAL SERVICE FORCE
CHEMICAL EQUIPMENT

1 Item	2 Allow-ances	3 For Compu-tation	4 Basis of Issue and Remarks
Curtain, gas proof	2		

ENGINEER EQUIPMENT

1 Item	2 Allow-ances	3 For Compu-tation	4 Basis of Issue and Remarks
Compass, lensatic, luminous dial with case	2		1 per indiv.

MEDICAL EQUIPMENT

1 Item	2 Allow-ances	3 For Compu-tation	4 Basis of Issue and Remarks
Brassard, Geneva Convention	2		1 per indiv. (Med & Dent serv) asgd to T of Opns
Equipment, regimental, special, "A"	1		
Kit, medical, NCO	1		1 per med NCO.
Kit, medical, officer	1		1 per med O.
Machine, imprinting	1		For use with indiv. identification tags.

ORDNANCE EQUIPMENT
a. Organizational Equipment

1 Item	2 Allow-ances	3 For Compu-tation	4 Basis of Issue and Remarks
Binoculars, M3	1		1 per O.
Pistol, automatic, cal. .45, M1911A1	2		1 per indiv. (See SNL B-6.)
Watch, wrist, 7 or more jewels	1		1 per EM.
Watch, wrist 15 or more jewels	1		1 per O.

24-33340   - 11 -

ORDNANCE EQUIPMENT
b. Motor transport equipment

1 Item	2 Allowances	3 For Computation	4 Basis of Issue and Remarks
Carrier, cargo, light, T-15, complete with tools and equipment	1		
Tube, flexible nozzle, for refillable gasoline drums	1		1 per cargo carrier, T-15.

QUARTERMASTER EQUIPMENT

1 Item	2 Allowances	3 For Computation	4 Basis of Issue and Remarks
Axe, ice, mountain	2		
Bucket, water, canvas, 18-qt	1		1 per cargo carrier, T-15.
Carrier, shovel, intrenching, rucksack	1		1 per shovel, intrenching, M1910.
Case, canvas, dispatch, M1938	1		1 per O.
Container, fuel, 1-qt	2		2 per stove, cooking, gasoline, 1-burner, M1941.
Cookset, mountain	1		1 per 2 indiv.
Crampons, mountain pr	2		
Drum, inflammable liquid (gasoline), steel, w/carrying handle, capacity 5-gal.	4		4 per cargo carrier, T-15.
Flag, Geneva Convention, Red Cross, bunting	1		
Hammer, piton, mountain	1		
Kit, repair, ski	1		1 per 2 indiv.
Lantern, electric, portable	1		
Lantern, gasoline, w/mantle and pump	1		

QUARTERMASTER EQUIPMENT (Cont'd)

1 Item	2 Allowances	3 For Computation	4 Basis of Issue and Remarks
Ropes, climbing, set	1		
Saw, buck, lightweight	1		
Shovel, intrenching, M1910	1		
Snaplink, mountain	2		
Stove, cooking, gasoline, 1-burner, M1942	1		1 per 2 indiv.
Tent, mountain, 2-man, complete with pins and poles	2		1 per O; 1 per 2 EM.
Whistle, Thunderer	2		1 per indiv.

SIGNAL EQUIPMENT

1 Item	2 Allowances	3 For Computation	4 Basis of Issue and Remarks
Flashlight, TL-122-A	2		1 per indiv.
Radio set, SCR-536	1		
Radio set, SCR-694	1		Installed in cargo carrier, T-15.

REGIMENTAL SUPPLY DETACHMENT, COMBAT ECHELON FIRST SPECIAL SERVICE FORCE
CHEMICAL EQUIPMENT

Item	Allowances	For Computation	Basis of Issue and Remarks
Apparatus, decontaminating, 3-gallon	6		
Kit, repair, gas mask, universal, M8	1		
Kit, service, for portable flame thrower, M1	2		1 per 10 flame throwers or fraction thereof.

ENGINEER EQUIPMENT

1 Item	2 Allowances	3 For Computation	4 Basis of Issue and Remarks
Compass, lensatic, luminous dial with case	19		1 per indiv.
Crimper, cap, with fuse cutter combination	6		3 per sec.

MEDICAL EQUIPMENT

Item	Allowances	For Computation	Basis of Issue and Remarks
Litter, folding	12		6 per sec.

ORDNANCE EQUIPMENT
a. Organizational Equipment

Item	Allowances	For Computation	Basis of Issue and Remarks
Bayonet, M-1905, and Scabbard, bayonet, M3	18		1 per EM.
Binoculars, M3	13		1 per O; 6 per sec.
Carbine, cal. .30, M1A1	1		1 per O; see SNL B-28.
Knife, fighting, Type V-42, with sheath	19		1 per indiv.
Pistol, automatic, cal. .45, M1911A1	19		1 per indiv; see SNL B-6.
Projector, signal, ground, M4	2		1 per sec; see SNL B-24.
Rifle, U S, Cal. .30, M1	18		1 per EM; see SNL B-21.
Watch, wrist, 7 or more jewels	16		1 per EM not furnished watch, wrist, 15-jewel.
Watch, wrist, 15 or more jewels	3		1 per O; C of sec.

ORDNANCE EQUIPMENT
b. Motor transport equipment

1 Item	2 Allowances	3 For Computation	4 Basis of Issue and Remarks
Carrier, cargo, light, T-15, complete with tools and equipment	13		
Tool set, Motor vehicle mechanic's (complete with tools)	2		1 per mech, mtr.
Tube, flexible nozzle, for refillable gasoline drums	13		1 per cargo carrier, T-15.

QUARTERMASTER EQUIPMENT

Item	Allowances	For Computation	Basis of Issue and Remarks
Axe, ice, mountain	6		3 per sec.
Axe, intrenching, M1910	2		1 per sec.
Bag, canvas, water sterilizing, complete with cover and hanger	1		
Bucket, water, canvas, 18-qt	13		1 per cargo carrier, T-15.
Carrier, axe, intrenching, M1910	2		1 per axe, intrenching, M1910.
Carrier, cutter, wire, M1938	2		1 per cutter, wire, M1938.
Carrier, pickmattock, intrenching, M1910	4		1 per pickmattock, intrenching, M1910.
Carrier, shovel, intrenching, rucksack	10		1 per shovel, intrenching, M1910.
Case, canvas, dispatch, M1938	3		1 per O; C of sec.
Case, magazine, 30-round, with shoulder strap	13		1 per cargo carrier, T-15.
Clipper, hair	1		(when authorized by CO.)

QUARTERMASTER EQUIPMENT (Cont'd)

Item	Allow-ances	For Compu-tation	Basis of Issue and Remarks
Container, fuel, 1-qt	20		2 per stove, cooking, gas-oline, 1-burner, M1941.
Cookset, mountain	10		1 per 2 indiv.
Crampons, mountain pr	6		3 per sec.
Cutter, wire, M1938	2		1 per sec.
Drum, inflammable, liquid (gasoline), steel, with car-rying handle, capacity 5-gal	52		4 per cargo carrier, T-15.
Hammer, piton, mountain	6		3 per sec.
Kit, repair, ski	10		1 per 2 indiv.
Lantern, electric, protable	3		1 per det hq; sec.
Machete, 18", M1942	2		1 per sec.
Paulin, canvas, 12' x 17', OD	2		
Pickmattock, intrenching, M1910	4		2 per sec.
Ropes, climbing set	6		3 per sec.
Saw, buck, lightweight	6		3 per sec.
Sheath, machete, leather, 18"	2		1 per machete, 18", M1942.
Shovel, intrenching, M1910	10		5 per sec.
Snaplink, mountain	12		6 per sec.
Stove, cooking, gasoline, 1-burner, M1941	10		1 per 2 indiv.
Tent, mountain, 2-man, complete with pins and poles	10		1 per O; 1 per 2 EM.
Whistle, Thunderer	3		1 per O; C of sec.

24-33340   - 16 -

SIGNAL EQUIPMENT

Item	Allow-ances	For Compu-tation	Basis of Issue and Remarks
Chest, BC-5	4		
Flashlight, TL-122-A	7		1 per O; C of sec; mech, mtr; repairman, rad.
Radio set, SCR-536	3		1 per det hq; sec.
Radio set, SCR-694	1		1 per det hq. (Installed in cargo carrier, T-15.)
Radio set, SCR-714	12		1 per cargo carrier, T-15, except in det hq. (In-stalled in cargo carrier, T-15.)
Signal lamp equipment, SE-11	1		
Tool equipment, TE-33	2		1 per repairman, rad.

BATTALION HEADQUARTERS DETACHMENT, COMBAT ECHELON FIRST SPECIAL SERVICE FORCE
ENGINEER EQUIPMENT

Item	Allow-ances	For Compu-tation	Basis of Issue and Remarks
Compass, lensatic, luminous dial, with case	6		1 per indiv.
Glass, magnifying, self-illuminated	1		
Glass, reading, 4 1/2", with case	1		
Sketching equipment	1		
Stereoscope, magnifying, pocket	1		
Tube, tin, map-storage, water-proof, 4" x 39"	1		

24-33340   - 17 -

ORDNANCE EQUIPMENT
a. Organizational Equipment

Item	Allow-ances	For Compu-tation	Basis of Issue and Remarks
Bayonet, M1905 and scabbard bayonet, M3	4		1 per EM.
Binoculars, M3	6		1 per indiv.
Carbine, cal. .30, M1A1	2		1 per O. See SNL B-28.
Knife, fighting, Type V-42 with sheath	6		1 per indiv.
Pistol, automatic, cal. .45, M1911A1	6		1 per indiv. See SNL B-6.
Projector, signal, ground, M4	1		See SNL B-24.
Rifle, U S, cal. .30, M1	4		1 per EM. See SNL B-21.
Watch, wrist, 7 or more jewels	4		1 per EM.
Watch, wrist, 15 or more jewels	2		1 per O.

b. Motor Transport Equipment

Item	Allow-ances	For Compu-tation	Basis of Issue and Remarks
Carrier, cargo, light, t-15, T-15, complete with tools and equipment	3		
Tube, flexible nozzle, for refillable gasoline drums	3		1 per cargo carrier, T-15.

QUARTERMASTER EQUIPMENT

Item	Allow-ances	For Compu-tation	Basis of Issue and Remarks
Axe, ice, mountain	2		
Axe, intrenching, M1910	1		

24-33340   - 18 -

QUARTERMASTER EQUIPMENT (Cont'd)

Item	Allow-ances	For Compu-tation	Basis of Issue and Remarks
Bucket, water, canvas, 18-qt	3		1 per cargo carrier, T-15.
Carrier, axe, intrenching, M1910	1		1 per axe, intrenching, M1910.
Carrier, cutter, wire, M1938	1		1 per cutter, wire, M1938.
Carrier, pickmattock, intrenching M1910	1		1 per pickmattock, intrench-ing, M1910.
Carrier, shovel, intrenching, rucksack	2		1 per shovel, intrenching, M1910.
Case, canvas, dispatch, M1938	3		1 per O. 1 per opns sgt.
Case, magazine, 30 round with shoulder strap	3		1 per cargo carrier, T-15.
Container, fuel, 1-qt	6		2 per stove, cooking, gas-oline, 1-burner, M1941.
Cookset, mountain	3		1 per 2 indiv.
Crampons, mountain pair	2		
Cutter, wire, M1938	1		

SIGNAL EQUIPMENT

Item	Allow-ances	For Compu-tation	Basis of Issue and Remarks
Flag set, M-133	1		
Flashlight, TL-122-A	6		1 per indiv.
Panel set, AP-30-C	1		
Panel set, AP-30-D	1		
Radio set, SCR-536	2		

24-33340   - 19 -

Appendix II: Historical Document #7 - Table of Equipment

Item	Allow-ances	For Compu-tation	Basis of Issue and Remarks
Radio set, SCR-694	1		Installed in cargo carrier, T-15.
Radio set, SCR-714	2		Installed in cargo carrier, T-15.
Signal lamp equipment, SE-11	1		

COMPANY, COMBAT, ECHELON
FIRST SPECIAL SERVICE FORCE
CHEMICAL EQUIPMENT

Item	Allow-ances	For Compu-tation	Basis of Issue and Remarks
Alarm, gas M1	1		
Apparatus, decontaminating 3 gallon	1		
Flame thrower, portable, M1	3		1 per plat.
Kit, HS, vapor detector, M4	1		

ENGINEER EQUIPMENT

Item	Allow-ances	For Compu-tation	Basis of Issue and Remarks
Compass, lensatic, luminous dial, with case	77		1 per indiv.
Crimper, cap, with fuse cutter combination	12		2 per Sec.
Glass, magnifying, self-illuminated	1		
Tube, tin, map storage, water-proof, 4" x 39"	1		Co hq.

24-33340
-20-

ORDNANCE EQUIPMENT
a. Organizational Equipment.

Item	Allow-ances	For Compu-tation	Basis of Issue and Remarks
Bayonet, M-1905, and Scabbard, bayonet, M3	66		1 per EM (except sec ldr).
Binoculars, M3	37		1 per O; 1st sgt; com sgt; 6 per sec.
Carbine, cal. .30, M1A1	5		1 per O. See SNL B-28.
Gun, machine, cal. .30, Browning, M1919A4.	6		1 per sec. See SNL A-6.
Gun, submachine, cal. .45, M3.	6		1 per sec ldr.
Knife, fighting, Type V-42, with sheath	77		1 per indiv.
Launcher, rocket, AT, 2.36", M1	6		1 per sec. See SNL B-36.
Mortar, 60-mm and mount M-2.	3		1 per Plat. See SNL A-43.
Mount, tripod, MG, cal. .30, M-2	6		1 per LMG. See SNL A-6.
Pistol, automatic, cal. .45, M1911A1.	77		1 per indiv. See SNL B-6.
Projector, signal, ground, M-4	10		1 per co hq; plat hq; sec. See SNL B-24.
Rifle, U S, cal. .30, M1	66		1 per EM (except sec ldr) see SNL B-21.
Watch, pocket, 7 or more jewels	65		1 per EM (except 1st sgt and sec ldr).
Watch, wrist, 15 or more jewels	12		1 per O; 1st sgt; sec ldr.

b. Motor transport equipment

Item	Allow-ances	For Compu-tation	Basis of Issue and Remarks
Carrier, cargo, light, T-15, complete with tools and equipment.	37		1 per plat hq; 2 per co hq; 2 spare; 5 per sec.

24-33340
- 21 -

Item	Allow-ances	For Compu-tation	Basis of Issue and Remarks
Tool set, Motor vehicle mechanic's (complete with tools)	6		1 per sec.

QUARTERMASTER EQUIPMENT

Item	Allow-ances	For Compu-tation	Basis of Issue and Remarks
Axe, ice, mountain	12		2 per sec.
Axe, intrenching, M1910	6		1 per sec.
Bag, canvas, water steriliz-ing, complete with cover and hanger	1		
Bucket, water, canvas, 18-qt.	37		1 per cargo carrier, T-15.
Carrier, axe, intrenching, M1910	6		1 per axe, intrenching, M1910.
Carrier, cutter, wire M1938	13		1 per cutter, wire, M1938.
Carrier, grenade	12		2 per sec.
Carrier, pickmattock, intrench-ing, M1910.	13		1 per pickmattock, in-trenching, M1910.
Carrier, shovel, intrenching, rucksack	41		1 per shovel, intrench-ing, M1910.
Case, canvas, dispatch, M1938	12		1 per O; 1st sgt; sec ldr.
Case, flag, duck, cotton, guidon	1		1 per guidon.
Case, magazine, 30-round, with shoulder strap	37		1 per cargo carrier, T-15.
Clippers, hair	3		1 per plat (when authorized by CO).
Container, fuel, 1-qt.	78		2 per stove, cooking, gas-oline, 1-burner, M1941.

24-33340
- 22 -

Item	Allow-ances	For Compu-tation	Basis of Issue and Remarks
Cookset, mountain	39		1 per 2 indiv.
Crampons, mountain pr	24		4 pr per sec.
Cutters, wire, M1938	13		1 per co hq; 2 per sec.
Drums, inflammable, liquid (gasoline), steel, with car-rying handle, capacity 5-gal	148		4 per cargo carrier, T-15.
Flag, guidon, bunting	1		
Flagstaff, guidon	1		
Hammer, piton, mountain	12		2 per sec.
Kit, repair, ski	39		1 per 2 indiv.
Lantern, electric, portable	1		
Machete, 18", M1942	6		1 per sec.
Mittens, asbestos, M1942	24		4 per sec.
Paulin, canvas, 12' x 17', OD	1		
Pickmattock, intrenching, M1910	13		1 per co hq; 2 per sec.
Ropes, climbing set	12		2 per sec.
Saw, buck, light-weight	6		1 per sec.
Sheath, machete, leather, 18"	6		1 per machete, 18", M1942.
Shovel, intrenching, M1910	41		1 per plat hq; 2 per co hq; 6 per sec.
Sling, carrying, MG and am-munition	224		4 per sec.
Snaplink, mountain	24		4 per sec.
Stove, cooking, gasoline, 1-burner, M1941	39		1 per 2 indiv.
Tent, mountain, 2-man, complete with pins and poles	41		1 per O; 1 per 2 EM.

24-33340
- 23 -

QUARTERMASTER EQUIPMENT (Cont'd)

1	2	3	4
Item	Allow-ances	For Compu-tation	Basis of Issue and Remarks
Whistle, Thunderer	12		1 per O; 1st sgt; sec ldr.

SIGNAL EQUIPMENT

1	2	3	4
Flag, set, M-133.	1		per co hq.
Flashlight, TL-122-A	12		1 per O; 1st sgt; sec ldr.
Radio set, SCR-536	4		1 per co hq; plat hq.
Radio set, SCR-694	4		1 per co hq; plat hq. (installed in cargo carrier T-15).
Radio set, SCR-714	33		1 per co hq; 5 per sec; 2 spare; (installed in cargo carrier, T-15).
Signal lamp equipment, SE-11	4		1 per co hq; plat hq.

AIR DETACHMENT, COMBAT ECHELON
FIRST SPECIAL SERVICE FORCE
ARMY AIR FORCES EQUIPMENT

1	2	3	4
Airplane	6		Ln and obsn types in accordance with mission asgd Force.
Bag, flyer's kit, Type A-3	12		1 per prcht.
Cover, engine, warning	6		1 per ap.
Emergency equipment for airplanes			To be in accordance with type of ap asgd.
Heater, engine warming	6		1 per ap.
Kit, air, message (T.O. 00-30-37)	30		5 per ap.

24-33340

- 24 -

ARMY AIR FORCES EQUIPMENT (Cont'd)

1	2	3	4
Item	Allow-ances	For Compu-tation	Basis of Issue and Remarks
Kit, airplane mooring	6		1 per ap in addition to that carried with ap.
Kit, crash tools and equipment, ground (T. O.00-30-44)	1		
Kit, flyer's emergency (T. O. 00-30-49)	18		3 per ap.
Kit, navigation, pilot (T. O. 00-30-63)	6		1 per pilot.
Parachute, seat, Type S-1 or S-2, complete	12		1 per pilot; ap.
Paulin, airplane protective, (Weather)	a		As required to cover aircraft.
Truck, oil-service, 2 1/2-ton, Type L-2 (Spec 3140)	1		
Truck, tractor, gasoline, 4 - 5 tons, with 2 semi-trailers, tank	1		
Vest, life preserver, Type B-4	8		1 per indiv.

CHEMICAL EQUIPMENT

Item	Allow-ances		
Alarm, Gas, M1	1		
Apparatus, decontaminat-ing, 3-gal, M1	3		

24-33340

- 25 -

ENGINEER EQUIPMENT

1	2	3	4
Item	Allow-ances	For Compu-tation	Basis of Issue and Remarks
Compass, lensatic, luminous dial, with case	8		1 per indiv.

ORDNANCE EQUIPMENT
a. Organizational Equipment

1	2	3	4
Bayonet, M1905 Scabbard, bayonet, M3	2		1 per EM.
Binoculars, M-3	7		1 per O; det.
Carbine, cal. .30, M1	6		1 per O (see SNL B-28).
Gun, machine, Browning cal. .30, M2, aircraft			As required for ap asgd (see SNL A-28).
Gun, machine, Browning cal. .50, M2, aircraft			As required for ap asgd (see SNL A-38).
Pistol, automatic, cal. .45, M1911A1	8		1 per indiv. (see SNL B-6)
Pistol, pyrotechnic M8, with Mount	6		1 per ap (see SNL B-18).
Rifle, U S, Cal. .30, M1	2		1 per EM (see SNL B-3).
Watch, wrist, 7 or more jewels	2		1 per EM.
Watch, wrist, 15 or more jewels	6		1 per O.

24-33340

- 26 -

ORDNANCE EQUIPMENT (Cont'd)
b. Motor Transport Equipment

1	2	3	4
Item	Allow-ances	For Compu-tation	Basis of Issue and Remarks
Carrier, cargo, light, T-15, complete with tools and equipment	1		
Tube, flexible nozzle, for refillable gasoline drums	27		4 per ap; 1 per cargo carrier, T-15; trk.

QUARTERMASTER EQUIPMENT

Item	Allow-ances	For Compu-tation	Basis of Issue and Remarks
Axe, ice, mountain	2		
Bucket, water, canvas, 18-qt	1		1 per cargo carrier, T-15.
Carrier, Shovel, intrench-ing, rucksack	2		1 per shovel, intrenching, M1910.
Case, canvas, dispatch, M1938	8		1 per O; NCO, first 3 gr.
Container, fuel, 1-qt	8		2 per stove, cooking, gas-oline, 1-burner, M1942.
Cookset, mountain	4		1 per 2 indiv.
Crampons, mountain pr	2		
Desk, field, empty, fiber, company	1		
Drums, inflammable liquid (gasoline), steel, with carrying handle, capacity 5-gal.	32		2 per trk, 2 1/2 ton and larger; 4 per cargo car-rier, T-15; 4 per ap.
Hammer, Piton, mountain	1		
Lantern, electric, portable	2		
Ropes, climbing, set	1		

24-33340

- 27 -

Appendix II: Historical Document #7 - Table of Equipment

QUARTERMASTER EQUIPMENT (Cont'd)

Item	Allowances	For Computation	Basis of Issue and Remarks
1	2	3	4
Saw, buck, lightweight	1		
Shovel, intrenching, M1910	2		
Snaplink, mountain	2		
Stove, cooking, gasoline, 1-burner, M1942	4		1 per 2 indiv.
Tent, mountain, 2-man, complete with pins and poles	7		1 per O; 1 per 2 EM.
Typewriter, portable, elite type, standard keyboard, with carrying case	1		
Whistle, Thunderer	6		1 per O.

SIGNAL EQUIPMENT

Item	Allowances	For Computation	Basis of Issue and Remarks
Flashlight, TL-122-A	8		1 per indiv.
Radio set, SCR-694	1		Installed in cargo, carrier, T-15.

COMMUNICATIONS DETACHMENT: COMBAT ECHELON
FIRST SPECIAL SERVICE FORCE
CHEMICAL EQUIPMENT

Item	Allowances	For Computation	Basis of Issue and Remarks
Curtain, gas proof, M1	2		

ENGINEER EQUIPMENT

Item	Allowances	For Computation	Basis of Issue and Remarks
Compass, lensatic, luminous dial, with case	4		1 per indiv.

24-33340
- 28 -

ORDNANCE EQUIPMENT
a. Organizational Equipment

Item	Allowances	For Computation	Basis of Issue and Remarks
1	2	3	4
Bayonet, M-1905 and Scabbard, bayonet, M3	3		1 per EM.
Binoculars, M3	2		1 per O; det.
Carbine, cal. .30, M1A1	1		1 per O (see SNL B-28).
Knife, fighting, Type V-42, with sheath	4		1 per indiv.
Pistol, automatic, cal. .45, M1911A1	4		1 per indiv. (see SNL B-6)
Projector, signal, ground, M4	1		See SNL B-24.
Rifle, U S, cal. .30, M1	3		1 per EM (see SNL B-21).
Watch, wrist, 7 or more jewels	3		1 per EM.
Watch, wrist, 15 or more jewels	1		1 per O.

b. Motor Transport Equipment

Item	Allowances	For Computation	Basis of Issue and Remarks
Carrier, cargo, light, T-15, complete with tools and equipment	2		

QUARTERMASTER EQUIPMENT

Item	Allowances	For Computation	Basis of Issue and Remarks
Bucket, water, canvas, 18-qt	2		1 per cargo carrier T-15.
Carrier, pickmattock, intrenching, M1910	1		1 per pickmattock, intrenching, M1910.
Carrier, shovel, intrenching, rucksack	2		1 per shovel, intrenching, M1910.

24-33340
- 29 -

QUARTERMASTER EQUIPMENT (Cont'd)

Item	Allowances	For Computation	Basis of Issue and Remarks
1	2	3	4
Case, canvas, dispatch, M1938.	1		1 per O.
Container, fuel, 1-qt.	4		2 per stove, cooking, gasoline, M1941.
Cookset, mountain.	2		1 per 2 indiv.
Drum, inflammable liquid (gasoline), steel, with carrying handle, capacity 5-gal.	8		4 per cargo carrier, T-15.
Kit, repair, ski	2		1 per 2 indiv.
Lantern, electric, portable	1		
Machete, 18'', M1942	1		
Pickmattock, intrenching, M1910	1		
Sheath, machete, leather, 18''	1		1 per machete, 18'', M1942.
Shovel, intrenching, M1910	2		
Stove, cooking, gasoline, 1-burner, M1942.	2		1 per 2 indiv.
Tent, Mountain, 2-man, complete with pins and poles	3		1 per O; 1 per 2 EM.
Typewriter, portable, Elite type, standard keyboard, with carrying case.	1		
Whistle, Thunderer	1		1 per O.

SIGNAL EQUIPMENT

Item	Allowances	For Computation	Basis of Issue and Remarks
Chest, BC-5	2		
Flag set, M-133	1		

24-33340
- 30 -

SIGNAL EQUIPMENT (Cont'd)

Item	Allowances	For Computation	Basis of Issue and Remarks
1	2	3	4
Flashlight TL-122-A	4		1 per indiv.
Frequency meter set, SCR-211	1		
Holder M-167	1		1 per rad set, SCR-188.
Radio set, SCR-188	1		
Radio set, SCR-536	1		
Radio set, SCR-694	1		Installed in cargo carrier, T-15.
Radio set, SCR-714	1		Installed in cargo carrier, T-15.
Signal lamp equipment, EE-84	1		
Signal lamp equipment, SE-11	1		
Tool equipment, TE-33	3		1 per EM.

HEADQUARTERS AND HEADQUARTERS COMPANY, SERVICE BATTALION
FIRST SPECIAL SERVICE FORCE
CHEMICAL EQUIPMENT

Item	Allowances	For Computation	Basis of Issue and Remarks
Alarm, gas, M1	1		
Apparatus, decontaminating, 3-gal, M1	3		
Curtain, gas-proof, M1	2		
Kits, HS, vapor detector, M4	1		

ENGINEER EQUIPMENT

Item	Allowances	For Computation	Basis of Issue and Remarks
Board, drawing, 31'' x42'', with folding trestle	1		Force hq.

24-33340
- 31 -

Appendix II: Historical Document #7 - Table of Equipment

ENGINEER EQUIPMENT (Cont'd)

1	2	3	4
Item	Allow-ances	For Compu-tation	Basis of Issue and Remarks
Compass, lensatic, luminous dial, with case	11		1 per O (except Ch.)
Compass, watch	60		1 per Ch; 1st sgt; com C; msgr; lineman; EM of gd plat.
Drafting and duplicating, equipment, complete	1		Force hq.
Duplicating equipment, gelatin process, 22'' x 33''	1		Force hq.
Pen, lettering with guides	1		Force hq.
Tape, measuring, woven-metallic, 50-foot	1		Force hq.

MEDICAL EQUIPMENT

Item	Allow-ances		Basis of Issue and Remarks
Brassard, Geneva Convention	2		1 per Ch.

ORDNANCE EQUIPMENT

Item	Allow-ances		Basis of Issue and Remarks
Bayonet, M1905 and Scabbard bayonet M3	144		1 per EM.
Binoculars, M3	14		1 per O; 1st sgt.
Bicycle	4		4 per co.
Carbine, cal. .30, M1	11		1 per O (except Ch), see SNL B-28.
Gun, machine, Browning, cal. .30, M1919A4	6		See SNL A-6.
Mount, tripod, MG, cal. .30, M2	6		1 per LMG, see SNL A-6.

24-33340   - 32 -

ORDNANCE EQUIPMENT (Cont'd)

1	2	3	4
Item	Allow-ances	For Compu-tation	Basis of Issue and Remarks
Pistol, automatic, cal. .45, M1911A1	53		1 per indiv. of gd plat, see SNL B-6.
Projector, signal, ground, M4	1		Com plat; see SNL B-24.
Rifle, Browning, automatic cal. .30, M1918A2	5		See SNL A-4.
Rifle, U S, cal. .30, M1	144		1 per EM, see SNL B-21.
Watch, wrist, 7 or more jewels	31		1 per O; NCO, first 3 gr; 1 per rad opr; sb opr.

QUARTERMASTER EQUIPMENT

Item	Allow-ances		Basis of Issue and Remarks
Axe, handled, chopping, singlebit, 4-lb	2		
Axe, intrenching, M1910	14		1 per 10 EM.
Bag, canvas, water, steril-izing, complete with cover and hanger.	2		1 per 100 indiv or fraction thereof.
Belt, magazine, BAR, M1937	10		2 per BAR.
Bucket, general purpose, Type II, w/o lip, 14-qt.	2		
Carrier, axe, intrenching, M1910	14		1 per axe, intrenching, M1910.
Carrier, cutter, wire, M1938	14		1 per cutter, wire, M1938.
Carrier, pickmattock, intrenching, M1910	43		1 per pickmattock, intrench-ing, M1910.
Carrier, shovel, intrenching, rucksack	87		1 per shovel, intrenching, M1910.
Case, canvas dispatch, M1938	21		1 per O; NCO, first 3 gr.

24-33340   - 33 -

QUARTERMASTER EQUIPMENT (Cont'd)

1	2	3	4
Item	Allow-ances	For Compu-tation	Basis of Issue and Remarks
Case, flag, duck, cotton, colors	1		
Case, flag, duck, cotton, guidon	1		
Chair, folding	12		Force hq.
Chest, record, fiber	12		Force hq.
Cutter, wire, M1938	14		1 per 10 EM.
Desk, field, empty, fiber, company.	5		2 per Force hq; 1 per co hq; com plat; hq serv bn.
Desk, field, empty, fiber, headquarters.	6		Force hq.
Flag, guidon, bunting	1		
Flag, national colors, service	1		
Flagstaff, colors	1		
Flagstaff, guidon	1		
Flagstaff, marker	2		1 per flag, Ch.
Lantern, electric, portable	16		1 per co hq; 4 per gd plat; 4 per com plat; 6 per Force hq.
Lantern, gasoline, with mantle and pump.	8		1 per co hq; com plat; 6 per Force hq.
Machete, 18'', M1942	14		1 per 10 EM.
Machine, duplicating, fluid process.	1		Force hq.
Mittens, asbestos, M-1935 pr	6		1 pr per LMG.
Outfit, chaplain, Christian	2		1 per Ch, Christian faith.
Paulin, canvas, 12' x 17', OD	2		

24-33340   - 34 -

QUARTERMASTER EQUIPMENT (Cont'd)

1	2	3	4
Item	Allow-ances	For Compu-tation	Basis of Issue and Remarks
Pick, handled, RR, 6-7 lbs	2		
Pickmattock, intrenching, M1910	43		3 per 10 EM.
Safe, field, key-lock	3		Force hq.
Screen, latrine, complete with pins and poles	2		1 per Force hq; hq co.
Sheath, machete, leather, 18''	14		1 per machete, 18'', M1942.
Shovel, general purpose, D-handled, strap-back, round point, No. 2	2		
Shovel, intrenching, M1910	87		6 per 10 EM.
Sling, carrying, MG and am-munition.	24		4 per LMG.
Sling, color, web, OD	1		
Stamp, official, rubber	3		Force hq.
Stove, tent, complete with ac-cessory equipment.	9		1 per tent, comd post; tent, wall, small.
Table, camp, folding	12		Force hq.
Tent, command post complete with pins and poles	6		1 per hq serv bn; 5 per Force hq.
Tent, mountain, 2-man, com-plete with pins and poles.	85		1 per O; 1 per 2 EM.
Tent, wall, small, complete with fly, pins and poles.	3		1 per hq serv bn; 2 per Force hq.
Tool kit, carpenter's, complete with tools.	1		
Typewriter, nonportable	6		
Typewriter, portable, Elite Type, standard keyboard, with carrying case.	20		1 per desk, fiber, fld hq; outfit, Ch; com plat; co hq; 10 per Force hq.

24-33340   - 35 -

Appendix II: Historical Document #7 - Table of Equipment

QUARTERMASTER EQUIPMENT (Cont'd)

1	2	3	4
Item	Allow-ances	For Compu-tation	Basis of Issue and Remarks
Whistle, Thunderer	72		1 per O; NCO, first 3 gr; 1 per EM, gd plat, below grade 3.

SIGNAL EQUIPMENT

1	2	3	4
Item	Allow-ances	For Compu-tation	Basis of Issue and Remarks
Axle, RL-27-A	2		Com plat.
Camera equipment, PH-104, complete	1		Photo sec.
Chest, BC-5	10		5 per Force hq; com plat.
Converter, M-209, or cipher device, M-94.	1		
Exposure meter, PH-77-C	1		Photo sec.
Flashlight, TL-122-A	47		1 per O; NCO, first 3 gr; Lineman; sb; rad set, SCR-188; 20 per gd plat.
Holder, M-187	4		2 per com plat; 1 per rad set, SCR-188.
Lineman's equipment, TE-21	2		1 per lineman.
Panel set, AP-30-C	1		Com plat.
Panel set, AP-30-D	1		Com plat.
Radio set, SCR-188	2		Com plat.
Radio set, SCR-536	3		Com plat.
Reel unit, RL-31	2		Com plat.
Signal lamp equipment, EE-84	1		Com plat.
Signal lamp equipment, SE-11	1		Com plat.
Switchboard, BD-72	2		Com plat.

24-33340   - 36 -

SIGNAL EQUIPMENT (Cont'd)

1	2	3	4
Items	Allow-ances	For Compu-tation	Basis of Issue and Remarks
Telephone, EE-8	28		Com plat.
Tool equipment, TE-33	15		Com plat.
Typewriter, MC-88	1		Com plat.
Wire, W-130, on reel miles DR-4	30		Com plat.
Wire pike, MC-123	1		Com plat.

SERVICE COMPANY, SERVICE BATTALION
FIRST SPECIAL SERVICE FORCE
ARMY AIR FORCES EQUIPMENT

1	2	3	4
Item	Allow-ances	For Compu-tation	Basis of Issue and Remarks
Bag, flyer's kit, Type A-3.	3,104		Para packing plat (1 per prcht, personnel).
Container, assembly, aerial delivery, Type A-3.	80		Para packing plat for combat ech.
Container, assembly, aerial delivery, Type A-4.	160		Para packing plat for combat ech.
Container, assembly, aerial delivery, Type A-5.	750		Para packing plat for combat ech.
Container, assembly, aerial delivery, Type A-6.	160		Para packing plat for combat ech.
Container, assembly, aerial delivery, Type A-7, cal. .30 ammunition sling.	750		Para packing plat for combat ech.
Container, assembly, aerial delivery, Type A-7, cal. .45 ammunition sling.	200		Para packing plat for combat ech.
Container, assembly, aerial delivery, Type A-8.	350		Para packing plat for combat ech.
Container, individual, aerial, delivery, rifle.	1,519		Para packing, plat (1 per indiv in combat ech) (except Med O, Med EM. and pilots).

24-33340   - 37 -

ARMY AIR FORCES EQUIPMENT (Cont'd)

1	2	3	4
Item	Allow-ances	For Compu-tation	Basis of Issue and Remarks
Drill Press, bench type, motor-driven, complete with drills 1/64" to 1/2"	1		Para packing plat.
Grinder, bench type, 2-wheel motor-driven.	1		Para packing plat.
Goggles, assembly, Type B-7, flying.	50		Para packing plat.
Hot plate, electric, 1-unit 660-watt.	1		Para packing plat.
Hot plate, electric, 1-unit 1,000-watt.	1		Para packing plat.
Kit, parachute maintenance, special.	1		Para packing plat.
Kit, parachute rigger, com-plete.	30		1 per para rigger.
Lamp assembly, identifi-cation, aerial delivery container, Type A-1.	2,450		1 per container assembly, aerial delv.
Machine, stencil cutting, hand-operated, 1/2"	1		Para packing plat.
Machine, stencil cutting, hand-operated, 1"	1		Para packing plat.
Parachute, back, Type B-7, complete	50		Para packing plat.
Parachute, cargo, 24'	2,450		1 per container assembly, aerial delv (color as ordered).
Parachute, cargo, 48', white canopy	3,000		4 per cargo carrier, T-15
Parachute, seat, Type S-1 or S-2.	4		Para packing plat.

24-33340   -38-

ARMY AIR FORCES EQUIPMENT (Cont'd)

1	2	3	4
Item	Allow-ances	For Compu-tation	Basis of Issue and Remarks
Parachute, troop, Type T-5, modified	3,050		2 per indiv of combat ech, except pilots.
Pot, heating, pressure, gasoline burning	1		Para packing plat.
Press, eyelet setting, foot-operated, Carr fastener, M-46	1		Para packing plat.
Sewing machine, Singer Type 97-10, complete with motor	1		Para packing plat.
Sewing machine, Singer, Type 112-W-116, complete with motor.	1		Para packing plat.
Sewing machine, Singer, Type 31-15, foot-powered, with bobbin winder and knee lift	1		Para packing plat.
Sewing machine, Singer, Type 111-W-151, complete with motor.	1		Para packing plat.
Table, para packing, folding 10' x 36" x 30"	120		Para packing plat (local manufacture and purchase).
Table, work, 48" x 24" x 30", folding	4		Para packing plat (local manufacture and purchase).
Tension board, standard type	30		1 per para rigger (local manufacture and purchase).
Vest, life preserver, Type B-3 or B-4.	1,598		Para packing plat (1 per indiv of combat ech and para packing plat (when auth-orized by CO).
Vise, bench, machine, swivel base, 3 1/2" jaws	1		Par packing plat.

24-33340   - 39 -

Appendix II: Historical Document #7 - Table of Equipment

CHEMICAL EQUIPMENT

1	2	3	4
Item	Allowances	For Computation	Basis of Issue and Remarks
Alarm, gas, M1	1		
Apparatus, decontaminating, 3-gal, M1	3		
Kit, HS, vapor detector, M4	1		
Kit, repair, gas mask, universal, M-8	1		

ENGINEER EQUIPMENT

Compass, lensatic, luminous dial, with case	7		1 per O.
Compass, watch	19		1 per NCO, first 3 gr.
Demolition kit, infantry	6		

ORDNANCE EQUIPMENT

Bayonet, M1905 and Scabbard, bayonet, M3	320		1 per EM.
Binoculars, M3	8		1 per O; 1st sgt.
Carbine, cal. .30, M1	7		1 per O (see SNL B-28)
Gun, machine, Browning, cal. .30 M1919A4	12		See SNL A-6.
Mount, tripod, MG, cal. .30	12		1 per IMG (see SNL A-6).
Rifle, Browning, automatic cal. .30, M1918A2.	10		See SNL A-4.
Rifle, U S, cal. .30, M1	320		1 per EM (see SNL B-21).
Watch, wrist, 7 or more jewels	26		1 per O; NCO, first 3 gr.

- 40 -

QUARTERMASTER EQUIPMENT

1	2	3	4
Item	Allowances	For Computation	Basis of Issue and Remarks
Axe, handled, chopping, singlebit, 4-lb.	34		1 per co, combat ech; 4 per regtl sup det, combat ech; 4 per serv co.
Axe, intrenching, M1910	32		1 per 10 EM.
Bag, canvas, water, sterilizing, complete with cover and hanger.	3		1 per 100 indiv.
Belt, magazine, BAR, M1937	20		2 per BAR.
Bucket, general purpose, heavy-weight, Type II, w/o lip, 14-qt.	38		
Can, corrugated, nesting, with cover:			
10-gal	21		1 per co mess.
16-gal	21		Do.
24-gal	21		Do.
32-gal	21		Do.
Carrier, axe, intrenching, M1910	32		1 per axe, intrenching, M1910.
Carrier, cutter, wire, M1938	32		1 per cutter, wire, M1938.
Carrier, pickmattock, intrenching, M1910.	96		1 per pickmattock, intrenching, M1910.
Carrier, shovel, intrenching, rucksack	192		1 per shovel, intrenching M1910.
Case, canvas, dispatch, M1938	26		1 per O; NCO, first 3 gr.
Case, flag, duck, cotton, guidon.	1		1 per guidon.
Chest, commissary, complete with equipment	1		

- 41 -

QUARTERMASTER EQUIPMENT (Cont'd)

1	2	3	4
Item	Allowances	For Computation	Basis of Issue and Remarks
Chest, record, fiber	4		1 per para packing plat; 3 per sup plat.
Container, round, insulated M1941, with insert.	88		2 per 50 indiv.
Container, water, 5-gal	417		1 per 5 indiv not to exceed 36 per co.
Cutter, wire, M1938	32		1 per 10 EM.
Desk, field, empty, fiber, company	4		1 per co hq; para packing plat; 2 per Force sup plat.
Flag, guidon, bunting	1		
Flagstaff, guidon	1		1 per guidon.
Fly, tent, wall, large, complete with fly, pins and poles	21		1 per co.
Gauntlets, barbed wire pr	20		
Heater, water, for range, field M1937	63		3 per range, fld, M1937.
Lantern, electric, portable	22		2 per co hq; 6 per sup plat; 6 per para packing plat; 8 per utility plat.
Lantern, gasoline, with mantle and pump	37		2 per co hq; 4 per sup plat; 6 per para packing plat; 25 per utility plat.
Machete, 18", M1942	32		1 per 10 EM.
Mittens, asbestos, M1942 pr	12		1 pr per IMG.
Musical instruments, fife-and-drum set	1		
Outfit, officer's mess	11		1 per bn hq; regtl hq; 2 per Force hq.

- 42 -

QUARTERMASTER EQUIPMENT (Cont'd)

1	2	3	4
Item	Allowances	For Computation	Basis of Issue and Remarks
Paulin, canvas, 12' x 17', OD	10		
Pick, handled, RR, 6-7 lbs.	52		2 per co, combat ech; 4 per regtl sup det, combat ech; 4 per serv co.
Pickmattock, intrenching, M1910	32		1 per 10 EM.
Puller, nail, 18"	3		1 per sec, sup plat.
Range, field, M1937:			
2-unit set	18		1 per combat co mess.
3-unit set	2		1 per hq co mess; maint co mess.
4-unit set	1		1 per serv co mess.
Saw, buck, light-weight	6		Utility plat.
Saw, cross cut, Type L, 2-man, 6'	1		Utility plat.
Scales, weighing, platform, folding, Army-and-Navy type, 300-lb.	2		1 per sup plat; para packing plat.
Screen, latrine, complete with pins and poles	26		1 per co, combat ech; 2 per regtl sup det, combat ech (for regtl & bn hq); 2 per serv co.
Sheath, machete, leather, 18"	32		1 per machete, 18", M1942.
Shovel, general purpose, D-handled, strapback, round point, No. 2	58		2 per co, combat ech; 4 per serv co; 6 per regtl sup det, combat ech.
Shovel, intrenching, M1910.	192		6 per 10 EM.
Sling, carrying, MG and ammunition	48		4 per IMG.
Stencil outfit, complete with figures and letters, 1/2" and 1"	2		Sup plat.

- 43 -

298

QUARTERMASTER EQUIPMENT (Cont'd)

1	2	3	4
Item	Allow-ances	For Compu-tation	Basis of Issue and Remarks
Stretcher, shoe (1 #0, 1 #00, 1 #1)	4		Utility plat.
Tent, mountain, 2-man, complete with pins and poles.	167		1 per O; 1 per 2 EM.
Tool kit, carpenters', complete with tools	4		Utility plat.
Tool set, carpenters' and wheelrights', complete with tools	1		Utility plat.
Trumpet, "G", with-slide-to "F".	6		1 per bglr.
Typewriter, portable, elite type, standard keyboard, with carrying case.	15		1 per para packing plat; 6 per supply plat; 8 per utility plat.
Whistle, Thunderer	26		1 per O; NCO, first 3 gr.

SIGNAL EQUIPMENT

1	2	3	4
Flashlight, TL-122-A	26		1 per O; NCO, first 3 gr.

MAINTENANCE COMPANY
SERVICE BATTALION
FIRST SPECIAL SERVICE FORCE
CHEMICAL EQUIPMENT

1	2	3	4
Alarm, gas, M1	1		
Apparatus, decontaminating, 1 1/2-qt, M2 w/ funnel	59		1 per fuel-consuming mtr vehicle (except cargo carrier, T-15).
Apparatus, decontaminating, 3-gal, M1	6		

24-33340   - 44 -

CHEMICAL EQUIPMENT (Cont'd)

1	2	3	4
Item	Allow-ances	For Compu-tation	Basis of Issue and Remarks
Kit, HS, vapor detector, M4	1		
Respirator, dust	59		1 per fuel-consuming mtr vehicle (except cargo carrier, T-15).

ENGINEER EQUIPMENT

1	2	3	4
Compass, lensatic, luminous dial, with case	5		1 per O.
Compass, watch	29		1 per 1st sgt; cfr.
Net, camouflage, cotton, shrimp:			
22' x 22'	10		1 per trk, 1/4-ton.
29' x 29'	44		1 per amb; tlr, 1-ton; trk, 3/4-ton.
36' x 44'	39		1 per trk, 2 1/2-ton, cargo; trk, 4-ton, wkr; trk, gasoline, 750-gal; trk, SA rep.
			(Net, cam, cotton, shrimp will be issued in OD or sand, solid color, when and as authorized by T of Opns comdr.)

MEDICAL EQUIPMENT

1	2	3	4
Kit, first-aid, motor vehicle, 12-unit	59		1 per fuel-consuming mtr vehicle (except cargo carrier, T-15).

24-33340   - 45 -

ORDNANCE EQUIPMENT
a. Organizational Equipment

1	2	3	4
Item	Allow-ances	For Compu-tation	Basis of Issue and Remarks
Bayonet, M-1905 and Scabbard, bayonet, M3	146		1 per EM.
Binoculars, M3	6		1 per O; 1st sgt.
Carbine, cal. .30, M1	5		1 per O (see SNL B-28)
Gun, machine, Browning, Cal. .30, M1919A4	6		See SNL A-6.
Kit, armorers', complete with tools	4		Ord. rep plat (in addition to kits with trk, SA rep, M7).
Mount, tripod, MG, cal. .30, M2	6		1 per LMG (see SNL A-6)
Mount, truck, M32	17		1 per 2 trks, 2 1/2-ton (see SNL A-55).
Rifle, Browning, automatic, cal. .30, M1918A2	15		See SNL A-4:
Rifle, U S, cal. .30, M1	146		1 per EM (SNL B-21.)
Scabbard, rifle, M1938	58		1 per fuel-consuming mtr vehicle (except cargo carrier, T-15).
Watch, wrist, 7 or more jewels	13		1 per O; NCO, first 3 gr.

b. Motor Transport Equipment

1	2	3	4
Bars, towing universal type	1		1 per co.
Chain, motor vehicle, towing, 16' x 7/16"	19		1 per trk, 2 1/2-ton, gasoline, tank and cargo, w/o WN.
Ord. Maint. Set "D" Cabinets Spare Parts Set complete	1		1 per ord maint plat.

24-33340   - 46 -

ORDNANCE EQUIPMENT
b. Motor Transport Equipment (Cont'd)

1	2	3	4
Item	Allow-ances	For Compu-tation	Basis of Issue and Remarks
Rope, towing, 1" diam, 20'	20		1 per fuel-consuming mtr vehicle under 1 1/2-ton capacity (except cargo carrier, T-15).
Tool set, Battery experts', complete with tools	1		Vehicle maint plat.
Tool set, Blacksmiths', No. 2, complete with tools	1		Vehicle maint plat.
Tool set, Electrical and carburetor mechanics', complete with tools	1		Vehicle maint plat.
Tool set, Motor Vehicle mechanics', complete with tools	30		1 per mech, mtr, in vehicle maint plat.
Tool set, Pioneer equipment, motor vehicle, Set No. 1, complete with tools	49		1 per fuel-consuming mtr vehicle (except passenger car, trk, 1/4-ton, and cargo carrier, T-15 and Ord tech trks).
Tool set, Unit equipment, 3d Echelon Set No. 1, complete with tools	1		Vehicle maint plat.
Tube, flexible nozzle, for refillable gasoline drums	63		1 per fuel-consuming vehicle; cargo carrier, T-15.
Vehicles, motor:			
Ambulance, 3/4-ton	2		Force mtr pool, for med det Base ech.
Carrier, cargo, light, T-15.	4		Force mtr pool, for combat ech.
Trailer, 1-ton, 2-wheel, cargo	34		Force mtr pool.
Truck, 1/4-ton, 4x4	10		Force mtr pool.

24-33340   - 47 -

Appendix II: Historical Document #7 - Table of Equipment

ORDNANCE EQUIPMENT
b. Motor Transport Equipment (Cont'd)

Item	Allowances	For Computation	Basis of Issue and Remarks
Truck, 3/4-ton, 4x4, command	6		Force mtr pool, for com plat hq co.
Truck, 3/4-ton, 4x4, weapons carrier, complete with Ord. Maint Set "B"	2		Force mtr pool, ord repair plat for emerg rep.
Truck, 2 1/2-ton, 6x6, with winch	18		Force mtr pool.
Truck, 2 1/2-ton, 6x6, cargo w/o winch	17		Force mtr pool.
Truck, 2 1/2-ton, 6x6, gasoline tank, 750-gal	2		Force mtr pool.
Truck, 4-ton, 6x6, wrecker, with winch	1		Force mtr pool, for vehicle maint plat.
Truck, small arms repair, M7	1		Force mtr pool, for ord rep plat.

QUARTERMASTER EQUIPMENT

Item	Allowances	For Computation	Basis of Issue and Remarks
Axe, handled, chopping, single-bit, 4-lb	2		
Axe, intrenching, M1910	15		1 per 10 EM.
Bag, canvas, water, sterilizing, complete with cover and hanger	1		
Belt, magazine, BAR, M1937	30		2 per BAR.
Bucket, general purpose, heavy-weight, Type II, w/o lip, 14-qt	2		
Bucket, water, canvas, 18-qt	63		1 per fuel-consuming mtr vehicle; cargo carrier T-15.

24-33340   - 48 -

QUARTERMASTER EQUIPMENT (Cont'd)

Item	Allowances	For Computation	Basis of Issue and Remarks
Carrier, axe, intrenching, M1910	15		1 per axe, intrenching, M1910.
Carrier, cutter, wire, M1938	15		1 per cutter, wire, M1938.
Carrier, pickmattock, intrenching, M1910	44		1 per pickmattock, intrenching, M1910.
Carrier, shovel, intrenching, rucksack	87		1 per shovel, intrenching, M1910.
Case, canvas, dispatch, M1938	6		1 per O; 1st sgt.
Case, flag, duck, cotton, guidon	1		
Cutter, wire, M-1938	15		1 per 10 EM.
Desk, field, empty, fiber, company	4		1 per co hq; vehicle maint plat; ord rep plat; sig rep plat.
Drum, inflammable liquid (gasoline), steel, with carrying handle, capacity 5-gal	114		1 per trk, 1/4-ton, 4x4; trk, 3/4-ton; 2 per trk, 2 1/2-ton and larger, 6x6; 4 per cargo carrier, T-15.
Flag, guidon, bunting	1		
Flagstaff, automobile	1		Force mtr pool.
Flagstaff, guidon	1		
Goggles, M1942, complete	60		1 per fuel-consuming mtr vehicle (except cargo carrier, T-15).

24-33340   - 49 -

QUARTERMASTER EQUIPMENT (Cont'd)

Item	Allowances	For Computation	Basis of Issue and Remarks
Lantern, electric, portable	11		1 per co hq; 2 per Force mtr pool; ord rep plat; sig rep plat; 4 per vehicle maint plat.
Lantern, gasoline, with mantle and pump	10		1 per co hq; Force mtr pool; 2 per ord rep plat; sig rep plat; 4 per vehicle maint plat.
Machete, 18", M1942	15		1 per 10 EM.
Mittens, asbestos, M1942 pr	6		1 per LMG.
Paulin, canvas, 12' x 17', OD	7		1 per sig rep plat; 2 per ord rep plat; 4 per vehicle maint plat.
Picks, handled, RR, 6-7 lbs	2		
Pickmattock, intrenching, M1910	44		3 per 10 EM.
Plates, distinguishing, automobile, 6" x 9", Brig Gen	1		Force mtr pool.
Plates, distinguishing, automobile, 6" x 9", unit	1		Force mtr pool.
Screen, latrine, complete with pins and poles	1		
Sheath, machete, leather, 18"	15		1 per machete, 18", M1942.
Shovel, general purpose, D-handled, strap-back, round point, No.2	12		1 per trk, 1/4-ton, 4x4; 2 per maint co.
Shovel, intrenching, M1910	87		6 per 10 EM.
Sling, carrying, MG and ammunition	24		4 per LMG.

24-33340   - 50 -

QUARTERMASTER EQUIPMENT (Cont'd)

Item	Allowances	For Computation	Basis of Issue and Remarks
Tent, mountain, 2-man, complete with pins and poles	78		1 per O; 1 per 2 EM.
Tool kit, carpenters', complete with tools	1		
Typewriter, portable, elite type, standard keyboard, with carrying case.	4		1 per maint co; vehicle maint plat; ord rep plat; sig rep plat.
Whistle, Thunderer	13		1 per O; NCO, first 3 gr.

SIGNAL EQUIPMENT

Item	Allowances	For Computation	Basis of Issue and Remarks
Chest, BC-5	12		Sig rep plat.
Flashlight, TL-122-A	112		1 per O; NCO; mech (014); 1 per fuel-consuming mtr vehicle (except cargo carrier T-15).
Maintenance Equipment, ME-9	1		Sig rep plat.
Power Unit PE-75	1		Sig rep plat.
Radio set, SCR-714	4		Sig rep plat (installed in cargo carrier T-15).
Signal generator, I-72-A	1		Sig rep plat.
Test equipment, IE-9	1		Sig rep plat.
Test equipment, IE-17-A	2		Sig rep plat.
Tool equipment, TE-33	14		1 per EM of sig rep plat.
Tool equipment, TE-36	3		Sig rep plat.
Tool equipment, TE-41	3		Sig rep plat.

24-33340   - 51 -

Appendix II: Historical Document #7 - Table of Equipment

SIGNAL EQUIPMENT (Cont'd)

1 Item	2 Allowances	3 For Computation	4 Basis of Issue and Remarks
Tool equipment, TE-46	1		Sig rep plat.
Tool equipment, TE-48	5		Sig rep plat.
Voltameter, I-50	1		Sig rep plat.

MEDICAL DETACHMENT SERVICE BATTALION
FIRST SPECIAL SERVICE FORCE
CHEMICAL EQUIPMENT

1 Item	2 Allowances	3 For Computation	4 Basis of Issue and Remarks
Alarm, gas, M1	1		
Apparatus, decontaminating, 3-gal, M1	1		
Curtain, gas proof, M1	2		

ENGINEER EQUIPMENT

1 Item	2 Allowances	3 For Computation	4 Basis of Issue and Remarks
Compass, watch	6		1 per O; NCO.

MEDICAL EQUIPMENT

1 Item	2 Allowances	3 For Computation	4 Basis of Issue and Remarks
Blanket set, small	18		
Brassard, Geneva Convention	19		1 per indiv.
Chest, MD No. 1	2		
Chest, MD No. 2	1		
Chest, MD No. 4	1		
Chest, MD No. 60	2		1 per dent O.
Cocoa unit	2		

24-33340   - 52 -

MEDICAL EQUIPMENT (Cont'd)

1 Item	2 Allowances	3 For Computation	4 Basis of Issue and Remarks
Kit, dental, officer	2		1 per dent O.
Kit, dental, private	2		1 per dent techn.
Kit, medical, NCO	2		1 per med NCO.
Kit, medical, officer	2		1 per med O.
Kit, medical, private	11		1 per techn, dent; techn surg; ofr; pharmacist; bs
Lantern set	2		
Litter, folding	20		
Machine, imprinting	2		For use with indiv identification tags.
Splint set, Army folding splints	6		

ORDNANCE EQUIPMENT

1 Item	2 Allowances	3 For Computation	4 Basis of Issue and Remarks
Watch, wrist, 7 or more jewels	6		1 per O; NCO.

QUARTERMASTER EQUIPMENT

1 Item	2 Allowances	3 For Computation	4 Basis of Issue and Remarks
Axe, handled, chopping, single-bit, 4-lb	2		
Axe, intrenching, M1910	2		1 per 10 EM.
Bag, canvas, water, sterilizing, complete with cover and hanger	1		

24-33340   - 53 -

QUARTERMASTER EQUIPMENT (Cont'd)

1 Item	2 Allowances	3 For Computation	4 Basis of Issue and Remarks
Bucket, general purpose, heavy-weight, type 11, w/o lip, 14-qt	3		
Bucket, water, canvas, 18-qt	2		
Carrier, axe, intrenching, M1910	2		1 per axe, intrenching, M1910.
Carrier, cutter, wire, M1938	1		1 per cutter, wire, M1938.
Carrier, pickmattock, intrenching, M1910	4		1 per pickmattock, intrenching, M1910.
Carrier, shovel, intrenching, rucksack	9		1 per shovel, intrenching, M1910.
Case, canvas, dispatch, M1938	5		1 per O; NCO, first 3 gr.
Chest, record, fiber	1		
Cutter, wire, M1938	1		1 per 10 EM.
Desk, empty, field, fiber, company	1		
Flag, Geneva Convention, Red Cross bunting, Ambulance-and-marker	3		1 per amb; med det.
Flagstaff, marker	1		
Lantern, electric, portable	2		
Lantern, gasoline, with mantle and pump	2		
Machete, 18", M1942	1		1 per 10 EM.
Pick, handled, RR, 6-7 lbs	1		
Pickmattock, intrenching, M1910	4		3 per 10 EM.

24-33340   - 54 -

QUARTERMASTER EQUIPMENT (Cont'd)

1 Item	2 Allowances	3 For Computation	4 Basis of Issue and Remarks
Screen, latrine, complete with pins and poles.	1		
Sheath, machete, leather, 18"	1		1 per machete, 18", M1942.
Shovel, general purpose, D-handled, strap-back, round point, No. 2	2		
Shovel, intrenching, M1910	9		6 per 10 EM.
Stove, tent, complete with equipment	4		2 per tent, sqd.
Tent, mountain, 2-man, complete with pins and poles	12		1 per O; 1 per 2 EM.
Tent, squad, M1942	2		
Typewriter, portable, elite type, standard keyboard, with carrying case	1		
Whistle, Thunderer	6		1 per O; NCO.

SIGNAL EQUIPMENT

1 Item	2 Allowances	3 For Computation	4 Basis of Issue and Remarks
Flashlight, TL-122	10		1 per O; NCO; 4 per det.

(A.G. 320.2(2-10-43).)

By order of the Secretary of War:

G. C. MARSHALL,
Chief of Staff.

Official:
J. A. ULIO,
Major General,
The Adjutant General.

24-33340   - 55 -

Appendix III: Historical Document #8 - Change in Status of Units

HEADQUARTERS, DEPARTMENT OF THE ARMY
Office of The Adjutant General
Washington 25, D. C.

AGAO-O (M) (14 Apr 60)   14 April 1960

SUBJECT: Change in Status of Units

TO: The Adjutant General

    1. Effective 15 April 1960, the 1st Special Service Force (less Service Battalion) is reconstituted.

    2. Effective 15 April 1960, Headquarters, 1st Special Service Force is redesignated as Headquarters, 1st Special Forces.

    3. Effective 15 April 1960, the units listed in column (1) are consolidated with the units listed in column (2) and designated as indicated in column (3):

(1)	(2)	(3)
1st Special Service Force:		1st Special Forces:
Hq & Hq Det, 1st Bn, First Regt	Hq & Hq Co, 1st Ranger Inf Bn	Hq & Hq Co, 8th Sp Forces Gp
Co 1, 1st Bn, First Regt	Co A, 1st Ranger Inf Bn	Hq & Hq Co, 7th Sp Forces Gp
Co 2, 1st Bn, First Regt	Co B, 1st Ranger Inf Bn	Hq & Hq Co, 1st Sp Forces Gp
Co 3, 1st Bn, First Regt	Co C, 1st Ranger Inf Bn	Hq & Hq Co, 9th Sp Forces Gp
Hq & Hq Det, 2d Bn, First Regt	Hq & Hq Co, 2d Inf Bn	Hq & Hq Co, 2d Sp Forces Gp
Co 4, 2d Bn, First Regt	Co A, 2d Inf Bn	Hq & Hq Co, 10th Sp Forces Gp
Co 5, 2d Bn, First Regt	Co B, 2d Inf Bn	Hq & Hq Co, 11th Sp Forces Gp
Co 6, 2d Bn, First Regt	Co C, 2d Inf Bn	Hq & Hq Co, 12th Sp Forces Gp
Hq & Hq Det, 1st Bn, Second Regt	Hq & Hq Co, 3d Ranger Inf Bn	Hq & Hq Co, 3d Sp Forces Gp
Co 1, 1st Bn, Second Regt	Co A, 3d Ranger Inf Bn	Hq & Hq Co, 13th Sp Forces Gp
Co 2, 1st Bn, Second Regt	Co B, 3d Ranger Inf Bn	Hq & Hq Co, 14th Sp Forces Gp
Co 3, 1st Bn, Second Regt	Co C, 3d Ranger Inf Bn	Hq & Hq Co, 15th Sp Forces Gp
Hq & Hq Det, 2d Bn, Second Regt	Hq & Hq Co, 4th Ranger Inf Bn	Hq & Hq Co, 4th Sp Forces Gp
Co 4, 2d Bn, Second Regt	Co A, 4th Ranger Inf Bn	Hq & Hq Co, 16th Sp Forces Gp
Co 5, 2d Bn, Second Regt	Co B, 4th Ranger Inf Bn	Hq & Hq Co, 17th Sp Forces Gp
Co 6, 2d Bn, Second Regt	Co C, 4th Ranger Inf Bn	Hq & Hq Co, 18th Sp Forces Gp
Hq & Hq Det, 1st Bn, Third Regt	Hq & Hq Co, 5th Ranger Inf Bn	Hq & Hq Co, 5th Sp Forces Gp
Co 1, 1st Bn, Third Regt	Co A, 5th Ranger Inf Bn	Hq & Hq Co, 19th Sp Forces Gp
Co 2, 1st Bn, Third Regt	Co B, 5th Ranger Inf Bn	Hq & Hq Co, 20th Sp Forces Gp
Co 3, 1st Bn, Third Regt	Co C, 5th Ranger Inf Bn	Hq & Hq Co, 21st Sp Forces Gp
Hq & Hq Det, 2d Bn, Third Regt	Hq & Hq Co, 6th Ranger Inf Bn	Hq & Hq Co, 6th Sp Forces Gp
Co 4, 2d Bn, Third Regt	Co A, 6th Ranger Inf Bn	Hq & Hq Co, 22d Sp Forces Gp
Co 5, 2d Bn, Third Regt	Co B, 6th Ranger Inf Bn	Hq & Hq Co, 23d Sp Forces Gp
Co 6, 2d Bn, Third Regt	Co C, 6th Ranger Inf Bn	Hq & Hq Co, 24th Sp Forces Gp

    4. Effective 15 April 1960, the following units are disbanded:

    Co D, F and Med Det, 1st Ranger Inf Bn
    559th Inf Rifle Plat
    Co D, E, F and Med Det, 3d Ranger Inf Bn
    Co D, E, F and Med Det, 4th Ranger Inf Bn
    Co D, E, F and Med Det, 5th Ranger Inf Bn
    Co D, E, F and Med Det, 6th Ranger Inf Bn

    By Order of Wilber M. Brucker, Secretary of the Army:

Adjutant General

Appendix IV: Addendum to Personnel Roster

Listed below are Forcemen whose names did not appear as part of the "Personnel Roster of Former Members of the First Special Service Force" in Robert D. Burhans, *The First Special Service Force, A War History of the North Americans 1942-1944*, (Washington: Infantry Journal Press, Inc., 1947).

Rance J. Adcock, Jr.
Ken Ault
Paul Bauer
Howard Bell
Roy Bellefeuille
David L. Bens
Pat Bertolucci
George Blair
George Bodine
W.R. Bonnycastle
Sam Borod (Boroditsky)
Dave Boyer
Robert Bray
Charles Brendle
Donald Bricker
Ken Brookover
Ralph Brouillard
Warren Bullin
Elbert C. Bush, Sr.
Lorenzo Cervantes
Richard B. Cart
Murray L. Chambers
Walter L. Christie
Reginal Currier
Lloyd Dabell
William Davis
Fred Deckert
Ron Dionne
William H. Dixon
Richard Dooley
Charles Dunlop
August C. Erdbrink
Walter Falkenberg
Jim Fetherston
Theodore S. Fleser

Dennis Flynn
Norbert Frank
Norman Gabriel
Gerald Garton
John Gorski
Roy Habermehl
Eugene Hall
John Hein, Jr.
Thomas Herbert
Elton Hesner
William D. Hill
Thomas W. Hope
Morton Jacobs
Richard Jenkins
Francis Johnson
Bernard Kassoy
Thomas Kelly
W. Kenneth
Theodore Kramer
Bernard Kwasek
William Leaver
Albert Lewis
Larry Lytle
A.J. Mackie
William J. MacLean
Hector Macrae
David Massey
Dan McCall
Alan McCririck
E. Reg Miller
W.B.I. Morrison
Herbert B. Nichols
Sealy Nicholson
Robert Oleson
Walter Palmer

James Paton
George Pellerman
Raymond Peterson
Charles Phillips
C.C. Privette
Thomas Prudhomme
Woodrow Pyles
Edward Ratliff
Larry Reed
Bert Renny
Mervin Ringlero
George Ropert
Hermann Ross (Rosenstein)
John Rowe
Stanly Sabens
Benjamin Saylor
William Searle
Arthur Seymour
John Shaw
Andrew Shontz
Frank Simmons
William Sobuliak
A.R. Spidle
Ed Step
Frank Stewart
Tibor Szego
Duncan Taylor
William P. Taylor
Charles Thein
Roger Twig
Virgil Vetters
T.D. Woods
Dale Youngern

Bibliographical Notes

Bibliographical Notes: Introduction

1. Churchill, Winston S., *Their Finest Hour*, (Houghton Mifflin Company, Boston, 1949), pp. 246-247; Quoted from Churchill, Winston S., *The Grand Alliance*, (Haughton Mifflin Company, Boston, 1951), p. 539; McMichael, Scott R., *A Historical Perspective On Light Infantry, Combat Studies Institute Research Survey No 6*, (Command and General Staff College, Fort Leavenworth, 1987), p. 169.

2. Miller, Russell, *World War II, The Commandos*, (Time-Life Books, USA, 1981), p. 8.

3. Baudot, Marcel, Editor, et. al., *The Historical Encyclopedia of World War II*, (Greenwich House, New York, 1980), p. 109; Churchill, Winston S., *Their Finest Hour*, (Houghton Mifflin Company, Boston, 1949), pp. 165-166, 246-247.

4. McMichael, Scott R., *A Historical Perspective On Light Infantry, Combat Studies Institute Research Survey No 6*, (Command and General Staff College, Fort Leavenworth, 1987), p. 169.

5. Churchill, Winston S., *Their Finest Hour*, (Houghton Mifflin Company, Boston, 1949), p. 247; Miller, Russell, *World War II, The Commandos*, (Time-Life Books, USA, 1981), p. 8; Stanton, Shelby L., *World War II Order of Battle*, (Galahad Books, New York, 1984), p. 14.

6. McMichael, Scott R., *A Historical Perspective On Light Infantry, Combat Studies Institute Research Survey No 6*, (Command and General Staff College, Fort Leavenworth, 1987), p. 171.

7. Quoted from Burhans, Robert D., *The First Special Service Force, A War History of the North Americans 1942-1944*, (Washington: Infantry Journal Press, Inc., 1947), p. 47.

8. Burhans, Robert D., *The First Special Service Force, A War History of the North Americans 1942-1944*, (Washington: Infantry Journal Press, Inc., 1947), p. 47.

9. McMichael, Scott R., *A Historical Perspective On Light Infantry, Combat Studies Institute Research Survey No 6*, (Command and General Staff College, Fort Leavenworth, 1987), p. 169.

Bibliographical Notes: Chapter 1

1. Burhans, Robert D., *The First Special Service Force, A War History of the North Americans 1942-1944*, (Washington: Infantry Journal Press, Inc., 1947), p. 30; Eisenhower, Dwight D., *Crusade in Europe*, (Doubleday & Company, Inc., Garden City, 1948), p. 38; Baudot, Marcel, Editor, et. al., *The Historical Encyclopedia of World War II*, (Greenwich House, New York, 1980).

2. McMichael, Scott R., *A Historical Perspective On Light Infantry, Combat Studies Institute Research Survey No 6*, (Command and General Staff College, Fort Leavenworth, 1987), p. 169; Thomas, Ed, Speech to 5th Special Forces Group (Airborne), Fort Campbell, Kentucky, 19 December 1996, p. 1.

3. Burhans, Robert D., *The First Special Service Force, A War History of the North Americans 1942-1944*, (Washington: Infantry Journal Press, Inc., 1947), p. 30; Dziuban, Stanley W., *Military Relations Between the United States and Canada 1939-1945*, (Washington: Office of the Chief of Military History, 1959), p. 259.

4. Burhans, Robert D., *The First Special Service Force, A War History of the North Americans 1942-1944*, (Washington: Infantry Journal Press, Inc., 1947), pp. 9-10; World War II with Walter Cronkite, Volume IV, Battleground: Italy/Air War Over Europe (Video Series); Baudot, Marcel, Editor, et. al., *The Historical Encyclopedia of World War II*, (Greenwich House, New York, 1980), pp. 37, 359-360; Thomas, Ed, Speech to 5th Special Forces Group (Airborne), Fort Campbell, Kentucky, 19 December 1996, p. 4.

5. Thomas, Ed, Speech to 5th Special Forces Group (Airborne), Fort Campbell, Kentucky, 19 December 1996, p. 2; Burhans, Robert D., *The First Special Service Force, A War History of the North Americans 1942-1944*, (Washington: Infantry Journal Press, Inc., 1947), p. 5; Dziuban, Stanley W., *Military Relations Between the United States and Canada 1939-1945*, (Washington: Office of the Chief of Military History, 1959), p. 260.

6. Lampe, David, *Pyke, the Unkown Genius*, (Hazell Watson and Viney LTD, Aylesbury, 1959), pp. 115-116, 119.

7. Burhans, Robert D., *The First Special Service Force, A War History of the North Americans 1942-1944*, (Washington: Infantry Journal Press, Inc., 1947), pp. 5-6, 8, 12, 43; Dawson, John R., and Kutemeier, Don, *First Special Service Force, 1942-44 (I)*, (Military Illustrated, Past and Present, August/September, 1986).

8. Ellis, Charles, *Military Transport of World War II*, (The MacMillan Company, New York, 1971). p. 155; Quoted from Lampe, David, *Pyke, the Unkown Genius*, (Hazell Watson and Viney LTD, Aylesbury, 1959), pp. 156-157.

9. Story, William S., Editor, *The First Special Service Force, A Commemorative History, July 1942-January 1945*, (Taylor Publishing Company, Dallas, 1995), p. 1; Adleman, Robert H. and Walton, Colonel George, *The Devil's Brigade*, (Chilton Books, Philadelphia, 1966), pp. 27-29.

10. Burhans, Robert D., *The First Special Service Force, A War History of the North Americans 1942-1944*, (Washington: Infantry Journal Press, Inc., 1947), p. 9.

11. Dawson, John R., and Kutemeier, Don, *First Special Service Force, 1942-44 (I)*, (Military Illustrated, Past and Present, August/September, 1986).

12. Wickham, Kenneth G., Speech to 1st Special Service Force Reunion, 1986, p. 5; Burhans, Robert D., *The First Special Service Force, A War History of the North Americans 1942-1944*, (Washington: Infantry Journal Press, Inc., 1947), p. 10; Adleman, Robert H. and Walton, Colonel George, *The Devil's Brigade*, (Chilton Books, Philadelphia, 1966), pp. 29-33; Story, William S., Editor, *The First Special Service Force, A Commemorative History, July 1942-January 1945*, (Taylor Publishing Company, Dallas, 1995), p. 1; Thomas, Ed, Speech to 5th Special Forces Group (Airborne), Fort Campbell, Kentucky, 19 December 1996, p. 2.

Bibliographical Notes: Chapter 2

1. Quoted from Burhans, Robert D., *The First Special Service Force, A War History of the North Americans 1942-1944*, (Washington: Infantry Journal Press, Inc., 1947), pp. 11-13, 25; Wickham, Kenneth G., Transcript of Speech to 1st Special Service Force Reunion, 1986, pp. 5-7; Memorandum to the Commanding General, Army Air Forces from Lt. Colonel Robert T. Frederick, 8 July 1942; Memorandum for the Commanding Officer, Plough Project from Colonel O.A. Anderson, 24 July 1942.

2. Burhans, Robert D., *The First Special Service Force, A War History of the North Americans 1942-1944*, (Washington: Infantry Journal Press, Inc., 1947), p. 13; Wickham, Kenneth G., Transcript of Speech to 1st Special Service Force Reunion, 1986, p. 6; Merha, Les Wayne, *The Service Battalion: Supporting Unit for the First Special Service Force*, (Unpublished Manuscript, No Date), p. 2.

3. Merha, Les Wayne, *The Service Battalion: Supporting Unit for the First Special Service Force*, (Unpublished Manuscript, No Date), p. 6.

4. Dziuban, Stanley W., *Military Relations Between the United States and Canada 1939-1945*, (Washington: Office of the Chief of Military History, 1959), p. 260; Dancocks, Daniel G., *The D-Day Dodgers, The Canadians In Italy: 1943-1945*, (McClelland & Stewart, Inc., Toronto, Ontario, 1991), p. 193.

5. Dziuban, Stanley W., *Military Relations Between the United States and Canada 1939-1945*, (Washington: Office of the Chief of Military History, 1959), p. 260; Wickham, Kenneth G., Transcript of Speech to 1st Special Service Force Reunion, 1986, p. 9; Lampe, David, *Pyke, the Unkown Genius*, (Hazell Watson and Viney LTD, Aylesbury, 1959), p. 122.

6. Wickham, Kenneth G., Transcript of Speech to 1st Special Service Force Reunion, 1986, p. 7.

7. Wickham, Kenneth G., Transcript of Speech to 1st Special Service Force Reunion, 1986, p. 7; Burhans, Robert D., *The First Special Service Force, A War History of the North Americans 1942-1944*, (Washington: Infantry Journal Press, Inc., 1947), p. 15.

8. Wickham, Kenneth G., Transcript of Speech to 1st Special Service Force Reunion, 1986, pp. 7-9.

9. Wickham, Kenneth G., Transcript of Speech to 1st Special Service Force Reunion, 1986, pp. 8-9, 11; Burhans, Robert D., *The First Special Service Force, A War History of the North Americans 1942-1944*, (Washington: Infantry Journal Press, Inc., 1947), p. 23.

10. Burhans, Robert D., *The First Special Service Force, A War History of the North Americans 1942-1944*, (Washington: Infantry Journal Press, Inc., 1947), p. 46; 452.1, 7-8-42, Duties of the Army Air Forces in regards to furnishing planes, personnel, etc. for the 1st Special Service Force; Story, William S., Notes from telephone interview with author regarding the FSSF Air Detachment, 28 August 1997.

11. Wickham, Kenneth G., Transcript of Speech to 1st Special Service Force Reunion, 1986, p. 10; Dziuban, Stanley W., *Military Relations Between the United States and Canada 1939-1945*, (Washington: Office of the Chief of Military History, 1959), pp. 262-264. Note: While administrative details posed "no particular problem for the U.S. component, for the force trained and operated within the framework of the logistical and supporting U.S. Army establishment," the complicated channels of communication that Canadian administrative personnel operated within, particularly in Europe, "caused difficulty through considerable delays in reporting casualties and other matters, [but this] had no practical impact on the force's fighting capabilities." Quoted from Dziuban, Stanley W., *Military Relations Between the United States and Canada 1939-1945*, (Washington: Office of the Chief of Military History, 1959), pp. 263-264. "The matter of relative pay scales, which favored the Americans, was apparently the only unhappy aspect of the relationship of the force to its two sponsoring governments. Repeated efforts were made to place the Canadian personnel on the same pay scale as the Americans. Every effort was disapproved by the Department of National Defense in Ottawa, which saw no more justification in this situation than in others where Canadian served alongside Americans. Fortunately the different rates, though a source of typical soldier griping, did not affect force morale seriously even when the force moved overseas and U.S. pay scales were augmented by 10 percent for officers and 20 percent for enlisted men." Quoted from Dziuban, Stanley W., *Military Relations Between the United States and Canada 1939-1945*, (Washington: Office of the Chief of Military History, 1959), p. 263.

12. Wickham, Kenneth G., Transcript of Speech to 1st Special Service Force Reunion, 1986, pp. 9-11; Burhans, Robert D., *The First Special Service Force, A War History of the North Americans 1942-1944*, (Washington: Infantry Journal Press, Inc., 1947), p. 22.

13. Wickham, Kenneth G., Transcript of Speech to 1st Special Service Force Reunion, 1986, p. 12; Burhans, Robert D., *The First Special Service Force, A War History of the North Americans 1942-1944*, (Washington: Infantry Journal Press, Inc., 1947), p. 14.

14. Wickham, Kenneth G., Transcript of Speech to 1st Special Service Force Reunion, 1986, pp. 11-12; Burhans, Robert D., *The First Special Service Force, A War History of the North Americans 1942-1944*, (Washington: Infantry Journal Press, Inc., 1947), p. 14.

15. Wickham, Kenneth G., Transcript of Speech to 1st Special Service Force Reunion, 1986, pp. 11-12; Burhans, Robert D., *The First Special Service Force, A War History of the North Americans 1942-1944*, (Washington: Infantry Journal Press, Inc., 1947), p. 31; Thomas, Ed, Transcript of Speech to 5th Special Forces Group (Airborne), Fort Campbell, Kentucky, 19 December 1996, p. 4.

16. Dziuban, Stanley W., *Military Relations Between the United States and Canada 1939-1945*, (Washington: Office of the Chief of Military History, 1959), p. 261; Wickham, Kenneth G., Transcript of Speech to 1st Special Service Force Reunion, 1986, p. 13.

17. Thomas, Ed, Transcript of Speech to 5th Special Forces Group (Airborne), Fort Campbell, Kentucky, 19 December 1996, p. 4.

18. Quoted from 353, 16 November 1943, Training - First Special Service Force; Burhans, Robert D., *The First Special Service Force, A War History of the North Americans 1942-1944*, (Washington: Infantry Journal Press, Inc., 1947), p. 23.

19. Quoted from Thomas, Ed, Transcript of Speech to 5th Special Forces Group (Airborne), Fort Campbell, Kentucky, 19 December 1996, p. 4.

20. Thomas, Ed, Transcript of Speech to 5th Special Forces Group (Airborne), Fort Campbell, Kentucky, 19 December 1996, p. 4.

21. Story, William S., At the Beginning, The First Special Service Force, p. 5; Burhans, Robert D., *The First Special Service Force, A War History of the North Americans 1942-1944*, (Washington: Infantry Journal Press, Inc., 1947), p. 48; Cottingham, Peter Layton, *Once Upon a Wartime, A Canadian Who Survived the Devil's Brigade*, (Privately Published: Neepawa, Manitoba, 1996), pp. 41-56.

22. Cottingham, Peter Layton, *Once Upon a Wartime, A Canadian Who Survived the Devil's Brigade*, (Privately Published: Neepawa, Manitoba, 1996), p. 46; Wickham, Kenneth G., Major General, Notes from telephone interview with author regarding FSSF organization, etc., 22 May 1998; Wickham, Kenneth G., Transcript of Speech to 1st Special Service Force Reunion, 1986, p. 13.

23. Hope, Thomas W., Letter to author regarding his assignment to and experiences with the FSSF, Headquarters Company, Photo Unit at Fort William Henry Harrison, Montana, 24 February 1999.

24. Cottingham, Peter Layton, *Once Upon a Wartime, A Canadian Who Survived the Devil's Brigade*, (Privately Published: Neepawa, Manitoba, 1996), p. 33; Wickham, Kenneth G., Major General, *An Adjutant General Remembers*, (The Adjutant General's Corps Regimental Association, Fort Harrison, Indiana, 1991), p. 25.

25. Frederick, Robert T., Audio tape recording of radio broadcast interview with Joe Pine, (No Date); Thomas, Ed, Transcript of Speech to 5th Special Forces Group (Airborne), Fort Campbell, Kentucky, 19 December 1996, p. 5; Burhans, Robert D., *The First Special Service Force, A War History of the North Americans 1942-1944*, (Washington: Infantry Journal Press, Inc., 1947), pp. 28-29, 35-37.

26. Thomas, Ed, Transcript of Speech to 5th Special Forces Group (Airborne), Fort Campbell, Kentucky, 19 December 1996, p. 5; Dziuban, Stanley W., *Military Relations Between the United States and Canada 1939-1945*, (Washington: Office of the Chief of Military History, 1959), pp. 260-261.

27. Burhans, Robert D., *The First Special Service Force, A War History of the North Americans 1942-1944*, (Washington: Infantry Journal Press, Inc., 1947), pp. 42, 49, 60, Quoted from Burhans, p. 42; Cottingham, Peter Layton, *Once Upon a Wartime, A Canadian Who Survived the Devil's Brigade*, (Privately Published: Neepawa, Manitoba, 1996), p. 56.

28. Quoted from 353, 16 November 1942, Training - First Special Service Force, Memoradum for the Deputy Chief of Staff from Colonel Robert T. Frederick; Cottingham, Peter Layton, *Once Upon a Wartime, A Canadian Who Survived the Devil's Brigade*, (Privately Published: Neepawa, Manitoba, 1996), p. 41-56; Story, William S., Editor, *The First Special Service Force, A Commemorative History, July 1942-January 1945*, (Taylor Publishing Company, Dallas, 1995), pp. 3-8; 319.1, 28 July 1942, Progress Report for the 1st Special Service Force for General McNarney.

29. Cottingham, Peter Layton, *Once Upon a Wartime, A Canadian Who Survived the Devil's Brigade*, (Privately Published: Neepawa, Manitoba, 1996), p. 41-56; Story, William S., Editor, *The First Special Service Force, A Commemorative History, July 1942-January 1945*, (Taylor Publishing Company, Dallas, 1995), pp. 3-8; Burhans, Robert D., *The First Special Service Force, A War History of the North Americans 1942-1944*, (Washington: Infantry Journal Press, Inc., 1947), pp. 39, 43.

30. 353, 16 November 1942, Training - First Special Service Force, Memoradum for the Deputy Chief of Staff from Colonel Robert T. Frederick; Burhans, Robert D., *The First Special Service Force, A War History of the North Americans 1942-1944*, (Washington: Infantry Journal Press, Inc., 1947), p. 23.

31. 319.1, 28 July 1942, Progress Report for the 1st Special Service Force for General McNarney; Story, William S., Editor, *The First Special Service Force, A Commemorative History, July 1942-January 1945*, (Taylor Publishing Company, Dallas, 1995), pp. 3-8, 154; Burhans, Robert D., *The First Special Service Force, A War History of the North Americans 1942-1944*, (Washington: Infantry Journal Press, Inc., 1947), p. 40; Cottingham, Peter Layton, *Once Upon a Wartime, A Canadian Who Survived the Devil's Brigade*, (Privately Published: Neepawa, Manitoba, 1996), p. 41-56.

32. Quoted from 353, 16 November 1942, Training - First Special Service Force, Memoradum for the Deputy Chief of Staff from Colonel Robert T. Frederick; Burhans, Robert D., *The First Special Service Force, A War History of the North Americans 1942-1944*, (Washington: Infantry Journal Press, Inc., 1947), pp. 23-24.

33. Burhans, Robert D., *The First Special Service Force, A War History of the North Americans 1942-1944*, (Washington: Infantry Journal Press, Inc., 1947), p. 49; Cottingham, Peter Layton, *Once Upon a Wartime, A Canadian Who Survived the Devil's Brigade*, (Privately Published: Neepawa, Manitoba, 1996), p. 46.

34. Quoted from 14 July 1942, Memorandum for the Commanding General, Services of Supply from Colonel Robert T. Frederick; Cottingham, Peter Layton, *Once Upon a Wartime, A Canadian Who Survived the Devil's Bri-*

gade, (Privately Published: Neepawa, Manitoba, 1996), p. 41-56; Letter of 30 July 1942, from Russell B. Reynolds to Commanding Officer, First Special Service Force; Quoted from Dziuban, Stanley W., *Military Relations Between the United States and Canada 1939-1945*, (Washington: Office of the Chief of Military History, 1959), p. 262.

35. Dziuban, Stanley W., *Military Relations Between the United States and Canada 1939-1945*, (Washington: Office of the Chief of Military History, 1959), p. 262, Burhans, Robert D., *The First Special Service Force, A War History of the North Americans 1942-1944*, (Washington: Infantry Journal Press, Inc., 1947), p. 53; Quoted from 353, 23 March 1943, Amphibious Training.

36. Burhans, Robert D., *The First Special Service Force, A War History of the North Americans 1942-1944*, (Washington: Infantry Journal Press, Inc., 1947), p. 53, Quoted from p. 56; Quoted from 353, 23 March 1943, Amphibious Training; 353/177 (S)-GNGCT, Special Amphibious-Airborne Directive, 8 April 1943, Letter to Commanding General, Second Army, Memphis, Tennessee, from Lt. General McNair.

37. Burhans, Robert D., *The First Special Service Force, A War History of the North Americans 1942-1944*, (Washington: Infantry Journal Press, Inc., 1947), p. 56.

38. MacGarrigle, George L., *Aleutian Islands, 3 June 1942-24 August 1943*, (United States Government Printing Office, Washington, 1992), p. 5; Thomas, Ed, Transcript of Speech to 5th Special Forces Group (Airborne), Fort Campbell, Kentucky, 19 December 1996, p. 5; Burhans, Robert D., *The First Special Service Force, A War History of the North Americans 1942-1944*, (Washington: Infantry Journal Press, Inc., 1947), pp. 51-52.

Bibliographical Notes: Chapter 3

1. Quoted from George L. MacGarrigle, *Aleutian Islands, 3 June 1942-24 August 1943*, (United States Government Printing Office, Washington, 1992), p. 10; pp. 3-4, 9.

2. "How the Japanese Escaped From Kiska Through Our Heavy Blockading Forces", *Shipmate News*, 8th Reunion, Issue No. 3, July 1997, p. 5.

3. Lael Morgan, "The Aleutians, Alaska's Far-Out Islands," *National Geographic Magazine*, September 1983, p. 343; George L. MacGarrigle, *Aleutian Islands, 3 June 1942-24 August 1943*, (United States Government Printing Office, Washington, 1992), p. 26; "How the Japanese Escaped From Kiska Through Our Heavy Blockading Forces", *Shipmate News*, 8th Reunion, Issue No. 3, July 1997, p. 5.

4. George L. MacGarrigle, *Aleutian Islands, 3 June 1942-24 August 1943*, (United States Government Printing Office, Washington, 1992), p. 23.

5. George L. MacGarrigle, *Aleutian Islands 3 June 1942-24 August 1943*, (United States Government Printing Office, Washington, 1992), pp. 9, 13, 24; "How the Japanese Escaped From Kiska Through Our Heavy Blockading Forces", *Shipmate News*, 8th Reunion, Issue No. 3, July 1997, p. 5.

6. Peter Layton Cottingham, *Once Upon a Wartime, A Canadian Who Survived the Devil's Brigade*, (Privately Published: Neepawa, Manitoba, 1996), p. 65; Robert D. Burhans, *The First Special Service Force, A War History of the North Americans 1942-1944*, (Washington: Infantry Journal Press, Inc., 1947), pp. 60, 71; Les Wayne Merha, *The Service Battalion: Supporting Unit for the First Special Service Force*, (Unpublished Manuscript, No Date), pp. 41-42.

7. *The Aleutians Campaign, June 1942-August 1943*, (United States Government Printing Office, Washington, 1993), pp. 123-124; 595.013 (D2) Report on the activities of the 1st Canadian Special Service Battalion, Kiska, 1943, period 1 August through 30 September 1943.

8. 1st Lieutenant William S. Story, Oral History Interview with Dr. Joseph R. Fischer, 9 June 1997, p. 55.

9. Robert D. Burhans, *The First Special Service Force, A War History of the North Americans 1942-1944*, (Washington: Infantry Journal Press, Inc., 1947), pp. 64-65; Les Wayne Merha, *The Service Battalion: Supporting Unit for the First Special Service Force*, (Unpublished Manuscript, No Date), pp. 42-43.

10. J.D. Mitchell, *The War As I Saw It From My Foxhole*, (Privately Published, No Date), p. 26.

11. "The Training Films," Motion Picture History of the First Special Service Force; J.D. Mitchell, *The War As I Saw It From My Foxhole*, (Privately Published, No Date), pp. 25-28; Robert D. Burhans, *The First Special Service Force, A War History of the North Americans 1942-1944*, (Washington: Infantry Journal Press, Inc., 1947), p. 72; 1st Lieutenant William S. Story,

Oral History Interview with Dr. Joseph R. Fischer, 9 June 1997, pp. 57-58; Les Wayne Merha, *The Service Battalion: Supporting Unit for the First Special Service Force*, (Unpublished Manuscript, No Date), p. 46.

12. Robert H. Adleman and Colonel George Walton, *The Devil's Brigade*, (Chilton Books, Philadelphia, 1966), p. 100.

13. "The Training Films," Motion Picture History of the First Special Service Force.

14. Peter Layton Cottingham, *Once Upon a Wartime, A Canadian Who Survived the Devil's Brigade*, (Privately Published: Neepawa, Manitoba, 1996), p. 72.

15. "The Training Films," Motion Picture History of the First Special Service Force; Peter Layton Cottingham, *Once Upon a Wartime, A Canadian Who Survived the Devil's Brigade*, (Privately Published: Neepawa, Manitoba, 1996), pp. 74, 153-154; J.D. Mitchell, *The War As I Saw It From My Foxhole*, (Privately Published, No Date), p. 28.

16. George I. Ruddell, Notes from telephone interview with author regarding 18th Fighter Squadron at Kiska, Aleutian Islands July-August 1943, 23 February 1998; Robert D. Burhans, *The First Special Service Force, A War History of the North Americans 1942-1944*, (Washington: Infantry Journal Press, Inc., 1947), p. 69; Masataka Chihaya, "Mysterious Withdrawal from Kiska," *Naval Proceedings*, :31-47, February 1958, p. 35.

17. Robert D. Burhans, *The First Special Service Force, A War History of the North Americans 1942-1944*, (Washington: Infantry Journal Press, Inc., 1947), p. 70; Les Wayne Merha, *The Service Battalion: Supporting Unit for the First Special Service Force*, (Unpublished Manuscript, No Date), p. 45; Robert H. Adleman and Colonel George Walton, *The Devil's Brigade*, (Chilton Books, Philadelphia, 1966), pp. 102-103.

18. *The Aleutians Campaign, June 1942-August 1943*, (U.S. Government Printing Office, Washington, 1993), p. 124.

19. 595.013 (D2) Report on the activities of the 1st Canadian Special Service Battalion, Kiska, 1943, period 1 August through 30 September 1943.

20. "The Training Films," Motion Picture History of the First Special Service Force; J.D. Mitchell, *The War As I Saw It From My Foxhole*, (Privately Published, No Date), p. 29.

21, 22, 23. Robert D. Burhans, *The First Special Service Force, A War History of the North Americans 1942-1944*, (Washington: Infantry Journal Press, Inc., 1947), pp. 67-74; George L. MacGarrigle, *Aleutian Islands 3 June 1942-24 August 1943*, (United States Government Printing Office, Washington, 1992), p. 24; 595.013 (D2) Report on the activities of the 1st Canadian Special Service Battalion, Kiska, 1943, period 1 August through 30 September 1943; T. Mark Radcliffe, Captain FSSF, Notes from telephone interview with author regarding operations in Kiska, Aleutian Islands, Alaska, 24 June 1998.

24, 25. *The Aleutians Campaign, June 1942-August 1943*, (U.S. Government Printing Office, Washington, 1993), p. 125; Robert D. Burhans, *The First Special Service Force, A War History of the North Americans 1942-1944*, (Washington: Infantry Journal Press, Inc., 1947), p. 76.

26. *The Aleutians Campaign, June 1942-August 1943*, (U.S. Government Printing Office, Washington, 1993), p. 126; Robert D. Burhans, *The First Special Service Force, A War History of the North Americans 1942-1944*, (Washington: Infantry Journal Press, Inc., 1947), pp. 76-79; 595.013 (D2) Report on the activities of the 1st Canadian Special Service Battalion, Kiska, 1943, period 1 August through 30 September 1943; General Paul D. Adams, Interview no. 1 with Colonel Irving Monclova and Lieutenant Colonel Marvin C. Lang, 5 May 1975. Photocopied transcript on file at the U.S. Army Military History Institute, Carlisle Barracks, PA, p. 2, Section 2.

27. T. Mark Radcliffe, Captain FSSF, Notes from telephone interview with author regarding operations in Kiska, Aleutian Islands, Alaska, 24 June 1998; Robert D. Burhans, *The First Special Service Force, A War History of the North Americans 1942-1944*, (Washington: Infantry Journal Press, Inc., 1947), pp. 76-78.

28. Robert D. Burhans, *The First Special Service Force, A War History of the North Americans 1942-1944*, (Washington: Infantry Journal Press, Inc., 1947), pp. 76-78; General Paul D. Adams, Interview no. 1 with Colonel Irving Monclova and Lieutenant Colonel Marvin C. Lang, 5 May 1975. Photocopied transcript on file at the U.S. Army Military History Institute, Carlisle Barracks, PA, p. 2, Section 2; "The Training Films," Motion Picture History of the First Special Service Force; *The Aleutians Campaign, June 1942-August 1943*, (U.S. Government Printing Office, Washington, 1993), p. 126.

29, 30. Masataka Chihaya, "Mysterious Withdrawal from Kiska," *Naval Proceedings*, :31-47, February 1958, p. 47.

31. Herb Peppard, *The Light Hearted Soldier*, (Nimbus Publishing, Ltd., Halifax NS, 1994), p. 74; Robert D. Burhans, *The First Special Service Force, A War History of the North Americans 1942-1944*, (Washington: Infantry Journal Press, Inc., 1947), pp. 76-84; Masataka Chihaya, "Mysterious Withdrawal from Kiska," *Naval Proceedings*, :31-47, February 1958, p. 47; George L. MacGarrigle, *Aleutian Islands, 3 June 1942-24 August 1943*, (United States Government Printing Office, Washington, 1992), p. 24; 1st Lieutenant William S. Story, Oral History Interview with Dr. Joseph R. Fischer, 9 June 1997, p. 61; Robert H. Adleman and Colonel George Walton, *The Devil's Brigade*, (Chilton Books, Philadelphia, 1966), p. 108; Les Wayne Merha, *The Service Battalion: Supporting Unit for the First Special Service Force*, (Unpublished Manuscript, No Date), p. 48.

32, 33. Robert D. Burhans, *The First Special Service Force, A War History of the North Americans 1942-1944*, (Washington: Infantry Journal Press, Inc., 1947), pp. 76-84.

34. Masataka Chihaya, "Mysterious Withdrawal from Kiska," *Naval Proceedings*, :31-47, February 1958, pp. 34-35, 44.

Bibliographical Notes: Chapter 4

1. Cottingham, Peter Layton, *Once Upon a Wartime, A Canadian Who Survived the Devil's Brigade*, (Privately Published: Neepawa, Manitoba, 1996), pp. 93-95; Story, 1st Lieutenant William S., Oral History Interview with Dr. Joseph R. Fischer, 9 June 1997, pp. 64-65; Merha, Les Wayne, *The Service Battalion: Supporting Unit for the First Special Service Force*, (Unpublished Manuscript, No Date), pp. 49-50.

2. Adams, Paul D., General. Interview no. 1 with Colonel Irving Monclova and Lieutnant Colonel Marvin C. Lang, 5 May 1975. Photocopied transcript on file at the U.S. Army Military History Institute, Carlisle Barracks, PA, p. 8; Story, 1st Lieutenant William S., Oral History Interview with Dr. Joseph R. Fischer, 9 June 1997, p. 65; Burhans, Robert D., *The First Special Service Force, A War History of the North Americans 1942-1944*, (Washington: Infantry Journal Press, Inc., 1947), p. 85.

3. Mitchell, J.D., *The War As I Saw It From My Foxhole*, (Privately Published, No Date), pp. 35-36; Merha, Les Wayne, *The Service Battalion: Supporting Unit for the First Special Service Force*, (Unpublished Manuscript, No Date), pp. 51-52.

4. Mitchell, J.D., *The War As I Saw It From My Foxhole*, (Privately Published, No Date), pp. 36, 39; Adleman, Robert H. and Walton, Colonel George, *The Devil's Brigade*, (Chilton Books, Philadelphia, 1966), p. 112; Burhans, Robert D., *The First Special Service Force, A War History of the North Americans 1942-1944*, (Washington: Infantry Journal Press, Inc., 1947), p. 85; Merha, Les Wayne, *The Service Battalion: Supporting Unit for the First Special Service Force*, (Unpublished Manuscript, No Date), pp. 52-53.

5. Mitchell, J.D., *The War As I Saw It From My Foxhole*, (Privately Published, No Date), pp. 39-41; Burhans, Robert D., *The First Special Service Force, A War History of the North Americans 1942-1944*, (Washington: Infantry Journal Press, Inc., 1947), p. 86; Merha, Les Wayne, *The Service Battalion: Supporting Unit for the First Special Service Force*, (Unpublished Manuscript, No Date), p. 56; Narrative Report, 1st Special Service Force, 17 November 1943-1 February 1944, p. 1; Cottingham, Peter Layton, *Once Upon a Wartime, A Canadian Who Survived the Devil's Brigade*, (Privately Published: Neepawa, Manitoba, 1996), p. 101.

6. Burhans, Robert D., *The First Special Service Force, A War History of the North Americans 1942-1944*, (Washington: Infantry Journal Press, Inc., 1947), p. 88; Story, 1st Lieutenant William S., Oral History Interview with Dr. Joseph R. Fischer, 9 June 1997, pp. 71-73.

7. Narrative Report, 1st Special Service Force, 17 November 1943-1 February 1944, p. 1; Merha, Les Wayne, *The Service Battalion: Supporting Unit for the First Special Service Force*, (Unpublished Manuscript, No Date), pp. 57-59; Story, 1st Lieutenant William S., Oral History Interview with Dr. Joseph R. Fischer, 9 June 1997, pp. 72-74; Wickham, Kenneth G., Major General, *An Adjutant General Remembers*, (The Adjutant General's Corps Regimental Association, Fort Harrison, Indiana, 1991), pp. 41-43; "The Training Films", 16mm Color and Black & White Motion Picture Film History of the First Special Service Force; Underhill, Heat, letter to Bill Story regarding First Sergeant I.P. Fox, 2-2 FSSF, 20 January 1989, pp. 2-3.

8. Blumenson, Martin, *Bloody River: The Real Tragedy of the Rapido*, (Hougton Mifflin Company, Boston, 1970), p. 31; Blumenson, Martin, *U.S. Army in World War Two, Mediterranean Theatre of Operation, Salerno to Cassino*, (Washington: Office of the Cheif of Military History, 1969), pp. 236-255.

9. Blumenson, Martin, *Bloody River: The Real Tragedy of the Rapido*, (Hougton Mifflin Company, Boston, 1970), p. 32.

10. Blumenson, Martin, *Bloody River: The Real Tragedy of the Rapido*, (Hougton Mifflin Company, Boston, 1970), p. 39.

11. Blumenson, Martin, *Bloody River: The Real Tragedy of the Rapido*, (Hougton Mifflin Company, Boston, 1970), pp. 32-33, 36.

12. *Fifth Army At the Winter Line, 15 November 1943-15 January 1944*, (Center of Military History, United States Army, Washington, 1990), p. 4; Blumenson, Martin, *Bloody River: The Real Tragedy of the Rapido*, (Hougton Mifflin Company, Boston, 1970), pp. 37-38; *Road To Rome*, Fifth Army, In the Field, Italy (No Date), p. 18; Laurie, Clayton D., *Rome-Arno 22 January-9 Spetmeber 1944*, (United States Government Printing Office, Washington, No Date), p. 3-5.

13. Blumenson, Martin, *Bloody River: The Real Tragedy of the Rapido*, (Hougton Mifflin Company, Boston, 1970), p. 38.

14. Blumenson, Martin, *Bloody River: The Real Tragedy of the Rapido*, (Hougton Mifflin Company, Boston, 1970), p. 38; Narrative Report, 1st Special Service Force, 17 November 1943-1 February 1944, p. 1.

15. *Fifth Army At the Winter Line, 15 November 1943-15 January 1944*, (Center of Military History, United States Army, Washington, 1990), p. 79.

16. *Fifth Army At the Winter Line, 15 November 1943-15 January 1944*, (Center of Military History, United States Army, Washington, 1990), pp. 16, 79; Blumenson, Martin, *Bloody River: The Real Tragedy of the Rapido*, (Hougton Mifflin Company, Boston, 1970), p. 38; Narrative Report, 1st Special Service Force, 17 November 1943-1 February 1944, p. 1.

17. Blumenson, Martin, *Bloody River: The Real Tragedy of the Rapido*, (Hougton Mifflin Company, Boston, 1970), pp. 15, 17, 39; *Road To Rome*, Fifth Army, In the Field, Italy (No Date), p. 20; *Fifth Army At the Winter Line, 15 November 1943-15 January 1944*, (Center of Military History, United States Army, Washington, 1990), pp. 4, 16.

18. *Fifth Army At the Winter Line, 15 November 1943-15 January 1944*, (Center of Military History, United States Army, Washington, 1990), pp. 116-117; Laurie, Clayton D., *Rome-Arno 22 January-9 Spetmeber 1944*, (United States Government Printing Office, Washington, No Date), p. 3-5.

19. Narrative Report, 1st Special Service Force, 17 November 1943-1 February 1944, p. 1; Blumenson, Martin, *Bloody River: The Real Tragedy of the Rapido*, (Hougton Mifflin Company, Boston, 1970), pp. 39, 44-45.

20. *Fifth Army At the Winter Line, 15 November 1943-15 January 1944*, (Center of Military History, United States Army, Washington, 1990), p. 17; Field Order 14 w/attached annexes, First Special Service Force, 29 November 1943 (Operation RAINCOAT).

21. Adams, Paul D., General. Interview no. 1 with Colonel Irving Monclova and Lieutnant Colonel Marvin C. Lang, 5 May 1975. Photocopied transcript on file at the U.S. Army Military History Institute, Carlisle Barracks, PA, part II, p. 10.

22. Story, 1st Lieutenant William S., Oral History Interview with Dr. Joseph R. Fischer, 9 June 1997, p. 74; Quoted from Adams, Paul D., General. Interview no. 1 with Colonel Irving Monclova and Lieutnant Colonel Marvin C. Lang, 5 May 1975. Photocopied transcript on file at the U.S. Army Military History Institute, Carlisle Barracks, PA, part II, pp. 9-10; Field Order 14 w/ attached annexes, First Special Service Force, 29 November 1943 (Operation RAINCOAT); Peppard, Herb, *The Light Hearted Soldier*, (Nimbus Publishing, Ltd., Halifax NS 1994), p. 80.

23. Quoted from "The Training Films", 16mm Color and Black & White Motion Picture Film History of the First Special Service Force.

24. Field Order 14 w/attached annexes, First Special Service Force, 29 November 1943 (Operation RAINCOAT); "The Training Films", 16mm Color and Black & White Motion Picture Film History of the First Special Service Force.

25. Field Order 14 w/attached annexes, First Special Service Force, 29 November 1943 (Operation RAINCOAT).

26. Narrative Report, 1st Special Service Force, 17 November 1943-1 February 1944, p. 1; Story, 1st Lieutenant William S., Oral History Interview with Dr. Joseph R. Fischer, 9 June 1997, p. 77; MacKinnon, Donald, 1st Company, Second Regiment, FSSF, *Memories of the Battle of Monte la Difensa, December 2-8, 1943*, (No Date), p. 4.

27. Thomas, Ed, Notes from telephone interview with author regarding First Special Service Force action at Monte la Difensa - Monte la Remetanea, 19 July 1998; Story, William S., Editor, *The First Special Service Force, A Commemorative History, July 1942-January 1945*, (Taylor Publishing Company, Dallas, 1995), pp. 96, 158.

28. Website: www.digitalhistory.org/quebec59.html, regarding General James Wolfe at the Battle of Quebec, 1759. *"Wolfe had in the meantime made an important discovery. He had found an inlet two miles west of Quebec with an overgrown path winding up the cliff face. The top was guarded by a company of Canadian militia under Captain Duchambon de Vergor. It was here that Wolfe found the soft underbelly of Quebec's defenses."*; Adams, Paul D., General. Interview no. 1 with Colonel Irving Monclova and Lieutenant Colonel Marvin C. Lang, 5 May 1975. Photocopied transcript on file at the U.S. Army Military History Institute, Carlisle Barracks, PA, part II, p. 10; Story, 1st Lieutenant William S., Oral History Interview with Dr. Joseph R. Fischer, 9 June 1997, p. 77.

29. Thomas, Ed, Notes from telephone interview with author regarding First Special Service Force action at Monte la Difensa - Monte la Remetanea, 19 July 1998; MacKinnon, Donald, 1st Company, Second Regiment, FSSF, *Memories of the Battle of Monte la Difensa, December 2-8, 1943*, (No Date), p. 2.

30. Thomas, Ed, Notes from telephone interview with author regarding First Special Service Force action at Monte la Difensa - Monte la Remetanea, 19 July 1998; MacKinnon, Donald, 1st Company, Second Regiment, FSSF, *Memories of the Battle of Monte la Difensa, December 2-8, 1943*, (No Date), p. 2; Story, 1st Lieutenant William S., Oral History Interview with Dr. Joseph R. Fischer, 9 June 1997, p. 78; Dancocks, Daniel G., *The D-Day Dodgers, The Canadians In Italy: 1943-1945*, (McClelland & Stewart, Inc., Toronto, Ontario, 1991), p. 197.

31. Quoted from Blumenson, Martin, *U.S. Army in World War Two, Mediterranean Theatre of Operation, Salerno to Cassino*, (Washington: Office of the Cheif of Military History, 1969), p. 265.

32. Cottingham, Peter Layton, *Once Upon a Wartime, A Canadian Who Survived the Devil's Brigade*, (Privately Published: Neepawa, Manitoba, 1996), p. 102; Adams, Paul D., General. Interview no. 1 with Colonel Irving Monclova and Lieutnant Colonel Marvin C. Lang, 5 May 1975. Photocopied transcript on file at the U.S. Army Military History Institute, Carlisle Barracks, PA, part II, p. 10; War Diary of the 1st Canadian Special Service Battalion.

33. MacKinnon, Donald, 1st Company, Second Regiment, FSSF, *Memories of the Battle of Monte la Difensa, December 2-8, 1943*, (No Date), pp. 3-4; Adams, Paul D., General. Interview no. 1 with Colonel Irving Monclova and Lieutnant Colonel Marvin C. Lang, 5 May 1975. Photocopied transcript on file at the U.S. Army Military History Institute, Carlisle Barracks, PA, part II, p. 11; Burhans, Robert D., *The First Special Service Force, A War History of the North Americans 1942-1944*, (Washington: Infantry Journal Press, Inc., 1947), p. 102.

34. Story, William S., Notes from telephone interview with author regarding Second Regiment attack on Hill 960, etc., 15 January 1999; Burhans, Robert D., *The First Special Service Force, A War History of the North Americans 1942-1944*, (Washington: Infantry Journal Press, Inc., 1947), p. 103.

35. Story, 1st Lieutenant William S., Oral History Interview with Dr. Joseph R. Fischer, 9 June 1997, p. 79; Story, William S., Editor, *The First Special Service Force, A Commemorative History, July 1942-January 1945*, (Taylor Publishing Company, Dallas, 1995), p. 158; MacKinnon, Donald, 1st Company, Second Regiment, FSSF, *Memories of the Battle of Monte la Difensa, December 2-8, 1943*, (No Date), pp. 3-5; Burhans, Robert D., *The First Special Service Force, A War History of the North Americans 1942-1944*, (Washington: Infantry Journal Press, Inc., 1947), p. 104.

36. Story, William S., Notes from telephone interview with author regarding Second Regiment attack on Hill 960, etc., 15 January 1999; Mitchell, J.D., *The War As I Saw It From My Foxhole*, (Privately Published, No Date), p. 50.

37. Dawson, John R., *Legend of the First Special Service Force*, (Unpublished Manuscript, 1986); Story, William S., Notes from telephone interview with author regarding Second Regiment attack on Hill 960, etc., 15 January 1999; Mitchell, J.D., *The War As I Saw It From My Foxhole*, (Privately Published, No Date), p. 50.

38. Story, 1st Lieutenant William S., Oral History Interview with Dr. Joseph R. Fischer, 9 June 1997, pp. 79-80; Mitchell, J.D., *The War As I Saw It From My Foxhole*, (Privately Published, No Date), p. 45; Dancocks, Daniel G., *The D-Day Dodgers, The Canadians In Italy: 1943-1945*, (McClelland & Stewart, Inc., Toronto, Ontario, 1991), p. 197; MacKinnon, Donald, 1st Company, Second Regiment, FSSF, *Memories of the Battle of Monte la Difensa, December 2-8, 1943*, (No Date), p. 5; Burhans, Robert D., *The First Special Service Force, A War History of the North Americans 1942-1944*, (Washington: Infantry Journal Press, Inc., 1947), p. 104; Story, William S., Notes from telephone interview with author regarding Second Regiment attack on Hill 960, etc., 15 January 1999.

39. Eisenhower, Dwight D., *Crusade in Europe*, (Doubleday & Company, Inc., Garden City, 1948), p. 203; Story, 1st Lieutenant William S., Oral History Interview with Dr. Joseph R. Fischer, 9 June 1997, p. 80; Dancocks, Daniel G., *The D-Day Dodgers, The Canadians In Italy: 1943-1945*, (McClelland & Stewart, Inc., Toronto, Ontario, 1991), p. 197; MacKinnon, Donald, 1st Company, Second Regiment, FSSF, *Memories of the Battle of Monte la Difensa, December 2-8, 1943*, (No Date), p. 5; Burhans, Robert D., *The First Special Service Force, A War History of the North Americans 1942-1944*, (Washington: Infantry Journal Press, Inc., 1947), p. 104.

40. Quoted from G-3 Journal, Headquarters 36th Infantry Division, 0001, 01 December 1943 to 2400, 08 December 1943.

41. Burhans, Robert D., *The First Special Service Force, A War History of the North Americans 1942-1944*, (Washington: Infantry Journal Press, Inc., 1947), p. 107-108; Story, 1st Lieutenant William S., Oral History Interview with Dr. Joseph R. Fischer, 9 June 1997, p. 87.

Bibliographical Notes: Chapter 5

1. Story, 1st Lieutenant William S., Oral History Interview with Dr. Joseph R. Fischer, 9 June 1997, p. 87; Thomas, Ed, Notes from telephone interview with author regarding action on Monte la Difensa on 3/4 December 1943, 13 April 1999.

2. Moore, Colonel Robert S., Notes from telephone conversations with author regarding battle of Monte la Difensa, 7 & 29 September 1999.

3. Burhans, Robert D., *The First Special Service Force, A War History of the North Americans 1942-1944*, (Washington: Infantry Journal Press, Inc., 1947), pp. 106-107; Story, 1st Lieutenant William S., Oral History Interview with Dr. Joseph R. Fischer, 9 June 1997, p. 87.

4. G-3 Journal, Headquarters 36th Infantry Division, 0001, 01 December 1943 to 2400, 08 December 1943; Blumenson, Martin, *U.S. Army in World War Two, Mediterranean Theatre of Operation, Salerno to Cassino*, (Washington: Office of the Cheif of Military History, 1969), p. 266; Story, 1st Lieutenant William S., Oral History Interview with Dr. Joseph R. Fischer, 9 June 1997, pp. 80, 87; Burhans, Robert D., *The First Special Service Force, A War History of the North Americans 1942-1944*, (Washington: Infantry Journal Press, Inc., 1947), pp. 107-110.

5. Cottingham, Peter Layton, *Once Upon a Wartime, A Canadian Who Survived the Devil's Brigade*, (Privately Published: Neepawa, Manitoba, 1996), pp. 132-133; Peppard, Herb, *The Light Hearted Soldier*, (Nimbus Publishing, Ltd., Halifax NS 1994), p. 87; Burhans, Robert D., *The First Special Service Force, A War History of the North Americans 1942-1944*, (Washington: Infantry Journal Press, Inc., 1947), pp. 110-111.

6. McFadden, Major Jerry, Diary from 1 December 1943 through 9 December 1943.

7. Quoted from Peppard, Herb, *The Light Hearted Soldier*, (Nimbus Publishing, Ltd., Halifax NS 1994), p. 80.

8. McFadden, Major Jerry, Notes from telephone conversation with author regarding First Regiment during Difensa operation, 10 February 1999; Burhans, Robert D., *The First Special Service Force, A War History of the North Americans 1942-1944*, (Washington: Infantry Journal Press, Inc., 1947), p. 111; Cottingham, Peter Layton, *Once Upon a Wartime, A Canadian Who Survived the Devil's Brigade*, (Privately Published: Neepawa, Manitoba, 1996), p. 103; Peppard, Herb, *The Light Hearted Soldier*, (Nimbus Publishing, Ltd., Halifax NS 1994), pp. 80-82.

9. McFadden, Major Jerry, Diary from 1 December 1943 through 9 December 1943.

10. G-3 Journal, Headquarters 36th Infantry Division, 0001, 01 December 1943 to 2400, 08 December 1943.

11. Thomas, Ed, Notes from telephone interview with author regarding action on Monte la Difensa on 3/4 December 1943, 13 April 1999; War Diary of the 1st Canadian Special Service Battalion.

12. Burhans, Robert D., *The First Special Service Force, A War History of the North Americans 1942-1944*, (Washington: Infantry Journal Press, Inc., 1947), pp. 113-114; Story, William S., Notes from telephone interview with author regarding Second Regiment attack on Hill 960, etc., 15 January 1999; Story, 1st Lieutenant William S., Oral History Interview with Dr. Joseph R. Fischer, 9 June 1997, p. 85; G-3 Journal, Headquarters 36th Infantry Division, 0001, 01 December 1943 to 2400, 08 December 1943.

13. Wickham, Kenneth G., Major General, *An Adjutant General Remembers*, (The Adjutant General's Corps Regimental Association, Fort Harrison, Indiana, 1991), p. 42.

14. Quoted from Story, 1st Lieutenant William S., Oral History Interview with Dr. Joseph R. Fischer, 9 June 1997, p. 92.

15. Wickham, Kenneth G., Major General, *An Adjutant General Remembers*, (The Adjutant General's Corps Regimental Association, Fort Harrison, Indiana, 1991), p. 43; Story, 1st Lieutenant William S., Oral History Interview with Dr. Joseph R. Fischer, 9 June 1997, p. 92.

16. Story, William S., Notes from telephone interview with author regarding Second Regiment attack on Hill 960, etc., 15 January 1999; Burhans, Robert D., *The First Special Service Force, A War History of the North Americans 1942-1944*, (Washington: Infantry Journal Press, Inc., 1947), pp. 117-118.

17, 18. Burhans, Robert D., *The First Special Service Force, A War History of the North Americans 1942-1944*, (Washington: Infantry Journal Press, Inc., 1947), pp. 119-124.

19. Burhans, Robert D., *The First Special Service Force, A War History of the North Americans 1942-1944*, (Washington: Infantry Journal Press, Inc., 1947), p. 112; The Training Films; Narrative Report, 1st Special Service Force, 17 November 1943-1 February 1944, p. 2.

Bibliographical Notes: Chapter 6

1. Narrative Report, 1st Special Service Force, 17 November 1943-1 February 1944, p. 2; *Fifth Army At the Winter Line, 15 November 1943-15 January 1944*, (Center of Military History, United States Army, Washington, 1990), pp. 45-46, 52.

2. *Fifth Army At the Winter Line, 15 November 1943-15 January 1944*, (Center of Military History, United States Army, Washington, 1990), pp. 48, 51.

3. *Fifth Army At the Winter Line, 15 November 1943-15 January 1944*, (Center of Military History, United States Army, Washington, 1990), pp. 45-68.

4. Burhans, Robert D., *The First Special Service Force, A War History of the North Americans 1942-1944*, (Washington: Infantry Journal Press, Inc., 1947), pp. 131, 140; Narrative Report, 1st Special Service Force, 17 November 1943-1 February 1944, p. 2; Merha, Les Wayne, *The Service Battalion: Supporting Unit for the First Special Service Force*, (Unpublished Manuscript, No Date), pp. 66, 70; Mitchell, J.D., *The War As I Saw It From My Foxhole*, (Privately Published, No Date), p. 50. Note: Frederick saw to it that Colonel D.D. Williamson was quickly and quietly ushered out of the Force – under the pretext of stomach ulcers – after, according to Forceman, J.D. Mitchell, Williamson's "less than spectacular performance" on Monte la Difensa. This was done, one could accurately infer, for political reasons. After all, Williamson was the senior Canadian officer. The Force had always been under intense scrutiny by American, and especially Canadian officials with its disbanding a constant specter.

5. *Fifth Army At the Winter Line, 15 November 1943-15 January 1944*, (Center of Military History, United States Army, Washington, 1990), p. 82; Burhans, Robert D., *The First Special Service Force, A War History of the North Americans 1942-1944*, (Washington: Infantry Journal Press, Inc., 1947), pp. 131-134.

6. Narrative Report, 1st Special Service Force, 17 November 1943-1 February 1944, p. 2; Burhans, Robert D., *The First Special Service Force, A War History of the North Americans 1942-1944*, (Washington: Infantry Journal Press, Inc., 1947), pp. 134-139.

7. Narrative Report, 1st Special Service Force, 17 November 1943-1 February 1944, p. 2; Qouted from Burhans, Robert D., *The First Special Service Force, A War History of the North Americans 1942-1944*, (Washington: Infantry Journal Press, Inc., 1947), p. 139.

8. Quoted from *Fifth Army At the Winter Line, 15 November 1943-15 January 1944*, (Center of Military History, United States Army, Washington, 1990), p. 93.

9. *Fifth Army At the Winter Line, 15 November 1943-15 January 1944*, (Center of Military History, United States Army, Washington, 1990), pp. 91, 95; Burhans, Robert D., *The First Special Service Force, A War History of the North Americans 1942-1944*, (Washington: Infantry Journal Press, Inc., 1947), pp. 140-141, 143.

10. *Fifth Army At the Winter Line, 15 November 1943-15 January 1944*, (Center of Military History, United States Army, Washington, 1990), p. 96; Burhans, Robert D., *The First Special Service Force, A War History of the North Americans 1942-1944*, (Washington: Infantry Journal Press, Inc., 1947), pp. 140-141, 143, 146.

11. *Fifth Army At the Winter Line, 15 November 1943-15 January 1944*, (Center of Military History, United States Army, Washington, 1990), p. 97; Narrative Report, 1st Special Service Force, 17 November 1943-1 February 1944, p. 2; Burhans, Robert D., *The First Special Service Force, A War History of the North Americans 1942-1944*, (Washington: Infantry Journal Press, Inc., 1947), pp. 143, 145-146.

12. Quoted From Narrative Report, 1st Special Service Force, 17 November 1943-1 February 1944, p. 3; Robert D., *The First Special Service Force, A War History of the North Americans 1942-1944*, (Washington: Infantry Journal Press, Inc., 1947), pp. 148-149.

13. Burhans, Robert D., *The First Special Service Force, A War History of the North Americans 1942-1944*, (Washington: Infantry Journal Press, Inc., 1947), p. 150.

14. Quoted from Burhans, Robert D., *The First Special Service Force, A War History of the North Americans 1942-1944*, (Washington: Infantry Journal Press, Inc., 1947), pp. 151-152.

15. Narrative Report, 1st Special Service Force, 17 November 1943-1 February 1944, p. 2; *Fifth Army At the Winter Line, 15 November 1943-15 January 1944*, (Center of Military History, United States Army, Washington, 1990), pp. 98-99; Burhans, Robert D., *The First Special Service Force, A War History of the North Americans 1942-1944*, (Washington: Infantry Journal Press, Inc., 1947), p. 152, and quoted from Burhans, p. 154; Mitchell, J.D., *The War As I Saw It From My Foxhole*, (Privately Published, No Date), pp. 63-66; Dancocks, Daniel G., *The D-Day Dodgers, The Canadians In Italy: 1943-1945*, (McClelland & Stewart, Inc., Toronto, Ontario, 1991), p. 199.

16. *Fifth Army At the Winter Line, 15 November 1943-15 January 1944*, (Center of Military History, United States Army, Washington, 1990), p. 99; Narrative Report, 1st Special Service Force, 17 November 1943-1 February 1944, p. 2; Burhans, Robert D., *The First Special Service Force, A War History of the North Americans 1942-1944*, (Washington: Infantry Journal Press, Inc., 1947), pp. 153-156; McFadden, Major Jerry, Notes from speech honoring Colonel A.C. Marshall, (No date), p. 2.

17. Burhans, Robert D., *The First Special Service Force, A War History of the North Americans 1942-1944*, (Washington: Infantry Journal Press, Inc., 1947), pp. 156-157, and quoted from Burhans, p. 156; *Fifth Army At the Winter Line, 15 November 1943-15 January 1944*, (Center of Military History, United States Army, Washington, 1990), p. 95.

18. Excerpt from (Canada, Department of National Defense, General Staff, Historical Section, "The 1st Canadian Special Service Battalion", Report no. 5, p. 38, quoted from McMichael, Scott R., *A Historical Perspective On Light Infantry, Combat Studies Institute Research Survey No 6*, (Command and General Staff College, Fort Leavenworth, 1987), p. 191; Burhans, Robert D., *The First Special Service Force, A War History of the North Americans 1942-1944*, (Washington: Infantry Journal Press, Inc., 1947), pp. 157-159; Narrative Report, 1st Special Service Force, 17 November 1943-1 February 1944, p. 2.

19. Burhans, Robert D., *The First Special Service Force, A War History of the North Americans 1942-1944*, (Washington: Infantry Journal Press, Inc., 1947), pp. 158-159; Narrative Report, 1st Special Service Force, 17 November 1943-1 February 1944, p. 3; McMichael, Scott R., *A Historical Perspective On Light Infantry, Combat Studies Institute Research Survey No 6*, (Command and General Staff College, Fort Leavenworth, 1987), p. 192.

20. Mitchell, J.D., *The War As I Saw It From My Foxhole*, (Privately Published, No Date), p. 66; Burhans, Robert D., *The First Special Service Force, A War History of the North Americans 1942-1944*, (Washington: Infantry Journal Press, Inc., 1947), p. 154, 159; Narrative Report, 1st Special Service Force, 17 November 1943-1 February 1944, p. 2.

21. Narrative Report, 1st Special Service Force, 17 November 1943-1 February 1944, p. 3; Burhans, Robert D., *The First Special Service Force, A War History of the North Americans 1942-1944*, (Washington: Infantry Journal Press, Inc., 1947), pp. 160-161; *Fifth Army At the Winter Line, 15 November 1943-15 January 1944*, (Center of Military History, United States Army, Washington, 1990), p. 109.

22. Burhans, Robert D., *The First Special Service Force, A War History of the North Americans 1942-1944*, (Washington: Infantry Journal Press, Inc., 1947), pp. 128-129, 162; Narrative Report, 1st Special Service Force, 17 November 1943-1 February 1944, p. 3.

23. Burhans, Robert D., *The First Special Service Force, A War History of the North Americans 1942-1944*, (Washington: Infantry Journal Press, Inc., 1947), p. 162; Narrative Report, 1st Special Service Force, 17 November 1943-1 February 1944, p. 3; *Fifth Army At the Winter Line, 15 November 1943-15 January 1944*, (Center of Military History, United States Army, Washington, 1990), pp. 111-112.

24. Quoted from Burhans, Robert D., *The First Special Service Force, A War History of the North Americans 1942-1944*, (Washington: Infantry Journal Press, Inc., 1947), p. 162.

25. Dziuban, Stanley W., *Military Relations Between the United States and Canada 1939-1945*, (Washington: Office of the Chief of Military History, 1959), p. 265

26. Note: Although some 750 Weasels (of the T-24 variant) were delivered to the Santa Maria base camp to be used by the First Special Service Force, according to Force Supply Officer, Colonel O.J. Baldwin, only a handful were ever uncrated, and then only for the purpose of training newly arrived replacements. In only one instance, when Forcemen volunteered to drive the Weasels, in order to move supplies forward across the flood plain of the Rapido River in support of its crossing by elements of the 36th Division, were they used during actual operations. Otherwise, their poor performance over the jagged, rock studded Italian terrain made them all but useless. Upon the Force's movement to southern France, the entire stock of weasels was left behind with Army Ordnance. Dawson, John R., and Kutemeier, Don, *First Special Service Force, 1942-44 (I)*, (Military Illustrated, Past and Present, August/September, 1986).

27. Adams, Paul D., General. Interview no. 1 with Colonel Irving Monclova and Lieutnant Colonel Marvin C. Lang, 5 May 1975. Photocopied transcript on file at the U.S. Army Military History Institute, Carlisle Barracks, PA., Part II, pp. 16-19; Adleman, Robert H. and Walton, Colonel George, *Rome Fell Today*, (Boston: Little, Brown, & Company, 1968), p. 156.

28. Narrative Report, 1st Special Service Force, 17 November 1943-1 February 1944, p. 4, and quoted from Narrative Report, p. 4; Merha, Les Wayne, *The Service Battalion: Supporting Unit for the First Special Service Force*, (Unpublished Manuscript, No Date), p. 80; Story, William S., Editor, *The First Special Service Force, A Commemorative History, July 1942-January 1945*, (Taylor Publishing Company, Dallas, 1995), p. 27; McMichael, Scott R., *A Historical Perspective On Light Infantry, Combat Studies Institute Research Survey No 6*, (Command and General Staff College, Fort Leavenworth, 1987), p. 193; Wickham, Kenneth G., Major General, *An Adjutant General Remembers*, (The Adjutant General's Corps Regimental Association, Fort Harrison, Indiana, 1991), p. 43.

Bibliographical Notes: Chapter 7

1. Summary of Operations Reports, 1 February 1944-28 November 1944; World War II with Walter Cronkite, Volume IV, Battleground: Italy/Air War Over Europe (Video Series); Story, William S., Editor, *The First Special Service Force, A Commemorative History, July 1942-January 1945*, (Taylor Publishing Company, Dallas, 1995), pp. 27-28.

2. Summary of Operations Reports, 1 February 1944-28 November 1944; Merha, Les Wayne, *The Service Battalion: Supporting Unit for the First Special Service Force*, (Unpublished Manuscript, No Date), p. 80; McFadden, Jerry, notes to author regarding remembrances of Anzio; Mitchell, J.D., *The War As I Saw It From My Foxhole*, (Privately Published, No Date), p. 73.

3. Quoted from Summary of Operations Reports, 1 February 1944-28 November 1944; Merha, Les Wayne, *The Service Battalion: Supporting Unit for the First Special Service Force*, (Unpublished Manuscript, No Date), p. 86; Story, William S., Editor, *The First Special Service Force, A Commemorative History, July 1942-January 1945*, (Taylor Publishing Company, Dallas, 1995), p. 28; Peppard, Herb, *The Light Hearted Soldier*, (Nimbus Publishing, Ltd., Halifax NS 1994), p. 104.

4. Story, William S., Editor, *The First Special Service Force, A Commemorative History, July 1942-January 1945*, (Taylor Publishing Company, Dallas, 1995), p. 28; Summary of Operations Reports, 1 February 1944-28 November 1944; McMichael, Scott R., *A Historical Perspective On Light Infantry, Combat Studies Institute Research Survey No 6*, (Command and General Staff College, Fort Leavenworth, 1987), p. 193.

5. Merha, Les Wayne, *The Service Battalion: Supporting Unit for the First Special Service Force*, (Unpublished Manuscript, No Date), pp. 78-79; McMichael, Scott R., *A Historical Perspective On Light Infantry, Combat Studies Institute Research Survey No 6*, (Command and General Staff College, Fort Leavenworth, 1987), p. 193; Summary of Operations Reports, 1 February 1944-28 November 1944.

6. Quoted from Frederick, Robert T., Major General. Interview at the Pentagon, 7 January 1949. Photocopied transcript on file at the U.S. Army Military History Institute, Carlisle Barracks, PA, p. 4.

7, 8. Quoted from Summary of Operations Reports, 1 February 1944-28 November 1944.

9. McMichael, Scott R., *A Historical Perspective On Light Infantry, Combat Studies Institute Research Survey No 6*, (Command and General Staff College, Fort Leavenworth, 1987), p. 193.

10, 11, 12. Summary of Operations Reports, 1 February 1944-28 November 1944.

13. Summary of Operations Reports, 1 February 1944-28 November 1944; Peppard, Herb, *The Light Hearted Soldier*, (Nimbus Publishing, Ltd., Halifax NS 1994), p. 105; Story, William S., Editor, *The First Special Service Force, A Commemorative History, July 1942-January 1945*, (Taylor Publishing Company, Dallas, 1995), p. 29; Burhans, Robert D., *The First Special Service Force, A War History of the North Americans 1942-1944*, (Washington: Infantry Journal Press, Inc., 1947), pp. 184-185.

14. Peppard, Herb, *The Light Hearted Soldier*, (Nimbus Publishing, Ltd., Halifax NS 1994), pp. 107-108; Dancocks, Daniel G., *The D-Day Dodgers, The Canadians In Italy: 1943-1945*, (McClelland & Stewart, Inc., Toronto, Ontario, 1991), pp. 225-226.

15. Quoted from Dancocks, Daniel G., *The D-Day Dodgers, The Canadians In Italy: 1943-1945*, (McClelland & Stewart, Inc., Toronto, Ontario, 1991), pp. 225-226.

16. Burhans, Robert D., *The First Special Service Force, A War History of the North Americans 1942-1944*, (Washington: Infantry Journal Press, Inc., 1947), p. 185.

17. Merha, Les Wayne, *The Service Battalion: Supporting Unit for the First Special Service Force*, (Unpublished Manuscript, No Date), pp. 81, 92.

18. Summary of Operations Reports, 1 February 1944-28 November 1944.

19. Quoted from Burhans, Robert D., *The First Special Service Force, A War History of the North Americans 1942-1944*, (Washington: Infantry Journal Press, Inc., 1947), p. 197.

20. World War II with Walter Cronkite, Volume IV, Battleground: Italy/Air War Over Europe (Video Series).

21. Summary of Operations Reports, 1 February 1944-28 November 1944.

22. Burhans, Robert D., *The First Special Service Force, A War History of the North Americans 1942-1944*, (Washington: Infantry Journal Press, Inc., 1947), pp. 204, 206-207.

23. Quoted from Lyons, Joseph, Letter with notes on the 456th and 463rd Parachute Field Artillery Battalions, and the Parachute Field Artillery Test Battalion with Pictures, etc., 02 February 1998.

24. Quoted from Peppard, Herb, *The Light Hearted Soldier*, (Nimbus Publishing, Ltd., Halifax NS 1994), p. 111.

25. Wickham, Kenneth G., Major General, *An Adjutant General Remembers*, (The Adjutant General's Corps Regimental Association, Fort Harrison, Indiana, 1991), p. 45; Peppard, Herb, *The Light Hearted Soldier*, (Nimbus Publishing, Ltd., Halifax NS 1994), p. 105.

26. Quoted from Summary of Operations Reports, 1 February 1944-28 November 1944; Merha, Les Wayne, *The Service Battalion: Supporting Unit for the First Special Service Force*, (Unpublished Manuscript, No Date), p. 94.

27. Frederick, Robert T., Major General. Interview at the Pentagon, 7 January 1949. Photocopied transcript on file at the U.S. Army Military History Institute, Carlisle Barracks, PA, p. 4; Summary of Operations Reports, 1 February 1944-28 November 1944; Merha, Les Wayne, *The Service Battalion: Supporting Unit for the First Special Service Force*, (Unpublished Manuscript, No Date), p. 90.

28. Allen, William Lusk, *Anzio: Edge of Disaster*, (E.P. Dutton, New York, 1978), pp. 75-77; World War II with Walter Cronkite, Volume IV, Battleground: Italy/Air War Over Europe (Video Series); Story, William S., Editor, *The First Special Service Force, A Commemorative History, July 1942-January 1945*, (Taylor Publishing Company, Dallas, 1995), pp. 27-28.

29. Quoted from Summary of Operations Reports, 1 February 1944-28 November 1944.

30. Frederick, Robert T., Major General. Interview at the Pentagon, 7 January 1949. Photocopied transcript on file at the U.S. Army Military History Institute, Carlisle Barracks, PA, p. 6; Summary of Operations Reports, 1 February 1944-28 November 1944; Altiere, James, *The Spearheaders*, (The Bobbs-Merrill Company, Inc., Indianapolis, 1960), pp. 315-316; Wickham, Kenneth G., Major General, *An Adjutant General Remembers*, (The Adjutant General's Corps Regimental Association, Fort Harrison, Indiana, 1991), p. 45; Burhans, Robert D., *The First Special Service Force, A War History of the North Americans 1942-1944*, (Washington: Infantry Journal Press, Inc., 1947), p. 203.

31. Summary of Operations Reports, 1 February 1944-28 November 1944; Dancocks, Daniel G., *The D-Day Dodgers, The Canadians In Italy: 1943-*

1945, (McClelland & Stewart, Inc., Toronto, Ontario, 1991), p. 297; McMichael, Scott R., *A Historical Perspective On Light Infantry, Combat Studies Institute Research Survey No 6*, (Command and General Staff College, Fort Leavenworth, 1987), p. 197.

32. Merha, Les Wayne, *The Service Battalion: Supporting Unit for the First Special Service Force*, (Unpublished Manuscript, No Date), pp. 77, 79-80, 84-85; Summary of Operations Reports, 1 February 1944-28 November 1944.

33. Quoted from Merha, Les Wayne, *The Service Battalion: Supporting Unit for the First Special Service Force*, (Unpublished Manuscript, No Date), p. 88.

34. Merha, Les Wayne, *The Service Battalion: Supporting Unit for the First Special Service Force*, (Unpublished Manuscript, No Date), pp. 88-90.

35. World War II with Walter Cronkite, Volume IV, Battleground: Italy/ Air War Over Europe (Video Series).

36. Merha, Les Wayne, *The Service Battalion: Supporting Unit for the First Special Service Force*, (Unpublished Manuscript, No Date), pp. 77-78, 82-84; World War II with Walter Cronkite, Volume IV, Battleground: Italy/Air War Over Europe (Video Series); Story, William S., Editor, *The First Special Service Force, A Commemorative History, July 1942-January 1945*, (Taylor Publishing Company, Dallas, 1995), p. 29; Burhans, Robert D., *The First Special Service Force, A War History of the North Americans 1942-1944*, (Washington: Infantry Journal Press, Inc., 1947), pp. 180-181.

37. World War II with Walter Cronkite, Volume IV, Battleground: Italy/ Air War Over Europe (Video Series); Merha, Les Wayne, *The Service Battalion: Supporting Unit for the First Special Service Force*, (Unpublished Manuscript, No Date), p. 97.

38. Summary of Operations Reports, 1 February 1944-28 November 1944.

39. Quoted from Lyons, Joseph, Letter with notes on the 456th and 463rd Parachute Field Artillery Battalions, and the Parachute Field Artillery Test Battalion with Pictures, etc., 02 February 1998; Summary of Operations Reports, 1 February 1944-28 November 1944.

40. Lyons, Joseph, Letter with notes on the 456th and 463rd Parachute Field Artillery Battalions, and the Parachute Field Artillery Test Battalion with Pictures, etc., 02 February 1998.

41. Summary of Operations Reports, 1 February 1944-28 November 1944.

42. Frederick, Robert T., Major General. Interview at the Pentagon, 7 January 1949. Photocopied transcript on file at the U.S. Army Military History Institute, Carlisle Barracks, PA, p. 4; Summary of Operations Reports, 1 February 1944-28 November 1944.

Bibliographical Notes: Chapter 8

1. Allen, William Lusk, *Anzio: Edge of Disaster*, (E.P. Dutton, New York, 1978). p. 146.

2. Laurie, Clayton D., *Rome-Arno 22 January-9 Spetmeber 1944*, (United States Government Printing Office, Washington, No Date), pp. 17-18; Allen, William Lusk, *Anzio: Edge of Disaster*, (E.P. Dutton, New York, 1978). p. 142.

3. Quoted from Laurie, Clayton D., *Rome-Arno 22 January-9 Spetmeber 1944*, (United States Government Printing Office, Washington, No Date), p. 18.

4. Laurie, Clayton D., *Rome-Arno 22 January-9 Spetmeber 1944*, (United States Government Printing Office, Washington, No Date), pp. 19-20.

5. Quoted from Allen, William Lusk, *Anzio: Edge of Disaster*, (E.P. Dutton, New York, 1978). p. 116.

6. Allen, William Lusk, *Anzio: Edge of Disaster*, (E.P. Dutton, New York, 1978). pp. 142-143; Laurie, Clayton D., *Rome-Arno 22 January-9 Spetmeber 1944*, (United States Government Printing Office, Washington, No Date), p. 20.

7. Allen, William Lusk, *Anzio: Edge of Disaster*, (E.P. Dutton, New York, 1978). pp. 147-149; Laurie, Clayton D., *Rome-Arno 22 January-9 Spetmeber 1944*, (United States Government Printing Office, Washington, No Date), pp. 23-24.

8. Quoted from Frederick, Robert T., Major General. Interview at the Pentagon, 7 January 1949. Photocopied transcript on file at the U.S. Army Military History Institute, Carlisle Barracks, PA, p. 2.

9. Frederick, Robert T., Major General. Interview at the Pentagon, 7 January 1949. Photocopied transcript on file at the U.S. Army Military History Institute, Carlisle Barracks, PA, p. 2; Sheldon, W.G., Battle - 1944 - Anzio To Rome, (No Date), pp. 1-2.

10. Merha, Les Wayne, *The Service Battalion: Supporting Unit for the First Special Service Force*, (Unpublished Manuscript, No Date), pp. 100-101.

11. Summary of Operations Reports, 1 February 1944-28 November 1944; Sheldon, W.G., Battle - 1944 - Anzio To Rome, (No Date), pp. 1-2; Frederick, Robert T., Major General. Interview at the Pentagon, 7 January 1949. Photocopied transcript on file at the U.S. Army Military History Institute, Carlisle Barracks, PA, p. 7; Sheldon, W.G., Battle - 1944 - Anzio To Rome, (No Date), p. 2.

12. Frederick, Robert T., Major General. Interview at the Pentagon, 7 January 1949. Photocopied transcript on file at the U.S. Army Military History Institute, Carlisle Barracks, PA, "23 May," p. 1; Summary of Operations Reports, 1 February 1944-28 November 1944; Sheldon, W.G., Battle - 1944 - Anzio To Rome, (No Date), p. 2.

13. Frederick, Robert T., Major General. Interview at the Pentagon, 7 January 1949. Photocopied transcript on file at the U.S. Army Military History Institute, Carlisle Barracks, PA, Section, p. 7, "23 May," pp. 1-2.

14. Frederick, Robert T., Major General. Interview at the Pentagon, 7 January 1949. Photocopied transcript on file at the U.S. Army Military History Institute, Carlisle Barracks, PA, p. 7; Burhans, Robert D., *The First Special Service Force, A War History of the North Americans 1942-1944*, (Washington: Infantry Journal Press, Inc., 1947), pp. 212-214.

15. Peppard, Herb, *The Light Hearted Soldier*, (Nimbus Publishing, Ltd., Halifax NS 1994), pp. 118-119.

16. Frederick, Robert T., Major General. Interview at the Pentagon, 7 January 1949. Photocopied transcript on file at the U.S. Army Military History Institute, Carlisle Barracks, PA, "23 May," p. 3; Sheldon, W.G., Battle - 1944 - Anzio To Rome, (No Date), pp. 2-4; Burhans, Robert D., *The First Special Service Force, A War History of the North Americans 1942-1944*, (Washington: Infantry Journal Press, Inc., 1947), p. 215.

17. Cottingham, Peter Layton, *Once Upon a Wartime, A Canadian Who Survived the Devil's Brigade*, (Privately Published: Neepawa, Manitoba, 1996), p. 127; Frederick, Robert T., Major General. Interview at the Pentagon, 7 January 1949. Photocopied transcript on file at the U.S. Army Military History Institute, Carlisle Barracks, PA, "23 May," pp. 3-4.

18. Sheldon, W.G., Battle - 1944 - Anzio To Rome, (No Date), pp. 4-6; . Frederick, Robert T., Major General. Interview at the Pentagon, 7 January 1949. Photocopied transcript on file at the U.S. Army Military History Institute, Carlisle Barracks, PA, "23 May," p. 4.

19. Summary of Operations Reports, 1 February 1944-28 November 1944; Frederick, Robert T., Major General. Interview at the Pentagon, 7 January 1949. Photocopied transcript on file at the U.S. Army Military History Institute, Carlisle Barracks, PA, pp. 7-8; Sheldon, W.G., Battle - 1944 - Anzio To Rome, (No Date), pp. 4-6.

20. Summary of Operations Reports, 1 February 1944-28 November 1944; Frederick, Robert T., Major General. Interview at the Pentagon, 7 January 1949. Photocopied transcript on file at the U.S. Army Military History Institute, Carlisle Barracks, PA, pp. 7-8, and "23 May," pp. 6-7; Sheldon, W.G., Battle - 1944 - Anzio To Rome, (No Date), pp. 4-6.

21. Frederick, Robert T., Major General. Interview at the Pentagon, 7 January 1949. Photocopied transcript on file at the U.S. Army Military History Institute, Carlisle Barracks, PA, p. 8; Dancocks, Daniel G., *The D-Day Dodgers, The Canadians In Italy: 1943-1945*, (McClelland & Stewart, Inc., Toronto, Ontario, 1991), p. 280; Sheldon, W.G., Battle - 1944 - Anzio To Rome, (No Date), pp. 6-8; Burhans, Robert D., *The First Special Service Force, A War History of the North Americans 1942-1944*, (Washington: Infantry Journal Press, Inc., 1947), p. 217.

22. Frederick, Robert T., Major General. Interview at the Pentagon, 7 January 1949. Photocopied transcript on file at the U.S. Army Military History Institute, Carlisle Barracks, PA, pp. 8-9; Dancocks, Daniel G., *The D-Day Dodgers, The Canadians In Italy: 1943-1945*, (McClelland & Stewart, Inc., Toronto, Ontario, 1991), p. 280; Sheldon, W.G., Battle - 1944 - Anzio To Rome, (No Date), pp. 6-9; Burhans, Robert D., *The First Special Service Force, A War History of the North Americans 1942-1944*, (Washington: Infantry Journal Press, Inc., 1947), p. 217.

23. Frederick, Robert T., Major General. Interview at the Pentagon, 7 January 1949. Photocopied transcript on file at the U.S. Army Military History Institute, Carlisle Barracks, PA, pp. 8-9, "23 May," p. 7; Sheldon, W.G., Battle - 1944 - Anzio To Rome, (No Date), pp. 8-9.

24. Frederick, Robert T., Major General. Interview at the Pentagon, 7 January 1949. Photocopied transcript on file at the U.S. Army Military History Institute, Carlisle Barracks, PA, "23 May," p. 10; Sheldon, W.G., Battle -

1944 - Anzio To Rome, (No Date), pp. 8-9; Allen, William Lusk, *Anzio: Edge of Disaster*, (E.P. Dutton, New York, 1978), p. 151; Burhans, Robert D., *The First Special Service Force, A War History of the North Americans 1942-1944*, (Washington: Infantry Journal Press, Inc., 1947), p. 219.

25. Sheldon, W.G., Battle - 1944 - Anzio To Rome, (No Date), pp. 9-10; Laurie, Clayton D., *Rome-Arno 22 January-9 Spetmeber 1944*, (United States Government Printing Office, Washington, No Date), p. 20.

26. Sheldon, W.G., Battle - 1944 - Anzio To Rome, (No Date), p. 10; Summary of Operations Reports, 1 February 1944-28 November 1944; Mitchell, J.D., *The War As I Saw It From My Foxhole*, (Privately Published, No Date), p. 104; Burhans, Robert D., *The First Special Service Force, A War History of the North Americans 1942-1944*, (Washington: Infantry Journal Press, Inc., 1947), p. 221.

27. Summary of Operations Reports, 1 February 1944-28 November 1944; Burhans, Robert D., *The First Special Service Force, A War History of the North Americans 1942-1944*, (Washington: Infantry Journal Press, Inc., 1947), pp. 224-225.

28. Allen, William Lusk, *Anzio: Edge of Disaster*, (E.P. Dutton, New York, 1978). p. 157; Burhans, Robert D., *The First Special Service Force, A War History of the North Americans 1942-1944*, (Washington: Infantry Journal Press, Inc., 1947), p. 225.

29. Summary of Operations Reports, 1 February 1944-28 November 1944; Quoted from Allen, William Lusk, *Anzio: Edge of Disaster*, (E.P. Dutton, New York, 1978). p. 158.

30. Summary of Operations Reports, 1 February 1944-28 November 1944; Burhans, Robert D., *The First Special Service Force, A War History of the North Americans 1942-1944*, (Washington: Infantry Journal Press, Inc., 1947), p. 226.

31. Cottingham, Peter Layton, *Once Upon a Wartime, A Canadian Who Survived the Devil's Brigade*, (Privately Published: Neepawa, Manitoba, 1996), p. 135; Summary of Operations Reports, 1 February 1944-28 November 1944; Burhans, Robert D., *The First Special Service Force, A War History of the North Americans 1942-1944*, (Washington: Infantry Journal Press, Inc., 1947), p. 229.

32, 33, 34. Summary of Operations Reports, 1 February 1944-28 November 1944.

35. Burhans, Robert D., *The First Special Service Force, A War History of the North Americans 1942-1944*, (Washington: Infantry Journal Press, Inc., 1947), p. 235; Summary of Operations Reports, 1 February 1944-28 November 1944.

36. Summary of Operations Reports, 1 February 1944-28 November 1944; Burhans, Robert D., *The First Special Service Force, A War History of the North Americans 1942-1944*, (Washington: Infantry Journal Press, Inc., 1947), pp. 235-236.

37. Laurie, Clayton D., *Rome-Arno 22 January-9 Spetmeber 1944*, (United States Government Printing Office, Washington, No Date), p. 23; Burhans, Robert D., *The First Special Service Force, A War History of the North Americans 1942-1944*, (Washington: Infantry Journal Press, Inc., 1947), p. 211.

38. Summary of Operations Reports, 1 February 1944-28 November 1944.

39. Summary of Operations Reports, 1 February 1944-28 November 1944; Mitchell, J.D., *The War As I Saw It From My Foxhole*, (Privately Published, No Date), p. 108; Cottingham, Peter Layton, *Once Upon a Wartime, A Canadian Who Survived the Devil's Brigade*, (Privately Published: Neepawa, Manitoba, 1996), p. 139.

40. Summary of Operations Reports, 1 February 1944-28 November 1944; Mitchell, J.D., *The War As I Saw It From My Foxhole*, (Privately Published, No Date), p. 108.

41. Quoted from Adleman, Robert H. and Walton, Colonel George, *The Devil's Brigade*, (Chilton Books, Philadelphia, 1966), p. 211.

42. Quoted from Adleman, Robert H. and Walton, Colonel George, *The Devil's Brigade*, (Chilton Books, Philadelphia, 1966), p. 211; Laurie, Clayton D., *Rome-Arno 22 January-9 Spetmeber 1944*, (United States Government Printing Office, Washington, No Date), p. 23.

43. Adleman, Robert H. and Walton, Colonel George, *Rome Fell Today*, (Boston: Little, Brown, & Company, 1968), p. 249; Allen, William Lusk, *Anzio: Edge of Disaster*, (E.P. Dutton, New York, 1978). p. 172.

44. Summary of Operations Reports, 1 February 1944-28 November 1944; Adleman, Robert H. and Walton, Colonel George, *Rome Fell Today*, (Boston: Little, Brown, & Company, 1968), p. 254.

45. Summary of Operations Reports, 1 February 1944-28 November 1944; Adleman, Robert H. and Walton, Colonel George, *Rome Fell Today*, (Boston:

Little, Brown, & Company, 1968), p. 254; Burhans, Robert D., *The First Special Service Force, A War History of the North Americans 1942-1944*, (Washington: Infantry Journal Press, Inc., 1947), pp. 239-244.

46. Quoted from Adleman, Robert H. and Walton, Colonel George, *Rome Fell Today*, (Boston: Little, Brown, & Company, 1968), p. 254.

47. Adleman, Robert H. and Walton, Colonel George, *The Devil's Brigade*, (Chilton Books, Philadelphia, 1966), pp. 216-217; Burhans, Robert D., *The First Special Service Force, A War History of the North Americans 1942-1944*, (Washington: Infantry Journal Press, Inc., 1947), pp. 244-245.

48. Summary of Operations Reports, 1 February 1944-28 November 1944; Burhans, Robert D., *The First Special Service Force, A War History of the North Americans 1942-1944*, (Washington: Infantry Journal Press, Inc., 1947), p. 245.

49. Quoted from Adleman, Robert H. and Walton, Colonel George, *The Devil's Brigade*, (Chilton Books, Philadelphia, 1966), p. 218.

50. Summary of Operations Reports, 1 February 1944-28 November 1944.

Bibliographical Note: Chapter 9

1. Quoted from Summary of Operations Reports, 1 February 1944-28 November 1944.

2. Story, 1st Lieutenant William S., Oral History Interview with Dr. Joseph R. Fischer, 9 June 1997, p. 122.

3. Quoted from Summary of Operations Reports, 1 February 1944-28 November 1944; SSFE-1-3.13 (19061) Training Memos-Section V, 12 June 1944-26 August 1944.

4. SSFE-1-3.13 (19061) Training Memos-Section V, 12 June 1944-26 August 1944.

5. Summary of Operations Reports, 1 February 1944-28 November 1944.

6. Quoted from General Frederick and His North Americans, Reader's Digest 45:99-102, November 1944, p. 101.

7. Wickham, Kenneth G., Major General, *An Adjutant General Remembers*, (The Adjutant General's Corps Regimental Association, Fort Harrison, Indiana, 1991), p. 47.

8. Story, William S., Editor, *The First Special Service Force, A Commemorative History, July 1942-January 1945*, (Taylor Publishing Company, Dallas, 1995), p. 43.

9. Wickham, Kenneth G., Major General, *An Adjutant General Remembers*, (The Adjutant General's Corps Regimental Association, Fort Harrison, Indiana, 1991), p. 47.

10. Summary of Operations Reports, 1 February 1944-28 November 1944. Note: Prior to the invasion of south France, there were too many non-parachute qualified replacements within the FSSF, and neither the time nor facility to train them, to use the unit for a parachute operation. As such, a more suitable mission was selected.

11, 12. Quoted from Summary of Operations Reports, 1 February 1944-28 November 1944.

13, 14. Summary of Operations Reports, 1 February 1944-28 November 1944.

15. McMichael, Scott R., *A Historical Perspective On Light Infantry, Combat Studies Institute Research Survey No 6*, (Command and General Staff College, Fort Leavenworth, 1987), p. 202.

16. Summary of Operations Reports, 1 February 1944-28 November 1944; Robichon, Jacques, *The Second D-Day*, (Walker and Company, New York, 1962), pp. 78, 90, 115.

17. Summary of Operations Reports, 1 February 1944-28 November 1944; Breuer, William B., *Operation Dragoon, The Allied Invasion of the South of France*, (Presidio Press, Novato, 1987), p. 85; Robichon, Jacques, *The Second D-Day*, (Walker and Company, New York, 1962), p. 116.

18. Quoted from Robichon, Jacques, *The Second D-Day*, (Walker and Company, New York, 1962), p. 116; Robichon, pp. 114-115.

19. Quoted from Robichon, Jacques, *The Second D-Day*, (Walker and Company, New York, 1962), p. 119.

20. McMichael, Scott R., *A Historical Perspective On Light Infantry, Combat Studies Institute Research Survey No 6*, (Command and General Staff College, Fort Leavenworth, 1987), p. 201; Robichon, Jacques, *The Second D-Day*, (Walker and Company, New York, 1962), pp. 114, 118, 254.

21. Breuer, William B., *Operation Dragoon, The Allied Invasion of the South of France*, (Presidio Press, Novato, 1987), p. 85; Robichon, Jacques, *The Second D-Day*, (Walker and Company, New York, 1962), p. 116.

22. Burhans, Robert D., *The First Special Service Force, A War History of the North Americans 1942-1944*, (Washington: Infantry Journal Press, Inc., 1947), pp. 253-255.

23. Summary of Operations Reports, 1 February 1944-28 November 1944; Breuer, William B., *Operation Dragoon, The Allied Invasion of the South of France*, (Presidio Press, Novato, 1987), p. 86; Robichon, Jacques, *The Second D-Day*, (Walker and Company, New York, 1962), p. 90; Burhans, Robert D., *The First Special Service Force, A War History of the North Americans 1942-1944*, (Washington: Infantry Journal Press, Inc., 1947), p. 258; *The Operations of the 1st Battalion, 1st Regiment (First Special Service Force) At Ile de Port Cros, Off the South Coast of France, 14-17 August 1944*. General Subjects Section, Academic Department, The Infantry School, Fort Benning, Georgia. Advanced Infantry Officers Course, 1947-1948, pp. 17-18.

24. Robichon, Jacques, *The Second D-Day*, (Walker and Company, New York, 1962), p. 115.

25. Quoted from Breuer, William B., *Operation Dragoon, The Allied Invasion of the South of France*, (Presidio Press, Novato, 1987), pp. 86-87.

26. Robichon, Jacques, *The Second D-Day*, (Walker and Company, New York, 1962), pp. 115-117; Summary of Operations Reports, 1 February 1944-28 November 1944.

27. Summary of Operations Reports, 1 February 1944-28 November 1944; Burhans, Robert D., *The First Special Service Force, A War History of the North Americans 1942-1944*, (Washington: Infantry Journal Press, Inc., 1947), p. 263; Story, William S., Editor, *The First Special Service Force, A Commemorative History, July 1942-January 1945*, (Taylor Publishing Company, Dallas, 1995), p. 44; Breuer, William B., *Operation Dragoon, The Allied Invasion of the South of France*, (Presidio Press, Novato, 1987), pp. 85, 87; Robichon, Jacques, *The Second D-Day*, (Walker and Company, New York, 1962), p. 254.

28. Summary of Operations Reports, 1 February 1944-28 November 1944; Robichon, Jacques, *The Second D-Day*, (Walker and Company, New York, 1962), p. 117; Burhans, Robert D., *The First Special Service Force, A War History of the North Americans 1942-1944*, (Washington: Infantry Journal Press, Inc., 1947), pp. 257, 263-264.

29. Summary of Operations Reports, 1 February 1944-28 November 1944; Cottingham, Peter Layton, *Once Upon a Wartime, A Canadian Who Survived the Devil's Brigade*, (Privately Published: Neepawa, Manitoba, 1996), pp. 156-157; Burhans, Robert D., *The First Special Service Force, A War History of the North Americans 1942-1944*, (Washington: Infantry Journal Press, Inc., 1947), p. 264.

30. Cottingham, Peter Layton, *Once Upon a Wartime, A Canadian Who Survived the Devil's Brigade*, (Privately Published: Neepawa, Manitoba, 1996), p. 157.

31. Burhans, Robert D., *The First Special Service Force, A War History of the North Americans 1942-1944*, (Washington: Infantry Journal Press, Inc., 1947), p. 262; Story, 1st Lieutenant William S., Oral History Interview with Dr. Joseph R. Fischer, 9 June 1997, p. 149.

32. Quoted from Breuer, William B., *Operation Dragoon, The Allied Invasion of the South of France*, (Presidio Press, Novato, 1987), p. 89.

33. Burhans, Robert D., *The First Special Service Force, A War History of the North Americans 1942-1944*, (Washington: Infantry Journal Press, Inc., 1947), pp. 262, 264-265.

34. Burhans, Robert D., *The First Special Service Force, A War History of the North Americans 1942-1944*, (Washington: Infantry Journal Press, Inc., 1947), p. 266; Cottingham, Peter Layton, *Once Upon a Wartime, A Canadian Who Survived the Devil's Brigade*, (Privately Published: Neepawa, Manitoba, 1996), p. 159; Breuer, William B., *Operation Dragoon, The Allied Invasion of the South of France*, (Presidio Press, Novato, 1987), p. 237.

35. Quoted from Adleman, Robert H. and Walton, Colonel George, *The Devil's Brigade*, (Chilton Books, Philadelphia, 1966), p. 230.

36. Burhans, Robert D., *The First Special Service Force, A War History of the North Americans 1942-1944*, (Washington: Infantry Journal Press, Inc., 1947), p. 266.

37. Burhans, Robert D., *The First Special Service Force, A War History of the North Americans 1942-1944*, (Washington: Infantry Journal Press, Inc., 1947), p. 267; Cottingham, Peter Layton, *Once Upon a Wartime, A Canadian Who Survived the Devil's Brigade*, (Privately Published: Neepawa, Manitoba, 1996), p. 158.

38. Quoted from Cottingham, Peter Layton, *Once Upon a Wartime, A Canadian Who Survived the Devil's Brigade*, (Privately Published: Neepawa, Manitoba, 1996), p. 158.

39. Story, William S., Editor, *The First Special Service Force, A Commemorative History, July 1942-January 1945*, (Taylor Publishing Company, Dallas, 1995), p. 45; Burhans, Robert D., *The First Special Service Force, A War History of the North Americans 1942-1944*, (Washington: Infantry Journal Press, Inc., 1947), p. 267.

40. Breuer, William B., *Operation Dragoon, The Allied Invasion of the South of France*, (Presidio Press, Novato, 1987), pp. 237-238; Summary of Operations Reports, 1 February 1944-28 November 1944; Robichon, Jacques, *The Second D-Day*, (Walker and Company, New York, 1962), p. 254.

41. Summary of Operations Reports, 1 February 1944-28 November 1944; Burhans, Robert D., *The First Special Service Force, A War History of the North Americans 1942-1944*, (Washington: Infantry Journal Press, Inc., 1947), pp. 266-267, 270.

42. Summary of Operations Reports, 1 February 1944-28 November 1944.

43, 44. Quoted from Summary of Operations Reports, 1 February 1944-28 November 1944.

45. Summary of Operations Reports, 1 February 1944-28 November 1944.

46. Quoted from McMichael, Scott R., *A Historical Perspective On Light Infantry, Combat Studies Institute Research Survey No 6*, (Command and General Staff College, Fort Leavenworth, 1987), p. 203.

Bibliographical Notes: Epilogue

1, 2, 3, 4. Summary of Operations Reports, 1 February 1944-28 November 1944.

5. Quoted from Summary of Operations Reports, 1 February 1944-28 November 1944.

6, 7. Summary of Operations Reports, 1 February 1944-28 November 1944.

8. Dziuban, Stanley W., *Military Relations Between the United States and Canada 1939-1945*, (Washington: Office of the Chief of Military History, 1959), pp. 257-258.

9. Quoted from McMichael, Scott R., *A Historical Perspective On Light Infantry, Combat Studies Institute Research Survey No 6*, (Command and General Staff College, Fort Leavenworth, 1987), p. 204.

10. Dancocks, Daniel G., *The D-Day Dodgers, The Canadians In Italy: 1943-1945*, (McClelland & Stewart, Inc., Toronto, Ontario, 1991), p. 374.

11. "The Training Films," Motion Picture History of the First Special Service Force; The Last Parade, (First Special Service Force Association, No Date).

12. "The Training Films," Motion Picture History of the First Special Service Force; Merha, Les Wayne, *The Service Battalion: Supporting Unit for the First Special Service Force*, (Unpublished Manuscript, No Date), pp. 143-144.

13. Quoted from The Last Parade, (First Special Service Force Association, No Date).

14. Cottingham, Peter Layton, *Once Upon a Wartime, A Canadian Who Survived the Devil's Brigade*, (Privately Published: Neepawa, Manitoba, 1996), pp. 180-182.

15. "The Training Films," Motion Picture History of the First Special Service Force.

16. Burhans, Robert D., *The First Special Service Force, A War History of the North Americans 1942-1944*, (Washington: Infantry Journal Press, Inc., 1947), pp. 316-320.

17. Quoted from McMichael, Scott R., *A Historical Perspective On Light Infantry, Combat Studies Institute Research Survey No 6*, (Command and General Staff College, Fort Leavenworth, 1987), p. 209.

18. Quoted from Dawson, John R., *Legend of the First Special Service Force*, (Unpublished Manuscript, 1986), p. 30.

19. Quoted from McMichael, Scott R., *A Historical Perspective On Light Infantry, Combat Studies Institute Research Survey No 6*, (Command and General Staff College, Fort Leavenworth, 1987), p. 211.

20. Quoted from Dawson, John R., *Legend of the First Special Service Force*, (Unpublished Manuscript, 1986), p. 30.

21. Quoted from Dawson, John R., *Legend of the First Special Service Force*, (Unpublished Manuscript, 1986), pp. 4-5.

Bibliographical Notes: Special Feature #2

1. Quoted from 421.7, 25 July 1942, Force Insignia: Coat of Arms for the Color of the 1st Special Service Force.
2. 421.7, 25 July 1942, Force Insignia: Coat of Arms for the Color of the 1st Special Service Force.
2. 421.7, 25 July 1942, Force Insignia: Coat of Arms for the Color of the 1st Special Service Force; Quoted from Wickham, Kenneth G., Transcript of Speech to 1st Special Service Force Reunion, 1986, p. 2.
3. Story, William S., Editor, *The First Special Service Force, A Commemorative History, July 1942-January 1945*, (Taylor Publishing Company, Dallas, 1995), p. 63.
4. Windrow, Richard, *The World War II GI*, (Motorbooks International Publishers & Wholesalers, Osceola, 1993), p. 15; Burhans, Robert D., *The First Special Service Force, A War History of the North Americans 1942-1944*, (Washington: Infantry Journal Press, Inc., 1947), p. 16; 421.7, 25 July 1942, Force Insignia: Coat of Arms for the Color of the 1st Special Service Force.

Bibliographical Note: Special Feature #3

1. Whelan, Richard, *Robert Capa: A Biography*, (University of Nebraska Press, Lincoln, 1994); Whelan, Richard, *Robert Capa/Photographs* (Introduction), (Aperture Foundation, New York, No Date); It's A Tough War, *Life Magazine*, Photographs by Robert Capa, 16:5, 31 January 1944.

Bibliographical Notes: Special Feature #4

1. Burhans, Robert D., *The First Special Service Force, A War History of the North Americans 1942-1944*, (Washington: Infantry Journal Press, Inc., 1947).
2. Dancocks, Daniel G., *The D-Day Dodgers, The Canadians In Italy: 1943-1945*, (McClelland & Stewart, Inc., Toronto, Ontario, 1991).
3. Quoted from Frederick, Robert T., Audio tape recording of radio broadcast interview with Joe Pine, (No Date).
4. Adleman, Robert H. and Walton, Colonel George, *Rome Fell Today*, (Boston: Little, Brown, & Company, 1968).

Bibliographical Note: Special Feature #6

1. Quoted from Adleman, Robert H. and Walton, Colonel George, *Rome Fell Today*, (Boston: Little, Brown, & Company, 1968), p. 253; Summary of Operations Reports, 1 February 1944-28 November 1944.

Bibliographical Note: Special Feature #7

1, 2, 3, 4. Bens, David L., Notes from telephone interview with author regarding the FSSF Cannon Company, 6 January 1998; Fleser, Theodore S., Notes from telephone interview with author regarding the FSSF Cannon Company, 16 January 1998.

Bibliographical Notes: Special Feature #8

1. Quoted from Story, William S., At the Beginning, The First Special Service Force.
2. Cottingham, Peter Layton, *Once Upon a Wartime, A Canadian Who Survived the Devil's Brigade*, (Privately Published: Neepawa, Manitoba, 1996), p. 44.
3. Quoted from Story, William S., At the Beginning, The First Special Service Force.
4. 472.5, 15 February 1943, Request that 125 Johnson Light Machine Gun be transferred from the Marine Corps; Fitzsimons, Bernard, *Weapons and Warfare, Volume 14*, (Phoebus Publishing Company, New York, 1978), p. 1505; Dawson, John R., and Kutemeier, Don, *First Special Service Force, 1942-44 (II)*, (Military Illustrated, Past and Present, August/September, 1986).
5. Myatt M.C., Major Frederick, *Modern Small Arms*, (Crescent Books, New York, 1978), pp. 188-189.
6. Forty, George, *Army Handbook 1939-1945*, (Alan Sutton Publishing Limited, Phoenix Mill, 1995), p. 131; Quoted from Myatt M.C., Major Frederick, *Modern Small Arms*, (Crescent Books, New York, 1978), pp. 232-233.
7. Forty, George, *Army Handbook 1939-1945*, (Alan Sutton Publishing Limited, Phoenix Mill, 1995), p. 127; Windrow, Richard, *The World War II GI*, (Motorbooks International Publishers & Wholesalers, Osceola, 1993), p. 104; Black, Robert W., *Rangers In World War II*, (Ballantine Books, New York, 1992), p. 357.
8. Black, Robert W., *Rangers In World War II*, (Ballantine Books, New York, 1992), p. 345; Myatt M.C., Major Frederick, *Modern Small Arms*, (Crescent Books, New York, 1978), p. 218.
9. Myatt M.C., Major Frederick, *Modern Small Arms*, (Crescent Books, New York, 1978), p. 141.
10. Black, Robert W., *Rangers In World War II*, (Ballantine Books, New York, 1992), pp. 355-356.
11. Black, Robert W., *Rangers In World War II*, (Ballantine Books, New York, 1992), p. 357; Myatt M.C., Major Frederick, *Modern Small Arms*, (Crescent Books, New York, 1978), pp. 94-95.

Acknowledgments

Were it not for the help of a great many people, this project could not have been accomplished. To all I express my grateful appreciation.

Allen Aiken; Dr. William F. Atwater, Curator, Sergeant First Class Steven P. Klein, and the Staff of the U.S. Army Ordnance Museum; Colonel Aussavy, Lieutenant-Colonel Boitard, and the staff of Establissement Cinematographique et Photographique des Armées; Scott Belliveau; Ken Bennett; David L. Bens; Richard Boyland, and the staffs of the National Archives Textual Reference and Still Pictures Branches; Brigadier General Edward Burka (USA Ret); Cornell Capa; Richard R. Cart; Peter L. Cottingham; John R. Dawson; J.G.H. Edwards; August C. Erdbrink; Theodore S. Fleser; Ann Frederick-Hicks; Thomas W. Hope; Mark Gatlin; Pete Johnston; Bernard Kassoy; C.V. "Sid" Krotzer; Bob Kuhlmann and UMBC; Herb Langdon; Joe Lyons; Hayes Outopalik; Major Jerry McFadden (Ret); Les Wayne Merha; Lewis J. Merrim; Roxanne Merritt, Curator, and the staff of the John F. Kennedy Special Warfare Museum; W. Michael Meyers; J.D. Mitchell; Colonel Robert S. Moore; Jessica Murray, and Magnum Photos, Inc.; Alastair Neely; Charles E. Nesbitt; Stacey Niemann, Dawn W. Stitzel, and the staff of the United States Naval Institute Photo Archives; Herbert G. Peppard; Robert E. Pettit for information and statistics featured on his website; Gabe Piselli; Queen Anne's County Public Library; Joe Ranoia; T. Mark Radcliffe; Leslie K. Redman, and the staff of the Canadian War Museum; Kirk B. Ross; Alese Ross, and Henninger Digital Audio; George I. Ruddell; William G. Sheldon; David Scrutski and Rieger Communications; Brigadier General Edward H. Thomas (USA Ret); Richard Whelan; Major General Kenneth G. Wickham (USA Ret); Charles W. Wietscher; Michael J. Winey, Curator, John J. Slonaker, and the staff of the U.S. Army Military History Institute; Henly P. Woods; and Paul Lemieux, Michel Wyczynski, Marc Frève, and the staff of the National Archives of Canada.

• • •

I would like to express my particular thanks to Mr. William S. Story
for his support throughout.

A noteworthy portion of the photographs contained in this book were taken by the men of the Force Photo Detachment. For their fine work, the author is deeply indebted. Here, Private Thomas W. Hope films Force activity, Fort William Henry Harrison, Montana, c. August 1942. (Bernard Kassoy, FSSF Photo Detachment)

The Force Photo Detachment. L-r: Irwin Cinatl, Frank Lenon, Edward Gielow, Lewis Merrim, Burton Wollenzien, Ollie Stripling, and Tom Hope. Photo unit personnel, in addition to their job of documenting the formation of the First Special Service Force, were to maintain and store photographs and equipment and to handle the numerous training films used for classroom instruction. (Thomas W. Hope)

Bernard Kassoy, Force Photo Detachment, with cameras ready to record in-plane parachuting procedures, c. August 1942. Kassoy stayed with the Force until 4 October 1942 when a broken leg caused his separation from the unit. (Courtesy Bernard Kassoy)

Addendum to Special Feature #6

Elements of the 91st Cavalry Reconnaissance Squadron (Mechanized), part of the Ellis Task Force, on the outskirts of Rome. Ahead of this group, an M-4 medium tank of the Task Force burns on the roadside in the wake of a counterattack by German tanks and infantry, 3 June 1944. (National Archives)

At 0600 hours on 4 June 1944, jeeps of Captain Mark Radcliffe's II Corps patrol pass under the gate at Via Tuscolana entering Rome proper. (National Archives)

Within the city, members of Radcliffe's patrol are mobbed by jubilant Roman civilians. (National Archives)

Standing aside the turret of this M-8 armored car, a member of Radcliffe's patrol raises the flags of the United States and Canada so that they may be documented by the accompanying photographers. (National Archives)

Addendum to Special Feature #7

```
                    H.Q. CANNON COMPANY
                    1ST SPECIAL SERVICE FORCE

          ARMORED                    RECONNAISSANCE
```

At 1215 on the 27th of August, 1944, we started from the town of Valvonne, France, on an armored reconnaissance to contact the enemy and find out exactly what type of opposition to expect from them. Our primary mission, however, was to make a reconnaissance of the main roads and bridges in the area which FSSF was expected to pass through. Our reconnaissance party consisted of two half tracks with 75mm rifles on them, and two half tracks (personnel carriers) carrying one platoon of FSSF men. In addition were attached two M-10 tank destroyers. Our first objective was the town of La Colle, we entered the town and met no opposition so then pushed on to our second objective which was the town of St. Paul. We met no opposition there either but were informed by the civilians the enemy (about 30 strong) had left just a short while before and that we could expect opposition from them on ahead. Our third objective was the bridge located at (462719). When we gained this objective we found the enemy had destroyed it by demolitions. But by fording the stream at another point without encountering mines we were able to continue on to our next objective which is a road crossing at (464793). We were informed by civilians there that the road leading up to the crossing would probably be mined but we proceeded on and found there were no mines and that the road crossing was in fairly good condition. This information we then radioed back to FSSF C.P. and proceeded on to our fifth objective, the town of Villeneuve-Loubet. This objective we also gained without meeting any enemy opposition, so we located at (483763).

At this time we received a new mission by radio from Colonel Walker. He informed us there was an enemy armored column reported proceeding down the beach road from the town of St. Laurent to Cagnes. We then loaded a full company of FSSF men on all our vehicles and advanced to meet the enemy. We gained the town of Cagnes where we deposited all but one platoon of infantry to hold the town and protect our rear then continued on towards the Var River. Here we met enemy opposition in the form of deadly cross fire from three enemy machine guns. One gun firing from our right front and the other two enemy guns

firing from our left flank. Immediately our radio peep dropped back and radioed the FSSF advanced C.P. giving them the location and type of opposition encountered. This opposition consisted of three light machine guns manned by twelve to fifteen men. In the meantime our two personnel tracks stopped and the platoon of infantry deployed in a skirmish line facing the enemy on our left flank, taking advantage of protective cover behind the railroad bridge and embankment on the left of the road, firing their small arms at the machine gun positions until the second half track backed around into firing position and destroyed them. In coordination with this the lead track engaged the machine gun on the right front making them retreat to safety from our cannon fire. From there we continued on our way to St. Laurent located at (516769). There we joined forces with a party of French partisans. They informed us of another machine gun strong point further up the road. Due to the enemy behind us we at this point left the two M-10s to protect our rear and then proceeded up the road with the section of Cannon Company and the section of infantry plus a few French partisans. We had gone but a short distance when we came under fire from this enemy machine gun and also from the party of enemy demolition men from the rear which we had driven from the bridge they had hoped to blow up outside of Cagnes. At that time we did not know they were in the vicinity. This group of enemy we estimated to be six or seven strong and we did not return their fire, however, we managed to destroy the machine gun in front of us, which during the brief encounter, had succeeded in killing one and wounding one of the French partisans.

Not contacting the reported enemy armored column we were now deep into enemy territory, approximately 15 or more kilometers. We had completely destroyed three enemy machine gun strong points, prevented the enemy from demolishing important bridges, and killed or wounded an unknown number of enemy personnel. During the day's operations we covered approximately 40 kilometers of road net in front of the FSSF advance positions. We were in need of fuel, ammunition, and medical attention for the partisans who were wounded, so at this point we returned to FSSF C.P. which was located at St. Paul and gave a report of our actions and information to Colonel Walker at 2000 hours.

-1-

-2-

Additional transportation is commandeered by crew of "Hearts" 'track. Left to right: Greenwald, Rice, Balcom, Bens, (an unidentified French lieutenant), and "Boston" Cleary, 28 September 1944, southern France. (David L. Bens)

Forcemen David L. Bens (right) and Sidney I. Zitrin, fire an 81mm mortar near Mount Ours, southern France, c. September-October 1944. Note Ranger scroll over the Force spearhead on Bens' shoulder and their half-track parked in the background. (David L. Bens)

OPPOSITE: Crew of "Spades" 'track pounds distant target with indirect fire, southern France, November 1944. (Courtesy U.S. Army Military History Institute)